CREATIONS

CREA

THE QUEST FOR
IN STORY AN

CROWN PUBLISHERS, INC.

ORIGINS

SCIENCE

T I O N S

With Introduction and
Notes by ISAAC ASIMOV

Edited by ISAAC ASIMOV,
GEORGE ZEBROWSKI,
MARTIN GREENBERG

NEW YORK

Introduction © 1983 by Isaac Asimov
Copyright © 1983 by Isaac Asimov,
George Zebrowski, and Martin H. Greenberg
All rights reserved. No part of this book may be reproduced or
transmitted in any form or by any means, electronic or mechanical,
including photocopying, recording, or by any information storage and
retrieval system, without permission in writing from the publisher.
Published by Crown Publishers, Inc.,
One Park Avenue, New York, New York 10016
and simultaneously in Canada by General Publishing Company Limited
Printed in the United States of America
Library of Congress Cataloging in Publication Data
Creations: the quest for origins in story and science.
Bibliography: p.
1. Cosmogony—Literary collections.   2. Creation—
Literary collections.   I. Asimov, Isaac, 1920—
II. Greenberg, Martin Harry.   III. Zebrowski, George, 1945—
PN6071.C76C73 1983   808.8'038   83-2114
ISBN 0-517-54861-5
Book design by Camilla Filancia
10   9   8   7   6   5   4   3   2   1
First Edition

PERMISSIONS

CONTENTS

INTRODUCTION
ISAAC ASIMOV

It is an almost inevitable part of our growing up that there comes a time when the young child asks, "Where did I come from?"

And just as inevitably, the child is told fanciful tales about storks, cabbage leaves, doctors' black bags, and so on. The most saccharine tale is likely to be about angels bringing down lovely little babies from heaven.

What the child is *not* told (except, very circumspectly, by self-consciously "modern" parents) are the straightforward mechanics of sexual intercourse.

Let us generalize, then. People are fascinated by creations. It is possible to be satisfied about individual creation, since in the end, one way or another, the "facts of life" (a familiar euphemism concerning a subject that seems to consist only of euphemisms) are revealed. But what about other such questionings?

Where did the human species come from? How did life originate? Where did the Earth and the Sun and the entire Universe come from?

For these questions there are no parents to turn to. To begin with, no one knew; no one had the faintest idea. But the question was asked—urgently, insistently—and if the answer was not known, it was guessed at and imagined, and the "stork" equivalent was supplied.

Straightforward analogy seemed the safest way of proceeding. Human beings by the use of human intelligence and human abilities built imposing structures and whole cities; therefore superhuman beings by the use of superhuman intelligence and superhuman abilities could build the entire Earth and all the objects in the sky as well. In particular, human potters and sculptors could form objects, including representations of the human form, out of clay; and it followed that a superhuman potter or sculptor could shape an actual living human being out of clay.

Various human cultures have rung changes upon this basic scheme. Sometimes humanity is seen as the climax toward which all creation is aimed, as in the Biblical scheme; sometimes humanity appears as an afterthought, as in the Greek myths, in which the minor god, Prometheus, shapes humanity, rather to the irritation of the Olympians. Sometimes the gods themselves are formed as part of a creation process, and chance, rather than intelligence, shapes the scheme.

None of this is an actual "denial of origins" as is the stork story that an inquiring child is told. After all, the human beings who invented creation tales involving gods, demons, and monsters of all varieties had no idea of what the true story of creation might be. They could not deny what they did not know.

But the time came when inquiring people discovered the equivalent of "parents-who-knew-the-answer." The answers to questions concerning creation were to be found in the things created. One could put the question to the Universe. The Universe would not willingly respond, nor would it speak plainly, but within it were hints that could be interpreted, little by little, through the labors of many inquirers spread through space and time.

Biologists, geologists, chemists, physicists, and astronomers cooperated to discover that life had arisen spontaneously, given the energy of the Sun and the chemistry of the primordial sea, and had then developed slowly and evolved continuously over billions of years; that the Earth and the solar system generally, had evolved out of a swirling and slowly contracting mass of dust and gas, the contraction initiated, perhaps, by a passing supernova; that the Universe as a whole was created in an incredibly vast explosion of which the present-day galaxies, racing outward and away from each other, are the most visible evidence—and a thin background of radio waves, reaching us equally from all directions, is the most subtle evidence.

The scientific answer to the riddles of creation, obtained by skilled questioning of the Universe, has a scope and grandeur, a vista of enormous stretches of space and time, and of vast permutations and changes involving incredible quantities of mass and energy, which dwarfs everything the prescientific human imagination had brought forth. (We might except the concept of an omnipotent, omniscient, omnipresent, eternal deity, which science cannot match, but certainly the concept is itself barren when the described deeds of such a deity are trivial compared to the science-described Universe.)

Nevertheless, even science does not fill in all the details and, perhaps, never can. There is always room for speculation and more interesting varieties of it now that so much more is known (or thought to be known) of the various aspects of creation.

Science itself speculates where knowledge fails, and, with far greater freedom, science-fiction writers speculate.

This anthology is devoted, then, to speculations on creation and origins by scientists and science-fiction writers. Nor does it totally ignore the speculations of the prescientific age. It is divided into four parts that successively narrow and restrict the question of creation—yet does this in a way that makes it progressively more important to ourselves by focusing attention increasingly in our own direction. We begin with the creation of the Universe as a whole; then with the creation of the solar system; then with the creation of life upon Earth; and, finally, with the creation of humanity.

And throughout, remember, we must deal with what we might call the "denial of origins." Just as the true creation of the individual through sexual intercourse is deliberately denied by parents dealing with the inquiring child, so the scientific creation of various aspects of the Universe is denied by many, and for the same reason. The truth (or the nearest approach we have to it) is uncomfortable. It is too complicated to explain. It deprives one of emotional solace. It subtracts from our own imagined importance. And this anthology deals with that phenomenon as well.

PART I

THE ORIGIN AND NATURE OF THE UNIVERSE

Let's begin by admitting one thing that may be central to any thought we have about beginnings. Whether it is the mythic concept of divine power or the scientific concept of sheer vastness, we end up with something we cannot conceive.

We can put matters into words, numbers, expressions, formulas, but does that help? And if you cannot grasp it—

IMAGINE*

JAMES E. GUNN

IMAGINE ALL THE MATTER IN EXISTENCE GATHERED
TOGETHER
IN THE CENTER OF THE UNIVERSE—
ALL THE METEORS
COMETS
MOONS
PLANETS
STARS
NEBULAS
THE MYRIAD GALAXIES
ALL COMPACTED INTO ONE GIANT PRIMORDIAL ATOM,
ONE MONOBLOC, MASSIVE BEYOND COMPREHENSION,
DENSE BEYOND BELIEF . . .
THINK OF WHITE DWARFS, THINK OF NEUTRON STARS,
THEN MULTIPLY BY INFINITY. . . .

THE CENTER OF THE UNIVERSE? THE UNIVERSE ITSELF.
NO LIGHT, NO ENERGY COULD LEAVE, NONE ENTER.
PERHAPS TWO UNIVERSES, ONE WITHIN THE GIANT EGG
WITH EVERYTHING
AND ONE OUTSIDE WITH ALL NOTHING . . .
DISTINCT, UNTOUCHABLE . . .
IMAGINE!
ARE YOU IMAGINING?

ALL THE MATTER BROUGHT TOGETHER,
THE UNIVERSE A SINGLE, INCREDIBLE MONOBLOC,

* Excerpted from *The Listeners*.

SEETHING WITH INCOMPREHENSIBLE FORCES AND
POTENTIALS
FOR COUNTLESS EONS OR FOR INSTANTS
(WHO MEASURES TIME IN SUCH A UNIVERSE?),
AND THEN . . .
BANG!
EXPLOSION!
BEYOND EXPLOSION!
TEARING APART THE MONOBLOC, THE PRIMORDIAL
ATOM,
THE GIANT EGG HATCHING WITH FIRE AND FURY,
CREATING
THE GALAXIES
THE NEBULAS
THE SUNS
THE PLANETS
THE MOONS
THE COMETS
THE METEORS
SENDING THEM HURTLING IN ALL DIRECTIONS INTO
SPACE
CREATING SPACE
CREATING THE EXPANDING UNIVERSE
CREATING EVERYTHING . . .
IMAGINE!

YOU CAN'T IMAGINE?
WELL, THEN, IMAGINE A UNIVERSE POPULATED WITH
STARS AND
GALAXIES, A UNIVERSE FOREVER EXPANDING,
UNLIMITED,
WHERE GALAXIES FLEE FROM EACH OTHER,
THE MOST DISTANT SO RAPIDLY
THAT THEY REACH THE SPEED OF LIGHT
AND DISAPPEAR FROM OUR UNIVERSE
AND WE FROM THEIRS . . .

IMAGINE MATTER BEING CREATED CONTINUOUSLY,
A HYDROGEN ATOM POPPING INTO EXISTENCE
HERE AND THERE,
HERE
     AND
        THERE,
PERHAPS ONE ATOM OF HYDROGEN A YEAR

WITHIN A SPACE THE SIZE OF THE HOUSTON
ASTRODOME,
AND OUT OF THESE ATOMS,
PULLED TOGETHER BY THE UNIVERSAL FORCE OF
GRAVITATION,
NEW SUNS ARE BORN,
NEW GALAXIES TO REPLACE THOSE FLED BEYOND
OUR PERCEPTION,
THE EXPANDING UNIVERSE
WITHOUT END,
WITHOUT BEGINNING . . .

YOU CAN'T IMAGINE?
WELL, PERHAPS IT IS ALL A FANTASY . . .

Of all the prescientific descriptions of beginnings, the account of the first chapter of Genesis seems to us to be the most majestic and rational. Perhaps this is a matter of cultural prejudice, since we are familiar with it and cannot help but absorb a certain awe concerning it from childhood conditioning, if from nothing else. Nevertheless, that is how it seems to us.

We have not chosen the King James version of the chapter, which is the one we are most familiar with, and which nothing is likely to surpass as sheer poetry. The King James, however, is laden with archaisms and the translations it uses are, in some cases, thought to be dubious by modern scholars. The New English Bible is in contemporary English, though it clings to the King James wherever possible.

The first nineteen verses deal with the creation of the inanimate Universe in four days. To be sure, when the dry land appears on the third day, vegetation springs forth upon it, but verses 11 and 12, which describe that event, do not refer to the plant world as alive, as the animal world will be so described later on. To the Biblical thinkers, only animals were alive, while plants served merely as food. This belief still clings to our language, for we make a clear distinction between "living" and "vegetating."

Note also that on the fourth day, there was created the Sun and the Moon. These are the only astronomical bodies mentioned specifically. There follows the clause, in verse 16, "and with them he made the stars."

Thus are the stars dismissed as a matter of small importance. We cannot too easily scoff at this, however. It was not until the twentieth century that astronomers freed themselves from this attitude; it was not until our own century that astronomical textbooks ceased to deal primarily with the solar system and to dismiss the stars in one or two concluding chapters.

GENESIS 1:1—19
NEW ENGLISH BIBLE

In the beginning of creation, when God made heaven and earth, the earth was without form and void, with darkness over the face of the abyss, and a mighty wind that swept over the surface of the waters. God said, "Let there be light," and there was light;

and God saw that the light was good, and he separated light from darkness. He called the light day, and the darkness night. So evening came, and morning came, the first day.

God said, "Let there be a vault between the waters, to separate water from water." So God made the vault, and separated the water under the vault from the water above it, and so it was; and God called the vault heaven. Evening came, and morning came, a second day.

God said, "Let the waters under heaven be gathered into one place, so that dry land may appear"; and so it was. God called the dry land earth, and the gathering of the waters he called seas; and God saw that it was good. Then God said, "Let the earth produce fresh growth, let there be on the earth plants bearing seed, fruit-trees bearing fruit each with seed according to its kind." So it was; the earth yielded fresh growth, plants bearing seed according to their kind and trees bearing fruit each with seed according to its kind; and God saw that it was good. Evening came, and morning came, a third day.

God said, "Let there be lights in the vault of heaven to separate day from night, and let them serve as signs both for festivals and for seasons and years. Let them also shine in the vault of heaven to give light on earth." So it was; God made the two great lights, the greater to govern the day and the lesser to govern the night; and with them he made the stars. God put these lights in the vault of heaven to give light on earth, to govern day and night, and to separate light from darkness; and God saw that it was good. Evening came, and morning came, a fourth day.

Modern skeptics are wont to smile at the Biblical tale that has the Universe created in six days. If we consider the Universe as it exists now, then, indeed, a six-day creation goes counter to all the physical evidence we have.

Suppose, though, we consider the Universe simply as having been created—never mind its state. In that case, it would seem, according to the best information that we now have, the Bible errs in the other direction. The Universe was created not in six days but in an instant of time, smaller than any we can imagine. That instant was the "big bang."

No one witnessed the big bang, any more than anyone witnessed the events described in Genesis, but it is possible to try to work out the events in the former case from the physical laws developed in connection with the present-day Universe. The events immediately after the instant of the big bang are bizarre and wonderful, as described by Weinberg—and uncertain, for it is not entirely certain how far the physical laws will apply, even if the application is entirely correct in the first place.

But it is the best we have right now and we will return to it for another look later on in the book.

THE FIRST ONE-HUNDREDTH SECOND

STEVEN WEINBERG

Our account of the first three minutes elsewhere did not begin at the beginning. Instead, we started at a "first frame" when the cosmic temperature had already cooled to 100,000 million degrees Kelvin, and the only particles present in large numbers were photons, electrons, neutrinos, and their corresponding antiparticles. If these really were the only types of particles in nature, we could perhaps extrapolate the expansion of the universe backward in time and infer that there must have been a real beginning, a state of infinite temperature and density, which occurred 0.0108 seconds before our first frame.

However, there are many other types of particles known to modern physics: muons, pi mesons, protons, neutrons, and so on. When we look back to earlier and earlier times, we encounter temperatures and densities so high that all of these particles would have been present in copious numbers in thermal equilibrium, and all in a state of continual mutual interaction. For reasons that I hope to make clear, we simply do not yet know enough about the physics of the elementary particles to be able to calculate the properties of such a melange with any confidence. Thus, our ignorance of microscopic physics stands as a veil, obscuring our view of the very beginning.

Naturally, it is tempting to try to peek behind this veil. The temptation is particularly strong for theorists like myself, whose work has been much more in elementary particle physics than in astrophysics. Many of the interesting ideas in contemporary particle physics have such subtle consequences that they are extraordinarily difficult to test in laboratories today, but their consequences are quite dramatic when these ideas are applied to the very early universe.

The first problem we face in looking back to temperatures above 100,000 million degrees is presented by the "strong interactions" of elementary particles. The strong interactions are the forces that hold neutrons and protons together in an atomic nucleus. They are not familiar in everyday life, in the way that the electromagnetic and gravitational forces are, because their range is extremely short, about one ten million millionth of a centimeter (10^{-13} cm). Even in molecules, whose nuclei are typically a few hundred millionths of a centimeter (10^{-8} cm) apart, the strong interactions between different nuclei have virtually no effect. However, as their name indicates, the strong interactions are very strong. When two protons are pushed close enough together, the strong interaction between them becomes about 100 times greater than the electrical repulsion; this is why the strong interactions are able to hold together atomic nuclei against the electrical repulsion of almost 100 protons. The explosion of a hydrogen bomb is caused by a rearrangement of neutrons and protons which allows them to be more tightly bound together by the strong interactions; the energy of the bomb is just the excess energy made available by this rearrangement.

It is the strength of the strong interactions that makes them so much more difficult to deal with mathematically than the electromagnetic interactions. When, for instance, we calculate the rate for scattering of two electrons due to the electromagnetic repulsion between them, we must add up an infinite number of contributions, each corresponding to a particular sequence of emission and absorption of photons and electron-positron pairs, symbolized in a "Feynman diagram" like those of Figure 1. (The method

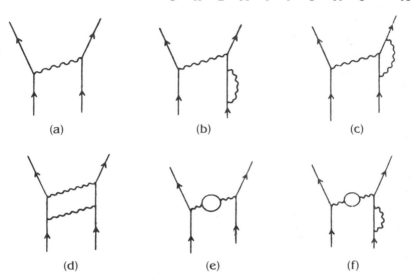

FIGURE 1. *Some Feynman Diagrams.* Shown here are some of the simpler Feynman diagrams for the process of electron-electron scattering. Straight lines denote electrons or positrons; wavy lines denote photons. Each diagram represents a certain numerical quantity which depends on the momenta and spins of the incoming and outgoing electrons; the rate of the scattering process is the square of the sum of these quantities, associated with all Feynman diagrams. The contribution of each diagram to this sum is proportional to a number of factors of 1/137 (the fine structure constant), given by the number of photon lines. Diagram (a) represents the exchange of a single photon and makes the leading contribution, proportional to 1/137. Diagrams (b), (c), (d), and (e) represent all the types of diagrams which make the dominant "radiative" corrections to (a); they all make contributions of order $(1/137)^2$. Diagram (f) makes an even smaller contribution, proportional to $(1/137)^3$.

of calculation that uses these diagrams was worked out in the late 1940s by Richard Feynman, then at Cornell. Strictly speaking, the rate for the scattering process is given by the *square* of a sum of contributions, one for each diagram). Adding one more internal line to any diagram lowers the contribution of the diagram by a factor roughly equal to a fundamental constant of nature, known as the "fine structure constant." This constant is quite small, about 1/137.036. Complicated diagrams therefore give small contributions, and we can calculate the rate of the scattering process to an adequate approximation by adding up the contributions from just a few simple diagrams. (This is why we feel confident that we can predict atomic spectra with almost unlimited precision.) However, for the strong interactions, the constant that plays the role of the fine structure constant is roughly equal to one, not 1/137, and complicated diagrams therefore make just as large a contribution as simple diagrams. This problem, the difficulty of calculating rates for processes involving strong interactions, has been the single greatest obstacle to progress in elementary particle physics for the last quarter-century.

Not all processes involve strong interactions. The strong interactions affect only a class of particles known as "hadrons": these include the nuclear particles and pi mesons, and other unstable particles known as K-mesons, eta mesons, lambda hyperons, sigma hyperons, and so on. The hadrons are generally heavier than the leptons (the name "lepton" is taken from the Greek word for "light"), but the really important difference between them is that hadrons feel the effects of the strong interactions, while the leptons—the neutrinos, electrons, and muons—do not. The fact that electrons do not feel the nuclear force is overwhelmingly important—together with the small mass of the electron, it is responsible for the fact that the cloud of electrons in an atom or a molecule is about 100,000 times larger than the atomic nuclei, and also that the chemical forces which hold atoms together in molecules are millions of times weaker than the forces which hold neutrons and protons together in nuclei. If the electrons in atoms and molecules felt the nuclear force, there would be no chemistry or crystallography or biology—only nuclear physics.

The temperature of 100,000 million degrees Kelvin was carefully chosen to be below the threshold temperature for all hadrons. (The lightest hadron, the pi meson, has a threshold temperature of about 1.6 million million degrees Kelvin.) Thus, the only particles present in large numbers were leptons and photons, and the interactions among them could safely be ignored.

How do we deal with higher temperatures, when hadrons and antihadrons would have been present in large numbers? There are two very different answers which reflect two very different schools of thought as to the nature of the hadrons.

According to one school, there really is no such thing as an "elementary" hadron. Every hadron is as fundamental as every other—not only stable and nearly stable hadrons like the proton and neutron, and not only moderately unstable particles like the pi mesons, K-mesons, eta mesons, and hyperons, which live long enough to leave measurable tracks in photographic films or bubble chambers, but even totally unstable "particles" like the rho mesons, which live just long enough so that at a speed near that of light they can barely cross an atomic nucleus. This doctrine was developed in the late 1950s and early 1960s, particularly by Geoffrey Chew of Berkeley, and is sometimes known as "nuclear democracy."

With such a liberal definition of "hadron," there are literally hundreds of known hadrons whose threshold temperature is less than 100 million million degrees Kelvin, and probably hundreds more yet to be discovered. In some theories there is an unlimited number of species: the number of types of particles will increase faster and faster as we explore higher and higher masses. It might seem hopeless to try to make sense out of such a world, but the very complexity of the particle spectrum might lead to a kind of simplicity. For instance, the rho meson is a hadron that can be thought of as an unstable composite of two pi mesons; when we include rho mesons explicitly in our calculations, we are already to some extent taking account of the strong interaction between pi mesons; perhaps by including *all* hadrons explicitly in our thermodynamic calculations, we can ignore *all* other effects of the strong interactions.

Further, if there really is an unlimited number of species of hadron, then when we put more and more energy in a given volume the energy does not go into increasing the random speeds of the particles, but goes instead into increasing the numbers of types of particles present in the volume. The temperature then does not go up as fast with increasing energy density as it would if the number of hadron species were fixed. In fact, in such theories there can be a *maximum* temperature, a value of the temperature at which the energy density becomes infinite. This would be as insuperable an upper bound on the temperature as absolute zero is a lower bound. The idea of a maximum temperature in hadron physics is originally due to R. Hagedorn of the CERN laboratory in Geneva, and has been further developed by other theorists, including Kerson Huang of M.I.T. and myself. There is even a fairly precise estimate of what the maximum temperature would be—it is surprisingly low, about two million million degrees Kelvin $(2 \times 10^{12} \, ^\circ K)$. As we look closer and closer to the beginning, the temperature would grow closer and closer to this maximum, and the variety of hadron types present would grow richer and richer. However, even under these exotic conditions there would still have been a beginning, a time of infinite energy density, roughly a hundredth of a second before the first frame.

There is another school of thought that is far more conventional, far closer to ordinary intuition than "nuclear democracy," and in my opinion also closer to the truth. According to this school, not all particles are equal; some really are elementary, and all the others are mere composites of the elementary particles. The elementary particles are thought to consist of the photon and all the known leptons, *but none of the known hadrons.* Rather, the hadrons are supposed to be composites of more fundamental particles, known as "quarks."

The original version of the quark theory is due to Murray Gell-Mann and (independently) George Zweig, both of Cal Tech. The poetic imagination of theoretical physicists has really run wild in naming the different sorts of quarks. The quarks come in different types, or "flavors," which are given names like "up," "down," "strange," and "charmed." Furthermore, each "flavor" of quark comes in three distinct "colors," which U.S. theorists usually call red, white, and blue. The small group of theoretical physicists in Peking has long favored a version of the quark theory, but they call them "stratons" instead of quarks because these particles represent a deeper stratum of reality than the ordinary hadrons.

If the quark idea is right, then the physics of the very early universe may be simpler than was thought. It is possible to infer something about the forces between quarks from their spatial distribution inside a nuclear particle, and this distribution can in turn be determined (if the quark model is true) from observations of high-energy collisions of electrons with nuclear particles. In this way, it was found a few years ago by an M.I.T.-Stanford Linear Accelerator Center collaboration that the force between quarks seems to disappear when the quarks are very close to each other. This suggests that at some temperature, around several million million degrees Kelvin, the hadrons would simply break up into their constituent quarks, just as atoms break up into electrons and nuclei at a few thousand degrees, and nuclei break up into protons and neutrons at a few thousand million degrees. According to this picture, at very early times the universe could be considered to consist of photons, leptons, antileptons, quarks, and antiquarks, all moving essentially as free particles, and each particle species therefore in effect furnishing just one more kind of black-body radiation. It is easy then to calculate that there must have been a beginning, a state of infinite density *and* infinite temperature, about one-hundredth of a second before the first frame.

These rather intuitive ideas have recently been put on a much firmer mathematical foundation. In 1973 it was shown by three young theorists—Hugh David Politzer of Harvard and David Gross and Frank Wilczek of Princeton—that, in a special class of quantum field theories, the forces between quarks do actually become weaker as the quarks are pushed closer together. (This class of theories is known as the "non-Abelian gauge theories" for reasons too technical to explain here.) These theories have the remarkable property of "asymptotic freedom": at asymptotically short distances or high energies, the quarks behave as free particles. It has even been shown by J. C. Collins and M. J. Perry at the University of Cambridge that in any asymptotically free theory, the properties of a medium at sufficiently high temperature and density are essentially the same as if the medium consisted purely of free particles. The asymptotic freedom of these non-Abelian gauge theories thus provides a solid mathematical justification for the very simple picture of the first hundredth of a second—that the universe was made up of free elementary particles.

The quark model works very well in a wide variety of applications. Protons and neutrons really do behave as if they consist of three quarks, rho mesons behave as if they consist of a quark and an antiquark, and so on. But despite this success, the quark model presents us with a great puzzle: even with the highest energies available from existing accelerators, it has so far proved impossible to break up any hadron into its constituent quarks.

The same inability to isolate free quarks also appears in cosmology. If hadrons really broke up into free quarks under the conditions of high temperature that prevailed in the early universe, then one might expect some free quarks to be left over at the present time. The Soviet astrophysicist Ya. B. Zeldovich has estimated that free leftover quarks should be roughly as common in the present universe as gold atoms. Needless to say, gold is not abundant, but an ounce of gold is a good deal easier to purchase than an ounce of quarks.

The puzzle of the nonexistence of isolated free quarks is one of the most important problems facing theoretical physics at the present moment. It has been suggested by Gross and Wilczek and by myself that "asymptotic freedom" provides a possible explanation. If the strength of the interaction between two quarks decreases as they are pushed close together, it also increases as they are pulled farther apart. The energy required to pull a quark away from the other quarks in an ordinary hadron therefore increases with increasing distance, and it seems eventually to become great enough to create new quark-antiquark pairs out of the vacuum. In the end, one winds up not with several free quarks but with several ordinary hadrons. It is exactly like trying to isolate one end of a piece of string: if you pull very hard, the string will break, but the result is two pieces of string, each with two ends! Quarks were close enough together in the early universe so that they did not feel these forces, and could behave like free particles. However, *every* free quark present in the very early universe must, as the universe expanded and cooled, have either annihilated with an antiquark or else found a resting place inside a proton or neutron.

So much for the strong interactions. There are further problems in store for us as we turn the clock back toward the very beginning.

One truly fascinating consequence of modern theories of elementary particles is that the universe may have suffered a *phase transition*, like the freezing water when it falls below 273 ° K (= 0 ° C). This phase transition is associated not with the strong interactions but with the other class of short-range interaction in particle physics, the *weak* interactions.

The weak interactions are those responsible for certain radioactive decay processes like the decay of a free neutron or, more generally, for any reaction involving a neutrino. As their name indicates, the weak interactions are much weaker than the electromagnetic or strong interactions. For instance, in a collision between a neutrino and an electron at an energy of one million electron volts, the weak force is about one ten-millionth (10^{-7}) of the electromagnetic force between two electrons colliding at the same energy.

Despite the weakness of the weak interactions, it has long been thought that there might be a deep relation between the weak and electromagnetic forces. A field theory which unifies these two forces was proposed in 1967 by myself, and independently in 1968 by Abdus Salam. This theory predicted a new class of weak interactions, the so-called neutral currents, whose existence was confirmed experimentally in 1973. It received further support from the discovery, starting in 1974, of a whole family of new hadrons. The key idea of this kind of theory is that nature has a very high degree of symmetry, which relates the various particles and forces, but which is obscured in ordinary physical phenomena. The field theories used since 1973 to describe the strong interactions are of the same mathematical type (non-Abelian gauge theories), and many physicists now believe that gauge theories may provide a unified basis for understanding all the forces of nature: weak, electromagnetic, strong, and perhaps gravitational forces.

For studies of the early universe, the important point about the gauge theories is that, as pointed out in 1972 by D. A. Kirzhnits and A. D. Linde of the Lebedev Physical Institute in Moscow, these theories exhibit a phase transition, a kind of freezing, at a "critical temperature" of about 3,000 million million degrees (3×10^{15} °K). At temperatures below the critical temperature, the universe was as it is now: weak interactions were weak, and of short range. At temperatures above the critical temperature, the essential unity between the weak and electromagnetic interactions was manifest: the weak interactions obeyed the same sort of inverse-square law as the electromagnetic interactions, and had about the same strength.

The analogy with a freezing glass of water is instructive here. Above the freezing point, liquid water exhibits a high degree of homogeneity: the probability of finding a water molecule at one point inside the glass is just the same as at any other point. However, when the water freezes, this symmetry among different points in space is partly lost: the ice forms a crystal lattice, with water molecules occupying certain regularly spaced positions, and with almost zero probability of finding water molecules anywhere else. In the same way, when the universe "froze" as the temperature fell below 3,000 million million degrees, a symmetry was lost —not its spatial homogeneity, as in our glass of ice, but the symmetry between the weak and the electromagnetic interactions.

It may be possible to carry the analogy even further. As everyone knows, when water freezes it does not usually form a perfect crystal of ice but something much more complicated: a great mess of crystal domains, separated by various types of crystal irregularities. Did the universe also freeze into domains? Do we live in one such domain, in which the symmetry between the weak and electromagnetic interactions has been broken in a particular way, and will we eventually discover other domains?

So far our imagination carried us back to a temperature of 3,000 million million degrees, and we have had to deal with the strong, weak, and electromagnetic interactions. What about the one other grand class of interactions known to physics, the gravitational interactions? Gravitation has of course played an important role in our story, because it controls the relation between the density of the universe and its rate of expansion. However, gravity has not yet been found to have any effect on the *internal* properties of any part of the early universe. This is because of the extreme weakness of the gravitational force; for instance, the gravitational force between the electron and the proton in a hydrogen atom is weaker than the electrical force by 39 powers of 10.

(One illustration of the weakness of gravitation in cosmological processes is provided by the process of particle production in gravitational fields. It has been pointed out by Leonard Parker of the University of Wisconsin that the "tidal" effects of the gravitational field of the universe would have been great enough, at a time about one million million million-millionth of a second (10^{-24} sec) after the beginning, to produce particle-antiparticle pairs out of empty space. However, gravitation was still so weak at these temperatures that the number of particles produced in this way made a negligible contribution to the particles already present in thermal equilibrium.)

Nevertheless, we can at least imagine a time when gravitational forces would have been as strong as the strong nuclear interactions discussed above. Gravitational fields are generated not only by particle masses but by all forms of energy. The earth is going around the sun a little faster than it otherwise would if the sun were not hot, because the energy in the sun's heat adds a little to the source of its gravitation. At superhigh temperatures the energies of particles in thermal equilibrium can become so large that the gravitational forces between them become as strong as any other forces. We can estimate that this state of affairs was reached at a temperature of about 100 million million million million million degrees (10^{32} ° K).

At this temperature all sorts of strange things would have been going on. Not only would gravitational forces have been strong and particle production by gravitational fields copious—the very idea of "particle" would not yet have had any meaning. The "horizon," the distance beyond which it is impossible yet to have received any signals, would at this time be closer than one wavelength of a typical particle in thermal equilibrium. Speaking loosely, each particle would be about as big as the observable universe!

We do not know enough about the quantum nature of gravitation even to speculate intelligently about the history of the universe before this time. We can make a crude estimate that the temperature of 10^{32} ° K was reached some 10^{-43} seconds after the beginning, but it is not really clear that this estimate has any meaning. Thus, whatever other veils may have been lifted, there is one veil, at a temperature of 10^{32} ° K, that still obscures our view of the earliest times.

However, none of these uncertainties make much difference to the astronomy of A.D. 1976. The point is that during the whole of the first second the universe was presumably in a state of thermal equilibrium, in which the numbers and distributions of all particles, even neutrinos, were determined by the laws of statistical mechanics, not by the details of their prior history. When we measure the abundance today of helium, or microwave radiation, or even of neutrinos, we are observing the relics of the state of thermal equilibrium which ended at the close of the first second. As far as we know, nothing that we can observe depends on the history of the universe prior to that time. (In particular, nothing we now observe depends on whether the universe was isotropic and homogeneous before the first second, except perhaps the photon-to-nuclear-particle ratio itself.) It is as if a dinner were prepared with great care—the freshest ingredients, the most carefully chosen spices, the finest wines—and then thrown all together in a great pot to boil for a few hours. It would be difficult for even the most discriminating diner to know what he was being served.

There is one possible exception. The phenomenon of gravitation, like that of electromagnetism, can be manifested in the form of waves as well as in the more familiar form of a static action at a distance. Two electrons at rest will repel each other with a static electric force that depends on the distance between them, but if we wiggle one electron back and forth, the other will not feel any change in the force acting on it until there is time for news of the change in separation to be carried on an electromagnetic wave from one particle to the other. It hardly needs to be said that these waves travel at the speed of light—they *are* light, although not necessarily visible light. In the same way, if some ill-advised giant were to wiggle the sun back and forth, we on earth would not feel the effect for eight minutes, the time required for a wave to travel at the speed of light from the sun to the earth. This is *not* a light wave, a wave of oscillating electric and magnetic fields, but rather a gravitational wave, in which the oscillation is in the gravitational fields. Just as for electromagnetic waves, we lump together gravitational waves of all wavelengths under the term "gravitational radiation."

Gravitational radiation interacts far more weakly with matter than electromagnetic radiation, or even neutrinos. (For this reason, although we are reasonably confident on theoretical grounds of the existence of gravitational radiation, the most strenuous efforts have so far apparently failed to detect gravitational waves from any source.) Gravitational radiation would therefore have gone out of thermal equilibrium with the other contents of the universe very early—in fact, when the temperature was about 10^{32} ° K. Since then, the effective temperature of the gravitational radiation has simply dropped in inverse proportion to the size of the universe. This is just the same law of decrease as obeyed by the temperature of the rest of the contents of the universe, except that the annihilation of quark-antiquark and lepton-antilepton pairs has heated the rest of the universe but not the gravitational radiation. Therefore, the universe today should be filled with gravitational radiation at a temperature similar to but somewhat less than that of the neutrinos or photons—perhaps about 1° K. Detection of this radiation would represent a direct observation of the very earliest moment in the history of the universe that can even be contemplated by present-day theoretical physics. Unfortunately there does not seem to be the slightest chance of detecting a 1° K background of gravitational radiation in the foreseeable future.

With the aid of a good deal of highly speculative theory, we have been able to extrapolate the history of the universe back in time to a moment of infinite density. But this leaves us unsatisfied. We naturally want to know what there was before this moment, before the universe began to expand and cool.

One possibility is that there never really was a state of infinite density. The present expansion of the universe may have begun at the end of a previous age of contraction, when the density of the universe had reached some very high but finite value.

However, although we do not know that it is true, it is at least logically possible that there *was* a beginning, and that time itself has no meaning before that moment. We are all used to the idea of an absolute zero of temperature. It is impossible to cool any-thing below $-273.16°$ C, not because it is too hard or because no one has thought of a sufficiently clever refrigerator, but because temperatures lower than absolute zero just have no meaning—we cannot have less heat than no heat at all. In the same way, we may have to get used to the idea of an absolute zero of time—a mo-ment in the past beyond which it is in principle impossible to trace any chain of cause and effect. The question is open, and may always remain open.

To me, the most satisfying thing that has come out of these speculations about the very early universe is the possible parallel between the history of the universe and its logical structure. Nature now exhibits a great diversity of types of particles and types of interactions. Yet we have learned to look beneath this diversity, to try to see the various particles and interactions as aspects of a simple unified gauge field theory. The present universe is so cold that the symmetries among the different particles and interactions have been obscured by a kind of freezing; they are not manifest in ordinary phenomena but have to be expressed mathematically, in our gauge field theories. That which we do now by mathematics was done in the very early universe by heat—physical phenomena directly exhibited the essential simplicity of nature. But no one was there to see it.

Lem is perhaps the cleverest satirist in science fiction. He can manage the wildest suggestions with an exuberance that skates over the thinnest of ice without disturbing plausibility one whit. You can believe the maddest of madness while he is writing. And a great deal of what he says is not invented. This business of violating the laws of conservation very briefly is correct, according to the Heisenberg principle of indeterminacy. However, the larger the mass, the briefer the time allowed for violation. For a mass the size of the Universe, the time for violation would be unimaginably small.

But never mind, satire has its point. How account for the imperfections in the Universe? That was the central question, after all, of the Book of Job, and in my opinion, the answer was fudged. The Jobian answer that humanity is too limited to understand may be true, but it is unsatisfactory. The Lemian answer may be false, but it is more acceptable.

PROJECT GENESIS *

(From the Memoirs of Ijon Tichy, Space Traveler)

STANISLAW LEM

The expedition I want to write about now was, in its consequences and scale, the greatest of my life. I am well aware that no one will believe me. But, paradoxical as it may seem, the Reader's disbelief will facilitate my task. Because I cannot claim that I achieved what I intended to achieve. To tell the truth, the whole thing turned out rather badly. The fact that it was not I who bungled, but certain envious and ignorant people who tried to thwart my plans, does not ease my conscience any.

So, then, the goal of this expedition was the creation of the Universe. Not some new, separate universe, one that never before existed. No. I mean this Universe we live in. On the face of it, an absurd, an insane statement, for how can one create what exists already and what is as ancient and irreversible as the Universe?

* Translated from the Polish by Joel Stern and Maria Swiecicka-Ziemianek.

Could this be—the Reader is likely to think—a wild hypothesis stating that till now nothing has existed except Earth, and that all the galaxies, suns, stellar clouds, and Milky Ways are only a mirage? But that's not it at all, because I really did create everything, absolutely Everything—and thus Earth, too, and the rest of the Solar System, and the Metagalaxy, which would certainly be cause for pride, if only my handiwork did not contain so many flaws. Some of these lie in the building material, but most are in the animate matter, particularly in the human race. This has been my greatest regret. True, the people I shall mention by name interfered in my efforts, but by no means do I consider myself thereby absolved. I should have planned, supervised, seen to everything more carefully. Especially since there is now no possibility for correction or improvement. Since October 20 of last year, I am to blame for all—and I mean all—the constructional defects in the Universe and the warps n human nature. There is no escape from that knowledge.

It began three years ago, when, through Professor Tarantoga, I met a certain physicst of Slavic descent from Bombay. A visiting professor. This scientist, Solon Razglaz, had spent thirty years in the study of cosmogony. that branch of astronomy that deals with the origin and early formation of the Universe.

Razglaz reached, after a thorough study of the subject, a conclusion that stunned even him. As we know, theories of cosmogony can be divided into two groups. One comprises those theories that regard the Universe as eternal—in other words, devoid of a beginning. The second holds that at one time the Universe arose in a violent manner from the explosion of a Protoatom. There have always been difficulties with both views. Regarding the first: science possesses a growing body of evidence that the visible Universe is from 12 to 20 billion years old. If something has a definite age, there is nothing simpler than to calculate back to its zero moment. But an eternal Universe can have no "zero," no beginning. Under the pressure of new information, most scientists now opt for a Universe that arose from 15 to 18 billion years ago. Initially, there was a substance—call it Ylem, the Protoatom, whatever—that exploded and gave rise to matter and energy, stellar clouds, spiral galaxies, and dark and bright nebulae, all floating in rarefied gas filled with radiation. This can be precisely and neatly determined as long as no one asks, "But where did the Proto-atom come from?" For there is no answer to this question. There are certain evasions, yes, but no self-respecting astronomer is satisfied with them.

Professor Razglaz, before taking up cosmogony, had for a long time studied theoretical physics, especially the so-called elementary particles. When his interest switched to the new subject, he quickly saw that the Universe unquestionably had a beginning. It obviously arose 18.5 billion years ago from a single Proto-atom. At the same time, however, the Proto-atom from which it sprang could not have existed. For who could have placed it in that emptiness? In the very beginning, there was nothing. Had there been something, that something, it is clear, would have begun developing at once, and the entire Universe would have arisen much earlier—infinitely earlier, to be exact! Why should a primordial Proto-atom remain inert, waiting motionless for unknown eons? And what in God's name could have wrenched it so, in that one moment, causing it to expand and fly apart into something so tremendous?

Learning of Razglaz's theory, I often questioned him about what led to his discovery. The origin of great ideas has always fascinated me, and surely it would be hard to find a greater revelation than Razglaz's cosmogonic hypothesis! The Professor, a quiet and extremely modest man, told me that his concept was, from the viewpoint of orthodox astronomy, quite outrageous. Every astronomer knows that the atomic seed from which the Universe is supposed to have sprung is a highly problematical thing. What do they do about this, then? They sidestep, they evade the issue, because it is inconvenient. Razglaz, on the other hand, dared to devote all his energy to it. The more he amassed facts, and the more he rummaged through libraries and built models, surrounding himself with a battery of the fastest computers, the more clearly he saw that there was something not right.

At first he hoped that eventually he would succeed in diminishing the contradiction, and perhaps even in resolving it. However, it kept increasing. Because all the data indicated that the Universe arose from a single atom but also that no such atom could have existed. Here an obvious explanation suggested itself, the God hypothesis, but Razglaz set it aside as a last resort. I remember his smile when he said, "We shouldn't pass the buck to God. Certainly an astrophysicist shouldn't. . . ." Pondering the dilemma for many months, Razglaz reviewed his previous research. Ask any physicist you know, if you do not believe me, and he will tell you that certain phenomena on the smallest scale occur, as it were, on credit. Mesons, those elementary particles, sometimes violate the laws of conservation, but they do this so incredibly fast that they hardly violate them at all. What is forbidden by the laws of physics they do with lightning speed, as though nothing could be more natural, and then they immediately submit to those laws again.

And so, on one of his morning strolls across the university campus, Razglaz asked himself: What if the Universe were doing the same thing on a large scale? If mesons can behave impossibly for a fraction of a second, a fraction so minuscule that a whole second would seem an eternity in comparison, then the Universe, given its dimensions, might behave in that forbidden way for a correspondingly longer period of time. For, say, 15 billion years. . . .

It arose, then, although it might well not have arisen, *there being nothing from which to arise*. The Universe is a *forbidden fluctuation*. It represents a momentary aberration, but an aberration of monumental proportions. It is no less a deviation from the laws of physics than, on the smallest scale, a meson! Suspecting he was on the right track, the professor immediately went to his laboratory and made some calculations, which, step by step, verified his idea. But even before he had finished, the realization came: the solution to the riddle of the origin of the Universe revealed a threat as great as could be imagined.

For the Universe exists *on credit*. It represents, with its constellations and galaxies, a monstrous debt, a pawn ticket, as it were, a promissory note that must ultimately be paid. The Universe is an illegal loan of matter and energy; its apparent "asset" is actually a "liability." Since the Universe is an Unlawful Anomaly, it will, one fine day, burst like a bubble. It will fall back into the Nonexistence from which it sprang. That moment will be a return to the Natural Order of Things!

That the Universe is so vast and that so much has taken place in it is due solely to the fact that we are dealing with a fluke on the largest possible scale. Razglaz immediately proceeded to calculate when the fatal term would come—that is, when matter, the Sun, the stars, the planets, and therefore Earth, along with all of us, would plunge into nothingness as though snuffed out. He learned that it was impossible to predict this. Of course impossible, given that the Universe was a fluke, a deviation from order! The danger revealed by his discovery kept him awake at night. After much inner struggle, he acquainted a few eminent astrophysicists with it. These scientists acknowledged the correctness of his theory and conclusions. At the same time, they felt that publication of his findings would plunge the world into spiritual chaos and alarm, the consequences of which could destroy civilization. What man would still desire to do anything—to move his little finger—knowing that at any second everything might vanish, himself included?

The matter came to a standstill. Razglaz, the greatest discoverer in all history, agreed with his learned colleagues. He decided, albeit reluctantly, not to publish his theory. Instead, he began searching the whole arsenal of physics for ways to assist the Universe somehow, to strengthen and maintain its debtor's life. But his efforts came to naught. It was impossible to cancel the cosmic debt by anything done in the present: the debt lay not within the Universe but at its origin—at that point in time when the Universe became the mightiest and yet most defenseless debtor to nothingness.

It was at this juncture that I met the Professor and spent many weeks in conversation with him. First he outlined for me the essential points of his discovery; then I went back to Bombay with him, and we worked together to find some means of deliverance.

Ah, I thought, returning to my hotel with fevered head and despairing heart, if only I could have been there, 20 billion years ago, for just a split second! That would be enough to place a single solitary atom in the void, and the Universe could grow from it as from a planted seed, now in a totally legitimate way, in accordance with the laws of physics and the principle of conservation of matter and energy. But how was I to get there?

The Professor, when I told him this idea, smiled sadly and explained to me that the Universe could not have arisen from any ordinary atom; the cosmic nucleus would have had to contain the energy of all the transformations and events that expanded to fill the metagalactic void. I saw my error but continued to mull over the problem. Then one afternoon, as I rubbed oil on my legs, which were swollen with mosquito bites, my mind wandered back to the old days, when, while flying through the spherical cluster of Canes Venatici, I had read theoretical physics for lack of anything better to do. I had been particularly engrossed in a volume devoted to elementary particles, and I recalled Feynman's hypothesis that there are particles that move "upstream" against the flow of time. When an electron moves in this manner, we perceive it then as an electron with a positive charge (a positron). I asked myself, with my feet in a washbasin: What if we took one electron and accelerated it, accelerated it so much that it would begin moving backward in time, faster and faster? Couldn't we give it such a tremendous impulse that it would fly back beyond the beginning of cosmic time to that point when there was still nothing? Couldn't the Universe arise from this accelerated positron?

I ran to the professor as I was, my bare feet dripping wet. He immediately realized the magnitude of my idea and without a word began to calculate. It turned out that the project was feasible; his calculations showed that the electron, as it moved against the flow of time, would gain greater and greater energy, so that when it reached beyond the beginning of the Universe, the force accumulated within it would split it apart, and the exploding particle would release the energy required to cancel the debt. The Universe then would be saved from collapse, since it would no longer exist on credit!

Now we had only to think about the practical side of the undertaking that was to legitimize the World—or, in short, to create it! As a man of integrity, Razglaz repeatedly said to Professor Tarantoga and to all his assistants and colleagues that it was I who had originated the concept of the Creation, and that therefore it was I, and not he, who deserved the double title of Creator and Saviour of the world. I mention this not to boast but to humble myself. Because the endless praise and appreciation that I received at that time in Bombay, well, I'm afraid it turned my head a little and caused me to neglect my work. I rested on my laurels, thinking that the most important part had been done—the intellectual part —and that what followed now would be the purely technical details, which others could take care of.

A fatal mistake! Throughout the summer and most of the fall, Razglaz and I determined the parameters, the characteristics and properties that were to be carried by the electron—the cosmic seed, or, perhaps more correctly, the constructional quantum. As for the mechanical aspect of Project Genesis, we took a huge university synchrophasetron and rebuilt it into a cannon aimed at the beginning of time. All its power, concentrated and focused in a single particle—the constructional quantum—was to be released on October 20. Professor Razglaz insisted that I, the author of the idea, fire the world-forming shot from the Chronocannon. Because, you see, this was a unique historical opportunity. Our machine, our mortar, was to shoot not just any random electron, but a particle suitably remade, reshaped, and remodeled to bring forth a *much more orderly and solid* Universe than the one that existed at present. And we paid particular attention to the *intermediate* and *late stages of Cosmocreation—the human race!*

Of course, to program and pack such an ungodly wealth of information into one electron was no easy task. I must confess that I did not do everything myself. Razglaz and I shared the work; I thought up the improvements and corrections, and he translated them into the precise language of physics, the theory of vacuums, the theory of electrons, positrons, and sundry other trons. We also set up a kind of incubator where we kept test particles in strict isolation. We would choose from among them the most successful particle, which, as I said, was to give birth to the Universe on October 20.

What good, what wonderful things I planned during those hectic days! How often did I work late into the night poring over books on physics, ethics, and zoology in order to gather, combine, and concentrate the most valuable information, which the Professor, starting at dawn, fashioned into the electron, the cosmic nucleus! We wanted, among other things, to have the Universe develop harmoniously, not as before; to prevent supernovas from jolting it too much; to eliminate the senseless waste of quasar and pulsar energy; to keep stars from sparking and smoking like damp candlewicks; and to shorten interstellar distances, which would facilitate space travel and thus bring together and unify sentient races. It would take volumes to tell of all the corrections I managed to plan in a relatively short time. But these were not the most important things. I need not explain why I concentrated on the human race; to improve it, I changed the principle of natural evolution.

Evolution, as we know, is, in animals, either the wholesale devouring of the weaker by the stronger (zoocide) or the conspiracy of the weaker, which attack the stronger from within (parasitism). Only green plants are moral, living as they do at their own expense, on solar energy. I therefore provided for the chlorophyllization of all living things; in particular, I devised the Foliated Man. Since this meant that the stomach had to go, I transferred to its location a suitably enlarged nerve center. I did not do all this directly, of course, having at my disposal only one electron. I simply established, in cooperation with the Professor, that the fundamental law of evolution in the new, debt-free Universe would be the rule of decent behavior of every life form toward every other. I also designed a much more aesthetic body, a more refined sexuality, and numerous other improvements I will not even mention, for my heart bleeds at the recollection of them. Suffice it to say that by the end of September we had completed the world-creating cannon and its electron bullet. There were still some highly complicated calculations to make; these were done by the professor and his assistants, because aiming for a target in time (or, in this case, before time) was an operation requiring the utmost precision.

I should have stayed on the premises and watched over everything, in view of my tremendous responsibility. But no, I wanted to unwind . . . and went to a small resort. Actually—to tell the truth —I was all swollen with mosquito bites, and that was why I longed for a dip in the cool ocean. If it hadn't been for those damned mosquitoes . . . But I'm not going to put the blame on anything or anyone else; it was all my fault. Just before I left, I had a quarrel with one of the professor's colleagues, a certain Aloysius Bunch. Actually, he was not even a colleague, only a lab assistant, but a fellow-countryman of Razglaz's. This individual, whose job it was to monitor the equipment, demanded—out of the blue—that he be included in the list of Creators. Because—he said—if it weren't for him the cryotron wouldn't work, and if the cryotron didn't work the electron wouldn't act properly . . . etc. I laughed at him, naturally, and he appeared to back down, but evidently the man began to make his own plans in secret. He could do nothing intelligent himself, but he formed a conspiracy with two acquaintances, types who hung around the Nuclear Research Institute in Bombay in hopes of finding a sinecure. They were the German Ast A. Roth and the American Lou Cipher.

As was shown by the inquiry conducted after the event, Bunch let them into the lab at right, and the rest was due to the carelessness of Professor Razglaz's junior assistant, a doctoral candidate named Sarpint. Sarpint had left the keys to the safe on a desk, which made the intruders' task all the easier. He later pleaded illness and presented medical evidence, but the whole institute knew that the jerk was involved with a certain married woman, one Eve Addams, and was so busy groveling at her feet that he neglected his official duties. Bunch led his accomplices to the cryotron; they removed the Dewar vessel from the cryotron, extracted from the vessel the box containing the priceless bullet, and made their infamous parametric "adjustments," the results of which anyone can see. All you have to do is look around you. Afterward, they pleaded, each upstaging the others, that they had had the "best intentions," and had also hoped for glory (!), especially since there were *three* of them.

A fine Trinity! As they admitted under the weight of evidence and under the fire of cross-examination, they had divided up the work. Herr Roth, a former student at Göttingen (but Heisenberg himself had booted him out for putting pornographic pictures in the Aston Spectograph), handled the physical side of Creation and made a royal mess of it. It is because of him that the so-called weak interactions do not correspond to the strong, and that the symmetry of the laws of conservation is imperfect. Any physicist will immediately know what I mean. This same Roth, who made a mistake in simple addition, is responsible for the fact that the electron charge, when it is calculated now, gains an *infinite* value. It is also thanks to this blockhead that one cannot find quarks anywhere, although in theory they exist! The ignoramus forgot to make a correction in the dispersion formula! He also deserves "credit" for the fact that interfering electrons blatantly contradict logic. And to think that the dilemma over which Heisenberg racked his brains his whole life long was caused by his worst and dullest student!

But he committed a far more serious crime. My Creation plan

provided for nuclear reactions, for without them there would be no radiant energy of stars, but I eliminated the elements of the uranium group, so that mankind would be unable to produce atom bombs in the mid-twentieth century—that is, prematurely. Mankind was to harness nuclear energy only as the synthesis of the hydrogen nuclei into the helium, and since that is more difficult, the discovery could not be expected before the twenty-first century. Roth, however, brought the uranides *back into the project.* Unfortunately, I was unable to prove that he had been put up to this by agents of a certain imperialist intelligence agency in connection with plans of military supremacy. . . . The man ought to have been tried for genocide; but for him the Japanese cities would not have been bombed in the Second World War.

The second "expert" in this select trio, Cipher, had finished medical school, but his license to practice was revoked for numerous violations. Cipher handled the biological side and made suitable "improvements" in it. My own reasoning had gone as follows: The world is the way it is, and mankind behaves the way it does, because everything arose by chance, that is, haphazardly, through the initial violation of fundamental laws. One has but to reflect a moment to see that under such conditions things could be worse! The determining factor, after all, was randomness—the "Creator" being the *fluctuational caprice of Nothingness,* which contracted a monstrous and nightmarish debt by inflating, without rhyme or reason, the metagalactic bubble!

I recognized, to be sure, that certain features of the Universe could be left as they were, with a little touching up and correction, so I filled in what was needed. But as far as Man went—ah, there I became radical. I crossed out all his vileness with one stroke. The foliation I mentioned above, which replaced body hair, would have helped establish a new ethics, but Mr. Cipher thought hair more important. He "missed" it, you see. One could make such nice fringes, whiskers, and other fancy things with it. On the one hand, my morality of fellowship and humanism; on the other, the value system of a hairdresser! I assure you, you would not know yourselves if it hadn't been for Lou Cipher, who copied back into the electron from a cassette all the hideous features that you behold in the mirror.

Finally, as for Lab Assistant Bunch, though he was not capable of doing anything himself, he demanded that his cronies immortalize his part in the Creation of the world. He wanted—and I shudder as I write this—he wanted his *name* to be visible from every corner of the firmament. When Roth explained to him that stars cannot form permanent monograms or letters, because of their movements, Bunch desired that they at least be grouped in large clusters, or bunches. This, too, was done.

On October 20, when I placed my finger on the button of the console, I had no idea what I was actually creating. It came to light a couple of days later, when we were checking the tapes and discovered what had been recorded, by the vile trio, in our positron. The Professor was crushed. As for me, I did not know whether to blow out my brains or someone else's. Eventually, reason prevailed over anger and despair, because I knew that nothing could be changed now. I did not even take part in the interrogation of the miscreants who had befouled the world I created. Professor Tarantoga told me about half a year later that the three intruders had played in the Creation a role that religion usually assigned to Satan. I shrugged. What sort of Satan did those three asses make? But the blame is mine; I was careless and left my post. If I wanted to look for excuses, I could say the culprit was the Bombay pharmacist who sold me, instead of decent mosquito repellent, an oil that attracted them as honey does bees. But in this way you could blame God-knows-whom for the flaws in existence. I do not intend to defend myself thus. I am responsible for the world as it is and for all human failing, since it was in my power to make both better.

It is possible in science fiction to include God, or a god, in connection with the beginning of the Universe.

Arthur Clarke has said that any technology, sufficiently advanced beyond one's own, is indistinguishable from magic. To a man of ancient Egypt, the appearance of light at the touch of a finger upon an unnoticed contact would appear magical, even godlike. And if there were a creature with so advanced a technology that with what seemed to us to be a pass of his hand, or a word of his mouth (or whatever the equivalent might be in connection with his physiology) he could create first light and then an entire Universe, that might seem to us, too, to be godlike.

Simak does in this story what a few other science-fiction writers have tried to do—convert God into a superscientist. If the story seems oddly unsophisticated in scientific terms, remember that it was written fifty years ago.

In this connection, by the way, I am reminded of a cartoon I once conceived but could not make actual because I cannot draw. It shows the globe of the Earth, and on it a tiny tree, with a serpent encircling a branch, and with a tiny man and woman, both nude, under it. Above the globe there hovers a beneficent being with a long white beard, dressed in a long white nightgown. Above him hovers a larger, more beneficent being, with a longer, whiter beard and a longer, whiter nightgown. The larger being above is speaking to the smaller being below, and the caption reads: "And for this you expect to earn a Ph.D.?"

THE CREATOR
CLIFFORD D. SIMAK

FOREWORD

This is written in the elder days as the Earth rides close to the rim of eternity, edging nearer to the dying Sun, into which her two inner companions of the solar system have already plunged to a fiery death. The Twilight of the Gods is history; and our planet drifts on and on into that oblivion from which nothing escapes, to which time itself may be dedicated in the final cosmic reckoning.

Old Earth, pacing her death march down the corridors of the

heavens, turns more slowly upon her axis. Her days have lengthened as she crawls sadly to her tomb, shrouded only in the shreds of her former atmosphere. Because her air has thinned, her sky has lost its cheerful blue depths and she is arched with a dreary gray, which hovers close to the surface, as if the horrors of outer space were pressing close, like ravening wolves, upon the flanks of this ancient monarch of the heavens. When night creeps upon her, stranger stars blaze out like a ring of savage eyes closing in upon a dying campfire.

Earth must mourn her passing, for she has stripped herself of all her gaudy finery and proud trappings. Upon her illimitable deserts and twisted ranges she has set up strange land sculptures. And these must be temples and altars before which she, not forgetting the powers of good and evil throughout the cosmos, prays in her last hours, like a dying man returning to his old faith. Mournful breezes play a hymn of futility across her barren reaches of sand and rocky ledges. The waters of the empty oceans beat out upon the treeless, bleak and age-worn coast a march that is the last brave gesture of an ancient planet which has served its purpose and treads the path to Nirvana.

Little half-men and women, final survivors of a great race, which they remember only through legends handed down from father to son, burrow gnomelike in the bowels of the planet which has mothered their seed from dim days when the thing which was destined to rule over all his fellow creatures crawled in the slime of primal seas. A tired race, they wait for the day legend tells them will come, when the sun blazes anew in the sky and grass grows green upon the barren deserts once again. But I know this day will never come, although I would not disillusion them. I know their legends lie, but why should I destroy the only solid thing they have left to round out their colorless life with the everlasting phenomena of hope?

For these little folks have been kind to me and there is a blood-bond between us that even the passing of a million years cannot erase. They think me a god, a messenger that the day they have awaited so long is near. I regret in time to come they must know me as a false prophet.

There is no point in writing these words. My little friends asked me what I do and why I do it and do not seem to understand when I explain. They do not comprehend my purpose in making quaint marks and signs upon the well-tanned pelts of the little rodents which overrun their burrows. All they understand is that when I have finished my labor they must take the skins and treasure them as a sacred trust I have left in their hands.

I have no hope the things I record will ever be read. I write my experiences in the same spirit and with the same bewildered purpose which must have characterized the first ancestor who chipped a runic message upon a stone.

I realize that I write the last manuscript. Earth's proud cities have fallen into mounds of dust. The roads that once crossed her surface have disappeared without a trace. No wheels turn, no engines drone. The last tribe of the human race crouches in its caves, watching for the day that will never come.

FIRST EXPERIMENTS

There may be some who would claim that Scott Marston and I have blasphemed, that we probed too deeply into mysteries where we had no right.

But be that as it may, I do not regret what we did and I am certain that Scott Marston, wherever he may be, feels as I do, without regrets.

We began our friendship at a little college in California. We were naturally drawn together by the similitude of our life, the affinity of our natures. Although our lines of study were widely separated (he majored in science and I in psychology), we both pursued our education for the pure love of learning rather than with a thought of what education might do toward earning a living.

We eschewed the society of the campus, engaging in none of the frivolities of the student body. We spent happy hours in the library and study hall. Our discussions were ponderous and untouched by thought of the college life which flowed about us in all its colorful pageantry.

In our last two years we roomed together. As we were poor, our quarters were shabby, but this never occurred to us. Our entire life was embraced in our studies. We were fired with the true spirit of research.

Inevitably, we finally narrowed our research down to definite lines. Scott, intrigued by the enigma of time, devoted more and more of his leisure moments to the study of that inscrutable element. He found that very little was known of it, beyond the perplexing equations set up by equally perplexed savants.

I wandered into as remote paths, the study of psychophysics and hypnology. I followed my research in hypnology until I came to the point where the mass of facts I had accumulated trapped me in a jungle of various diametrically opposed conclusions, many of which verged upon the occult.

It was at the insistence of my friend that I finally sought a solution in the material rather than the psychic world. He argued that if I were to make any real progress I must follow the dictate of pure, cold science rather than the elusive will-o'-the-wisp of an unproven shadow existence.

At length, having completed our required education, we were offered positions as instructors, he in physics and I in psychology. We eagerly accepted, as neither of us had any wish to change the routine of our lives.

Our new status in life changed our mode of living not at all. We continued to dwell in our shabby quarters, we ate at the same restaurant, we had our nightly discussions. The fact that we were no longer students in the generally accepted term of the word made no iota of difference to our research and study.

It was in the second year after we had been appointed instructors that I finally stumbled upon my "consciousness unit" theory. Gradually I worked it out with the enthusiastic moral support of my friend, who rendered me what assistance he could.

The theory was beautiful in simplicity. It was based upon the hypothesis that a dream is an expression of one's consciousness, that it is one's second self going forth to adventure and travel. When the physical being is at rest the consciousness is released and can travel and adventure at will within certain limits.

I went one step further, however. I assumed that the consciousness actually does travel, that certain infinitesimal parts of one's brain do actually escape to visit the strange places and encounter the odd events of which one dreams.

This was taking dreams out of the psychic world to which they had formerly been relegated and placing them on a solid scientific basis.

I speak of my theory as a "consciousness units" theory. Scott and I spoke of the units as "consciousness cells," although we were aware they could not possibly be cells. I thought of them as highly specialized electrons, despite the fact that it appeared ridiculous to suspect electrons of specialization. Scott contended that a wave force, an intelligence wave, might be nearer the truth. Which of us was correct was never determined, nor did it make any difference.

As may be suspected, I never definitely arrived at undeniable proof to sustain my theory, although later developments would seem to bear it out.

Strangely, it was Scott Marston who did the most to add whatever measure of weight I could ever attach to my hypothesis.

While I was devoting my time to the abstract study of dreams,

Scott was continuing with his equally baffling study of time. He confided to me that he was well satisfied with the progress he was making. At times he explained to me what he was doing, but my natural ineptitude at figures made impossible an understanding of the formidable array of formulas which he spread out before me.

I accepted as a matter of course his statement that he had finally discovered a time force, which he claimed was identical with a fourth-dimensional force. At first the force existed only in a jumble of equations, formulas, and graphs on a litter of paper, but finally we pooled our total resources and under Scott's hand a machine took shape.

Finished, it crouched like a malign entity on the worktable, but it pulsed and hummed with a strange power that was of no earthly source.

"It is operating on time, pure time," declared Scott. "It is warping and distorting the time pattern, snatching power from the fourth dimension. Given a machine large enough, we could create a time-stress great enough to throw this world into a new plane created by the distortion of the time-field."

We shuddered as we gazed upon the humming mass of metal and realized the possibilities of our discovery. Perhaps for a moment we feared that we had probed too deeply into the mystery of an element that should have remained forever outside the province of human knowlege.

The realization that he had only scratched the surface, however, drove Scott on to renewed efforts. He even begrudged the time taken by his work as instructor and there were weeks when we ate meager lunches in our rooms after spending all our available funds but a few pennies to buy some piece needed for the time-power machine.

Came the day when we placed a potted plant within a compartment in the machine. We turned on the mechanism and when we opened the door after a few minutes the plant was gone. The pot and earth within it was intact, but the plant had vanished. A search of the pot revealed that not even a bit of root remained.

Where had the plant gone? Why did the pot and earth remain?

Scott declared the plant had been shunted into an outré dimension, lying between the lines of stress created in the time pattern by the action of the machine. He concluded that the newly discovered force acted more swiftly upon a life organism than upon an inanimate object.

We replaced the pot within the compartment, but after twenty-four hours it was still there. We were forced to conclude the force had no effect upon inanimate objects.

We found later that here we touched close to the truth, but had failed to grasp it in its entirety.

THE DREAM

A year following the construction of the time-power machine, Scott came into an inheritance when a relative, whom he had almost forgotten but who apparently had not forgotten him, died. The inheritance was modest, but to Scott and me, who had lived from hand to mouth for years, it appeared large.

Scott resigned his position as instructor and insisted upon my doing the same in order that we might devote our uninterrupted time to research.

Scott immediately set about the construction of a larger machine, while I plunged with enthusiasm into certain experiments I had held in mind for some time.

It was not until then that we thought to link our endeavors. Our research had always seemed separated by too great a chasm to allow collaboration beyond the limited mutual aid of which we were both capable and which steadily diminished as our work progressed further and further, assuming greater and greater complications, demanding more and more specialization.

The idea occurred to me following repetition of a particularly vivid dream. In the dream I stood in a colossal laboratory, an unearthly laboratory, which seemed to stretch away on every hand for inconceivable distances. It was equipped with strange and unfamiliar apparatus and uncanny machines. On the first night the laboratory seemed unreal and filled with an unnatural mist, but on each subsequent occasion it became more and more real, until upon awakening I could reconstruct many of its details with surprising clarity. I even made a sketch of some of the apparatus for Scott and he agreed that I must have drawn it from the memory of my dream. No man could have imagined unaided the sketches I spread upon paper for my friend.

Scott expressed an opinion that my research into hypnology had served to train my "consciousness units" to a point where they had become more specialized and were capable of retaining a more accurate memory of their wandering. I formulated a theory that my consciousness units had actually increased in number, which would account in a measure for the vividness of the dream.

"I wonder," I mused, "if your time-power would have any influence upon the units."

Scott hummed under his breath. "I wonder," he said.

The dream occurred at regular intervals. Had it not been for my absorption in my work, the dream might have become irksome, but I was elated, for I had found in myself a subject for investigation.

One night Scott brought forth a mechanism resembling the headphones of early radio sets, on which he had been working for weeks. He had not yet explained its purpose.

"Pete," he said, "I want you to move your cot near the table and put on this helmet. When you go to sleep I'll plug it in the time-power. If it has any effect upon consciousness units, this will demonstrate it."

He noticed my hesitation.

"Don't be afraid," he urged. "I will watch beside you. If anything goes wrong, I'll jerk the plug and wake you."

So I put on the helmet and, with Scott Marston sitting in a chair beside my cot, went to sleep.

That night I seemed to actually walk in the laboratory. I saw no one, but I examined the place from end to end. I distinctly remember handling strange tools, the use of which I could only vaguely speculate upon. Flanking the main laboratory were many archways, opening into smaller rooms, which I did not investigate. The architecture of the laboratory and the archways was unbelievably alien, a fact I had noticed before but had never examined in such minute detail.

I opened my eyes and saw the anxious face of Scott Marston above me.

"What happened, Pete?" he asked.

I grasped his arm.

"Scott, I was there. I actually walked in the laboratory. I picked up tools. I can see the place now, plainer than ever before."

I saw a wild light come into his eyes. He rose from the chair and stood towering above me as I propped myself up on my arms.

"Do you know what we've found, Pete! Do you realize that we can travel in time, that we can explore the future, investigate the past? We are not even bound to this sphere, this plane of existence. We can travel into the multidimensions. We can go back to the first flush of eternity and see the cosmos born out of the womb of nothingness! We can travel forward to the day when all that exists comes to an end in the ultimate dispersion of wasted energy, when even space may be wiped out of existence and nothing but frozen time remains!"

"Are you mad, Scott?"

His eyes gleamed.

"Not mad, Pete. Victorious! We can build a machine large enough, powerful enough, to turn every cell of our bodies into consciousness units. We can travel in body as well as in thought. We can live thousands of lifetimes, review billions of years. We can visit undreamed-of planets, unknown ages. We hold time in our hands!"

He beat his clenched fists together.

"That plant we placed in the machine. My God, Pete, do you know what happened to it? What primordial memories did that plant hold? Where is it now? Is it in some swamp of the carboniferous age? Has it returned to its ancestral era?"

Years passed, but we scarcely noticed their passing.

Our hair grayed slightly at the temples and the mantle of youth dropped slowly from us. No fame came to us, for our research had progressed to a point where it would have strained even the most credulous mind to believe what we could have unfolded.

Scott built his larger time-power machine, experimented with it, devised new improvements, discovered new details . . . and rebuilt it, not once, but many times. The ultimate machine, squatting like an alien god in our workshop, bore little resemblance to the original model.

On my part, I delved more deeply into my study of dreams, relentlessly pursuing my theory of consciousness units. My progress necessarily was slower than that of my friend as I was dealing almost entirely with the abtruse although I tried to make it as practical as possible, while Scott had a more practical and material basis for his investigations.

Of course, we soon decided to make the attempt to actually transfer our bodies into the laboratory of my dreams. That is, we proposed to transform all the electrons, all the elements of our bodies, into consciousness units through the use of the time-power. A more daring scheme possibly had never been conceived by man.

In an attempt to impress upon my friend's mind a picture of the laboratory, I drew diagrams and pictures, visiting the laboratory many times, with the aid of the time-power, to gather more detailed data on the place.

It was not until I used hypnotism that I could finally transfer to Scott's mind a true picture of that massive room with its outré scientific equipment.

It was a day of high triumph when Scott, placed under the influence of the time-power, awoke to tell me of the place I had visited so often. It was not until then that we could be absolutely sure we had accomplished the first, and perhaps most difficult, step in our great experiment.

I plunged into a mad study of the psychology of the Oriental ascetic, who of all people was the furthest advanced in the matter of concentration, the science of willpower, and the ability to subjugate the body to the mind.

Although my studies left much to be desired, they nevertheless pointed the way for us to consciously aid the time-power element in reducing our corporeal beings to the state of consciousness units necessary for our actual transportation to the huge laboratory with which we had both grown so familiar.

There were other places than the dream-laboratory, of course. Both of us, in our half-life imparted by the time-power, visited other strange places, the location of which in time and space we could not determine. We looked upon sights which would have blasted our mortal sanity had we gazed upon them in full consciousness. There were times when we awoke with blanched faces and told each other in ghastly, fear-ridden whispers of the horrors that dwelled in some unprobed dimension of the unplumbed depth of the cosmos. We stared at shambling, slithering things which we recognized as the descendants of entities, or perhaps the very entities, which were related in manuscripts written by ancient men versed in the blackest of sorcery—and still remembered in the hag-ridden tales of people in the hinterlands.

But it was upon the mysterious laboratory that we centered all our efforts. It had been our first real glimpse into the vast vista to which we had raised the veil and to it we remained true, regarding those other places as mere side excursions into the recondite world we had discovered.

IN THE CREATOR'S LABORATORY

At last the day arrived when we were satisfied we had advanced sufficiently far in our investigations and had perfected our technique to a point where we might safely attempt an actual excursion into the familiar, yet unknown, realm of the dream-laboratory.

The completed and improved time-power machine squatted before us like a hideous relic out of the forgotten days of an earlier age, its weird voice filling the entire house, rising and falling, half the time a scream, half the time a deep murmur. Its polished sides glistened evilly and the mirrors set about it, at inconceivable angles in their relation to each other, caught the glare from the row of step-up tubes across the top, reflecting the light to bathe the entire creation in an unholy glow.

We stood before it, our hair tinged with gray, our faces marked by lines of premature age. We were young men grown old in the service of our ambition and vast curiosity.

After ten years we had created a thing that I now realize might have killed us both. But at that time we were superbly confident. Ten years of molding metal and glass, harnessing and taming strange powers! Ten years of molding brains, of concentrating and stepping up the sensitivity and strength of our consciousness until, day and night, there lurked in the back of our brains an image of that mysterious laboratory. As our consciousness direction had been gradually narrowed, the laboratory had become almost a second life to us.

Scott pressed a stud on the side of the machine and a door swung outward, revealing an interior compartment which yawned like a black maw. In that maw was no hint of the raw power and surging strength revealed by the exterior. Yet, to the uninitiate, it would have held a horrible threat of its own.

Scott stepped through the door into the pitch-black interior; gently he lowered himself into the reclining seat, reaching out to place his hands on the power controls.

I slid in beside him and closed the door. As the last ray of light was shut out, absolute blackness enveloped us. We fitted power helmets on our heads. Terrific energy poured through us, beating through our bodies, seeming to tear us to pieces.

My friend stretched forth a groping hand. Fumbling in the darkness, I found it. Our hands closed in a fierce grip, the handshake of men about to venture into the unknown.

I fought for control of my thoughts, centered them savagely upon the laboratory, recalling, with a supereffort, every detail of its interior. Then Scott must have shoved the power control full over. My body was pain-racked, then seemed to sway with giddiness. I forgot my body. The laboratory seemed nearer; it seemed to flash up at me. I was falling toward it, falling rapidly. I was a detached thought speeding along a directional line, falling straight into the laboratory . . . and I was very ill.

My fall was suddenly broken, without jar or impact.

I was standing in the laboratory. I could feel the cold of the floor beneath my feet.

I glanced sidewise and there stood Scott Marston and my friend was stark naked. Of course, we would be naked. Our clothing would not be transported through the time-power machine.

"It didn't kill us," remarked Scott.

"Not even a scratch," I asserted.

We faced each other and shook hands, solemnly, for again we had triumphed and that handshake was a self-imposed congratulation.

We turned back to the room before us. It was a colorful place. Varicolored liquids reposed in gleaming containers. The furniture, queerly carved and constructed along lines alien to any earthly standard, seemed to be of highly polished, iridescent wood. Through the windows poured a brilliant blue daylight. Great globes suspended from the ceiling further illuminated the building with a soft white glow.

A cone of light, a creamy white faintly tinged with pink, floated through an arched doorway and entered the room. We stared at it. It seemed to be light, yet was it light? It was not transparent and although it gave one the impression of intense brilliance, its color was so soft that it did not hurt one's eyes to look at it.

The cone, about ten feet in height, rested on its smaller end and advanced rapidly toward us. Its approach was silent. There was not even the remotest suggestion of sound in the entire room. It came to a rest a short distance in front of us and I had an uncanny sense that the thing was busily observing us.

"Who are you?"

The Voice seemed to fill the room, yet there was no one there but Scott and me, and neither of us had spoken. We looked at one another in astonishment and then shifted our gaze to the cone of light, motionless, resting quietly before us.

"I am speaking," said the Voice and instantly each of us knew that the strange cone before us had voiced the words.

"I am not speaking," went on the Voice. "That was a misstatement. I am thinking. You hear my thoughts. I can as easily hear yours."

"Telepathy," I suggested.

"Your term is a strange one," replied the Voice, "but the mental image the term calls up tells me that you faintly understand the principle.

"I perceive from your thoughts that you are from a place which you call the Earth. I know where the Earth is located. I understand you are puzzled and discomfited by my appearance, my powers, and my general disresemblance to anything you have ever encountered. Do not be alarmed. I welcome you here. I understand you worked hard and well to arrive here and no harm will befall you."

"I am Scott Marston," said my friend, "and this man is Peter Sands."

The thoughts of the light-cone reached out to envelop us and there was a faint tinge of rebuke, a timbre of pity at what must have appeared to the thing as unwarranted egotism on our part.

"In this place there are no names. We are known by our personalities. However, as your mentality demands an identifying name, you may think of me as the Creator.

"And now, there are others I would have you see."

He sounded a call, a weird call which seemed to incorporate as equally a weird name.

There was a patter of feet on the floor and from an adjoining room ran three animallike figures. Two were similar. They were pudgy of body, with thick, short legs which terminated in rounded pads that made sucking sounds as they ran. They had no arms, but from the center of their bulging chests sprang a tentacle, fashioned somewhat after the manner of an elephant's trunk, but with a number of small tentacles at its end. Their heads, rising to a peak from which grew a plume of gaily colored feathers, sat upon their tapering shoulders without benefit of necks.

The third was an antithesis of the first two. He was tall and spindly, built on the lines of a walking stick insect. His gangling legs were three-jointed. His grotesquely long arms dangled almost to the floor. Looking at his body, I believed I could have encircled it with my two hands. His head was simply an oval ball set on top of the sticklike body. The creature more nearly resembled a man than the other two, but he was a caricature of a man, a comic offering from the pen of a sardonic cartoonist.

The Creator seemed to be addressing the three.

"Here," he said, "are some new arrivals. They came here, I gather, in much the same manner you did. They are great scientists, great as yourselves. You will be friends."

The Creator turned his attention to us.

"These beings which you see came here as you did and are my guests as you are my guests. They may appear outlandish to you. Rest assured that you appear just as queer to them. They are brothers of yours, neighbors of yours. They are from your ———."

I received the impression of gazing down on vast space, filled with swirling motes of light.

"He means our solar system," suggested Scott.

Carefully I built up in my mind a diagram of the solar system.

"*No!*" The denial crashed like an angry thunderbolt upon us. Again the image of unimaginable space and of thousands of points of light—of swirling nebulae, of solar systems, mighty double suns and island universes.

"He means the universe," said Scott.

"Certainly they came from our universe," I replied. "The universe is everything, isn't it—all existing things?"

Again the negative of the Creator burned its way into our brains.

"You are mistaken, Earthman. Your knowledge here counts as nothing. You are mere infants. But come; I will show you what your universe consists of."

—OUR UNIVERSE?

Streamers of light writhed down from the cone toward us. As we shrank back they coiled about our waists and gently lifted us. Soothing thoughts flowed over us, instructions to commit ourselves unreservedly to the care of the Creator, to fear no harm. Under this reassurance, my fears quieted. I felt that I was under the protection of a benevolent being, that his great power and compassion would shield me in this strange world. A Creator, in very truth!

The Creator glided across the floor to set us on our feet on the top of a huge table, which stood about seven feet above the floor level.

On the tabletop, directly before me, I saw a thin oval receptacle, made of a substance resembling glass. It was about a foot across its greatest length and perhaps a little more than half as wide and about four inches deep. The receptacle was filled with a sort of grayish substance, a mass of puttylike material. To me it suggested nothing more than a mass of brain substance.

"There," said the Creator, pointing a light-streamer finger at the disgusting mass, "is your universe."

"What!" cried Scott.

"It is so," ponderously declared the Creator.

"Such a thing is impossible," firmly asserted Scott. "The universe is boundless. At one time it was believed that it was finite, that it was enclosed by the curvature of space. I am convinced, however, through my study of time, that the universe, composed of millions of overlapping and interlocking dimensions, can be nothing but eternal and infinite. I do not mean that there will not be a time when all matter will be destroyed, but I do maintain—"

"You are disrespectful and conceited," boomed the thought vibrations of the Creator. "That is your universe. I made it. I created it. And more. I created the life that teems within it. I was curious to learn what form that life would take, so I sent powerful thought vibrations into it, calling that life out. I had little hope that it had developed the necessary intelligence to find the road to my laboratory, but I find that at least five of the beings evolving from my created life possessed brains tuned finely enough to catch my vibrations and possessed sufficient intelligence to break out of their medium. You are two of these five. The other three you have just seen."

"You mean," said Scott, speaking softly, "that you created matter and then went further and created life?"

"I did."

I stared at the puttylike mass. The universe! Millions of galaxies composed of millions of suns and planets—all in that lump of matter!

"This is the greatest hoax I've ever seen," declared Scott, a deliberate note of scorn in his voice. "If that is the universe down there, how are we so big? I could step on that dish and break the universe all to smithereens. It doesn't fit."

The light-finger of the Creator flicked out and seized my friend, wafting him high above the table. The Creator glowed with dull flashes of red and purple.

His thought vibrations filled the room to bursting with their power.

"Presumptuous one! You defy the Creator. You call his great work a lie! You, with your little knowledge! You, a specimen of the artificial life I created, would tell me, your very Creator, that I am wrong!"

I stood frozen, staring at my friend, suspended above me at the end of the rigid light-streamer. I could see Scott's face. It was set and white, but there was no sign of fear upon it.

His voice came down to me, cold and mocking.

"A jealous god," he taunted.

The Creator set him down gently beside me. His thoughts came to us evenly, with no trace of his terrible anger of only a moment before.

"I am not jealous. I am above all your imperfect emotions. I have evolved to the highest type of life but one—pure thought. In time I will achieve that. I may grow impatient at times with your tiny brains, with your imperfect knowledge, with your egotism, but beyond that I am unemotional. The emotions have become unnecessary to my existence."

I hurried to intervene.

"My friend spoke without thinking," I explained. "You realize this is all unusual to us. Something beyond any previous experience. It is hard for us to believe."

"I know it must be hard for you to understand," agreed the Creator. "You are in an ultra-universe. The electrons and protons making up your body have grown to billions and billions of times their former size, with correspondingly greater distances between them. It is all a matter of relativity. I did not consciously create your universe, I merely created electrons and protons. I created matter. I created life—and injected it into the matter.

"I learned from the three who preceded you here that all things upon my electrons and protons, even my very created electrons and protons, are themselves composed of electrons and protons.

This I had not suspected. I am at a loss to explain it. I am beginning to believe that one will never find an end to the mysteries of matter and life. It may be that the electrons and protons you know are composed of billions of infinitely smaller electrons and protons."

"And I suppose," mocked Scott, "that you, the Creator, may be merely a bit of synthetic life living in a universe that is in turn merely a mass of matter in some greater laboratory."

"It may be so," said the Creator. "My knowledge has made me very humble."

Scott laughed.

"And now," said the Creator, "if you will tell me what food and other necessities you require to sustain life, I will see you are provided for. You also will wish to build the machine which will take you back to Earth once more. You shall be assigned living quarters and may do as you wish. When your machine is completed, you may return to Earth. If you do not wish to do so, you are welcome to remain indefinitely as my guests. All I wished you to come here for was to satisfy my curiosity concerning what forms my artificial life may have taken."

The tentacles of light lifted us carefully to the floor and we followed the Creator to our room, which adjoined the laboratory proper and was connected to it by a high, wide archway. What the place lacked in privacy, it made up in beauty. Finished in pastel shades, it was easy on the eyes and soothing to one's nerves.

We formed mind pictures of beds, tables, and chairs. We described our foods and their chemical composition. Water we did not need to describe. The Creator knew instantly what it was. It, of all the necessities of our life, however, seemed the only thing in common with our earth contained in this ultra-universe into which we had projected ourselves.

In what seemed to us a miraculously short time our needs were provided. We were supplied with furniture, food and clothing, all of which apparently was produced synthetically by the Creator in his laboratory.

Later we were to learn that the combining of elements and the shaping of the finished product was a routine matter. A huge, yet simple machine was used in the combination and fixing of the elements.

Steel, glass, and tools, shaped according to specifications given the Creator by Scott, were delivered to us in a large workroom directly off the laboratory where our three compatriots of the universe were at work upon their machines.

The machine being constructed by the lone gangling creature, which Scott and I had immediately dubbed the "walking-stick-man," resembled in structure the creature building it. It was shaped like a pyramid and into its assembly had gone hundreds of long rods.

The machine of the elephant-men was a prosaic affair, shaped like a crude box of some rubber material, but its inner machinery, which we found to be entirely alien to any earthly conceptions, was intricate.

From the first the walking-stick-man disregarded us except when we forced our attentions on him.

The elephant-men were friendly, however.

We had hardly been introduced into the workshop before the two of them attempted to strike up an acquaintaince with us.

We spoke to them as they stood before us, but they merely blinked their dull expressionless eyes. They touched us with their trunks, and we felt faint electric shocks which varied in intensity, like the impulses traveling along a wire, like some secret code tapped out by a telegrapher.

"They have no auditory sense," said Scott. "They talk by the transmission of electrical impulses through their trunks. There's no use talking to them."

"And in a thousand years we might figure out their electrical language," I replied.

After a few more futile attempts to establish communication Scott turned to the task of constructing the time-power machine, while the elephant-men padded back to their own work.

I walked over to the walking-stick-man and attempted to establish communication with him, but with no better results. The creature, seeming to resent my interruption of his work, waved his hands in fantastic gestures, working his mouth rapidly. In despair, I realized that he was talking to me, but that his jabbering was pitched too high for my ear to catch.

Here were representatives of three difference races, all three of a high degree of intelligence else they never would have reached this superplane, and not a single thought, not one idea could they interchange. Even had a communication of ideas been possible, I wondered if we could have found any common ground of understanding.

I stared at the machines. They were utterly different from each other and neither bore any resemblance to ours. Undoubtedly they all operated on dissimilar principles.

In that one room adjoining the main laboratory were being

constructed three essentially different types of mechanisms by three entirely different types of beings. Yet each machine was designed to accomplish the same result and each of the beings was striving for the same goal!

Unable to assist Scott in his building of the time-power machine, I spent the greater part of my waking hours in roaming about the laboratory, in watching the Creator at work. Occasionally I talked to him. At times he explained to me what he was doing, but I am afraid I understood little of what he told me.

One day he allowed me to look through a microscope at a part of the matter he had told us contained our universe.

I was unprepared for what I saw. As I peered into the complicated machine, I saw protons, electrons! Judged by earthly standards, they were grouped peculiarly, but their formation corresponded almost exactly to our planetary system. I sensed that certain properties in that master-microscope created an optical illusion by grouping them more closely than were their actual corresponding distances. The distance between them had been foreshortened to allow an entire group to be within a field of vision.

But this was impossible! The very lenses through which I was looking were themselves formed of electrons and protons! How could they have any magnifying power?

The Creator read my thoughts and tried to explain, but his explanation was merely a blur of distances, a mass of outlandish mathematical equations and a pyramiding of stupendous formulas dealing with the properties of light. I realized that, with the Creator, the Einstein equations were elementary, that the most intricate mathematics conceived by man were as rudimentary to him as simple addition.

He must have realized it, too, for after that he did not attempt to explain anything to me. He made it plain, however, that I was welcome to visit him at his work, and as time passed, he came to take my presence as a matter of course. At times he seemed to forget I was about.

The work on the time-power machine was progressing steadily under Scott's skillful hands. I could see that the other two machines were nearing completion, but that my friend was working with greater speed. I calculated that all three of the machines would be completed at practically the same time.

"I don't like this place," Scott confided to me. "I want to get the machine built and get out of here as soon as I can. The Creator is a being entirely different from us. His thought processes and emotional reflexes can bear little resemblance to ours. He is further advanced along the scale of life than we. I am not fool enough to believe he accepts us as his equals. He claims he created us.

Whether he did or not, and I can't bring myself to believe that he did, he nevertheless believes he did. That makes us his property —in his own belief, at least—to do with as he wishes. I'm getting out of here before something happens."

One of the elephant-men, who had been working with his partner, approached us as we talked. He tapped me gently with his trunk and then stood stupidly staring at us.

"Funny," said Scott. "That fellow has been bothering me all day. He's got something he wants to tell us, but he doesn't seem to be able to get it across"

Patiently I attempted an elementary language, but the elephant-man merely stared, unmoved, apparently not understanding.

The following day I secured from the Creator a supply of synthetic paper and a sort of black crayon. With these I approached the elephant-men and drew simple pictures, but again I failed. The strange creatures merely stared. Pictures and diagrams meant nothing to them.

The walking-stick-man, however, watched us from across the room and after the elephant-men had turned away to their work, he walked over to where I stood and held out his hands for the tablet and crayon. I gave them to him. He studied my sketches for a moment, ripped off the sheet and rapidly wielded the crayon. He handed back the tablet. On the sheet were a number of hieroglyphics. I could not make head or tail of them. For a long time the two of us labored over the tablet. We covered the floor with sheets covered with our scribbling, pictures, and diagrams. We quit in despair after advancing ro further than recognizing the symbols for the cardinal numbers.

It was apparent that not only the elephant-men but the walking-stick-man as well wished to communicate something to us. Scott and I discussed it often, racking our brains for some means to establish communication with our brothers in exile.

CREATION—AND DESTRUCTION

It was shortly after this I made the discovery that I was able to read the unprojected thoughts of the Creator. I imagine that this was made possible by the fact that our host paid little attention to me as he went about his work. Busy with his tasks, his thoughts must have seeped out as he mulled over the problems confronting him. It must have been through this thought seepage that I caught the first of his unprojected brain-images.

At first I received just faint impressions, sort of half-thoughts.

Realizing what was occurring, I concentrated upon his thoughts, endeavoring to bore into his brain, to probe out those other thoughts which lay beneath the surface. If it had not been for the intensive mind training which I had imposed upon myself prior to the attempt to project my body through the time-power machine, I am certain I would have failed. Without this training, I doubt if I would have been able to read his thoughts unbidden in the first place—certainly I could not have prevented him from learning that I had.

Recalling Scott's suspicions, I realized that my suddenly dis-covered ability might be used to our advantage. I also realized that this ability would be worthless should the Creator learn of it. In such case, he would be alert and would close his thought pro-cesses to me. My hope lay in keeping any suspicion disarmed. Therefore I must not only read his mind but must also keep a portion of mine closed to him.

Patch by patch I pieced his thoughts together like a jigsaw puzzle.

He was studying the destruction of matter, seeking a method of completely annihilating it. Having discovered a means of creat-ing matter, he was now experimenting with its destruction.

I did not share my secret with Scott, for I feared that he would unconsciously betray it to the Creator.

As days passed, I learned that the Creator was considering the destruction of matter without the use of heat. I knew that, even on Earth, it was generally conceded a temperature of 4 trillion de-grees Fahrenheit would absolutely annihilate matter. I had be-lieved the Creator had found some manner in which he could control such an excessive temperature. But to attempt to destroy matter without using heat at all—! I believe that it was not until then that I fully realized the great chasm of intelligence that lay between myself and this creature of light.

I have no idea how long we remained in the world of the Creator before Scott announced that the machine in which we expected to return to our universe was ready for a few tests. Time had the illusive quality in this queer place of slithering along without no-ticeably passing. Although I did not think of it at the time, I cannot recollect now that the Creator employed any means of measuring time. Perhaps time, so far as he was concerned, had become an unnecessary equation. Perhaps he was eternal and time held no significance for him in his eternity.

The elephant-men and the walking-stick-man had already com-pleted their machines, but they seemed to be waiting for us. Was it a gesture of respect? We did not know at the time.

While Scott made the final tests of our machine I walked into the laboratory. The Creator was at work at his accustomed place. Since our arrival he had paid little attention to us. Now that we were about to leave he made no expression of regret, no sign of farewell.

I approached him, wondering if I should bid him farewell. I had grown to respect him. I wanted to say goodbye, and yet. . . .

Then I caught the faintest of his thoughts and I stiffened. Instantly and unconsciously my mind thrust out probing fingers and grasped the predominant idea in the Creator's mind.

". . . Destroy the mass of created matter—the universe which I created . . . create matter . . . destroy it. It is a laboratory product. Test my destructive. . . ."

"Why, you damn murderer," I screamed, and threw myself at him.

Light fingers flicked out at me, whipped around my body, snapped me into the air and heaved me across the laboratory. I struck on the smooth floor and skidded across it to bring up with a crash against the wall.

I shook my head to clear it and struggled to my feet. We must fight the Creator! Must save our world from destruction by the very creature who had created it!

I came to my feet with my muscles bunched, crouched in a fighting posture.

But the Creator had not moved. He stood in the same position and a rod of purple light extended between him and the queer machine of the walking-stick man. The rod of light seemed to be holding him there, frozen, immovable. Beside the machine stood the walking-stick-man, his hand on the lever, a mad glare in his eyes.

Scott was slapping the gangling fellow on his slender back.

"You've got the goods, old man," he was shouting. "That's one trick old frozen face didn't learn from you."

A thunderous tumult beat through my head. The machine of the walking-stick-man was not a transmission machine at all. It was a weapon—a weapon that could freeze the Creator into rigid lines.

Weird colors flowed through the Creator. Dead silences lay over the room. The machine of the walking-stick-man was silent, with no noise to hint of the great power it must have been developing. The purple rod did not waver. It was just a rigid rod of purple which had struck and stiffened the Creator.

I screamed at Scott: "Quick! The universe! He is going to destroy it!"

Scott leaped forward. Together we raced toward the table where the mass of created matter lay in its receptacle. Behind us padded the elephant-men.

As we reached the table, I felt a sinuous trunk wrap about me. With a flip I was hurled to the tabletop. It was but a step to the dish containing the universe. I snatched it up, dish and all, and handed it down to Scott. I let myself over the table edge, hung by my hands for an instant, and dropped. I raced after the others toward the workshop.

As we gained the room, the walking-stick-man made an adjustment on his machine. The purple rod faded away. The Creator, a towering cone of light, tottered for a moment and then glided swiftly for the doorway.

Instantly a sheet of purple radiance filled the opening. The Creator struck against it and was hurled back.

The radiance was swiftly arching overhead and curving beneath us, cutting through the floor, walls, and ceiling.

"He's enclosing us in a globe of that stuff," cried Scott. "It must be an energy screen of some sort, but I can't imagine what. Can you?"

"I don't care what it is, just so it works," I panted, anxiously.

Through the steady purple light I could see the Creator. Repeatedly he hurled himself against the screen and each time he was hurled back.

"We're moving," announced Scott.

The great purple globe was ascending, carrying in its interior we five universe-men, our machines, and fragments of the room in which we but recently had stood. It was cutting through the building like the flame of a torch through soft steel. We burst free of the building into the brilliant blue sunlight of that weird world.

Beneath us lay the building, a marvel of outré architecture, but with a huge circular shaft cut through it—the path of the purple globe. All about the building lay a forest of red and yellow vegetation, shaped as no vegetation of Earth is shaped, bent into hundreds of strange and alien forms.

Swiftly the globe sprang upward to hang in the air some distance above the building. As far as the eye could see stretched the painted forest. The laboratory we had just quit was the only sign of habitation. No roads, no lakes, no rivers, no distant mountain —nothing relieved the level plain of red and yellow stretching away to faint horizons.

Was the Creator, I wondered, the sole denizen of this land? Was he the last survivor of a mystic race? Had there ever been a race at all? Might not the Creator be a laboratory product, even as the things he created were laboratory products? But if so, who or what had set to work the agents which resulted in that uncanny cone of energy?

My reflections were cut short as the walking-stick-man reached out his skinny hand for the mass of matter which Scott still held. As I watched him breathlessly, he laid it gently on a part of the floor which still remained in the globe and pulled a sliding rod from the side of the machine. A faint purple radiance sprang from the point of the rod, bathing the universe. The radiant purple surrounded the mass, grew thicker and thicker, seeming to congeal into layer after layer until the mass of matter lay sealed in a thick shell of the queer stuff. When I touched it, it did not appear to be hard or brittle. It was smooth and slimy to the touch, but I could not dent it with my fingers.

"He's building up the shell of the globe in just the same way," Scott said. "The machine seems to be projecting that purple stuff to the outside of the shell, where it is congealed into layers."

I noted that what he said was true. The shell of the globe had taken on a thickness that could be perceived, although the increased thickness did not seem to interfere with our vision.

Looking down at the laboratory, I could see some strange mechanism mounted on the roof of the building. Beside the massive mechanism stood the Creator.

"Maybe it's a weapon of some sort," suggested Scott.

Hardly had he spoken when a huge column of crimson light leaped forth from the machine. I threw up my hands to protect my eyes from the glare of the fiery column. For an instant the globe was bathed in the red glow, then a huge globule of red collected on its surface and leaped away, straight for the laboratory, leaving behind a trail of crimson.

The globe trembled at the force of the explosion as the ball of light struck. Where the laboratory had stood was merely a great hole, blasted to the primal rock beneath. The vegetation for great distances on either side was sifting ash. The Creator had disappeared. The colorful world beneath stretched empty to the horizon. The men of the universe had proven to be stronger than their Creator!

"If there's any more Creators around these parts," said Scott, smiling feebly, "they won't dare train another gun on this thing in the next million years. It gives them exactly what was meant for the other fellow; it crams their poison right down their own throats. Pete, that mass of matter, whether or not it is the universe, is saved. All hell couldn't get at it here."

The walking-stick-man, his mummylike face impassive as ever, locked the controls of the machine. It was, I saw, still operating, was still building up the shell of the globe. Second by second the globe was adding to its fortress—light strength. My mind reeled as I thought of it continuing thus throughout eternity.

The elephant-men were climbing into their machines.

Scott smiled wanly.

"The play is over," he said. "The curtain is down. It's time for us to go."

He stepped to the side of the walking-stick man.

"I wish you would use our machine." he said, evidently forgetting our friend could understand no word he spoke. "You threw away your chance back there when you built this contraption instead of a transmitter. Our machine will take you wherever you wish to go."

He pointed to the machine and to the universe, then tapped his head. With the strange being at his side, he walked to our machine, pointed out the controls, explained its uses in pantomime.

"I don't know if he understands," said Scott, "but I did the best I could."

As I walked past the walking-stick-man to step into the time-power machine, I believe I detected a faint flicker of a smile on his face. Of that, however, I can never be sure.

MAROONED IN TIME

I know how the mistake was made. I was excited when I stepped into the machine. My mind was filled with the many strange happenings I had witnessed. I thought along space directional lines, *but I forgot to reckon the factor of time.*

I thought of the Earth, but I did not consider time. I willed myself to be back on Earth, but I forgot to will myself in any particular time era. Consequently when Scott shoved over the lever, I was shot to Earth, but the time element was confused.

I realize that life in the superuniverse of the Creator, being billions of times larger than life upon the Earth, was correspondingly slower. Every second in the superuniverse was equal to years of Earth-time. My life in the Creator's universe had equaled millions of years of Terran existence.

I believe that my body was projected along a straight line and not along the curve which was necessary to place me back in the twentieth century.

This is theory, of course. There might have been some fault in the machine. The purple globe might have exerted some influence to distort our calculations.

Be that as it may, I reached a dying planet. It has been given to me, a man of the twentieth century, to live out the last years of my life on my home planet some millions of years later than the date of my birth. I, a resident of a comparatively young dynasty in the history of the Earth, now am tribal chieftain and demigod of the last race, a race that is dying even as the planet is dying.

As I sit before my cave or huddle with the rest of my clan around a feeble fire, I often wonder if Scott Marston was returned to Earth in his proper time. Or is he, too, a castaway in some strange time? Does he still live? Did he ever reach the Earth? I often feel that he may even now be searching through the vast corridors of time and the deserts of space for me, his one-time partner in the wildest venture ever attempted by man.

And often, too, I wonder if the walking-stick-man used our time-power machine to return to his native planet. Or is he a prisoner in his own trap, caught within the scope of the great purple globe? And I wonder how large the globe has grown.

I realize now that our effort to save the universe was unnecessary so far as the earth was concerned, for the earth, moving at its greater time-speed, would already have plunged into extinction in the flaming furnace of the sun before the Creator could carry out his destructive plans.

But what of those other worlds? What of those other planets which must surely swim around strange suns in the gulf of space? What of the planets and races yet unborn? What of the populations that may exist on the solar systems of island universes far removed from our own?

They are saved, saved for all time; for the purple globe will guard the handiwork of the Creator through eternity.

Which brings us back to the first item: Gunn's poem. That was a momentary vision; Benford gives us a painstaking comparison. Benford is a professional physicist and it is his job (when he is not writing science fiction) to try to make sense out of the subtle signals being sent us by the Universe.

There is no contract whereby the Universe agrees to make it simple for us, or to tell us anything in a way that makes sense. We have to squeeze information out of it, little by little, year by year, using our own ingenuity to force one more drop out of it, or, as an alternative, being the heir of unexplainable good luck.

There are mysteries and mysteries, and perhaps no matter the route by which we approach the moments of creation, we are forced to confront them. The route of science, however, offers us hope. Where God, in the Book of Job, tells us we can never understand, science seems to give us the assurance (false, perhaps, but not certainly false) that, given enough time, we will understand— and that, in any case, even if we never fully understand, each year we may understand a little more than the year before.

EXPOSURES
GREGORY BENFORD

Puzzles assemble themselves one piece at a time. Yesterday I began laying out the new plates I had taken up on the mountain, at Palomar. They were exposures of varying depth. In each, NGC 1097—a barred spiral galaxy about twenty megaparsecs away— hung suspended in its slow swirl.

As I laid out the plates I thought of the way our family had always divided up the breakfast chores on Sunday. On that ritual day our mother stayed in bed. I laid out the forks and knives and egg cups and formal off-white china, and then stood back in the thin morning light to survey my precise placings. Lush napkin pyramids perched on lace tablecloth, my mother's favorite. Through the kitchen door leaked the mutter and clang of a meal coming into being.

I put the exposures in order according to the spectral filters used, noting the calibrated photometry for each. The ceramic sounds of Bridge Hall rang in the tiled hallways and seeped through the door of my office: footsteps, distant talk, the scrape of chalk on slate, a banging door. Examining the plates through an eyepiece, I felt the galaxy swell into being, huge

The deep exposures brought out the dim jets I was after. There were four of them pointing out of NGC 1097, two red and two blue, the brightest three discovered by Wolsencroft and Zealey, the last red one found by Lorre over at JPL. Straight lines scratched across the mottling of foreground dust and stars. No one knew what colored a jet red or blue. I was trying to use the deep plates to measure the width of the jets. Using a slit over the lens, I had stopped down the image until I could employ calibrated photometry to measure the wedge of light. Still further narrowing might allow me to measure the spectrum to see if the blues and reds came from stars, or from excited clouds of gas.

They lanced out, two blue jets cutting through the spiral arms and breaking free into the blackness beyond. One plate, taken in that spectral space where ionized hydrogen clouds emit, giving H II radiation, showed a string of beads buried in the curling spiral lanes. They were vast cooling clouds. Where the jets crossed the H II regions, the spiral arms were pushed outward, or else vanished altogether.

Opposite each blue jet, far across the galaxy, a red jet glowed. They, too, snuffed out the H II beads.

From these gaps in the spiral arms I estimated how far the barred spiral galaxy had turned, while the jets ate away at them: about fifteen degrees. From the velocity measurements in the disk, using the Doppler shifts of known spectral lines, I deduced the rotation rate of the NGC 1097 disk: approximately 100 million years. Not surprising; our own sun takes about the same amount of time to circle around our galactic center. The photons which told me all these specifics had begun their steady voyage 60 million years ago, before there was a *New General Catalog of Nebulae and Clusters of Stars* to label them as they buried themselves in my welcoming emulsion. Thus do I know thee, NGC 1097.

These jets were unique. The brightest blue one doglegs in a right angle turn and ends in silvery blobs of dry light. Its counter-jet, offset a perverse eleven degrees from exact oppositeness, continues on a warmly rose-colored path over an immense distance, a span far larger than the parent galaxy itself. I frowned, puckered my lips in concentration, calibrated and calculated and refined. Plainly these ramrod, laconic patterns of light were trying to tell me something. But answers come when they will, one piece at a time.

I tried to tell my son this when, that evening, I helped him with his reading. Using what his mother now knowingly termed "word attack skills," he had mastered most of those tactics. The larger strategic issues of the sentence eluded him still. *Take it in phrases,* I urged him, ruffling his light brown hair, distracted, because I liked the nutmeg smell. (I have often thought that I could find my children in the dark, in a crowd, by my nose alone. Our genetic code colors the air.) He thumbed his book, dirtying a corner. Read the words between the commas, I instructed, my classroom sense of order returning. Stop at the commas, and then pause before going on, and think about what all those words mean. I sniffed at his wheatlike hair again.

I am a traditional astronomer, accustomed to the bitter cold of the cage at Palomar, the Byzantine marriage of optics at Kitt Peak, the muggy air of Lick. Through that long morning yesterday I studied the NGC 1097 jets, attempting to see with the quick eye of the theorist, "dancing on the data," as Roger Blandford down the hall had once called it. I tried to erect some rickety hypothesis that my own uncertain mathematical abilities could brace up. An idea came. I caught at it. But holding it close, turning it over, pushing terms about in an overloaded equation, I saw it was merely an old idea tarted up, already disproved.

Perhaps computer enhancement of the images would clear away some of my enveloping fog, I mused. I took my notes to the neighboring building, listening to my footsteps echo in the long arcade. The buildings at Caltech are mostly done in a pseudo-Spanish style, tan stucco with occasional flourishes of Moorish windows and tiles. The newer library rears up beside the crouching offices and classrooms, a modern extrusion. I entered the Alfred Sloan Laboratory of Physics and Mathematics, wondering for the nth time what a mathematical laboratory would be like, imagining Lewis Carroll in charge, and went into the new computer-terminal rooms. The indices which called up my plates soon stuttered across the screen. I used a median numerical filter, to suppress variations in the background. There were standard routines to subtract particular parts of the spectrum. I called them up, averaging away noise from dust and gas and the image-saturating spikes that were foreground stars in our own galaxy. Still, nothing dramatic emerged. Illumination would not come.

I sipped at my coffee. I had brought a box of crackers from my office; and I broke one, eating each wafer with a heavy crunch. I swirled the cup and the coffee swayed like a dark disk at the bottom, a scum of cream at the vortex curling out into gray arms. I drank it. And thumbed another image into being.

This was not NGC 1097. I checked the number. Then the log. No, these were slots deliberately set aside for later filing. They were not to be filled; they represented my allotted computer space. They should be blank.

Yet I recognized this one. It was a view of Sagittarius A, the intense radio source that hides behind a thick lane of dust in the Milky Way. Behind that dark obscuring swath that is an arm of our Galaxy, lies the center. I squinted. Yes: this was a picture formed from observations sensitive to the 21-centimeter wavelength line, the emission of nonionized hydrogen. I had seen it before, on exposures that looked radially inward at the Galactic core. Here was the red band of hydrogen along our line of sight. Slightly below was the well-known arm of hot, expanding gas, nine thousand light years across. Above, tinted green, was a smaller arm, a ridge of gas moving outward at 135 kilometers per second. I had seen this in seminars years ago. In the very center was the knot no more than a light-year or two across, the source of the 10^{40} ergs per second of virulent energy that drove the cooker that caused all this. Still, the energy flux from our Galaxy was ten million times less than that of a quasar. Whatever the compact energy source there, it was comparatively quiet. NGC 1097 lies far to the south, entirely out of the Milky Way. Could the aim of the satellite camera have strayed so much?

Curious, I thumbed forward. The next index number gave another scan of the Sagittarius region, this time seen by the spectral emissions from outward-moving clouds of ammonia. Random blobs. I thumbed again. A formaldehyde-emission view. But now the huge arm of expanding hydrogen was sprinkled with knots, denoting clouds which moved faster, Dopplered into blue.

I frowned. No, the Sagittarius A exposures were no aiming error. These slots were to be left open for my incoming data. Someone had co-opted the space. Who? I called up the identifying codes, but there were none. As far as the master log was concerned, these spaces were still empty.

I moved to erase them. My finger paused, hovered, went limp. This was obviously high-quality information, already processed. Someone would want it. They had carelessly dumped it into my territory, but . . .

My pause was in part that of sheer appreciation. Peering at the color-coded encrustations of light, I recalled what all this had often been like: impossibly complicated, ornate in its terms, caked with the eccentric jargon of long-dead professors, choked with thickets of atomic physics and thermodynamics, a web of complexity that finally gave forth mental pictures of a whirling, furious past, of stars burned now into cinders, of whispering, turbulent hydrogen that filled the void between the suns. From such numbers came the starscape that we knew. From a sharp scratch on a strip of film we could catch the signature of an element, deduce velocity from the Doppler shift, and then measure the width of that scratch to give the random component of the velocity, the random jigglings due to thermal motion, and thus the temperature. All from a scratch. No, I could not erase it.

When I was a boy of nine I was browbeaten into serving at the altar, during the unendurably long Episcopal services that my mother felt we should attend. I wore the simple robe and was the first to appear in the service, lighting candles with an awkward long device and its sliding wick. The organ music was soft and did not call attention to itself, so the congregation could watch undistracted as I fumbled with the wick and tried to keep the precarious balance between feeding it too much (so that, engorged, it bristled into a ball of orange) and the even worse embarrassment of snuffing it into a final accusing puff of black. Through the service I would alternately kneel and stand, murmuring the worn phrases as I thought of the softball I would play in the afternoon, feeling the prickly gathering heat underneath my robes. On a bad day the sweat would accumulate and a drop would cling to my nose. I'd let it hang there in mute testimony. The minister never seemed to notice. I would often slip off into decidedly untheological daydreams, intoxicated by the pressing moist heat, and miss the telltale words of the litany that signaled the beginning of communion. A whisper would come skating across the layered air and I would surface, to see the minister turned with clotted face toward me, holding the implements of his forgiving trade, waiting for me to bring the wine and wafers to be blessed. I would surge upward, swearing under my breath with the ardor only those who have just learned the words can truly muster, unafraid to be muttering these things as I snatched up the chalice and sniffed the too-sweet murky wine, fetching the plates of wafers, swearing that once the polished walnut altar rail was emptied of its upturned and strangely blank faces, once the simpering organ had ebbed into silence and I had shrugged off these robes swarming with the stench of mothballs, I would have no more of it, I would erase it.

I asked Redman who the hell was logging their stuff into my inventory spaces. He checked. The answer was: nobody. There were no recorded intrusions into those sections of the memory system. *Then look further,* I said, and went back to work at the terminal.

They were still there. What's more, some index numbers that had been free before were now filled.

NGC 1097 still vexed me, but I delayed working on the problem. I studied these new pictures. They were processed, Doppler-coded, and filtered for noise. I switched back to the earlier plates, to be sure. Yes, it was clear: these were different.

Current theory held that the arm of expanding gas was on the outward phase of an oscillation. Several hundred million years ago, so the story went, a massive explosion at the galactic center had started the expansion: a billowing, spinning doughnut of gas swelled outward. Eventually its energy was matched by the gravitational attraction of the massive center. Then, as it slowed and finally fell back toward the center, it spun faster, storing energy in rotational motion, until centrifugal forces stopped its inward rush. Thus the hot cloud could oscillate in the potential well of gravity, cooling slowly.

These computer-transformed plates said otherwise. The Doppler shifts formed a cone. At the center of the plate, maximum values far higher than any observed before, over a thousand kilometers per second, were recorded. That exceeded escape velocity from the Galaxy itself. The values tapered off to the sides, coming smoothly down to the shifts that were on the earlier plates.

I called the programming director. He looked over the displays, understanding nothing of what it meant but everything about how it could have gotten there, and his verdict was clean, certain: human error. But further checks turned up no such mistake. "Must be comin' in on the transmission from orbit," he mused. He seemed half asleep as he punched in commands, traced the intruders. These data had come in from the new combination optical, IR, and UV 'scope in orbit, and the JPL programs had obligingly performed the routine miracles of enhancement and analysis. But the orbital staff were sure no such data had been transmitted. In fact, the 'scope had been down for inspection, plus an alignment check, for over two days. The programming director shrugged and promised to look into it, fingering the innumerable pens clipped in his shirt pocket.

I stared at the Doppler cone, and thumbed to the next index number. The cone had grown, the shifts were larger. Another: still larger. And then I noticed something more; and a cold sensation seeped into me, banishing the casual talk and mechanical-printout stutter of the terminal room.

The point of view had shifted. All the earlier plates had shown a particular gas cloud at a certain angle of inclination. This latest plate was slightly cocked to the side, illuminating a clotted bunch of minor H II regions and obscuring a fraction of the hot, expanding arm. Some new features were revealed. If the JPL program had done such a rotation and shift, it would have left the new spaces blank, for there was no way of filling them in. These were not empty. They brimmed with specific shifts, detailed spectral indices. The JPL program would not have produced the field of numbers unless the raw data contained them. I stared at the screen for a long time.

That evening I drove home the long way, through the wide boulevards of Pasadena, in the gathering dusk. I remembered giving blood the month before, in the eggshell light of the Caltech dispensary. They took the blood away in a curious plastic sack, leaving me with a small bandage in the crook of my elbow. The skin was translucent, showing the riverwork of tributary blue veins, which—recently tapped—were nearly as pale as the skin. I had never looked at that part of me before and found it tender, vulnerable, an unexpected opening. I remembered my wife had liked being stroked there when we were dating, and that I had not touched her there for a long time. Now I had myself been pricked there, to pipe brimming life into a sack, and then to some other who could make use of it.

That evening I drove again, taking my son to Open House. The school bristled with light and seemed to command the neighborhood with its luminosity, drawing families out of their homes. My wife was taking my daughter to another school, and so I was unshielded by her ability to recognize people we knew. I could never sort out their names in time to answer the casual hellos. In our neighborhood the PTA nights draw a disproportionate fraction of technical types, like me. Tonight I saw them without the quicksilver verbal fluency of my wife. They had compact cars that seemed too small for their large families, wore shoes whose casualness offset the formal, just-come-from-work jackets and slacks, and carried creamy folders of their children's accumulated work, to use in conferring with the teachers. The wives were sun-darkened, wearing crisp, print dresses that looked recently put on, and spoke with ironic turns about PTA politics, bond issues, and class sizes. In his classroom my son tugged me from board to board, where he had contributed paragraphs on wildlife. The crowning exhibit was a model of Io, Jupiter's pizza-mocking moon, which he had made from a tennis ball and thick, sulfurous paint. It hung in a box painted black and looked remarkably, ethereally real. My son had won first prize in his class for the mockup moon, and his teacher stressed this as she went over the less welcome news that he was not doing well at his reading. Apparently he arranged the plausible phrases—A, then B, then C—into illogical combinations, C coming before A, despite the instructing commas and semicolons which should have guided him. It was a minor problem, his teacher assured me, but should be looked after. Perhaps a little more reading at home, under my eye? I nodded, sure that the children of the other scientists and computer programmers and engineers did not have this difficulty, and already knew what the instructing phrase of the next century would be, before the end of this one. My son took the news matter-of-factly, unafraid, and went off to help with the cake and Koolaid. I watched him mingle with girls whose awkwardness was lovely, like giraffes'. I remembered that his teacher (I had learned from gossip) had a mother dying of cancer, which might explain the furrow between her eyebrows that would not go away. My son came bearing cake. I ate it with him, sitting with knees slanting upward in the small chair; and quite calmly and suddenly an idea came to me and would not go away. I turned it over and felt its shape, testing it in a preliminary fashion. Underneath I was both excited and fearful and yet sure that it would survive: it was right. Scraping up the last crumbs and icing, I looked down, and saw my son had drawn a crayon design, an enormous father playing ball with a son, running and catching, the scene carefully fitted into the small compass of the plastic, throwaway plate.

The next morning I finished the data reduction on the slit-image exposures. By carefully covering over the Galaxy and background I had managed to take successive plates which blocked out segments of the space parallel to the brightest blue jet. Photometry of the resulting weak signal could give a cross section of the jet's intensity. Pinpoint calibration then yielded the thickness of the central jet zone.

The data was somewhat scattered, the error bars were larger than I liked, but still—I was sure I had it. The jet had a fuzzy halo and a bright core. The core was less than a hundred light years across, a thin filament of highly ionized hydrogen, cut like a swath through the gauzy dust beyond the galaxy. The resolute, ruler-sharp path, its thinness, its profile of luminosity: all pointed toward a tempting picture. Some energetic object had carved each line, moving at high speeds. It swallowed some of the matter in its path; and in the act of engorgement the mass was heated to incandescent brilliance, spitting UV and X-rays into an immense surrounding volume. This radiation in turn ionized the galactic gas, leaving a scratch of light behind the object, like picnickers dumping luminous trash as they pass by.

The obvious candidates for the fast-moving sources of the jets were black holes. And as I traced the slim profiles of the NGC 1097 jets back into the galaxy, they all intersected at the precise geometrical center of the barred spiral pattern.

Last night, after returning from the Open House with a sleepy boy in tow, I talked with my wife as we undressed. I described my son's home room, his artistic achievements, his teacher. My wife let slip offhandedly some jarring news. I had, apparently, misheard the earlier gossip; perhaps I had mused over some problem while she related the story to me over breakfast. It was not the teacher's mother who had cancer, but the teacher herself. I felt an instant, settling guilt. I could scarcely remember the woman's face, though it was a mere hour later. I asked why she was still working. Because, my wife explained with straightforward New England sense, it was better than staring at a wall. The chemotherapy took only a small slice of her hours. And anyway, she probably needed the money. The night beyond our windows seemed solid, flinty, harder than the soft things inside. In the glass I watched my wife take off a print press and stretch backward, breasts thinning into crescents, her knobbed spine describing a serene curve that anticipated bed. I went over to my chest of drawers and looked down at the polished walnut surface, scrupulously rectangular and arranged, across which I had tossed the residue of an hour's dutiful parenting: a scrawled essay on marmosets, my son's anthology of drawings, his reading list, and on top, the teacher's bland paragraph of assessment. It felt odd to have called these things into being, these signs of a forward tilt in a small life, by an act of love or at least lust, now years past. The angles appropriate to cradling my children still lived in my hands. I could feel clearly the tentative clutch of my son as he attempted some upright steps. Now my eye strayed to his essay. I could see him struggling with the notion of clauses, with ideas piled upon each other to build a point, and with the caged linearity of the sentence. On the page above, in the loops of the teacher's generous flow pen, I saw a hollow rotundity, a denial of any constriction in her life. She had to go on, this schoolgirlish penmanship said, to forcefully forget a gnawing illness among a roomful of bustling children. Despite all the rest, she had to keep on doing.

What could be energetic enough to push black holes out of the galactic center, up the slopes of the deep gravitational potential well? Only another black hole. The dynamics had been worked out years before—as so often happens, in another context—by William Saslaw. Let a bee-swarm of black holes orbit about each other, all caught in a gravitational depression. Occasionally, they veer close together, deforming the space-time nearby, caroming off each other like billiard balls. If several undergo these near-miss collisions at once, a black hole can be ejected from the gravitational trap altogether. More complex collisions can throw pairs of black holes in opposite directions, conserving angular momentum: jets and counterjets. But why did NGC 1097 display two blue jets and two red? Perhaps the blue ones glowed with the phosphorescent waste left by the largest, most energetic black holes; their counterjets must be, by some detail of the dynamics, always smaller, weaker, redder.

I went to the jutting, air-conditioned library, and read Saslaw's papers. Given a buzzing hive of black holes in a gravitational well —partly of their own making—many things could happen. There were compact configurations, tightly orbiting and self-obsessed, which could be ejected as a body. These close-wound families could in turn be unstable, once they were isolated beyond the galaxy's tug, just as the group at the center had been. Caroming off each other, they could eject unwanted siblings. I frowned. This could explain the astonishing right-angle turn the long blue jet made. One black hole thrust sidewise and several smaller, less energetic black holes pushed the opposite way.

As the galactic center lost its warped children, the ejections would become less probable. Things would die down. But how long did that take? NGC 1097 was no younger than our own Galaxy; on the cosmic scale, a 60-million-year difference was nothing.

In the waning of afternoon—it was only a bit more than twenty-four hours since I first laid out the plates of NGC 1097—the Operations report came in. There was no explanation for the Sagittarius A data. It had been received from the station in orbit and duly processed. But no command had made the 'scope swivel to that axis. Odd, Operations said, that it pointed in an interesting direction, but no more.

There were two added plates, fresh from processing. I did not mention to Redman in Operations that the resolution of these plates was astonishing, that details in the bloated, spilling clouds were unprecedented. Nor did I point out that the angle of view had tilted further, giving a better perspective on the outward-jutting inferno. With their polynomial percussion, the computers had given what was in the stream of downward-flowing data, numbers that spoke of something being banished from the pivot of our Galaxy.

Caltech is a compact campus. I went to the Athenaeum for coffee, ambling slowly beneath the palms and scented eucalyptus, and circumnavigated the campus on my return. In the varnished perspectives of these tiled hallways, the hammer of time was a set of Dopplered numbers, blue-shifted because the thing rushed toward us, a bulge in the sky. Silent numbers.

There were details to think about, calculations to do, long strings of hypothesis to unfurl like thin flags. I did not know the effect of a penetrating, ionizing flux on Earth. Perhaps it could affect the upper atmosphere and alter the ozone cap that drifts above our heedless heads. A long trail of disturbed, high-energy plasma could fan out through our benign spiral arm—odd, to think of bands of dust and rivers of stars as a neighborhood where you have grown up—churning, working, heating. After all, the jets of NGC 1097 had snuffed out the beaded HH II regions as cleanly as an eraser passing across a blackboard, ending all the problems that life knows.

The NGC 1097 data was clean and firm. It would make a good paper, perhaps a letter to *Astrophysical Journal Letters.* But the rest—there was no crisp professional path. These plates had come from much nearer the Galactic center. The information had come outward at light speed, far faster than the pressing bulge, and tilted at a slight angle away from the radial vector that led to Earth.

I had checked the newest Palomar plates from Sagittarius A this afternoon. There were no signs of anything unusual. No Doppler bulge, no exiled mass. They flatly contradicted the satellite plates.

That was the key: old reliable Palomar, our biggest ground-based 'scope, showed nothing. Which meant that someone in high orbit had fed data into our satellite 'scope—exposures that had to be made nearer the Galactic center and then brought here and deftly slipped into our ordinary astronomical research. Exposures that spoke of something stirring where we could not yet see it, beyond the obscuring lanes of dust. The plumes of fiery gas would take a while longer to work through that dark cloak.

These plain facts had appeared on a screen, mute and undeniable, keyed to the data on NGC 1097. Keyed to a connection that an eye other than mine could miss. Some astronomer laboring over plates of eclipsing binaries or globular clusters might well have impatiently erased the offending, multicolored spattering, not bothered to uncode the Dopplers, to note the persistent mottled red of the galactic dust arm at the lower right, and so not known what the place must be. Only I could have made the connection to NGC 1097, and guessed what an onrushing black hole could do to a fragile planet: burn away the ozone layer, hammer the land with high-energy particles, mask the sun in gas and dust.

But to convey this information in this way was so strange, so— yes, that was the word—so alien. Perhaps this was the way they had to do it: quiet, subtle, indirect. Using an oblique analogy which only suggested, yet somehow disturbed more than a direct statement. And of course, this might be only a phrase in a longer message. Moving out from the Galactic center, they would not know we were here until they grazed the expanding bubble of radio noise that gave us away, and so their data would use what they had, views at a different slant. The data itself, raw and silent, would not necessarily call attention to itself. It had to be placed in context, beside NGC 1097. How had they managed to do that? Had they tried before? What odd logic dictated this approach? How . . .

Take it in pieces. Some of the data I could use, some not. Perhaps a further check, a fresh look through the dusty Sagittarius arm, would show the beginnings of a ruddy swelling, could give a verification. I would have to look, try to find a bridge that would make plausible what I knew but could scarcely prove. The standards of science are austere, unforgiving—and who would have it differently? I would have to hedge, to take one step back for each two forward, to compare and suggest and contrast, always sticking close to the data. And despite what I thought I knew now, the data would have to lead, they would have to show the way.

There is a small Episcopal church, not far up Hill Street, which offers a Friday communion in early evening. Driving home through the surrounding neon consumer gumbo, musing, I saw the sign, and stopped. I had the NGC 1097 plates with me in a carrying case, ripe beneath my arm with their fractional visions, like thin sections of an exotic cell. I went in. The big oak door thumped solemnly shut behind me. In the nave two elderly men were passing woven baskets, taking up the offertory. I took a seat near the back. Idly I surveyed the people, distributed randomly like a field of unthinking stars, in the pews before me. A man came nearby and a pool of brassy light passed before me and I put something in, the debris at the bottom clinking and rustling as I stirred it. I watched the backs of heads as the familiar litany droned on, as devoid of meaning as before. I do not believe, but there is communion. Something tugged at my attention; one head turned a fraction. By a kind of triangulation I deduced the features of the other, closer to the ruddy light of the altar, and saw it was my son's teacher. She was listenly raptly. I listened, too, watching her, but could only think of the gnawing at the center of a bustling, swirling galaxy. The lights seemed to dim. The organ had gone silent. *Take, eat. This is the body and blood of* and so it had begun. I waited my turn. I do not believe, but there is communion. The people went forward in their turns. The woman rose; yes, it was she, the kind of woman whose hand would give forth loops and spirals and who would dot her *i*'s with a small circle. The faint timbre of the organ seeped into the layered air. When it was time I was still thinking of NGC 1097, of how I would write the paper— fragments skittered across my mind, the pyramid of the argument was taking shape—and I very nearly missed the gesture of the elderly man at the end of my pew. Halfway to the altar rail I realized that I still carried the case of NGC 1097 exposures, crooked into my elbow, where the pressure caused a slight ache to spread: the spot where they had made the transfusion in the clinic, transfer- ring a fraction of life, blood given. I put it beside me as I knelt. The robes of the approaching figure were cobalt blue and red, a change from the decades since I had been an acolyte. There were no acolytes at such a small service, of course. The blood would follow; first came the offered plate of wafers. Take, eat. Life calling out to life. I could feel the pressing weight of what lay ahead for me, the long roll of years carrying forward one hypothesis, and then, swallowing, knowing that I would never believe this and yet I would want it, I remembered my son, remembered that these events were only pieces, that the puzzle was not yet over, that I would never truly see it done, that as an astronomer I had to live with the knowledge forever partial and provisional, that science was not final results but instead a continuing meditation carried on in the face of enormous facts—*take it in phrases*—let the sen- tences of our lives pile up.

Again an attempt to assure us of mystery is followed by an attempt to penetrate the mystery. This essay is my own and you must remember that I am not a theoretical physicist. I don't speak with the personal authority of a Steven Weinberg.

However, I have gathered some of the current thinking on the creation of the Universe, and I have tried to apply it to the history of the Universe in general and not to merely the first fraction of a second. In doing so, I must warn you that I have indulged in speculations of my own, for which no one else should be asked to share the blame. In particular the notion of the logarithmic treatment of time as described in the article is my own.

THE CRUCIAL ASYMMETRY
ISAAC ASIMOV

On rare occasions I sit in a bar as a matter of social necessity, and a few nights ago such a necessity arose. I ordered my inevitable ginger ale and observed with scientific detachment (well, not quite) the beautiful barmaid, whose long legs were covered by nothing more than sheer hose for their full length.

I was moved to philosophical reflection and said, out loud, what I have often thought.

"The rewards in male-female relationships," I said, "seem to be weighted enormously in favor of the male. Consider the female leg—how utterly smooth, graceful, well-proportioned and (I happen to know) delightful to the touch. What do women get in return for what they have to offer? The male leg: hairy, bunchy, and (I suspect) equally repulsive to sight and touch."

Whereupon a young lady, who was also at the table, said in wide-eyed wonder, "How can you possibly manage to get the situation so completely reversed?"

That left me speechless, I assure you, but as I lingered over my ginger ale, I worked it out in my mind. The natural attachment of men for the consummate charms of women, as contrasted with the bizarre affection women feel for men, is a necessary and even crucial asymmetry that preserves the human species.

It's tough on women, of course, but apparently that is how it must be.

And having straightened that out, let us move on to a crucial asymmetry in the Universe that is even more broadly significant.

The Universe is thought to be about 15,000,000,000 years old in the sense that 15,000,000,000 years ago there was a "big bang." With the big bang, the Universe came into existence as an object with its present mass but with a diameter that was virtually zero and a temperature that was virtually infinite.

With incredible rapidity, it expanded and cooled, continuing to do so at a steadily slowing rate. It continues to expand and cool today, 15,000,000,000 years later.

At the start, with mass and energy unbelievably concentrated, changes naturally took place very rapidly. They had to. For one thing, all change is driven by energy, and there never was such a concentrated energy supply in our Universe as existed at the very start. Secondly, change is made easier and more rapid if the constituent bits that are being subjected to change are close together so that they can interact without undue delay, and there never was such closeness in our Universe as existed at the very start.

As the Universe expanded, its constituent bits spread farther apart and the energy concentration (temperature) declined. For both reasons, the rate of change in the Universe slowed with expansion.

Because of the enormous rate of change at the start, physicists talk about crucial events that happened only minutes after the beginning, and only seconds after, and only very tiny fractions of a second after. Carefully, they calculate what must have happened in less than a billionth of a billionth of a second after the big bang.

This shakes the mind. How can so much happen in such an ultrabrief interval?

Ah, but let's not consider time as a smoothly and evenly flowing stream, with every second just as filled with potential events as every other second. Let us not consider all seconds as tiny bags of events of precisely the same size.

We are lured into thinking of seconds as equally sized and equally eventful right now, because the expansion-cooling of the Universe is now proceeding at a rate so small compared to its present size and temperature that there is no perceptible change in the number of events a second can hold (on the average over the Universe generally) in a human lifetime or even in recorded history. There's not much change even over stretches of millions of years.

In the early beginnings of the Universe, however, seconds were incredibly crammed with events. An early second could hold trillions of times as many events as a contemporary second. A still earlier second could hold trillions of trillions of times as many events as a contemporary second. Judging by how many events they could hold, an early second was the equivalent of thousands of contemporary years in length, while a still earlier second was the equivalent of millions of contemporary years in length, and so on.

If we measure time by events, it would make more sense if we treat time logarithmically. Let us not suppose it behaves arithmetically, so that 1/15 of all the events that have ever taken place took place in the first billion years; another 1/15 in the second billion years; another 1/15 in the third billion years; and so on, until the final 1/15 took place in the fifteen billionth year, which brings us to now.

Let us suppose, instead, that half of all the events that took place in the Universe took place in the first 1/10 of the Universe's lifetime; that half of that half took place in the first 1/100 of the Universe's lifetime; that half of that half of that half took place in the first 1/1000 of the Universe's lifetime and so on. This is the logarithmic view.*

This means that half the events that have ever taken place in the Universe had taken place by 1,500,000,000 years after the big bang; a quarter of the events by 150,000,000 years after the big bang; an eighth of the events by 15,000,000 years after the big bang and so on.

But let's not work with all those zeros. Let's use exponential figures instead. In place of 15,000,000,000 years, we can say 1.5×10^{10} years, where 10^{10} is the product of ten tens multiplied together, or a one followed by ten zeros. Again, 1,500,000,000 years is 1.5×10^9; 150,000,000 years is 1.5×10^8; 15,000,000 years is 1.5×10^7; and so on. Now, we have exponents that go down smoothly from 10 to 9 to 8 and so on, and since exponents are very closely related to logarithms, this gives us a logarithmic scale.

For convenience, in fact, let us consider the age of the Universe in seconds. Each year is made up of 31,556,926 seconds so that 15,000,000,000 years is just about 470,000,000,000,000,000 (or 470 quadrillion) seconds long. Exponentially, we can write it as 4.7×10^{17} seconds.

Let us set up a logarithmic scale of time by drawing a straight

* Matching events by halves to durations by tenths is just a matter of convenience in calculation. The actual match may be different, and more complicated, but I am just me and not a theoretical physicist.

line divided into equal intervals marked 1, 2, 3, and so on up to 18, as in Figure 1.

FIGURE 1.   *Logarithmic Time.*

10 seconds	1
100 seconds	2
1,000 seconds	3
10,000 seconds	4
100,000 seconds	5
1,000,000 seconds	6
10,000,000 seconds	7
100,000,000 seconds	8
1,000,000,000 seconds	9
10,000,000,000 seconds	10
100,000,000,000 seconds	11
1,000,000,000,000 seconds	12
10,000,000,000,000 seconds	13
100,000,000,000,000 seconds	14
1,000,000,000,000,000 seconds	15
10,000,000,000,000,000 seconds	16 present
100,000,000,000,000,000 seconds	17 position of
1,000,000,000,000,000,000 seconds	18 the Universe

Point 1 would represent the time 10^1, or 10 seconds, after the big bang; point 2 would 10^2, or 100 seconds, after the big bang; point 3 would be 10^3, or 1,000 seconds, after the big bang; and so on up to point 18, which would be 10^{18} or 1,000,000,000,000,000,000 seconds after the big bang. The Universe at present is located at about 17 2/3.

Each time interval on the line would seem to be ten times as long as the one immediately above it by ordinary arithmetic. Thus, the interval between 2 and 3 is the interval from 10 to 100, or 90 seconds; while the interval between 1 and 2 is the interval from 1 to 10, or 9 seconds.

In terms of the number of events that took place within them, however, each interval may be considered as long as every other. As many events took place between 1 second and 10 seconds after the big bang as took place in all the billions of years representing the stretch between points 17 and 18 (100,000,000,000,000,000 seconds and 1,000,000,000,000,000,000 seconds).

Yet need we begin the logarithmic line of Figure 1 at 1? Might we not extend it further upward to 0?

Certainly we can—and the first thought might be that 0 represents the big bang itself, but it doesn't!

The 0 on the line is not an ordinary zero but an exponential zero, representing 10^0 seconds, and 10^0 is *not* zero, though that might seem logical at a quick glance. Since 10^2 (100) is 1/10 of 10^3 (1000), and 10^1 (10) is 1/10 of 10^2 (100), then it is reasonable to suppose that 10^0 is 1/10 of 10^1 (10). But 1/10 of 10 is 1; therefore 10^0 should be equal to 1, and 0 on the logarithmic scale should represent 1 second.

We can extend the scale still further upward, and have -1, -2, -3, and so on, with each figure representing a point ten times closer to the big bang than the one before. Thus -1 represents the point one-tenth of a second after the big bang, -2 the point one-hundredth of a second after the big bang, -3 the point one-thousandth of a second after the big bang, and so on (see Figure 2). From the standpoint of the number of events taking place, each of these new tiny intervals is as long as any of the others. As many events took place between a thousand-millionth of a second and a hundred-millionth of a second after the big bang as took place in the last 13.5 billion years.

FIGURE 2.   *Extended Logarithmic Time.*

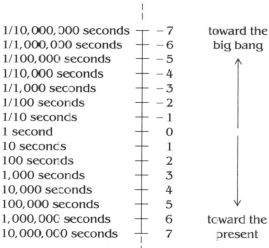

1/10,000,000 seconds	-7	toward the
1/1,000,000 seconds	-6	big bang
1/100,000 seconds	-5	
1/10,000 seconds	-4	
1/1,000 seconds	-3	
1/100 seconds	-2	
1/10 seconds	-1	
1 second	0	
10 seconds	1	
100 seconds	2	
1,000 seconds	3	
10,000 seconds	4	
100,000 seconds	5	
1,000,000 seconds	6	toward the
10,000,000 seconds	7	present

If we imagine ourselves moving along the logarithmic time-line toward larger and larger numbers, the Universe is expanding and cooling. At 17 2/3, where the Universe is now located, it is about 25,000,000,000 light-years in diameter and has an average temperature of 3° Kelvin: that is, 3 degrees above absolute zero. (Of course, there are places where the temperature is much higher than that in today's Universe, even very much higher, as at the center of the Sun, but we're talking average.)

If we imagine ourselves moving along the logarithmic time-line toward smaller and smaller numbers, the Universe is contracting and warming. (From our present taken-for-granted view, it would be like taking a film of the Universe as it expands and cools and running it backward.)

Suppose, then, we run the film backward until the Universe reaches point 12. At that point, the Universe is 10^{12} seconds (or about 100,000 years) after the big bang. When the Universe is that young it has had time to expand to a diameter of only about 200,000 light-years. Its total width is not very much greater than the total width of a large galaxy of the contemporary Universe. The average temperature of this small universe is estimated to be about $1,000°$ K.

If we imagine the Universe to have contracted to this size, there is no longer room for galaxies, or even stars. The Universe is a mere chaos of atoms. In fact, if we try to trace the Universe back to points smaller than 12, it becomes too hot and too crowded for matter to exist even as atoms.

In short, it is only 100,000 years after the big bang that atoms formed and ordinary matter began to exist. It was only after a period of further expansion and cooling that the atoms could gather into stars and galaxies. Those atoms, stars, and galaxies making up the Matter-Universe have existed for almost all the time of existence (considered arithmetically) of the Universe as a whole —14.9 out of the 15 billion years. All those billions of years, however, take up only the last 5 2/3 intervals of the logarithmic time-line.

What existed at points lower than 12? What existed before the Matter-Universe?

When the Universe was too small and too hot to contain atoms, it must have been made up of the various subatomic constituents of atoms. It must have been a melange of photons, electrons, neutrons, protons, and so on. Of these, the neutrons and protons make up the nuclei of normal atoms and are lumped together as "nucleons." They are the most massive particles at this stage and we can refer to the "Nucleon-Universe" as existing at points less than 12 on our logarithmic time-line.

If we imagine the Universe moving through points smaller and smaller than 12, the nucleons are pushed closer and closer together and the temperature gets higher and higher. By the time we reach −4 on the scale, the Universe is only about 250 kilometers across, no larger than an asteroid, though it still contains all the mass of the present-day Universe. The asteroid-size Universe has an average temperature of about $1,000,000,000,000°$ K (a trillion degrees).

At points smaller than -4, the Universe is too small and too hot for nucleons to exist. In other words, nucleons did not form until 1/10,000 seconds after the big bang. From 1/10,000 second to 100,000 years after the big bang we had the Nucleon-Universe and from 100,000 years after the big bang to the present, we have had the Matter-Universe.

In point of ordinary arithmetical time, the Matter-Universe has lasted 150,000 times as long as the Nucleon-Universe. What's more, the Matter-Universe is steadily, if slowly, increasing the ratio of endurance as it continues to exist for what will undoubtedly prove to be many billions of additional years.

On the logarithmic scale, however, which measures time by events rather than by arithmetical duration, the Nucleon-Universe has lasted for 16 intervals (-4 to 12) while the Matter-Universe has so far lasted 5 2/3 intervals (see Figure 3). This means that about three times as many events took place during the apparently short lifetime of the Nucleon-Universe as during the apparently long lifetime of the Matter-Universe. The Matter-Universe would have to continue to endure for something like 10,000,000,000,000,000,000,000 additional years in something like its present form in order to equal the Nucleon-Universe in event content.

FIGURE 3. *Nucleon-Universe.*

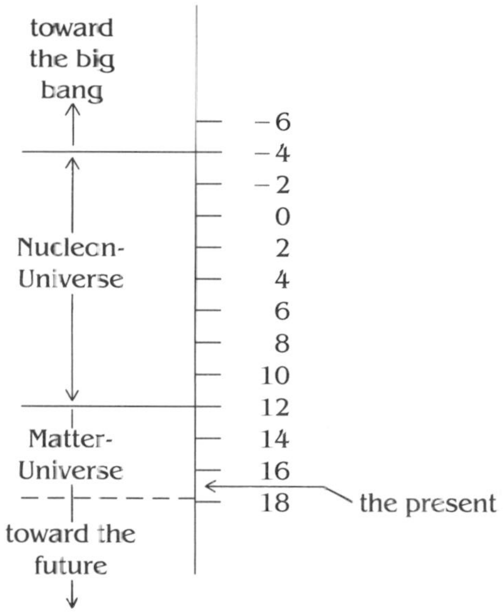

Until recently, physicists could only go back to about -4 on the logarithmic scale. They could not tell what was taking place within the first 1/10,000 seconds after the big bang, when the Universe was far smaller than a sizable asteroid and far hotter than a trillion degrees. All they could say was that nucleons could not exist.

The concept of quarks arose in the 1960s. They are the fundamental particles of which the nucleons are constructed. Unlike the nucleons, but like the electrons, the quarks are apparently point objects and do not take up volume.

During the first ten-thousandth of a second after the big bang, then, what exists are not nucleons but quarks, and in that interval, we have the Quark-Universe.

In the 1970s, new, very general theories have been devised covering three of the four known types of interactions in the Universe under an umbrella of similar mathematical treatment. Such Grand Unified Theories (GUTs) for the two nuclear interactions (the strong and the weak), and for the electromagnetic interactions as well, give some leads for treating the Quark-Universe.

Right now, the three interactions covered by GUTs are widely different in strength, with the strong interaction 137 times as strong as the electromagnetic interaction, which is in turn about 10,000,000,000,000 (ten trillion) times as strong as the weak interaction.

As the temperature gets higher and higher, however, the three forces become equal in strength and in other properties as well, fading into a single interaction.

It is thought that if the temperature gets high enough, even the gravitational interaction will join the rest. The gravitational interaction is the least intense of the four, being weaker than even the weak interaction by a factor of 1,000,000,000,000,000,000,000,000,000,000 (1 nonillion). Nevertheless, given a high enough temperature, it will strengthen and become part of the one primordial interaction. The only trouble is that nothing physicists can yet do has served to place the gravitational interaction under the same umbrella as the other three.

Making use of GUTs, which were worked out only to explain subatomic relationships, physicists find they can make apparently useful calculations tending to describe the properties of the very early Universe, though a lot depends on just which variety of GUTs they use.*

Right now, some physicists trace the Universe all the way back

* Which variety will win out depends on the exact results of delicate measurements of phenomena such as proton decay, which physicists hope eventually to be able to make.

to point −43 on the logarithmic scale. That point is $1/10^{43}$ seconds (one hundred duo decillionths of a second) after the big bang.

At 10^{-43} seconds, the Universe is of infinitesimal size compared even to a proton, for instance, and has an average temperature of $100,000,000,000,000,000,000,000,000,000,000$ ° K (100 nonillion degrees). At such a temperature, gravitational effects are strong enough to have to be taken into account, but the theory to do so is lacking. Physicists, therefore, cannot go to numbers smaller than point −43. The Quark-Universe goes from −43 to −4. Points smaller than −43 represent an unknown region (see Figure 4).

FIGURE 4.   *Quark-Universe.*

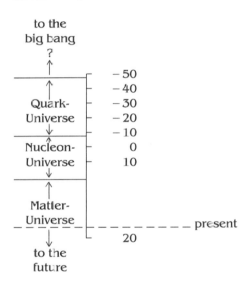

As you see, the Quark-Universe lasted 39 divisions on the scale as compared to 16 divisions for the Nucleon-Universe and 5 2/3 for the Matter-Universe. And who knows how many divisions the pre-Quark-Universe lasted or how many different types of Universe there were in the crucial duodecillionths of a second before quarks came into existence?

In fact, if we insist on looking backward in time through a logarithmic scale, it would seem that the Universe extends an infinite distance through a never-ending series of intervals, each equal in amount of change-content. To the left of −43 are −44, −45, and so on indefinitely. Can it be that we must conclude the big bang never really took place because it took place an infinite number of divisions ago containing an infinite number of events?

I don't believe that. Here's my own *guess* about it.*

As one moves farther and farther down the scale into smaller and smaller numbers, and the Universe becomes ever more compressed and ever hotter, there is a tendency to form more and more massive particles. These ultramassive particles could not possibly exist today because there is nowhere energy sufficiently concentrated to form them. Such an energy-concentration did exist in the very early Universe, however.

In that case, if we go far enough back in time, might not the Universe have been tiny enough and hot enough for a *single particle* to exist with the mass of the entire Universe? My own selection for the name of such a particle would be a "holon" (the "particle of the whole," so to speak).

Perhaps that is the ultimate retreat pastward on the logarithmic scale. The big bang consisted, we might speculate, in the creation of a holon with the mass of a hundred billion galaxies squeezed into a single particle with an unimaginably small volume; a particle as small relative to a proton, perhaps, as a proton is to the present-day Universe.

Suppose that if we go backward along the logarithmic scale into the far, far past, the compression and temperature at point -100 is enough to make it possible for the holon to exist. Why not consider that the big bang takes place at -100?

The holon is unstable and breaks down into smaller particles in an unimaginably brief moment of time. These smaller particles repel each other intensely so that the Universe spreads outward and, in consequence, cools. The smaller particles break down further in a slightly longer moment of time and so on. The expansion and cooling continues, and at -43, quarks are beginning to form and the single existing interaction divides into two forms, one of which rapidly weakens with falling temperature to become what we now recognize as the gravitational interaction.

As expansion-cooling continues, two other interactions break away and weaken, taking us on the high road to the present-day four interactions which, in the low temperatures of the contemporary Universe, seem irretrievably different.

Meanwhile, at -4, the quarks combine with each other to form nucleons, and at 12, the nucleons combine with each other or with electrons (or both) to form atoms and matter. As we progress past 12, the chaotic melange of atoms breaks up into galaxy-cluster-size turbulences and these condense into stars so that the Universe becomes the familiar one of today: the slow-changing,

---

* Most of the rest of this essay consists of my own guesses. No one else is to be blamed for it.

incredibly slow-motion appendix to the long, exciting, and immensely changeful Universes of the far past, all of which were over (by arithmetic time) in less time than Homo sapiens has existed.

At −4, where prequark particles form quarks for the first time, we are at an important crossroads, for here we encounter something we call "the law of conservation of baryon number." This law, deduced from observations in our contemporary Universe, states that the total number of baryons minus antibaryons in the Universe must remain constant. (An antibaryon is precisely the same as a corresponding baryon in almost all properties except a particularly important one, such as electric charge or magnetic orientation, in which it is precisely opposite.)

If a baryon is destroyed, a balancing antibaryon must be destroyed with it, and both converted into photons. If a baryon is brought into existence out of photons, then a balancing antibaryon must also be brought into existence. In either case, the total number of baryons minus antibaryons remains unchanged. Included among the baryons are the protons and neutrons, as well as the quarks that make them up.

Thus, a proton and antiproton can undergo mutual annihilation, as can a neutron and antineutron. In addition, a quark and antiquark of the same color and flavor can annihilate each other. Again protons and antiprotons must be produced in pairs, as is true of neutrons and antineutrons, and (given equivalence in flavor and color) quarks and antiquarks.

Consequently, when prequark particles break down, it would seem that they must form quarks and antiquarks in equal numbers. As the temperature drops further, those quarks and antiquarks would annihilate each other to produce photons. The Universe would end up with no nucleons at all, and therefore no atoms, and therefore no stars and galaxies. In short, the Universe, as we know it, would not exist.

Where, then, did the Universe come from?

GUTs make it plain, however, that the theory of conservation of baryon number is not true but only *almost* true. Thus, these new theories suggest that protons have a half-life of 10^{31} years, breaking down into nonbaryons such as positrons and neutrinos. It can do so even without the corresponding breakdown of antiprotons.

Similarly, it is possible for a baryon to be produced without the production of a corresponding antibaryon, though in a vanishingly small percentage of cases. As the temperature rises to dizzying heights, this asymmetric tendency grows more important, though it is never overwhelming.

Even at the many trillions of degrees of temperature under which the prequark particles are breaking down, the asymmetry would only be one part in a billion. For every 1,000,000,000 antiquarks formed, 1,000,000,001 quarks are formed.

This means that for every 1,000,000,000 antiquarks undergoing mutual annihilation with 1,000,000,000 quarks, 1 single and lonely quark is left over. The tiny percentage of leftover quarks is sufficient to produce enough nucleons to make up the stars and galaxies of our Universe. It is a small but crucial asymmetry (as I promised you in the introduction).

At the present moment, there are indeed about a billion photons in the Universe (formed from that primordial mutual annihilation) for every existing baryon. What's more, as nearly as we can tell, everything we know in the Universe seems to be composed of baryons just about exclusively, with virtually no samples of antibaryons existing. (This was something that badly puzzled physicists when the law of conservation of baryon number was thought to be absolute.)

But why is it quarks, nucleons, and matter that are produced in slight excess, rather than antiquarks, antinucleons, and antimatter?

My own guess is that this asymmetry is inherent in the original holon and that there might also be an antiholon in which antiquarks would appear in slight excess so that an Anti-Universe of antimatter would eventually be formed. (The photons of such an Anti-Universe would be identical with the photons of a Universe in all respects, however.)

If there are an infinite number of holons produced here and there in what I choose to call "hyperspace," half should be holons and half antiholons. In fact, I suspect that they are produced in pairs, with every big bang actually a double big bang, producing a holon/antiholon pair. Thus, for our Universe there is a corresponding Anti-Universe which we cannot reach or impinge on in any way —nor it on us.

But where does the vast mass of the holon/antiholon pair come from? Does it suddenly appear out of nothing? Or are we forced, finally, to postulate a Divine Creator?

I prefer to wonder if the holon/antiholon pair might not actually appear out of nothing.

Suppose there is such a thing as "negative energy" which has the property of being able to combine with ordinary energy and cancel it out, leaving nothing. For every holon/antiholon pair, there might be a negative-holon/negative-antiholon pair also formed; the two pairs together adding to nothing and therefore, mathematically at least, being equivalent to nothing. It would not be strange to have nothing appear out of nothing.

Thus, $(+1) + (-1) = 0$. If you have no money, you have nothing (fiscally speaking). If someone owes you a dollar and you owe someone else a dollar, you still have nothing—though you can now collect what is owed you and delay paying what you owe, so that you have a dollar to do something with.

In the same way, the quadruple holon is nothing, but the individual members can be played with for a time. The four holons appear out of nothing, each expanding in a quadruple big bang and playing out a temporary game as separate Universes, and each eventually contracting into a quadruple big crunch in which all the events of the expansion reverse themselves, right down to the final disappearance, into the nothingness from which they came. (And there may be an infinite number of such quadruple Universes, coming and going.)

This, you will note, repeats the thesis of my essay "I'm Looking Over a Four-Leaf Clover" which I still stand by.* In the earlier essay, I had to rely on the dubious concept of antigravity to separate matter and antimatter. Now I can accept, instead, the crucial asymmetry inherent in GUTs, which is a big improvement.

I must still make use of the dubious concept of antienergy, however. There I must wait longer for science to catch up.

* In my collection *Science, Numbers and I* (Doubleday, 1968).

There seems to be a rebellion against the notion of limits in the Universe. Going into the realm of the ultrasmall, we have not managed to come up against limits yet. We envisaged the atom as the ultimate unit of matter, and then it turned out to have structure. At the center of the atom was the much tinier nucleus, and the nucleus was made up of component parts: protons and neutrons. And each of these, it turns out, according to present notions, is composed of three quarks.

As of now it would seem that quarks and leptons (the latter including the electron) are fundamental bits of matter and are point-objects without structure. Really? At the moment, I'm not prepared to bet on it.

And there have been science-fiction writers who have decided that the atom with its central nucleus and its surrounding cloud of circling electrons is suspiciously like the Sun and its family of planets. Could each atom be a solar system, with each electron a planet (bearing life, perhaps), and with every particle made up of subatoms containing subnuclei and subelectrons, each subatom being a sub-solar system made up of sub-subatoms and so on, without end?

What if we go upward? The Sun is one of many stars that together make up our Milky Way galaxy. And that is one of a number of galaxies, which make up a cluster of galaxies, and these are grouped together into superclusters, and might there be no end to that? Might not every solar system be a superatom of a superuniverse, the components of which are super-superatoms of a super-superuniverse and so on, without end.

We have no evidence that any of this is so. In fact, atoms differ from solar systems in such fundamental ways, thanks to quantum theory, that it is inconceivable that they should form analogous structures differing only in scale.

And yet the speculation has such interest that we cannot resist continuing to play with such an infinitely hierarchical Universe in both directions. But if such an infinite arrangement of wheels within wheels existed, how would one work out the moment of creation of the whole? Would there be one?

THE LIVING GALAXY
LAURENCE MANNING

FOREWORD

It is impossible for me, as author, to write this story so that it is complete in itself; I must ask you, as reader, to lend a hand to the work. This is what must be done: Close your eyes and picture to yourself a classroom of children about six years of age. *You are one of these children.* You have a book open in front of you and, as you read it, a lecturer says the words of it out loud, so that the subject matter is impressed through ear as well as eye. The date is very far in the future—more than 500,000,000 years, and the Sun, Earth, Mars, Venus, and other ancient things have long since died and become as forgotten and legendary as the Garden of Eden. You, at the age of six, have played with strange toys—toys that would puzzle a skilled engineer today. You look forward to a whole century of study, research, sport, amusement, and philosophy. This first century is your childhood and it will end when you go to the great hospital to be operated upon and made bodily young once more. After that you are grown up and set about doing your work in the world—in whatever world you please, as a matter of fact, for there are billions of planets to choose from. You expect to live in this way forever, except for the risk of accidents. There is no hurry about learning or doing anything—but at six you are curious and ill-informed and this is the very first time you have been given any insight into the history of the human race, its habitations and its physical limits.

So you look around the room, with its bare green tinted walls, and gaze at the young face of the lecturer with awe, for his eyes are the most astonishingly intelligent things you have ever seen and they stare out from the youthful head with all the contrast and force of a scream coming out of the dark night. His name is History Zeta Nine and you have been told by one of your playmates that he is more than 100,000,000 years old. You did not believe it until he entered the room. Now you rather wonder if he can be as young as that! All through the reading, your eyes wander from the page every few minutes to steal a glance at this ancient man—just a glance, for you dread lest those burning eyes might meet yours.

Now, if you are ready, we will commence the history lesson:

As human beings, history must start for us upon a planet circling a small sun that has long since died. This sun was not located in our present universe, but very far away from here in a large cluster of stars known by courtesy as the "First Universe." In the Chart of Space it is known as Nebula X23G79 and is medium-size, slightly smaller than the one in which our sun and planets happen to be located. It will be the object of this first introduction to history to paint a brief picture of the progress of the race through space and to give some hints as to its final limits and their possible nature. When you have understood this general picture, we shall be in a position to go into more detail, but this is reserved for future lessons.

The planet on which the race first developed was called "Earth" and it possessed by nature a climate and an atmosphere suitable to human existence without any artificial aids. In all of Space, counting millions upon millions of Universes, such a condition has been noted only seventy-two times so that it may be considered extraordinary. Eight other planets circled the same sun and two of these called "Mars" and "Venus" (all ancient heavenly bodies were named instead of numbered) were colonized with great difficulty. This would have been the total distribution of humanity but for three prehistoric inventions that occurred among the ancients who inhabited the "Earth" planet. Let us examine these.

First came the release of atomic power, the first freeing of humanity from the necessity of using its manpower. The early engines and motors were, presumably, crude and dangerous but the result of the invention was, nevertheless, to enable power to be used to the limit of the raw material available in the planets. It rendered trips from one planet to another possible on a practical scale, instead of being gigantic adventures that could be afforded only once a century.

Second, arising out of the first, was atomic synthesis. This was observed as a phenomenon in the exhaust tubes of atomic rocket motors and it was found that the product could be controlled if the exhausts were surrounded by heavy induction magnets turned on and off with very high frequency. The "Earth" was now freed of its last need for labor. Food, metals, fabrics could be produced at will by atomic power using any handy raw material—rock and water being, of course, most common.

Now the "Earth" was deserted by thousands of explorers who settled down on the five remaining planets of the original solar system. These were not habitable without artificial air and heat, but the two great inventions mentioned above had solved all difficulties. One planet called "Mercury" was so near the sun of that system that it called for cooling and not until millions of years later was this perfected. The ability to reduce the heat of a body in isolated space is nowadays a mere technical commonplace—yet it involves transforming heat into energy and energy into matter.

We have, then, a human race existing on the planets of one star. The life of a man lasted little more than one century. For this reason, exploration of other stars came slowly, for a whole lifetime was used up in the mere trip. Had it not been for the third great invention, the human race might still have lived and died in one tiny corner of one universe. This invention was the rejuvenating operation which we all undergo every hundred years today. It came slowly and was not perfected without accident and many deaths. In principle, it is simple—being the familiar law of biology that hybridizing renews the youth of two aged parent races. The difficulty lay in its practice, for to hybridize the thousands of different cell types in the human body called for skill and technique then unknown. The result, historically, was to permit the long trips of exploration and colonization which in a few million years spread mankind over the planets of the "First Universe" and, subsequently, throughout all the universes and galaxies in space.

Of late, this steady, peaceful expansion has slowed down. The reason is that few new planets remain. In every direction we have spread to the very edge of matter and have come to a stop. For "space" as we know it is finite and its "curvature" that ancient men so brilliantly argued has been actually found and studied by us. As the very outermost planets grow more thickly populated and as further studies and observations are reported, we shall, perhaps, know more than now. What actually constitutes this end of matter is still a mystery. The action of light and electricity is warped and bent there, and so far, the only data available are due to the work of Bzonn, the chief actor in this lesson. His trip beyond space occupied a period of 15 million years and since one of the results was to prevent the destruction of the human race before it had spread outside of the stars of the "First Universe," he may be called the most important character in history.

Just at the time when the human race was engrossed in possibilities of new exploration in distant galaxies and universes, with thousands of huge rocket ships under construction, astronomers reported in alarm a violent "shift to the red" in one area of the sky. As all of you have had toy spectroscopes, you know what this means. Over an area ten degrees of arc across, the star background seemed to be flying apart at terrific speed—hundreds of times faster than anything ever observed. As the centuries passed, it was seen that a void was being created where once stars had been. A great black empty area thrust its way down toward the First Universe which then contained all the human race. It was like a vast cone, point down, and in it there appeared to be nothing—absolutely nothing. Beyond it the blank space extended to infinity and not even the most powerful telescopes showed any trace of distant stars.

As the years passed, it was seen that the cone's point would at its present rate touch the First Universe in a few more millions of years. Yet what action could be taken? Most scientists were resigned to the role of mere observers. Not so Bzonn!

He gathered together a dozen scientists—twelve men and women whose names are now unknown. They settled upon an uninhabited planetoid circling a small sun—a tiny planet not quite one hundred miles in diameter—and busied themselves in secret preparations. Atomic motors of huge size were constructed and the entire core of the planet scooped out and its stone transformed into metal. From the center, great rocket tubes flared out to the surface—fifty miles away—and the entire planet was in a few centuries made into a rocket ship. A mile below the surface they made themselves living quarters and were ready to start. The voyage they planned was, in those days, incredible. So much fuel would be needed that only a ship of planetary dimensions could have contained it and it would have been absurd to construct such a vehicle. The whole planet was set under motion by earthshaking blasts from the great rocket chamber and the voyage commenced. Its purpose was no less than to explore the edge of space and investigate the force that was driving the stars apart. Consider this at a time when the longest flight had been less than a thousand years! After the fashion of those days of naming everything, the planet ship was named the *Humanity*.

These twelve immortals and their leader, Bzonn, had wasted no time upon preparations. As soon as the blast chambers had been excavated by atomic motors in the core of the *Humanity*, they set off. For what remained to be done there would be ample time during the voyage. After continuous firing for thirty hours, they were traveling at the speed of 100,000 miles a second. The bulk of their ship had been reduced by one-quarter, in spite of the well-known efficiency of atomic power. For two hundred years they tore through the First Universe at this speed, often averting collisions by furious application of rocket power at the last second. During this time, the tiny planet ship had been converted into the most enormous power plant known to mankind. Its surface was gleaming with a silver tracery of beams and girders housing every known appliance for the use of power in attack and defense. It is said that a tenth of the weight of the *Humanity* could be converted into energy in one second—a greater outpouring of force than possessed by many of our stars.

When the gray stretches of intergalactic space were reached, a course was set to avoid all stars and the pace was speeded up to 150,000 miles a second, relative to its starting speed, in its orbit which was, of course, unknown in the absolute. Four million years were to elapse in this monotonous journey and, there being four females among the dozen scientists, a few hundred new humans were bred and educated during the first two or three centuries and the *Humanity* turned into a research laboratory in physics and related subjects. Several important inventions were given to the human race as a result, which you will learn about later in more technical courses. The only one I shall mention is the theory of gravitation diseases—that inexplicable effect upon stars and planets of Bzonn's "delayed" or static vortex. We now know that this effect on a minute scale is responsible for our atomic power. When applied to a sun, the result, after a delay of a century or two, is sudden expansion and deterioration until nothing remains but a vast cloud of bright gas. Since suns are rarely found outside of thickly starred systems, the net result is that several dozen suns are destroyed before the reaction is complete. The sending apparatus is extremely complicated and the power required to set up such a vortex is enormous.

It must not be thought that the opportunity for charting the galaxies was neglected. A small mountain of photographs was prepared during the four million years. Progress was made in every phase of art and science. It is regrettable that the colonization idea was not thought of until a million years had elapsed. This consisted of breeding a hundred humans and thoroughly educating them, stopping the *Humanity* in her course, entering a galaxy and finding a planet, and then leaving the hundred colonists on it to multiply and explore their new universe. This was done, Bzonn reports, more than 170 times in the last three million years of the voyage. Twice during this period, the *Humanity* was deserted for a new planet and fresh and improved machines and equipment were set up, the name and purpose in each case being transferred to the new planet ship, and the old one left with the current quota of colonists in the quickly deserted universe that then held them.

All dimensions, no matter how gigantic, have a definite end and the time came at last when, search as they might, no light of any sort could be seen beyond the edges of the last universe they had visited. Always before, though it might be a million years to the next star, the sky had shown dusty gray with distant pinpoints. This sky now showed blankly black—dead black—the unseeable darkness where light simply does not exist in any form, color, hue, or strength. They had arrived at the end of Matter and, by theory, also at the end of space itself. But of this latter point they were not yet certain, for though they saw this blank area, they had not yet reached it. At full speed they proceeded in its direction guided by the near stars. But before they passed these, fresh stars swung into view from the left or the right and seemed to move into the space ahead. This, Bzonn decided, must be caused by the curvature of space which seemed to be greatly magnified at its edges. To overcome this deceptive effect was impossible by physical means, for light waves and even motion itself were all equally distorted. A thousand years were spent in study and a corrective curve drawn painstakingly from empiric tests. For its solution it was necessary to solve the problem of three forces—three impinging curves, each of three dimensions, and this tedious mathematical task had to await the breeding and educating of a thousand new humans and the construction of countless elaborate calculating machines. When at length it was finished and a course could be set, it seemed so startling and disastrous in its implications that the work must needs be gone over again painstakingly.

There was no mistake; the course was correctly laid out. But it called for driving at full speed on a course that curved more sharply as the last fringe of stars were approached until at the last the course twisted back upon itself and would return them, seemingly, into the very universe from which they sought to escape! Seven hundred years were spent in completing the maneuver and at the end they were apparently driving with full power straight back toward a distant star. It was days before they suspected and months before they were certain of the amazing fact that the faster they drove toward it, the farther away it became! When it finally vanished as a far pinprick of light, they searched with the telescopes and took sufficient observations to orient themselves, afterward attempting to correct the photographs for light curvature. For they had passed beyond the stars.

And now picture these intrepid ones, gazing on one hand out upon nothingness and on the other upon a far distant wall of dusty light that was all that remained of Creation! This wall they imagined as a floor and across it they sped for a hundred thousand years searching for anything that might project above it—that might possibly explain the great shift to the red that had been the cause of their adventure. And they found it. What they found is, of course, still debatable. Ahead of them there loomed up a wall of distant starlight at right angles to the great floor beneath their planet-ship. This they approached not too closely but skirted it, and in the course of a million years completely circled the mass of star-matter. It rose about a million light-years in height and half that in diameter. Photographs of its contour were taken and by superimposing the outlines, a tiny model was created—a weird little thing that stood on their laboratory table. This sculpture you have all seen copied in the museums under the title of "The Living Galaxy." This is, of course, a misnomer, for upwards of fifty galaxies were noted in it. The title, however, clearly gives the idea of one theory of its origin, which is that the protuberance was a creature of life in some form which utilized solar systems after the fashion of atoms. This theory is much supported by the observed fact that photographic projections of its outline repeated at intervals of a hundred years showed clearly that the mass was in movement. For two million years it was studied with the most intense interest and a series of miniature statues were projected and photographed upon moving-picture film, one after the other, each in its proper attitude. It was found that when the film was viewed rapidly, the result was progressive movement.

Let us be as explicit as we may: The shape of this mass was that of a rounded cylinder, bulged out roughly above the center line. From this projected a streamer which tapered almost to nothingness. The motion observed was, briefly, a wriggling of the streamer (possibly a tentacle?) and a slow bending forward of the main body.

The next action of Bzonn upon establishing these facts was characteristic of the fearless and coldly scientific mind which drove him continuously throughout this extraordinary voyage. Straight down toward the wriggling tip of the tentacle of star-matter he sped his ship *Humanity.* The voyage lasted half a million years and as the last stars in the streamer came into view, it was noted that at its point commenced the enormous vacancy in the universes—that conical emptiness formerly occupied by countless stars that had first started them on their quest!

Here was (and still is) matter for the gravest minds to consider! Those who take the opposite view from Bzonn point out that it is inconceivable that this moving cluster of star groups could have held life. They argue by analogy that even if stars and planets could be substituted for atoms to make a scale of existence similar to our own, yet the number of stars involved was too few (relatively) to have created anything more than a very primitive microscopic creature—much too small to have fixed body parts such as tentacles. They also, by mathematics, seek to establish that there is so slight a resemblance between atoms and solar systems as to preclude the very possibility. Such reasons and arguments cannot be considered in an elementary treatise, but it must always be said that this occurred upon the edge of space—that light rays travel only a short distance outside of space (as was learned later and almost to their destruction) and that the rules and properties of such an existence cannot be yet established. On the other hand, Bzonn undoubtedly leaped to conclusions. His next action can hardly be condoned upon a scientific basis, for even if it averted destruction from a few billion or trillion humans, what is that? Humans can always be bred. And the phenomenon he destroyed was one that, to date, has not since been observed and may conceivably never again occur.

Ours is not to judge. Here to Bzonn seemed a clear issue. He had found a gigantic creature rooting dangerously with a tentacle among the stars that housed the human race. This he determined to stop if it lay in his power. It must be borne in mind that Bzonn felt no doubt that the star-mass composed a living intelligent creature. At the top of the rounded body must, he thought, lie some sort of brain and toward this he drove his mobile planetoid. Right up to the "head" of the creature he came and into it, observing no difference between the stars which formed it and those back in the more orderly portions of space. Possibly, he reported, the stars were more closely placed than might have been expected—no more than that. They were still more than two light-years apart at the closest and often as much as ten.

The task of destruction which he now set himself was simple—all that was necessary was to infect every tenth star he passed with his newly invented "delayed" vortex disease. There were by this time several thousand humans upon the *Humanity* of the moment. These were now divided into ten groups and each group established upon a suitable small planet as they passed among the suns. Each new planet was excavated for blast chambers of gigantic size and covered with huge engines for creating and releasing power. A hundred thousand years was spent in making these preparations, and upon an agreed day, the ten *Humanities* set off through the star-strewn space a hundred light-years apart, and as each selected star was passed, it was subjected to the terrific thrust of the disease-producing vortex. The violence and fury of this operation must be seen to be believed. Photographic reproductions are available at all museums and you are requested to view them before the next term. The ten planets shrank almost a tenth of their weight at each blast—shrank in one second! You may well believe what terrific earthquakes and storms racked them at that moment! The crew could not have lived upon them and did not attempt to. They set automatic controls an hour in advance and took themselves to small space ships which they guided to a few thousand miles distance and there they waited until the shock had passed before returning to their wrecked living quarters. In the two or three hundred years which had then to elapse before the next selected star approached, it was necessary to rebuild the machinery over the entire surface of each of the ten *Humanities.*

By the time the second blast was shot, it was possible to see in the telescopes the first signs of the vortex disease in the first infected suns they had left behind. When four blasts had been delivered by each of the ten planet ships, the distant stars were in violent disruption. On they sped, delivering in all six blasts apiece, and came out through the other side of the "Living Galaxy" and hastened away through the blackness beyond space, anxious to be well out of the way before that galaxy vanished in fiery vapor. On they continued until, with the naked eye they saw nothing but a distant hint of gray, and the telescopes showed only faint images of far stars. And as they proceeded to get clear of the danger zone, these faint images suddenly, inexplicably, and horrifyingly vanished!

Bzonn vividly recalls this scene in the following words: "Astronomy Gamma * first reported it to me and I did not believe him. It was not an hour before that I had used the telescope myself. He went away and returned with Astronomy Alpha himself and upon this I went to investigate and found it was even as I had been told. Through our most powerful electric telescope nothing—literally nothing—could be seen save for the other nine planets that formed our fleet. I signaled each of the nine in turn but not one reported any observation different from ours. The command to apply rocket power to bring our flight to a halt was a dangerous one—I dare not give it. How could we tell that direction might not be lost in the maneuver? One thing I did know and only one—if our rockets were kept shut off, our inertia would continue us in a straight line. Possibly large gyroscopes would hold direction and set us upon a return course. I proceeded at once to try them.

"By signal, I requested Physics Beta, who commanded one of the planetoids, to make the official tests, using the other nine ships to check direction. In a tenth of a year, he had completed his apparatus and the test was made. He found that the gyroscope retained its direction in spite of all manner of maneuvers to which

* A member of the crew.

he subjected his planetoid. The facts were signaled to all our con-
sorts and I delayed the command to return on our course only
long enough for Mechanics Delta to finish a gyroscope on my own
planet. This delay was fatal, as you shall see.

"All this time, it must be remembered, our planet-ships were
speeding outward in the blackness beyond space. Evidently, light
waves cease to function entirely when space completely ends.
Also, evidently, we had reached about then an absolutely blank
condition which, near or in space, only partially exists. Whatever
the exact reason, the fact is that, of a sudden, the other planets in
the fleet grew faint and dim and quite casually vanished. One of
them was less than a thousand miles away! Radio signals were
tried in vain. Our gyroscope was set in motion finally and I
changed course at once, hoping to come close enough to the
nearest planet ship to get into communication. Possibly her commander had the same idea—I may never know—but I never saw
him again.

"For a hundred thousand years, I searched through the black
fog in the most complete and utter fruitlessness. Finally, despairing of ever finding them, I gave the command for setting our
course back to our starting point. Of the other nine planets, eight
had not set up gyroscopes when the light failed and could only by
the merest chance ever hope to return to our familiar star universes. Physics Beta, of course, had a guide for his return and him
I expected to find later on. As a matter of fact, he returned to
human civilization half a million years before I did.

"For centuries we peered despairingly out at the desolate
wastes that lie there so emptily and blackly, searching for the first
distant hints that might indicate our approach to familiar space.
We gave up hope a dozen times, fearing that the gyroscope compass had failed, and a dozen times we kept grimly on, for what
else was there for us to do? Then came the glorious moment
when, with the naked eye, we all of us could make out the far floor
of light formed by all created matter and toward it we rushed until
the separate light-points showed us stars in the telescopes. And
where we entered space, there was a great rough lump of star-
clusters projecting above the level floor of stars and this we
photographed as we passed over and, laying silhouette upon silhouette, built up a tiny replica of its outline in our laboratory. It
had the appearance of a long, rounded body lying on its side with
a tentacle motionless on the floor beside it."

The remainder of Bzonn's narrative is an argument in favor of
his theory that he had slain a superbeast—a living galaxy of stars.

He warmly defended his action and insisted that a second beast doubtless exists somewhere and can be studied. He has made frequent expeditions to the edge of space in many directions but, so far, without success. At present, he has been absent 20 million years and is feared lost. But space has been conquered by many other explorers and there remains almost no star not already in our catalogs and almost no planet without its human settlement.

The next problem facing the human race is, is all this finite incurved group of star clusters we know as "space" merely one unit in infinity? Do there lie embedded in the dark nothingness beyond "space" incalculable other such units? Can we reach these other islands in chaos steering through the lightless areas with gyroscopes? Only time can tell.

AFTERWORD

When the voice of the teacher ceases, you look up, for the end of the chapter has been reached. You have been so excited by the substance of what has been read that you have lost your awe for this ancient man. Then his eyes sweep over the class and meet yours—just for an instant—and pass on to the door as he walks out of the room. And then a low babble of conversation breaks out among your six-year-old contemporaries and there is a general movement toward the door. You, reader, barely notice the others. Your chin is on your hands and your elbows on your desk. Your eyes stare through walls and pass through space until, in imagination, you see the warped and bulbous edge of space itself—see it as a fish sees the surface of water from beneath. How fine it would be, you think, to devote yourself forever to searching for the lost companions of Bzonn! But to do that one must wait until one knows enough and . . . there is the book before you. You are one of those who cannot wait for the next day to bring what it will—you must peer into the next chapter, driven by curiosity. For long hours you sit there over the book and I would give anything to know what you read there!

The advance of science has in no way wiped out the fundamental beliefs of religion. Indeed, the two apparently go along parallel, nonintersecting courses. Where they seem to intersect, it is usually a mistake and one or the other falls back baffled.

Today, for instance, we see attempts to deny scientific findings concerning the evolution of the Universe, of the solar system, of life, and of man. The current attempt, miscalled "scientific creationism," is actually an expression of prescientific mythology, an attempted "denial of origin." It cannot win. Even if it forces its beliefs on human beings through the use of terror, even if it forbids any other teaching, even if it blanks out all thought, nevertheless, as Galileo is supposed to have said when forbidden to teach that the Earth moves about the Sun: "Eppur si muove" ("And yet it moves even so"). And eventually the lie will break down under its own weight.

That is an example of a destructive collision. There are not wanting attempts at constructive collisions—attempts to reconcile the teachings of science and religion, while subverting neither.

The trouble with that is twofold. In the first place, science is always advancing. It never stands still long enough to be reconciled to anything. In the second place, there are many religions. Which one is to be reconciled?

Philo of Alexandria in the first century tried to reconcile Judaism with the Platonic philosophy of the Greeks; while in the twelfth century Thomas Aquinas tried to reconcile Catholic theology with Aristotelian philosophy.

Neither Plato nor Aristotle now represents the world view commonly accepted by scientific thinkers, and the modern fashion is not to seek reconciliation of science and Christianity, as much as of science and Eastern mysticism (as in that peculiar book, The Tao of Physics, *by Fritjof Capra).*

There's no reason why science-fiction writers should not seek their own way of reconciling science and religion, and here is one example of such an effort.

NON-ISOTROPIC
BRIAN ALDISS

The boy was first seen as a distant figure across sand. Behind him was water, then hills, green and tan. Beyond them, mountains, fading to blue, teased by cloud.

The boy was running wildly about a deep pool. As the viewpoint neared, it could be seen that he was laughing in excitement. He had a net which he jabbed inexpertly at the water. He jumped into the pool, to emerge shrieking with laughter.

The viewpoint moved remorselessly nearer, across the bare, wet sand. The boy stooped to make a trawl with his net. So close was the viewpoint that the serrations of the boy's backbone showed, white-knuckled. He straightened, lifting high a crab for the inspection of the hidden viewer.

Research vessel *Truganini* hung just beyond Home Galaxy, its antennae probing forward into the non-isotropic fault. It resembled a malformed spider, with its one extended leg housing delicate instruments protected from the artificial magnetosphere of the ship. Like certain kinds of spiders, the *Truganini* trailed a web. The web was designed to catch the fossil microwave radiation which powered it.

A lay brother switched the latest compread-out to the screen before which Priest Captain Shiva Askanza stood, talking with his chief navigator, Varga Bergwein. Captain and navigator briefly scanned the figures.

"We're at the extreme limit of safety," Askanza said. "There's the fault ahead of us. Nothing for it but to send out the drone and see where it gets us."

"If it can locate Cellini before it becomes inert, we're in God's luck."

Askanza bent over his panel and activated the auxiliary systems which controlled Drone A. The picture on the big screen jumped, and began to yield drone-oriented data as the machine nosed its way forward into space from its homing tube.

From the germanium brain of the drone came a simulation of the non-isotropic fault, writhing in concentric radiation contours shaped roughly like ram's horns. The fault was only some eighty light-years long at its longest, and fifty across. Its depth could not be estimated; conflicting readings suggested infinite depth. It was the first NIF to be discovered, and as shattering an event in its way as the discovery of the Expanding Universe two millennia ago.

The astrophysicist Rufort Cellini had developed the dislocation theory and the math behind it which postulated the existence of NIFS; he had gone out in a research vessel, ranging beyond the undetectable walls of the galaxy, and had verified his hypothesis —first, by finding the NIF, second by disappearing into it.

Drone A nudged forward from the *Truganini*, scattering a trail over Askanza's screen. The scatter cleared, the readings resumed, the simulation switching automatically from microwave to long wave to equivalent temperature to hadron to lepton to photon plot. The picture built up of a customary space trellis with average particle activity for such quadrants.

Askanza muttered a prayer. He found himself breathing more tightly as he watched the drone make its approach to the NIF. It took up a position almost stationary in relation to the fault, and then began to wind in sideways in response to Askanza's remote command.

The figures changed. The readings fell, all except the proton count. The temperature reading dropped to only a few decimal points off zero K.

Varga Bergwein grunted. Askanza shot him a glance, and by so doing almost missed the flash of red on the margin of the screen. It was there, it was gone.

The drone moved up against the fault in a shower of plummeting figures. It entered the fault. Readings and simulation ceased. A brilliant flash. The screen went dead. The drone had ceased to exist in relation to the isotropic universe.

In his ordinary voice, Askanza said into the phone, "Rerun of that, please, and the photorecord."

The photorecord came up first, corrected for visual frequencies. Clear through the fault, the viewers could see the shapes of two distant galaxies. The picture was steady, the NIF did not show. It had no refractive index, light traveled it unimpeded.

When the rerun appeared, Askanza slowed the picture and switched an auxiliary screen to infrared. When the flash of red showed again, he stopped the film and brought up magnification. There was no fuzziness. Limned in blue, there was the spider-shape of the *Poseidonian*.

"That's Cellini's ship right enough," said Bergwein. "There he is, but can we get him out?"

"Photons at least have the same properties in or out of non-isotropic space. Whatever goes on in there, we can see the ship. We can capture it and bring it and ourselves out again—provided our shield holds."

"You think Cellini will be alive, Captain?"

"Cellini was the theorist, the man with the hypotheses. Let's worry about him first and the hypotheses later."

He turned to the phone. "Switch on external amplifiers. Tell the crew to stand by. We are preparing to enter the NIF."

The boy had walked far across the stretch of sand. So low was the tide in the estuary that the channel of the river could hardly be seen from its banks. Several veins of water meandered through the sand, but the boy had now reached the deepest channel.

He was lost in thought. The viewpoint went to look over his bare shoulder and found him dredging pebbles out of the water and arranging them on the sharply defined edge of the sand. The water gurgled. A gull cried overhead.

He looked up and said, "It's glory here. I'd like to come here every holiday, really get to know the play of the tides, see how the sand patterns changed with the season. I just wish you could be here too, Father, to enjoy it with me. . . ."

The man said, "I'm sorry. I'm still sorry. Forever sorry . . ." He switched off the cube and sat with it under his palm. After a moment, he mastered himself and switched it on again.

The boy planted a big stone half in the river and against the bank, so as to watch the swirl of water undercut the sand, sharpening the miniature cliff. "Too bad you have to be away in space so long. I don't understand your dislocation theory too well—I guess I'll have to be older to do that. Right now, I don't ever want to leave Earth. It's so—it's so inexhaustible. I mean, just look at the dislocation I have here at this bank, between liquid and solid. One day I suppose I will understand the formula for this kind of thing, what makes solids solid and liquids liquid. I mean to understand if I can."

"Yes, yes, you mean to—for your father's sake," the man said, looking down with furrowed brow at the contents of the cube.

"I wish you were here to play with me," said the boy.

The man switched the holocube off. For a long time he sat staring blankly ahead. A tap at the door made him sit up and collect himself, instinctively covering the cube with one broad hand.

A messenger looked in.

"Captain Askanza, we are ready to ferry down to Earth if you're ready."

Askanza nodded curtly without speaking.

Omega was a mere chunk of inert rock some four hundred kilometers long and half as thick. It suited Rufort Cellini.

He anchored his vessel and set up some instruments on the rocky surface. The thickness of Omega cut out some of the background galactic radiation. He made observations. When he felt like it, he walked and thought. Cellini made a point of exercise, and derived pleasure from taking a stroll on the very edge of the galaxy.

When he walked in one direction, the cosmic night was there, intermittently lit by distant other galaxies. When he turned about and walked in the opposite direction, the great wheel of the Home Galaxy reared up, diamond bright and cruel, every nearer light with a cutting edge. From that wheel he received signals older than any light received from the most distant of galaxies to his rear.

Intergalactic space, he felt instinctively, was a gulf that mankind would never cross; there were burdens of distance too great for organic matter to shoulder. The galaxies had separated as thought separates, to further unity. All would become functions in his formulae. There was a solution to every mystery—even the Great Why itself—the solution that Rufort Cellini had set himself to discover, many years ago.

Certain basic equations had moved into his mind at the same time as the computer of the Congregation to which he belonged offered him the opportunity of a year's marriage.

Intellectual curiosity moved him to take up the year. He enjoyed sexual intercourse, he found the woman pleasant; but he experienced with her the same impatience he felt with his male friends: he could not bear idle conversation—and for Cellini most conversation was idle. He left her before the year had expired, but not before she became pregnant. It was social intercourse Cellini could not stand.

He had seen the child since then, spent time with it on his three visits back to Earth. The child he could tolerate. Growing organisms held some interest as a process, particularly when seen in temporal cross-section, as he saw his son. Unfortunately the child showed him affection and that was a claim Cellini was not prepared for. Only his work had his love.

That work, his lifetime's work, was now justified.

Reading his instruments, looking ahead into intergalactic space, Rufort Cellini trembled. He saw as clearly into his own brain as he saw into the universe ahead; indeed, the two views were disconcertingly parallel.

The insight brought recollections. He saw again the first nebulous intimations he had received in his teens that man's plan according to which the universe had been mapped held a dislocation, a fatal dislocation which prevented comprehension alike of the macroscopic and the microscopic and their extraordinary interrelationship: that the courses of the stars as well as the motions of the particles which constituted subnuclear physics were plotted according to a misapprehension that was almost fundamental to the mind of man. He remembered that fear, the burden of that knowledge which set him on a course further and further apart from his fellow humans. To him was given the task of correcting the misapprehension—and with it the basic comprehensions of mind.

Only gradually did Cellini perceive that the dislocation could be expressed in mathematics. But the mathematics which served to carry men in metal ships across their home galaxy was itself a product of the dislocation, and perpetuated the dislocation. He had to return to beginnings and invent a new mathematical language, the Cellini system, to formulate the divergences he began to see more and more clearly.

How lucid his brain had become, isolated despite his colleagues at the institute, despite his marriage period. It had worked without cease. Even the dream periods of sleep were oriented about his one central preoccupation, and were so oriented that they abolished the untidiness of normal human dreams.

Only in space, free of the irritating radiations of terrestrial life, had Cellini managed to complete his computations. He traveled in the *Poseidonian* at near light speed, willing his own generation left behind to age and die, seeing in their death his freedom from all emotional and human ties.

A new enlightenment overtook him. Remotely, he regarded the word "enlightenment" with sardonic amusement; it had been coined unknowingly long ago, specifically to describe his state of mind. For in his speeding brain photons themselves moved at a crawl: his thoughts traveled at near light speeds. There, his understanding and his Cellini system developed. Almost casually, he watched his computer spell out the syllables of the new equations that made the universe a different place.

Two voyages later he landed on Omega and set up his observatory. Confirmation in the real world of his abstractions was almost immediately forthcoming. He located a non-isotropic fault only a few light-years away.

The Cosmological Constant on which all astronomy and physics had been founded was wiped away. The universe was non-homogeneous and non-isotropic. Its composition was of energy in three great phase transitions: matter and energy, which had long been recognized—and consciousness.

At length, Cellini turned away and went back into his ship. His face was expressionless.

Sitting in his favorite chair, he came to a decision. Before returning to the inhabited planets, he would investigate the alien space himself and determine its properties. There was no need for further speculation; he could investigate this mysterious fault, this consciousness, in person.

There was a certain pride in the decision. He recognized it for what it was, a remnant of human weakness. He smiled, idly picking up the glassite cube by his right hand.

Well, it was fun to be a child some times. He pressed the holocube. Briefly, a boy ran on damp sand, smiling and beckoning, hardly expecting a response.

Prayers were said in the *Truganini* before it moved forward into the NIF. The prayers were amplified and broadcast throughout the research vessel. Amplifiers on the outside of the ship caused the prayers to be broadcast through space, so that the ship was surrounded by a field of prayer.

Everyone prayed. Only Askanza and Bergwein and other essential priest officers were excused as the great vessel accelerated gently.

The navigation officer said, "The holiness of this moment! If we survive, I shall go into isolation for the rest of my life, taking the Vow of Silence. Who can speak of such experience?"

Priest Captain Shiva Askanza was old. The hair on his head was sparse and gray, his shoulders were bent, but he straightened and said, "Cellini delivered not just humanity but the universe itself from materialism. Beyond doubt he has proved that the explosion which began the universe happened in the mind of God. So the universe has always been non-homogeneous, contrary to assumptions. We ourselves, our bodies, are composed of the consciousness of God in a phase transition."

"Quite. Consciousness, together with hydrogen, has been the basic building brick of the cosmos."

With awe and rejoicing in their hearts, they fell silent. The volume of prayer about them rose as the vessel moved toward the NIF. The NIF showed like a pulsating green wall on the screens before them.

The *Truganini* entered the fault.

Science and religion became one.

The prayer-field acted like a shield. Most of the instrumentation went dead as they penetrated the non-homogeneous matter. Photon count remained steady; they had a visual fix on Cellini's lost ship and moved steadily toward it with grappling magnets ready.

Glory moved in them. They were penetrated harmlessly by the fault.

In them was no fault. All the ancient ancestral ideas of God rose in their minds like birds from the surface of a lake. They were with God, with each other. Theirs was absolute comprehension. They traversed original undiluted godhead, which throughout the rest of the universe had been dispersed thinly. The Lord let his face to shine upon them.

Working in wonder, they reached the *Poseidonian*, matched velocities, secured it, brought it away.

The *Poseidonian* had had no prayer-shield. Cellini's mind had been burned out by glory.

He lay, a still youthful figure, sprawled on the floor of his cabin, clutching a holocube in his hand.

Safely back in normal space, back into the fringes of the Home Galaxy, Askanza and Bergwein reverently lifted the body out between them and carried it to the Captain's cabin. The crew, faces still transfigured, looked on.

Bergwein glanced from the youthful dead face to the gnarled old face of his priest captain. The resemblance prompted him to ask, "Forgive me, but why did you not take your father's illustrious name of Cellini?"

Askanza set the body reverently down and retrieved the cube from the dead hand.

"It would have been prideful so to do. My mother's name was Askanza; she was the one who cared for me. My father could only find the Truth by neglecting all else."

When he was left alone, and the *Truganini* had set its course for Earth, Askanza switched on the cube and watched his youthful self.

The boy had reached the remains of a wrecked ship. The bones of its hull curved out of the sand like ribs. It looked less like a vessel than the skeleton of a gigantic animal. The boy paced round it slowly.

After a while, he looked at the unseen viewer.

"I guess I should be able to grasp your dislocation theory or whatever you're going to call it. After all—solids and liquids, ships that don't make it home . . . The world's full of such things . . ."

He was silent for a moment, before adding apologetically, "And we two so far apart . . . Another dislocation." He sighed. "We just haven't recognized the principle behind such things before. Like it's proved impossible for most people to imagine God, though he's all around us."

The shallowest of waves lapped about his feet.

The boy looked embarrassed and prepared to flee.

"Maybe you don't even understand what I'm trying to say to you, Father. All these divisions . . . Anyhow, I hope that this holo-cube will catch up with you some day and give you a bit of company on your way."

Askanza switched off the cube and laid it beside his father's dead hand.

"Too late—as usual," he said. Over most of the universe God was spread in fossil radiation, too old, too thin.

Those people whose education and experience have been sharply limited to their own communities are apt to end with a totally self-contained view of the Universe. Their language is the only language. Why should anyone call a boy a knabe or a garçon, when a boy is manifestly a boy?

Again, people who believe that the Bible is the inspired word of God often believe that it is the King James Bible, specifically, that is so inspired, and turn away in horror from any attempt to correct or modernize what is after all merely a translation. Or as one aged parishioner said, waving his Bible, "If the King James was good enough for the prophets and apostles, it is good enough for me."

Yet there are sophisticated attempts at penetrating the mysteries of creation that are neither scientific nor Judeo-Christian, and here is one of them: a Hindu attempt.

There are points in it that resemble Genesis 1 (chaos and darkness first, and then light), and points that do not (the Universe first and gods next, rather than the reverse). The greatest difference, however, is that Genesis 1 states and is certain; whereas the account we now read questions and cheerfully admits uncertainty. It does not even end with the conventional "God knows," for even God might not.

THE SONG OF CREATION
HINDU RG-VEDA

Then was not nonexistent nor existent: there was no realm of air,
    no sky beyond it.
What covered in, and where? and what gave shelter? Was water
    there, unfathomed depth of water?

Death was not then, nor was there aught immortal: no sign was
    there, the day's and night's divider.
That one thing, breathless, breathed by its own nature: apart
    from it was nothing whatsoever.

Darkness there was: at first concealed in darkness, this All was
    indiscriminated chaos.

All that existed then was void and formless: by the great power of
warmth was born that unit.

Thereafter rose desire in the beginning, Desire, the primal seed
and germ of spirit.
Sages who searched with their heart's thought discovered the
existent's kinship in the nonexistent.

Transversely was their severing line extended: what was above it
then, and what below it?
There were begetters, there were mighty forces, free action here
and energy up yonder.

Who verily knows and who can here declare it, whence it was born
and whence came this creation?
The gods are later than this world's production. Who knows, then,
whence it first came into being?

He, the first origin of this creation, whether he formed it all or did
not form it,
Whose eye controls this world in highest heaven, he verily knows
it, or perhaps he knows not.

PART II

THE ORIGIN OF THE SOLAR SYSTEM

Now we limit ourselves. We forget the Universe and the big bang and descend to the smaller construct of the solar system. A few million years after the big bang, the Universe began to take on the shape it has now, as a thing of matter divided up into clusters of galaxies, each of which consisted of stars.

Yet even as long as 10 billion years after the big bang, the Sun still did not exist. In its place was a vast cloud of dust and gas, contaminated with the heavy-element debris blown into space by exploding supernovas. About 5 billion years ago, this vast cloud began to contract and to form, eventually, a central body that ignited into nuclear fire, and surrounding bits of matter that form the planets.

It is a magnificent scenario but it is hard to replace the one given us by Genesis 1: light, firmament, dry land, heavenly bodies, sea life and birds, animal life and man.

And yet if the solar system was formed by an omniscient God, why is life on Earth so manifestly imperfect; why is the history of humanity such a tissue of evils and lunacies? Science fiction is allowed any speculation and it might all rest in the nature of God.

KINDERGARTEN
JAMES E. GUNN

FIRST DAY

Teacher told my parent that I am the slowest youngster in my class, but today I made a star in the third quadrant of kindergarten.

Teacher was surprised. Teacher tried to hide it and said the solar phoenix reaction is artistic, but is it practical?

I don't care. I think it's pretty.

SECOND DAY

Today I made planets: four big ones, two middle-sized ones, and three little ones. Teacher laughed and said why did I make so many when all but three were too hot or too cold to support life and the big ones were too massive and poisonous for any use at all.

Teacher doesn't understand. There is more to creation than mere usefulness.

The rings around the sixth planet are beautiful.

THIRD DAY

Today I created life. I begin to understand why my people place creation above all else.

I have heard the philosophers discussing the purpose of existence, but I thought it was merely age. Before today joy was enough: to have fun with the other kids, to speed through endless space, to explode some unstable star into a nova, to flee before the outrage of some adult—this would fill eternity.

Now I know better. Life must have a function.

Teacher was right: only two of the middle-sized planets and one of the little ones were suitable for life. I made life for all three, but only on the third planet from the sun was it really successful.

I have given it only one function: survive!

FOURTH DAY

The third planet has absorbed all my interest. The soupy seas are churning with life.

Today I introduced a second function: multiply!

The forms developing in the seas are increasingly complex.

The kids are calling me to come and play, but I'm not going.

This is more fun.

FIFTH DAY

Time after time I stranded sea-creatures on the land and kept them alive long past the time when they should have died. At last I succeeded. Some of them have adapted.

I was right. The sea is definitely an inhibiting factor.

The success of the land-creatures is pleasing.

SIXTH DAY

Everything I did before today was nothing. Today I created intelligence.

I added a third function: know!

Out of a minor primate has developed a fabulous creature. It has two legs and walks upright and looks around it with curious

eyes. It has weak hands and an insignificant brain, but it is conquering all things. Most of all, it is conquering its environment.

It has even begun speculating about me!

SEVENTH DAY

Today there is no school.

After the pangs and labors of creation, it is fun to play again. It
is like escaping the gravitational field of a white dwarf and regain-
ing the dissipated coma.

Teacher talked to my parent again today. Teacher said I had
developed remarkably in the last few days but my creation was
hopelessly warped and inconsistent. Moreover, it was potentially
dangerous.

Teacher said it would have to be destroyed.

My parent objected, saying tht the solar phoenix reaction in the
sun would lead the dangerous life form on the third planet to
develop a thermonuclear reaction of its own. With the functions I
had given that life form, the problem would take care of itself.

It wasn't my parent's responsibility, Teacher said, and Teacher
couldn't take the chance.

I didn't hear who won the argument. I drifted away, feeling
funny.

I don't care, really. I'm tired of the old thing anyway. I'll make
a better one.

But it was the first thing I ever made, and you can't help feeling
a kind of sentimental attachment.

If anyone sees a great comet plunging toward the sun, it isn't
me.

EIGHTH DAY

Another way of speculating about creation is to suppose that it is an endless circle, that the creation produces something which in turn causes the creation. My own favorite story, of all those I have written, is "The Last Question," in which computers are described as gradually evolving through billions of years of human history into omniscience and omnipotence. Finally, when the Universe has completely run down, the ultimate computer says, "Let there be light," and the whole thing starts in again, following a line of development that will eventually create the ultimate computer who will say—

The thing to remember is that van Vogt's "The Seesaw" was written in 1941. In that year the dominant notion of the manner in which the solar system was created was that it came about through a near-collision of two stars. Enormous gravitational forces wrenched matter out of each, and this matter eventually formed the planets (some circling each star, presumably, as the two went their separate ways). It was not till 1944 that the German physicist Carl F. von Weizsacker worked out the modern version of the contracting gas-cloud theory of the creation of the solar system.

For that reason, the final catastrophe hinted at in the ending is out of place—or is it? What started the gas-cloud contracting so as to bring about the formation of the sun and planets? An increasingly attractive present-day notion is that it was the explosion of a nearby supernova that set up a pressure-wave in the cloud and began the process. And if so, the final catastrophe is correct, and we can marvel at the prescience of van Vogt.

Except that if I had been writing the story myself—and today —I would make the final catastrophe the big bang itself.

THE SEESAW
A. E. VAN VOGT

MAGICIAN BELIEVED TO HAVE
HYPNOTIZED CROWD

June 11, 1941—Police and newspapermen believe that Middle City will shortly be advertised as the next stopping place of a master magician, and they are prepared to extend him a hearty welcome if he will condescend to explain exactly how he fooled hundreds of people into believing they saw a strange building, apparently a kind of gun shop.

The building seemed to appear on the space formerly, and still, occupied by Aunt Sally's Lunch and Patterson Tailors. Only employees were inside the two aforementioned shops, and none noticed any untoward event. A large, brightly shining sign featured the front of the gun shop, which had been so miraculously conjured out of nothingness; and the sign constituted the first evidence that the entire scene was nothing but a masterly illusion. For from whichever angle one gazed at it, one seemed to be staring straight at the words, which read:

FINE WEAPONS
THE RIGHT TO BUY WEAPONS
IS THE RIGHT TO BE FREE

The window display was made up of an assortment of rather curiously shaped guns, rifles as well as small arms; and a glowing sign in the window stated:

THE FINEST ENERGY WEAPONS
IN THE KNOWN UNIVERSE

Inspector Clayton of the Investigation Branch attempted to enter the shop, but the door seemed to be locked; a few moments later, C. J. (Chris) McAllister, reporter of the *Gazette-Bulletin*, tried the door, found it open, and entered.

Inspector Clayton attempted to follow him, but discovered that the door was again locked. McAllister emerged after some time, and was seen to be in a dazed condition. All memory of the action had apparently been hypnotized out of him, for he could make no answer to the questions of the police and spectators.

Simultaneous with his reappearance, the strange building vanished as abruptly as it had appeared.

Police state they are baffled as to how the master magician created so detailed an illusion for so long a period before so large a crowd. They are prepared to recommend his show, when it comes, without reservation.

Author's Note: The foregoing account did not mention that the police, dissatisfied with the affair, attempted to contact McAllister for a further interview but were unable to locate him. Weeks passed, and he was still not to be found.

Herewith follows the story of what happened to McAllister from the instant that he found the door of the gun shop unlocked.

There was a curious quality about the gun shop door. It was not so much that it opened at his first touch as that, when he pulled, it came away like a weightless thing. For a bare instant, McAllister had the impression that the knob had freed itself into his palm.

He stood quite still, startled. The thought that came finally had to do with Inspector Clayton, who a minute earlier had found the door locked.

The thought was like a signal. From behind him boomed the voice of the inspector: "Ah, McAllister, I'll handle this now."

It was dark inside the shop beyond the door, too dark to see anything, and somehow his eyes wouldn't accustom themselves to the intense gloom. . . .

Pure reporter's instinct made him step forward toward the blackness that pressed from beyond the rectangle of door. Out of the corner of one eye, he saw Inspector Clayton's hand reaching for the door handle that his own fingers had let go a moment before; and quite simply he knew that if the police officer could prevent it, no reporter would get inside that building.

His head was still turned, his gaze more on the police inspector than on the darkness in front; and it was as he began another step forward that the remarkable thing happened.

The door handle would not allow Inspector Clayton to touch it. It twisted in some queer way, in some *energy* way, for it was still there, a strange, blurred shape. The door itself, without visible movement, so swift it was, was suddenly touching McAllister's heel.

Light, almost weightless, was that touch; and then, before he could think or react to what had happened, the momentum of his forward movement had carried him inside.

As he breasted the darkness, there was a sudden, enormous tensing along his nerves. Then the door shut tight, the brief, incredible agony faded. Ahead was a brightly lit shop; behind—were unbelievable things!

For McAllister, the moment that followed was one of blank impression. He stood, body twisted awkwardly, only vaguely conscious of the shop's interior, but tremendously aware, in the brief moment before he was interrupted, of what lay beyond the transparent panels of the door through which he had just come.

There was no unyielding blackness anywhere, no Inspector Clayton, no muttering crowd of gaping spectators, no dingy row of shops across the way.

It wasn't even remotely the same street. There was *no* street.

Instead, a peaceful park spread there. Beyond it, brilliant under a noon sun, glowed a city of minarets and stately towers—

From behind him, a husky, musical, woman's voice said, "You will be wanting a gun?"

McAllister turned. It wasn't that he was ready to stop feasting his eyes on the vision of the city. The movement was automatic reaction to a sound. And because the whole affair was still like a dream, the city scene faded almost instantly; his mind focused on the young woman who was advancing slowly from the rear section of the store.

Briefly, his thought wouldn't come clear. A conviction that he ought to say something was tangled with first impressions of the girl's appearance. She had a slender, well-shaped body; her face was creased into a pleasant smile. She had brown eyes, neat, wavy brown hair. Her simple frock and sandals seemed so normal at first glance that he gave them no other thought.

He was able to say: "What I can't understand is why the police officer who tried to follow me couldn't get in. And where is he now?"

To his surprise, the girl's smile became faintly apologetic. "We know that people consider it silly of us to keep harping on that ancient feud."

Her voice grew firmer: "We even know how clever the propaganda is that stresses the silliness of our stand. Meanwhile, we never allow any of *her* men in here. We continue to take our principles very seriously."

She paused as if she expected dawning comprehension from him, but McAllister saw from the slow puzzlement creeping into her eyes that his face must look as limp as were the thoughts behind it.

Her men! The girl had spoken the word as if she were referring to some personage, and in direct reply to his use of the words, police officer. That meant *her* men, whoever she was, were policemen; and they weren't allowed in this gun shop. So the door was hostile, and wouldn't admit them.

A strange emptiness struck into McAllister's mind, matching the hollowness that was beginning to afflict the pit of his stomach, a sense of unplumbed depths, the first, staggering conviction that all was not as it should be.

The girl was speaking in a sharper tone: "You mean you know nothing of all this, that for generations the gunmakers' guild has existed in this age of devastating energies as the common man's only protection against enslavement. The right to buy guns—"

She stopped again, her narrowed eyes searching him; then: "Come to think of it, there's something very illogical about you. Your outlandish clothes—you're not from the northern farm plains, are you?"

He shook his head dumbly, more annoyed with his reactions every passing second. But he couldn't help it. A tightness was growing in him, becoming more unbearable instant by instant, as if somewhere a vital mainspring were being wound to the breaking point.

The young woman went on more swiftly: "And come to think of it, it is astounding that a policeman should have tried the door and there was no alarm."

Her hand moved; metal flashed in it, metal as bright as steel in blinding sunlight. There was not the faintest hint of the apologetic in her voice as she said, "You will stay where you are, sir, till I have called my father. In our business, with our responsibility, we never take chances. Something is very wrong here."

Curiously, it was at that point that McAllister's mind began to function clearly; the thought that came paralleled hers: How had this gun shop appeared on a 1941 street? How had he come here into this fantastic world?

Something was very wrong indeed!

It was the gun that held his attention. A tiny thing it was, shaped like a pistol, but with three cubes projecting in a little half circle from the top of the slightly bulbous firing chamber.

And as he stared, his mind began to quiver on its base; for that wicked little instrument, glittering there in her browned fingers, was as real as she herself.

"Good Heaven!" he whispered. "What the devil kind of gun is it? Lower that thing and let's try to find out what all this is about."

She seemed not to be listening; and abruptly he noticed that her gaze was flicking to a point on the wall somewhat to his left. He followed her look—in time to see seven miniature white lights flash on.

Curious lights! Briefly, he was fascinated by the play of light and shade, the waxing and waning from one tiny globe to the next, a rippling movement of infinitesimal increments and decrements, an incredibly delicate effect of instantaneous reaction to some supersensitive barometer.

The lights steadied; his gaze reverted to the girl. To his surprise, she was putting away her gun. She must have noticed his expression.

"It's all right," she said coolly. "The automatics are on you now. If we're wrong about you, we'll be glad to apologize. Meanwhile, if you're still interested in buying a gun, I'll be happy to demonstrate."

So the automatics were on him, McAllister thought ironically. He felt no relief at the information. Whatever the automatics were, they wouldn't be working in his favor; and the fact that the young woman could put away her gun in spite of her suspicions spoke volumes for the efficiency of the new watchdogs.

There was absolutely nothing he could do but play out this increasingly grim and inexplicable farce. Either he was mad, or else he was no longer on Earth, at least not the Earth of 1941—which was utter nonsense.

He'd have to get out of this place, of course. Meanwhile, the girl was assuming that a man who came into a gun shop would, under ordinary circumstances, want to buy a gun.

It struck him suddenly that, of all the things he could think of, what he wanted to see was one of those strange guns. There were implications of incredible things in the very shape of the instruments. Aloud he said, "Yes, by all means show me."

Another thought occurred to him. He added: "I have no doubt your father is somewhere in the background making some sort of study of me."

The young woman made no move to lead him anywhere. Her eyes were dark pools of puzzlement, staring at him.

"You may not realize it," she said finally, slowly, "but you have already upset our entire establishment. The lights of the automatics should have gone on the moment father pressed the buttons, as he did when I called to him. They didn't! That's unnatural, that's alien.

"And yet"—her frown deepened—"if you were one of them, how did you get through that door? Is it possible that *her* scientists have discovered human beings who do not affect the sensitive energies? And that you are one of many such, sent as an experiment to determine whether or not entrance could be gained?

"Yet that doesn't make logic either.

"If they had even a hope of success, they would not risk so lightly the chance of an overwhelming surprise. Instead you would be the entering wedge of an attack on a vast scale. She is ruthless, she's brilliant; and she craves all power during her lifetime over poor saps like you who have no more sense than to worship her amazing beauty and the splendor of the Imperial Court."

The young woman paused, with the faintest of smiles. "There I go again, off on a political speech. But you can see that there are at least a few reasons why we should be careful about you."

There was a chair over in one corner; McAllister started for it. His mind was calmer, cooler.

"Look," he began, "I don't know what you're talking about. I don't even know how I came to be in this shop. I agree with you that the whole thing requires explanation, but I mean that differently than you do. In fact . . ."

His voice trailed. He had been half lowered over the chair, but instead of sinking into it, he came erect like an old, old man. His eyes fixed on lettering that shone above a glass case of guns behind her. He said hoarsely, "Is that—a calendar?"

She followed his gaze, puzzled: "Yes, it's June third. What's wrong?"

"I don't mean that. I mean—" He caught himself with a horrible effort. "I mean those figures above that. I mean—what year is this?"

The girl looked surprised. She started to say something, then stopped and backed away. Finally: "Don't look like that! There's nothing wrong. This is eighty-four of the four thousand seven hundredth year of the Imperial House of the Isher. It's quite all right."

There was no real feeling in him. Quite deliberately he sat down, and the conscious wonder came: Exactly how *should* he feel?

Not even surprise came to his aid. Quite simply, the whole pattern of events began to make a sort of distorted logic.

The building front superimposed on those two 1941 shops; the way the door had acted; the great exterior sign with its odd linking of freedom with the right to buy weapons; the actual display of weapons in the window, *the finest energy weapons in the known universe!*

He grew aware that minutes had passed while he sat there in slow, dumb thought. And that the girl was talking earnestly with a tall, gray-haired man who was standing on the open threshold of the door through which she had originally come.

There was an odd, straining tenseness in the way they were talking. Their low-spoken words made a curious blur of sound in his ears, strangely unsettling in effect—McAllister could not quite analyze the meaning of it until the girl turned; and, in a voice dark with urgency, said, "Mr. McAllister, my father wants to know what year you're from!"

Briefly, the sense of the sentence was overshadowed by that stark urgency; then: "Huh!" said McAllister. "Do you mean that you're responsible for—And how the devil did you know my name?"

The older man shook his head. "No, we're not responsible." His voice quickened but lost none of its gravity. "There's no time to explain. What has happened is what we gunmakers have feared for generations: that sooner or later would come one who lusted for unlimited power; and who, to attain tyranny, must necessarily seek first to destroy us.

"Your presence here is a manifestation of the energy force that she has turned against us—something so new that we did not even suspect it was being used against us. But now—I have no time to waste. Get all the information you can, Lystra, and warn him of his own personal danger."

The man turned. The door closed noiselessly behind his tall figure.

McAllister asked, "What did he mean—personal danger?"

He saw that the girl's brown eyes were uneasy as they rested on him.

"It's hard to explain," she began in an uncomfortable voice. "First of all, come to the window, and I'll try to make everything clear. It's all very confusing to you, I suppose."

McAllister drew a deep breath. "Now we're getting somewhere."

His alarm was gone. The older man seemed to know what it was all about; that meant there should be no difficulty getting home again. As for all this danger to the gunmakers' guild, that was their worry, not his. Meanwhile—

He stepped forward, closer to the girl. To his amazement, she cringed away as if he had struck at her.

As he stared blankly, she turned, and laughed a humorless, uncertain laugh; finally she breathed, "Don't think I'm being silly, don't be offended—but for your life's sake don't touch any human body you might come into contact with."

McAllister was conscious of a chill. It struck him with a sudden, sharp dismay that the expression of uneasiness in the girl's face was—fear!

His own fear fled before a wave of impatience. He controlled himself with an effort.

"Now, look," he began, "I want to get things clear. We can talk here without danger, providing I don't touch you or come near you. Is that straight?"

She nodded. "The floor, the walls, every piece of furniture, in fact the entire shop is made of perfect nonconducting material."

McAllister had a sudden sense of being balanced on a tightrope over a bottomless abyss. The way this girl could imply danger without making it clear what the danger was, almost petrified him.

He forced calm into his mind. "Let's start," he said, "at the beginning. How did you and your father know my name, and that I was not of"—he paused before the odd phrase, then went on—"of this time?"

"Father X-rayed you," the girl said, her voice as stiff as her body. "He X-rayed the contents of your pockets. That was how he first found out what was the matter. You see, the X-rays themselves became carriers of the energy with which you're charged. That's what was the matter; that's why the automatics wouldn't focus on you, and—"

"Just a minute!" said McAllister. His brain was a spinning world. "Energy—charged?"

The girl was staring at him. "Don't you understand?" she gasped. "You've come across five thousand years of time; and of all the energies in the universe, time is the most potent. You're charged with trillions of trillions of time-energy units. If you should step outside this shop, you'd blow up this city of the Isher and half a hundred miles of land beyond.

"You"—she finished on an unsteady, upward surge of her voice —"you could conceivably destroy the earth!"

He hadn't noticed the mirror before; funny, too, because it was large enough, at least eight feet high, and directly in front of him on the wall where a minute before—he could have sworn—had been solid metal.

"Look at yourself," the girl was saying soothingly. "There's nothing so steadying as one's own image. Actually your body is taking the mental shock very well."

It was! He stared in dimly gathering surprise at his image. There was a paleness in the lean face that stared back at him; but the body was not actually shaking as the whirling in his mind had suggested.

He grew aware again of the girl. She was standing with one finger on one of a series of wall switches. Abruptly, he felt better.

"Thank you," he said quietly. "I certainly needed that."

She smiled encouragingly; and he was able now to be amazed at her conflicting personality. There had been on the one hand her complete inability a few minutes earlier to get to the point of his danger, a distinct incapacity for explaining things with words; yet obviously her action with the mirror showed a keen understanding of human psychology. He said, "The problem now is, from your point of view, to circumvent this—Isher—woman, and to get me back to 1941 before I blow up the Earth of . . . of whatever year this is."

The girl nodded. "Father says that you can be sent back, but— as for the rest: watch!"

He had no time for relief at the knowledge that he could be returned to his own time. She pressed another button. Instantly the mirror was gone into the metallic wall. Another button clicked —and the wall vanished.

Literally vanished. Before him stretched a park similar to the one he had already seen through the front door—obviously an extension of the same gardenlike vista. Trees were there, and flowers, and green, green grass in the sun.

There was also the city again, nearer from this side, but not so pretty, immeasurably grimmer.

One vast building, as high as it was long, massively dark against the sky, dominated the entire horizon. It was a good quarter-mile away; and incredibly, it was at least that long and that high.

Neither near that monstrous building nor in the park was a living person visible. Everywhere was evidence of man's dynamic labor—but no men, not a movement; even the trees stood motionless in that strangely breathless sunlit day.

"Watch!" said the girl again, more softly.

There was no click this time. She made an adjustment on one of the buttons; and suddenly the view was no longer so clear. It wasn't that the sun had dimmed its bright intensity. It wasn't even that glass was visible where a moment before there had been nothing.

There was still no apparent substance between them and the gemlike park. But—

The park was no longer deserted!

Scores of men and machines swarmed out there. McAllister stared in frank amazement; and then as the sense of illusion faded, and the dark menace of those men penetrated, his emotion changed to dismay.

"Why," he said at last, "those men are soldiers, and the machines are—"

"Energy guns!" she said. "That's always been their problem: how to get their weapons close enough to our shops to destroy us. It isn't that the guns are not powerful over a very great distance. Even the rifles we sell can kill unprotected life over a distance of miles; but our gun shops are so heavily fortified that, to destroy us, they must use their biggest cannon at point-blank range.

"In the past, they could never do that because we own the surrounding park; and our alarm system was perfect—until now. The new energy they're using affects none of our protective instruments; and—what is infinitely worse—affords them a perfect shield against our own guns. Invisibility, of course, has long been known; but if you hadn't come, we would have been destroyed without ever knowing what happened."

"But," McAllister exclaimed sharply, "what are you going to do? They're still out there working—"

Her brown eyes burned with a fierce, yellow flame. "Where do you think Father is?" she asked. "He's warned the guild; and every member has now discovered that similar invisible guns are being set up outside his place by invisible men. Every member is working at top speed for some solution. They haven't found it yet."

She finished quietly: "I thought I'd tell you."

McAllister cleared his throat, parted his lips to speak—then closed them as he realized that no words were even near his lips. Fascinated, he watched the soldiers connecting what must have been invisible cables that led to the vast building in the background: foot-thick cables that told of the titanic power that was to be unleashed on the tiny weapon shop.

There was actually nothing to be said. The deadly reality out there overshadowed all conceivable sentences and phrases. Of all the people here, he was the most useless, his opinion the least worthwhile.

Oddly, he must have spoken aloud, but he did not realize that until the familiar voice of the girl's father came from one side of him. The older man said, "You're quite mistaken, McAllister. Of all the people here you are the *most* valuable. Through you we discovered that the Isher were actually attacking us. Furthermore, our enemies do not know of your existence, therefore have not yet realized the full effect produced by the new blanketing energy they have used.

"You, accordingly, constitute the unknown factor—our only hope, for the time left to us is incredibly short. Unless we can make immediate use of the unknown quantity you represent, all is lost!"

The man looked older, McAllister thought; there were lines of strain in his lean, sallow face, as he turned toward his daughter; and his voice, when he spoke, was edged with harshness: "Lystra, number seven!"

As the girl's fingers touched the seventh button, her father explained swiftly to McAllister: "The guild supreme council is holding an immediate emergency session. We must choose the most likely method of attacking the problem, and concentrate individually and collectively on that method. Regional conversations are already in progress, but only one important idea has been put forward as yet . . . ah, gentlemen!"

He spoke past McAllister, who turned with a start, then froze.

Men were coming out of the solid wall, lightly, easily, as if it were a door and they were stepping across a threshold. One, two, three—twelve.

They were grim-faced men, all except one who glanced at McAllister, started to walk past, then stopped with a half-amused smile.

"Don't look so blank. How else do you think we could have survived these many years if we hadn't been able to transmit material objects through space? The Isher police have always been only too eager to blockade our sources of supply. Incidentally, my name is Cadron—Peter Cadron!"

McAllister nodded in a perfunctory manner. He was no longer

genuinely impressed by the new machines. Here were endless products of the machine age; science and invention so stupendously advanced that men made scarcely a move that did not involve a machine. He grew aware that a heavy-faced man near him was about to speak.

The man began: "We are gathered here because it is obvious that the source of the new energy is the great building just outside this shop—"

He motioned toward the wall where the mirror had been a few minutes previously, and the window through which McAllister had gazed at the monstrous structure in question.

The speaker went on: "We've known, ever since that building was completed five years ago, that it was a power building aimed against us; and now from it new energy has flown out to engulf the world, immensely potent energy, so strong that it broke the very tension of time, fortunately only at this nearest gun shop. Apparently it weakens when transmitted over distance. It—"

"Look, Dresley!" came a curt interruption from a small, thin man. "What good is all this preamble? You have been examining the various plans put forward by regional groups. Is there, or isn't there, a decent one among them?"

Dresley hesitated. To McAllister's surprise, the man's eyes fixed doubtfully on him, his heavy face worked for a moment, then hardened.

"Yes, there is a method, but it depends on compelling our friend from the past to take a great risk. You all know what I'm referring to. It will gain us the time we need so desperately."

"Eh!" said McAllister, and stood stunned as all eyes turned to stare at him.

The seconds fled; and it struck McAllister that what he really needed again was the mirror—to prove to him that his body was putting up a good front. Something, he thought, something to steady him.

His gaze flicked over the faces of the men. The gunmakers made a curious, confusing pattern in the way they sat, or stood, or leaned against glass cases of shining guns; and there seemed to be fewer than he had previously counted. One, two—ten, including the girl. He could have sworn there had been fourteen.

His eyes moved on, just in time to see the door of the back room closing. Four of the men had obviously gone to the laboratory or whatever lay beyond the door. Satisfied, he forgot them.

Still, he felt unsettled; and briefly his eyes were held by the purely mechanical wonder of this shop, here in this vastly future world, a shop that was an intricate machine in itself and—

He discovered that he was lighting a cigarette; and abruptly realized that that was what he needed most. The first puff tingled deliciously along his nerves. His mind grew calm; his eyes played thoughtfully over the faces before him.

He said, "I can't understand how any one of you could even think of compulsion. According to you, I'm loaded with energy. I may be wrong, but if any of you should try to thrust me back down the chute of time, or even touch me, that energy in me would do devastating things—"

"You're damned right!" chimed in a young man. He barked irritably at Dresley: "How the devil did you ever come to make such a psychological blunder? You know that McAllister will have to do as we want, to save himself; and he'll have to do it fast!"

Dresley grunted under the sharp attack. "Hell," he said, "the truth is we have no time to waste, and I just figured there wasn't time to explain, and that he might scare easily. I see, however, that we're dealing with an intelligent man."

McAllister's eyes narrowed over the group. There was something phony here. They were talking too much, wasting the very time they needed, as if they were marking time, waiting for something to happen.

He said sharply, "And don't give me any soft soap about being intelligent. You fellows are sweating blood. You'd shoot your own grandmothers and trick me into the bargain, because the world you think right is at stake. What's this plan of yours that you were going to compel me to participate in?"

It was the young man who replied: "You are to be given insulated clothes and sent back into your own time—"

He paused. McAllister said, "That sounds okay, so far. What's the catch?"

"There is no catch!"

McAllister stared. "Now, look here," he began, "don't give me any of that. If it's as simple as that, how the devil am I going to be helping you against the Isher energy?"

The young man scowled blackly at Dresley. "You see," he said to the other, "you've made him suspicious with the talk of yours about compulsion."

He faced McAllister. "What we have in mind is an application of a sort of an energy lever and fulcrum principle. You are to be a 'weight' at the long end of a kind of energy 'crowbar,' which lifts the greater 'weight' at the short end. You will go back five thousand years in time; the machine in the great building to which your body is tuned, and which has caused all this trouble, will move ahead in time about two weeks."

"In that way," interrupted another man before McAllister could speak, "we shall have time to find a counteragent. There must be a solution, else our enemies would not have acted so secretly. Well, what do you think?"

McAllister walked slowly over to the chair that he had occupied previously. His mind was turning at furious speed, but he knew with a grim foreboding that he hadn't a fraction of the technical knowledge necessary to safeguard his interests.

He said slowly, "As I see it, this is supposed to work something like a pump handle. The lever principle, the o d idea that if you had a lever long enough, and a suitable fulcrum, you could move the Earth out of its orbit."

"Exactly!" It was the heavy-faced Dresley who spoke. "Only this works in time. You go five thousand years, the building goes a few wee . . ."

His voice faded, his eagerness drained from him as he caught the expression on McAllister's face.

"Look!" said McAllister, "there's nothing more pitiful than a bunch of honest men engaged in their first act of dishonesty. You're strong men, the intellectual type, who've spent your lives enforcing an idealistic conception. You've always told yourself that if the occasion should ever require it, you would not hesitate to make drastic sacrifices. But you're not fooling anybody. *What's the catch?"*

It was quite startling to have the suit thrust at him. He hadn't observed the men emerge from the back room; and it came as a distinct shock to realize that they had actually gone for the insulated clothes before they could have known that he would use them.

McAllister stared grimly at Peter Cadron, who held the dull, grayish, limp thing toward him. A very flame of abrupt rage held him choked; before he could speak, Cadron said in a tight voice, "Get into this, and get going! It's a matter of minutes, man! When those guns out there start spraying energy, you won't be alive to argue about our honesty."

Still he hesitated; the room seemed insufferably hot; and he was sick—sick with the deadly uncertainty. Perspiration streaked stingingly down his cheeks. His frantic gaze fell on the girl, standing silent and subdued in the background, near the front door.

He strode toward her; and either his glare or presence was incredibly frightening, for she cringed and turned white as a sheet.

"Look!" he said. "I'm in this as deep as hell. What's the risk in this thing? I've got to feel that I have some chance. Tell me, what's the catch?"

The girl was gray now, almost as gray and dead-looking as the suit Peter Cadron was holding. "It's the friction," she mumbled finally; "you may not get all the way back to 1941. You see, you'll be a sort of 'weight' and—"

McAllister whirled away from her. He climbed into the soft, almost flimsy suit, crowding the overall-like shape over his neatly pressed clothes. "It comes tight over the head, doesn't it?" he asked.

"Yes!" It was Lystra's father who answered. "As soon as you pull that zipper shut, the suit will become completely invisible. To outsiders it will seem just as if you have your ordinary clothes on. The suit is fully equipped. You could live on the Moon inside it."

"What I don't get," complained McAllister, "is why I have to wear it. I got here all right without it."

He frowned. His words had been automatic, but abruptly a thought came: "Just a minute. What becomes of the energy with which I'm charged when I'm bottled up in this insulation?"

He saw by the stiffening expressions of those around him that he had touched on a vast subject.

"So that's it!" he snapped. "The insulation is to prevent me losing any of that energy. That's how it can make a 'weight.' I have no doubt there's a connection from this suit to that other machine. Well, it's not too late. It's—"

With a desperate twist, he tried to jerk aside, to evade the clutching hands of the four men who leaped at him. Hopeless movement! They had him instantly; and their grips on him were strong beyond his power to break.

The fingers of Peter Cadron jerked the zipper tight, and Peter Cadron said, "Sorry, but when we went into that back room, we also dressed in insulated clothing. That's why you couldn't hurt us. Sorry, again!

"And remember this: There's no certainty that you are being sacrificed. The fact that there is no crater in *our* Earth proves that you did not explode in the past, and that you solved the problem in some other way. *Now, somebody open the door, quick!*"

Irresistibly he was carried forward. And then—

"Wait!"

It was the girl. The colorless gray in her face was a livid thing. Her eyes glittered like dark jewels; and in her fingers was the tiny, mirror-bright gun she had pointed in the beginning at McAllister.

The little group hustling McAllister stopped as if they had been struck. He was scarcely aware; for him there was only the girl, and the way the muscles of her lips were working, and the way her voice suddenly flamed: "This is utter outrage. Are we such cowards —is it possible that the spirit of liberty can survive only through a shoddy act of murder and gross defiance of the rights of the individual? I say no! Mr. McAllister must have the protection of the hypnotism treatment, even if we die during the wasted minutes."

"Lystra!" It was her father; and McAllister realized in the swift movement of the older man what a brilliant mind was there, and how quickly the older man grasped every aspect of the situation.

He stepped forward and took the gun from his daughter's fingers—the only man in the room, McAllister thought flashingly, who could dare approach her in that moment with the certainty she would not fire. For hysteria was in every line of her face, and the racking tears that followed showed how dangerous her stand might have been against the others.

Strangely, not for a moment had hope come. The entire action seemed divorced from his life and his thought; there was only the observation of it. He stood there for a seeming eternity and, when emotion finally came, it was surprise that he was not being hustled to his doom. With the surprise came awareness that Peter Cadron had let go his arm and stepped clear of him.

The man's eyes were calm, his head held proudly erect; he said, "You daughter is right, sir. At this point we rise above our petty fears, and we say to this unhappy man: 'Have courage! You will not be forgotten. We can guarantee nothing, cannot even state exactly what will happen to you. But we say: If it lies in our power to help you, that help you shall have.' And now—we must protect you from the devastating psychological pressures that would otherwise destroy you, simply but effectively."

Too late, McAllister noticed that the others had turned faces away from that extraordinary wall—the wall that had already displayed so vast a versatility. He did not even see who pressed the activating button for what followed.

There was a flash of dazzling light. For an instant he felt as if his mind had been laid bare; and against that nakedness the voice of Peter Cadron pressed like some ineradicable engraving stamp: "To retain your self-control and your sanity—this is your hope: This you will do in spite of everything! And, for your sake, speak of your experience only to scientists or to those in authority who you feel will understand and help. Good luck!"

So strong remained the effect of that brief flaring light that he felt only vaguely the touch of their hands on him, propelling him. He must have fallen, but there was no pain—

He grew aware that he was lying on a sidewalk. The deep, familiar voice of Police Inspector Clayton boomed over him: "Clear the way; no crowding now!"

McAllister climbed to his feet. A pall of curious faces gawked at him; and there was no park, no gorgeous city. Instead, a bleak row of one-story shops made a dull pattern on either side of the street.

He'd have to get away from here. These people didn't understand. Somewhere on Earth must be a scientist who could help him. After all, the record was that he hadn't exploded. Therefore, somewhere, somehow—

He mumbled answers at the questions that beat at him; and then he was clear of the disappointed crowd. There followed purposeless minutes of breakneck walking; the streets ahead grew narrower, dirtier—

He stopped, shaken. What was happening?

It was night, in a brilliant, glowing city. He was standing on an avenue that stretched jewellike into remote distance.

A street that lived, flaming with a soft light that gleamed up from its surface—a road of light, like a river flowing under a sun that shone nowhere else, straight and smooth and—

He walked along for uncomprehending minutes, watching the cars that streamed past—and wild hope came!

Was this again the age of the Isher and the gunmakers? It could be; it looked right, and it meant they had brought him back. After all, they were not evil, and they would save him if they could. For all he knew, weeks had passed in their time and—

Abruptly, he was in the center of a blinding snowstorm. He staggered from the first, mighty, unexpected blow of that untamed wind, then, bracing himself, fought for mental and physical calm.

The shining, wondrous night city was gone; gone too the glowing road—both vanished, transformed into this deadly, wilderness world.

He peered through the driving snow. It was daylight; and he could make out the dim shadows of trees that reared up through the white mist of blizzard less than fifty feet away.

Instinctively he pressed toward their shelter, and stood finally out of that blowing, pressing wind.

He thought: One minute in the distant future; the next—where?

There was certainly no city. Only trees, an uninhabited forest and winter—

The blizzard was gone. And the trees. He stood on a sandy beach; before him stretched a blue, sunlit sea that rippled over broken white buildings. All around, scattered far into that shallow, lovely sea, far up into the weed-grown hills, were the remnants of a once tremendous city. Over all clung an aura of incredible age; and the silence of the long-dead was broken only by the gentle, timeless lapping of the waves—

Again came that instantaneous change. More prepared this

time, he nevertheless sank twice under the surface of the vast, swift river that carried him on and on. It was hard swimming, but the insulated suit was buoyant with the air it manufactured each passing second; and, after a moment, he began to struggle purposefully toward the tree-lined shore a hundred feet to his right.

A thought came, and he stopped swimming. "What's the use!"

The truth was as simple as it was terrible. He was being shunted from the past to the future; he was the "weight"on the long end of an energy seesaw; and in some way he was slipping farther ahead and farther back each time. Only that could explain the catastrophic changes he had already witnessed. It a minute would come another change and—

It came! He was lying face downward on green grass. but there was no curiosity in him. He did not look up, but lay there hour after hour as the seesaw jerked on: past—future—past—future—

Beyond doubt, the gunmakers had won their respite; for at the far end of this dizzy teeter-totter was the machine that had been used by the Isher soldiers as an activating force; it too teetered up, then down, in a mad seesaw.

There remained the gunmakers' promise to help him, vain now; for they could not know what had happened. They could not find him ever in this maze of time.

There remained the mechanical law that forces must balance.

Somewhere, sometime, a balance would be struck, probably in the future—because there was still the fact that he hadn't exploded in the past. Yes, somewhere would come the balance when he would again face *that* problem. But now—

On, on, on the seesaw flashed; the world on the one hand grew bright with youth, and on the other dark with fantastic age.

Infinity yawned blackly ahead.

Quite suddenly it came to him that he knew where the seesaw would stop. It would end in the very remote past, with the release of the stupendous temporal energy he had been accumulating with each of those monstrous swings.

He would not witness, but he would cause, the formation of the planets.

The notion of a dying God is as old as mythology. My father, when I told him this once, was puzzled. He had been brought up in the sternest of monotheisms and he said, "How can God die? If he dies, he is not God." Many a Jew, uneducated outside Judaic doctrine, must have thought this when he hurried past a crucifix and must have known better than to voice his thoughts aloud.

And yet how else explain the cycle of the seasons? How else explain the fact that (in temperate regions, at least) vegetation dies with the approach of winter and then reappears with the spring? Surely it must be the reflection of the death and resurrection of a god. Death is no denial of godhood if it is followed by resurrection; rather it is the offer of a great hope to humanity that death can be conquered.

And so Osiris and Tammuz and Adonis and Persephone and many others die and are reborn, with the death and rebirth celebrated each year with sorrow followed by triumph. This is true of Jesus, too, except that Christians do not view it as a nature myth, but as an event of cosmic and nonrepeating significance. Nevertheless, the death and resurrection are celebrated each year.

But if gods can die, is it possible that the creator of the solar system can be less enduring than the creation, in a way? This is again a speculation that is made to order for science fiction.

HEATHEN GOD
GEORGE ZEBROWSKI

". . . every heathen deity has its place in the flow of existence."

The isolation station and preserve for alien flora and fauna on Antares IV had only one prisoner, a three-foot-tall gnomelike biped with skin like creased leather and eyes like great glass globes. His hair was silky white and reached down to his shoulders, and he usually went about the great natural park naked. He lived in a small white cell located in one of the huge blocklike administration modules. There was a small bed in the cell, and a small doorway which led out to the park. A hundred feet away from the door there was a small pool, one of many scattered throughout the park. It reflected the deep blue color of the sky.

The gnome was very old, but no one had yet determined quite how old. And there seemed to be no way to find out. The gnome himself had never volunteered any information about his past. In the one hundred years of his imprisonment he had never asked the caretaker for anything. It was rumored among the small staff of Earthmen and humanoids that the gnome was mad. Generally they avoided him. Sometimes they would watch his small figure gazing at the giant disk of Antares hanging blood-red on the horizon, just above the well-pruned trees of the park, and they would wonder what he might be thinking.

The majority of Earthpeoples spread over twelve star systems did not even know of the gnome's existence, much less his importance. A few knew, but they were mostly scholarly and political figures, and a few theologians. The most important fact about the alien was that sometime in the remote past he had been responsible for the construction of the solar system and the emergence of intelligent life on earth.

The secret had been well kept for over a century.

In the one hundred and fourth year of the alien's captivity, two men set out to visit him. The first man's motives were practical: the toppling of an old regime; the other man's goal was to ask questions. The first man's political enemies had helped him to undertake this journey, seeing that it would give them the chance to destroy him. The importance of gaining definitive information about the alien was in itself enough reason to send a mission, but combined with what they knew about the motives of the man they feared, this mission would provide the occasion to resolve both matters at the same time. The second man would bring back anything of value that they might learn about the gnome.

Everything had been planned down to the last detail. The first ship, carrying the two unsuspecting men, was almost ready to come out of hyperspace near Antares. Two hours behind it in the warp was a military vessel—a small troop ship. As the first vessel came out of nothingness into the brilliance of the great star, the commander of the small force ship opened his sealed orders.

As he came down the shuttle ramp with his two companions, Father Louis Chavez tried to prepare himself for what he would find here. It was still difficult to believe what his superiors had told him about the imprisoned alien. The morning air of Antares IV was fresh, and the immediate impression was one of stepping out into a warm botanical garden. At his left Sister Guinivere carried his small attaché case. On his right walked Benedict Compton, linguist, cultural anthropologist, and as everyone took for granted, eventual candidate for first secretary of Earth's Northern Hemisphere. Compton was potentially a religious man, but the kind who always demanded an advance guarantee before committing himself to anything. Chavez felt suspicious of him.

On earth the religiophilosophic system was a blend of evolutionary Chardinism and Christianity, an imposing intellectual structure that had been dominant for some two hundred years now. The political structure based its legitimacy and continuing policies on it. Compton, from what he had learned, had frightened some high authorities with the claim that the gnome creature here on Antares IV was a potential threat to the beliefs of mankind. This, combined with what was already known about the alien's past, was seemingly enough to send this fact-finding mission. Only a few men knew about it, and Chavez remembered the fear he had sensed in them when he had been briefed. Their greatest fear was that somehow the gnome's history would become public knowledge. Compton, despite his motives, had found a few more political friends. But Chavez suspected that Compton wanted power not for himself, but to do something about the quality of life on earth. He was sure the man was sincere. How little of the thought in our official faith filters out into actual policy, Chavez thought. And what would the government do if an unorganized faith—a heresy in the old sense—were to result from this meeting between Compton and the alien? Then he remembered how Compton had rushed this whole visit. He wondered just how far a man like Compton would go to have his way in the world.

Antares was huge on the horizon, a massive red disk against a deep blue sky. A slight breeze waved the trees around the landing square. The pathway, which started at the north corner, led to three brightly white buildings set on a neat lawn and surrounded by flowering shrubs and fruit-bearing trees. The walk was pleasant.

Rufus Kade, the caretaker, met them at the front entrance to the main building. He showed them into the comfortable reception room. He was a tall, thin botanist, who had taken the post because it gave him the opportunity to be near exotic plants. Some of the flora came from worlds as much as one hundred light-years away from Antares. After the introductions were over, Kade took the party to the garden where the gnome spent most of his time.

"Do you ever talk with him, Mr. Kade?" Father Chavez asked. The caretaker shook his head. "No," he said. "And now I hope you will all excuse me, I have work to do." He left them at the entrance to the garden path.

Compton turned to Father Chavez and said, "You are lucky, you're the only representative of any church ever to get a chance to meet what might be the central deity of that church." He smiled. "But I feel sorry for you—for whatever he is, he will not be what you expect, and most certainly he will not be what you want him to be."

"Let's wait and see," Chavez said. "I'm not a credulous man."

"You know, Chavez," Compton said in a more serious mood, "they let me come here too easily. What I mean is they took my word for the danger involved with little or no question."

"Should they have not taken your word? You are an important man."

Sister Guinivere led the way into the garden. On either side of them the plants were luxurious, with huge green leaves and strange varicolored flowers. The air was filled with rich scents, and the earth gave the sensation of being very moist and loosely packed. They came into the open area surrounding the pool. Sister Guinivere stood between the two men as they looked at the scene. The water was still, and the disk of Antares was high enough now in the morning sky to be reflected in it.

The gnome stood on the far side, watching them as they approached, as if he expected them at any moment to break into some words of greeting. It would be awkward standing before a member of a race a million years older than mankind and towering over him. It would be aesthetically banal, Chavez thought.

As they came to the other side of the pool Compton said, "Let me start the conversation, Father."

"If you wish," Chavez said. *Why am I afraid, and what does it matter who starts the conversation,* he thought.

Compton walked up to the gnome and sat down cross-legged in front of him. It was a diplomatic gesture. Father Chavez felt relieved and followed the example, motioning Sister Guinivere to do the same. They all looked at the small alien.

His eyes were deep-set and large; his hair was white, thin, and reached down to his shoulders. He had held his hands behind his back when they had approached, but now they were together in front of him. His shoulders were narrow and his arms were thin. He wore a one-piece coverall with short sleeves.

Chavez hoped they would be able to talk to him easily. The gnome looked at each of them in turn. It became obvious that he expected them to start the conversation.

"My name is Benedict Compton," Compton said, "and this is Father Chavez and Sister Guinivere, his secretary. We came here to ask you about your past, because it concerns us."

Slowly the gnome nodded his head, but he did not sit with them. Compton gave Chavez a questioning look.

"Could you tell us who you are?" Chavez asked. The gnome moved his head sharply to look at him. *It's almost as if I interrupted him at something,* Chavez thought. There was a sad look on the face now, as if in that one moment he had understood everything—why they were here and the part he would have to play.

Chavez felt his stomach grow tense. He felt as if he were being carefully examined. Compton was playing with a blade of grass. Sister Guinivere sat with her hands folded in her lap. Briefly he recalled the facts he knew about the alien—facts that only a few Earthmen had been given access to over the last century. Facts that demanded that some sort of official attitude be taken.

The best-kept secret of the past century was that this small creature had initiated the events which led to the emergence of intelligent life on Earth. In the far past he had harnessed his powers of imagination to a vast machine, which had been built for another purpose, and had used it to create much of the life on Earth. He had been caught at his experiments and exiled. Long before men had gone out to the stars he had been a wanderer in the galaxy, but in recent years he had been handed over to Earth authorities to keep at this extraterrestrial preserve. Apparently his people still feared his madness. This was all they had ever revealed to the few Earthmen who took charge of the matter.

It was conjectured that the gnome's race was highly isolationist; the gnome was the only member of it who had ever been seen by Earthmen. The opinion was that his culture feared contact with other intelligent life, and especially with this illegitimate creation. Of the few who knew about the case, one or two had expressed disbelief. It was, after all, Chavez thought, enough to make any man uneasy. It seemed safer to ignore the matter most of the time.

Since that one contact with Earth, the gnome's race had never come back for him. A century ago they had simply left him in Earth orbit, in a small vessel of undeniably superior workmanship. A recorded message gave all the information they had wanted to reveal. Their home world had never been found, and the gnome had remained silent. Benedict Compton had set up this meeting, and Chavez had been briefed by his superiors and instructed to go along as an observer.

Chavez remembered how the information had at first shaken and then puzzled him. The tension in his stomach grew worse. He wondered about Compton's motives, but he had not dared to question them openly. On Earth many scientists prized the alien as the only contact with a truly advanced culture, and he knew that more than one young student would do anything to unlock the secrets that must surely exist in the brain of the small being now standing in front of him. He felt sure that Compton was hoping for some such thing.

Suddenly the small figure took a step back from them. A small breeze waved his long white hair. His small, gnarly body took on a strange stature; his face was grief-stricken and his low voice was sad. It wavered as he spoke to them. "I made you to love each other, and through yourselves, me. I needed that love. No one can know how much I needed it, but it had to be freely given, so I had to permit the possibility of it being withheld. There was no other way, and there still is not."

Chavez looked at Compton. The big man sat very still. Sister Guinivere was looking down at the grass in front of her feet. Chavez felt a stirring of fear and panic in his insides. It felt as if the alien was speaking only to him—as if *he* could relieve the thirst that lived behind those deep-set eyes in that small head.

He felt the other's need. He felt the deprivation that was visible on that face, and he felt that at any moment he would feel the awesome rage that would spill out onto them. This then, he thought, is the madness that his race had spoken about. All the power had been stripped from this being, and now he was a beggar.

Instead of rage there was sadness. It was oppressive. What was Compton trying to uncover here? How could all this benefit anyone? Chavez felt his hand shaking, and he gripped it with the other hand.

The gnome raised his right hand and spoke again. *Dear God, help me,* Chavez prayed. *Help me to see this clearly.* "I fled from the hive mind which my race was working toward," the gnome said in a louder voice than before. "They have achieved it. They are one entity now. What you see in this dwarfed body are only the essentials of myself—the feelings mostly—they wait for the day when the love in my children comes to fruition and they will unite, thus recreating my former self—which is now in them. Then I will leave my prison and return to them to become the completion of myself. This body will die then. My longing for that time is without limit, and I will make another history like this one and see it through. Each time I will be the completion of a species and its moving spirit. And again they will give birth to me. Without this I am nothing."

There was a loud thunderclap overhead, the unmistakable sound of a shuttle coming through the atmosphere. But it was too early for the starship shuttle to be coming back for them, Chavez thought. Compton jumped up and turned to look toward the administration buildings. Chavez noticed that the gnome was looking at him. *Do your people worship a supreme being?* Chavez thought the question. *Do they have the idea of such a being? Surely you know the meaning of such a being?*

I don't know any such thing. The thought was clear in his head. *Do you know him?*

"It's a shuttle craft," Compton said.

Chavez got up. Sister Guinivere struggled to her feet.

"What is it?" she asked.

"I—I don't know who it could be," Compton said. Chavez noticed the lack of confidence in the other's voice. Behind them the gnome stood perfectly still, unaffected by the interruption.

"They've landed by now," Compton said. "It could only be one thing, Father—they've found out my plans for the gnome." Compton spoke in a low voice. "Father, this is the only way to get a change on earth—yes, it's what you think, a cult, with me as its head, but the cause is just. Join me now, Father!"

Then it's true, Chavez thought. *He's planning to bypass the lawful candidacy. Then why did they let him come here?*

There was a rustling in the shrubs around the pool area. Suddenly they were surrounded by armed men. Twenty figures in full battle gear had stepped out from the trees and garden shrubs. They stood perfectly still, waiting.

Antares was directly overhead now, a dark red circle of light covering 10 percent of the blue dome that was the sky. Noontime.

Compton's voice shook as he shouted, "What is *this?* Who the devil are you!"

A tall man immediately on the other side of the pool from them appeared to be the commanding officer. He wore no gear and there were no weapons in his hands. Instead he held a small piece of paper which he had just taken out of a sealed envelope.

"Stand away, Father, and you too, Sister!" the officer shouted. "This does not concern you." Then he looked down at the paper in his hand and read: "Benedict Compton, you have been charged with conspiracy to overthrow the government of the Northern Hemisphere on Earth by unlawful means, and you have been tried and convicted by the high court of North America for this crime. The crime involves the use of an alien being as your coconspirator to initiate a religious controversy through a personally financed campaign which would result in your becoming the leader of a subversive cult, whose aim would be to seize power through a carefully prepared hoax. You and your coconspirator are both mortal enemies of the state." The officer folded the paper and put it back in its envelope and placed it in his tunic.

Chavez noticed that Sister Guinivere was at his side, and he could tell that she was afraid.

Compton turned to Chavez. "Father, protect the gnome, whatever he is. Use what authority you have. They won't touch you."

"The execution order is signed by Secretary Alcibiad herself!" the tall officer shouted.

Chavez was silent.

"Father, please!" Compton pleaded. "You can't let this happen." Chavez heard the words, but he was numb with surprise. The words had transfixed him as effectively as any spear. He couldn't move, he couldn't think. Sister Guinivere held his arm.

Suddenly Compton was moving toward the gnome.

"Shoot!"

The lasers reached out like tongues.

The little figure fell. And the thought went out from him in one last effort, reaching light-years into space. *I loved you. You did not love me, or each other.* They all heard the thought, and it stopped them momentarily. Compton was still standing, but his right arm was gone, and he was bleeding noisily onto the grass.

"Shoot!"

Again the lasers lashed out. Compton fell on his back, a few yards from the gnome. Sister Guinivere collapsed to her knees, sobbing. She began to wail. The soldiers began to retreat. Father Chavez sat down on the ground. He didn't know what to do. He looked at the two bodies. There was smoke coming from Compton's clothing. The gnome's hair was aflame.

The tall officer now stood alone on the other side of the pool. Chavez knew that his orders had probably been sealed, and he only now felt their full force. After a few moments the tall officer turned and went after his men.

The alien knew this would happen, Chavez thought. *He knew, and that was why he told us everything.*

When the great disk of Antares was forty-five degrees above the horizon, Rufus Kade came out to them. He put the two bodies in plastic specimen bags. Sister Guinivere was calm now and was holding Father Chavez's hand. They both stood up when Kade finished with the bodies.

"They had an official pass from way up," Kade said. "I even checked back on it."

He walked slowly with them to the administration building.

Father Chavez sat alone in his small cabin looking at the small monitor which showed him where he had been. Soon now the brilliance of the stars would be replaced by the dull emptiness of hyperspace. Antares was a small red disk on the screen.

Momentarily Chavez resented the fact that he had been a mere creation to the gnome. In any case the alien had not been God. His future importance would be no greater than that of Christ— probably less. He had been only an architect, a mere shaper of materials which had existed long before even his great race had come into being. But still—was he not closer to God than any *man* had ever been? Or would be?

The completion for which the gnome had made man would never take place now. The point of mankind's existence as he had made it was gone. And the alien had not known God. If there was such a being, a greatest possible being, he now seemed hopelessly remote. . . .

O Lord, I pray for a sign! Chavez thought.

But he heard only his thoughts and nothing from the being who would surely have answered in a case like this. And he had stood by while they killed the gnome there in the garden by the pool, on that planet circling the red star whose diameter was greater than the orbit of Mars. Despite all his reasoning now, Chavez knew that he had stood back while they killed that part of the small creature which had loved humanity.

But what had he said? The *rest* of the gnome's being *was* humanity, and it still existed; except that now it would never be reunited with him. *"Do not fear,"* the holy Antony had said three thousand years ago, *"this goodness as a thing impossible, nor its pursuit as something alien, set a great way off: it hangeth on our own arbitrament. For the sake of the Greek learning men go overseas . . . but the city of God is everywhere . . . the kingdom of God is within. The goodness that is in us only asks the human mind."* What we can do for ourselves, Chavez thought, that's all that is ours now.

He took a deep breath as the starship slipped into the nothingness of hyperspace. He felt the burden of the political power which he now carried as a witness to the alien's murder, and he knew that Compton's life had not been for nothing. He would have to hide his intentions carefully, but he knew what he would have to do.

In time, he hoped anew, we may still give birth to the semblance of godhood that lives on in mankind, on that small world which circles a yellow sun.

For almost all the time that humanity's inquiring mind has studied the heavens, the Sun has been merely a circle of light, the Moon a sometime circle of light that waxes and wanes, and five of the planets merely dots of light, moving erratically across the sky. The sky had been studied about five thousand years before the first telescope came to the aid of human eyesight in 1609.

In the next 350 years, far more was learned about the solar system, thousands of times more, than had been or could have been learned in the previous five thousand.

And then after World War II, a whole new battery of tools came to the aid of the astronomer, with radio telescopes and planetary probes at the head of the list, so that in the last thirty-five years, far more has been learned about the solar system, thousands of times more, than had been or could have been learned in the previous 350.

As Carl Sagan has said, this is the most fortunate generation in which planetary astronomers (such as himself) could live. In previous generations, nothing really important was known about the planets. In subsequent generations, all will be old hat.

And it is Sagan who here presents an overview of the solar system and its origin, as it is currently known.

THE SUN'S FAMILY
CARL SAGAN

Like a shower of stars the worlds whirl, borne along by the winds of heaven, and are carried down through immensity; suns, earths, satellites, comets, shooting stars, humanities, cradles, graves, atoms of the infinite, seconds of eternity, perpetually transform beings and things.　　　　CAMILLE FLAMMARION
Popular Astronomy, translated by J. E. Gore
(New York, D. Appleton & Company, 1894)

Imagine the Earth scrutinized by some very careful and extremely patient extraterrestrial observer: 4.6 billion years ago the planet is observed to complete its condensation out of interstellar gas and dust, the final planetesimals falling in to make the Earth produce enormous impact craters; the planet heats internally from the gravitational potential energy of accretion and from radioactive decay, differentiating the liquid iron core from the silicate mantle and crust; hydrogen-rich gases and condensible water are released from the interior of the planet to the surface; a rather humdrum cosmic organic chemistry yields complex molecules, which lead to extremely simple self-replicating molecular systems—the first terrestrial organisms; as the supply of impacting interplanetary boulders dwindles, running water, mountain building, and other geological processes wipe out the scars attendant to the Earth's origin; a vast planetary convection engine is established which carries mantle material up at the ocean floors and subducts it down at the continental margins, the collision of the moving plates producing the great folded mountain chains, and the general con-figuration of land and ocean, glaciated and tropical terrain varies continuously. Meanwhile, natural selection extracts out from a wide range of alternatives those varieties of self-replicating molec-ular systems best suited to the changing environments; plants evolve that use visible light to break down water into hydrogen and oxygen, and the hydrogen escapes to space, changing the chemi-cal composition of the atmosphere from reducing to oxidizing; organisms of fair complexity and middling intelligence eventually arise.

Yet in all the 4.6 billion years our hypothetical observer is struck by the isolation of the Earth. It receives sunlight and cosmic rays—both important for biology—and occasional impact of inter-planetary debris. But nothing in all those eons of time leaves the planet. And then the planet suddenly begins to fire tiny dispersules throughout the inner solar system, first in orbit around the Earth, then to the planet's blasted and lifeless natural satellite, the Moon. Six capsules—small, but larger than the rest—set down on the Moon, and from each, two tiny bipeds can be discerned, briefly exploring their surroundings and then hotfooting it back to the Earth, having extended tentatively a toe into the cosmic ocean. Eleven little spacecraft enter the atmosphere of Venus, a searing hellhole of a world, and six of them survive some tens of minutes on the surface before being fried. Eight spacecraft are sent to Mars. Three successfully orbit the planet for years; another flies past Venus to encounter Mercury, on a trajectory obviously chosen intentionally to pass by the innermost planet many times. Four others successfully traverse the asteroid belt, fly close to Jupiter and are there ejected by the gravity of the largest planet into inter-stellar space. It is clear that something interesting is happening lately on the planet Earth.

If the 4.6 billion years of the Earth history were compressed into a single year, this flurry of space exploration would have occupied the last tenth of a second, and the fundamental changes in attitude and knowledge responsible for this remarkable transformation would fill only the last few seconds. The seventeenth century saw the first widespread application of simple lenses and mirrors for astronomical purposes. With the first astronomical telescope Galileo was astounded and delighted to see Venus as a crescent, and the mountains and the craters of the Moon. Johannes Kepler thought that the craters were constructions of intelligent beings inhabiting that world. But the seventeenth-century Dutch physicist Christianus Huygens disagreed. He suggested that the effort involved in constructing the lunar craters would be unreasonably great, and also thought that he could see alternative explanations for these circular depressions.

Huygens exemplified the synthesis of advancing technology, experimental skills, a reasonable, hard-nosed, and skeptical mind, and an openness to new ideas. He was the first to suggest that we are looking at atmosphere and clouds on Venus; the first to understand something of the true nature of the rings of Saturn (which had seemed to Galileo as two "ears" enveloping the planet); the first to draw a picture of a recognizable marking on the Martian surface (Syrtis Major); and the second, after Robert Hooke, to draw the Great Red Spot of Jupiter. These last two observations are still of scientific importance because they establish the permanence at least for three centuries of these features. Huygens was of course not a thoroughly modern astronomer. He could not entirely escape the fashions of belief of his time. For example, he presented a curious argument from which we could deduce the presence of hemp on Jupiter; Galileo had observed that Jupiter has four moons. Huygens asked a question few modern planetary astronomers would ask: *Why* does Jupiter have four moons? An insight into this question, he thought, could be garnered by asking the same question of the Earth's single moon, whose function, apart from giving a little light at night and raising the tides, was to provide a navigational aid to mariners. If Jupiter has four moons, there must be many mariners on that planet. But mariners imply boats; boats imply sails; sails imply ropes; and, I suppose, ropes imply hemp. I wonder how many of our present highly prized scientific arguments will seem equally suspect from the vantage point of three centuries.

A useful index of our knowledge about a planet is the number of bits of information necessary to characterize our understanding of its surface. We can think of this as the number of black and white dots in the equivalent of a newspaper wirephoto which, held at arm's length, would summarize all existing imagery. Back in Huygens's day, about ten bits of information, all obtained by brief glimpses through telescopes, would have covered our knowledge of the surface of Mars. By the time of the close approach of Mars to Earth in the year 1877, this number had risen to perhaps a few thousand, if we exclude a large amount of erroneous information —for example, drawings of the "canals," which we now know to be entirely illusory. With further visual observations and the development of ground-based astronomical photography, the amount of information grew slowly until a dramatic upturn in the curve occurred, corresponding to the advent of space-vehicle exploration of the planet.

The twenty photographs obtained in 1965 by the Mariner 4 fly-by comprised five million bits of information, roughly comparable to all previous photographic knowledge about the planet. The coverage was still only a tiny fraction of the planet. The dual fly-by mission, Mariners 6 and 7 in 1969, increased this number by a factor of 100, and the Mariner 9 orbiter in 1971 and 1972 increased it by another factor of 100. The Mariner 9 photographic results from Mars correspond roughly to 10,000 times the total previous photographic knowledge of Mars obtained over the history of mankind. Comparable improvements apply to the infrared and ultraviolet spectroscopic data obtained by Mariner 9, compared with the best previous ground-based data.

Going hand in hand with the improvement in the quantity of our information is the spectacular improvement in its quality. Prior to Mariner 4, the smallest feature reliably detected on the surface of Mars was several hundred kilometers across. After Mariner 9, several percent of the planet had been viewed at an effective resolution of 100 meters, an improvement in resolution of a factor of 1,000 in the last ten years, and a factor of 10,000 since Huygens's time. Still further improvements were provided by Viking. It is only because of this improvement in resolution that we today know of vast volcanoes, polar laminae, sinuous tributaried channels, great rift valleys, dune fields, crater-associated dust streaks, and many other features, instructive and mysterious, of the Martian environment.

Both resolution and coverage are required to understand a newly explored planet. For example, even with their superior resolution, by an unlucky coincidence the Mariner 4, 6, and 7 spacecraft observed the old, cratered and relatively uninteresting part of Mars and gave no hint of the young and geologically active third of the planet revealed by Mariner 9.

Life on Earth is wholly undetectable by orbital photography until about 100-meter resolution is achieved, at which point the urban and agricultural geometrizing of our technological civilization becomes strikingly evident. Had there been a civilization on Mars of comparable extent and level of development, it would not have been detected photographically until the Mariner 9 and Viking missions. There is no reason to expect such civilizations on the nearby planets, but the comparison strikingly illustrates that we are just beginning an adequate reconnaissance of neighboring worlds.

There is no question that astonishments and delights await us as both resolution and coverage are dramatically improved in photography, and comparable improvements are secured in spectroscopic and other methods.

The largest professional organization of planetary scientists in the world is the Division for Planetary Sciences of the American Astronomical Society. The vigor of this burgeoning science is apparent in the meetings of the society. In the 1975 annual meeting, for example, there were announcements of the discovery of water vapor in the atmosphere of Jupiter, ethane on Saturn, possible hydrocarbons on the asteroid Vesta, an atmospheric pressure approaching that of the Earth on the Saturnian moon Titan, decameter-wavelength radio bursts from Saturn, the radar detection of the Jovian moon Ganymede, the elaboration of the radio emission spectrum of the Jovian moon Callisto, to say nothing of the spectacular views of Mercury and Jupiter (and their magnetospheres) presented by the Mariner 10 and Pioneer 11 experiments. Comparable advances were reported in subsequent meetings.

In all the flurry and excitement of recent discoveries, no general view of the origin and evolution of the planets has yet emerged, but the subject is now very rich in provocative hints and clever surmises. It is becoming clear that the study of any planet illuminates our knowledge of the rest, and if we are to understand Earth thoroughly, we must have a comprehensive knowledge of the other planets. For example, one now fashionable suggestion, which I first proposed in 1960, is that the high temperatures on the surface of Venus are due to a runaway greenhouse effect in which water and carbon dioxide in a planetary atmosphere impede the emission of thermal infrared radiation from the surface to space; the surface temperature then rises to achieve equilibrium between the visible sunlight arriving at the surface and the infrared radiation leaving it; this higher surface temperature results in a higher vapor pressure of the greenhouse gases, carbon dioxide and water; and so on, until all the carbon dioxide and water vapor is in the vapor phase, producing a planet with high atmospheric pressure and high surface temperature.

Now, the reason that Venus has such an atmosphere and Earth does not seems to be a relatively small increment of sunlight. Were the Sun to grow brighter or Earth's surface and clouds to grow darker, could Earth become a replica of the classical vision of Hell? Venus may be a cautionary tale for our technical civilization, which has the capability to alter profoundly the environment of Earth.

Despite the expectation of almost all planetary scientists, Mars turns out to be covered with thousands of sinuous tributaried channels probably several billion years old. Whether formed by running water or running CO_2, many such channels probably could not be carved under present atmospheric conditions; they require much higher pressures and probably higher polar temperatures. Thus the channels—as well as the polar laminated terrain on Mars —may bear witness to at least one, and perhaps many, previous epochs of much more clement conditions, implying major climatic variations during the history of the planet. We do not know if such variations are internally or externally caused. If internally, it will be of interest to see whether the Earth might, through the activities of man, experience a Martian degree of climatic excursions— something much greater than the Earth seems to have experienced at least recently. If the Martian climatic variations are externally produced—for example, by variations in solar luminosity— then a correlation of Martian and terrestrial paleoclimatology would appear extremely promising.

Mariner 9 arrived at Mars in the midst of a great global dust storm, and the Mariner 9 data permit an observational test of whether such storms heat or cool a planetary surface. Any theory with pretensions to predicting the climatic consequences of increased aerosols in the Earth's atmosphere had better be able to provide the correct answer for the global dust storm observed by Mariner 9. Drawing upon our Mariner 9 experience, James Pollack of NASA Ames Research Center, Brian Toon of Cornell and I have calculated the effects of single and multiple volcanic explosions on the Earth's climate and have been able to reproduce, within experimental error, the observed climatic effects after major explosions on our planet. The perspective of planetary astronomy, which permits us to view a planet as a whole, seems to be very good training for studies of the Earth. As another example of this feedback from planetary studies on terrestrial observations, one of the major groups studying the effect on the Earth's ozonosphere of the use of halocarbon propellants from aerosol cans is headed by M. B. McElroy at Harvard University—a group that cut its teeth for this problem on the aeronomy of the atmosphere of Venus.

We now know from space-vehicle observations something of the surface density of impact craters of different sizes for Mercury, the Moon, Mars and its satellites; radar studies are beginning to provide such information for Venus, and although it is heavily eroded by running water and tectonic activity, we have some information about craters on the surface of the Earth. If the population of objects producing such impacts were the same for all these planets, it might then be possible to establish both an absolute and a relative chronology of cratered surfaces. But we do not yet know whether the populations of impacting objects are common —all derived from the asteroid belt, for example—or local; for example, the sweeping up of rings of debris involved in the final stages of planetary accretion.

The heavily cratered lunar highlands speak to us of an early epoch in the history of the solar system when cratering was much more common than it is today; the present population of interplanetary debris fails by a large factor to account for the abundance of the highland craters. On the other hand, the lunar maria have a much lower crater abundance, which can be explained by the present population of interplanetary debris, largely asteroids and possibly dead comets. It is possible to determine, for planetary surfaces that are not so heavily cratered, something of the absolute age, a great deal about the relative age, and in some cases, even something about the distribution of sizes in the population of objects that produced the craters. On Mars, for example, we find the flanks of the large volcanic mountains are almost free of impact craters, implying their comparative youth; they were not around long enough to accumulate very much in the way of impact scars. This is the basis for the contention that volcanoes on Mars are a comparatively recent phenomenon.

The ultimate objective of comparative planetology is, I suppose, something like a vast computer program into which we put a few input parameters—perhaps the initial mass, composition, angular momentum, and population of neighboring impacting objects—and out comes the time evolution of the planet. We are very far from having such a deep understanding of planetary evolution at the present time, but we are much closer than would have been thought possible only a few decades ago.

Every new set of discoveries raises a host of questions which we were never before wise enough even to ask. I will mention just a few of them. It is now becoming possible to compare the compositions of asteroids with the compositions of meteorites on

Earth. Asteroids seem to divide neatly into silicate-rich and organic matter—rich objects. One immediate consequence appears to be that the asteroid Ceres is apparently undifferentiated, while the less massive asteroid Vesta is differentiated. But our present understanding is that planetary differentiation occurs above a certain critical mass. Could Vesta be the remnant of a much larger parent body now gone from the solar system? The initial radar glimpse of the craters of Venus shows them to be extremely shallow. Yet there is no liquid water to erode the Venus surface, and the lower atmosphere of Venus seems to be so slow-moving that dust may not be able to fill the craters. Could the source of the filling of craters of Venus be a slow molasses-like collapse of a very slightly molten surface?

The most popular theory on the generation of planetary magnetic fields invokes rotation-driven convection currents in a conducting planetary core. Mercury, which rotates once every fifty-nine days, was expected in this scheme to have no detectable magnetic field. Yet such a field is manifestly there, and a serious reappraisal of theories of planetary magnetism is in order. Only Saturn and Uranus have rings. Why? There is on Mars an exquisite array of longitudinal sand dunes nestling against the interior ramparts of a large eroded crater. There is in the Great Sand Dunes National Monument near Alamosa, Colorado, a very similar set of sand dunes nestling in the curve of the Sangre de Cristo mountains. The Martian and the terrestrial sand dunes have the same total extent, the same dune-to-dune spacing and the same dune heights. Yet the Martian atmospheric pressure is 1/200 that on Earth, the winds necessary to initiate the saltation of sand grains are ten times that for Earth, and the particle-size distribution may be different on the two planets. How, then, can the dune fields produced by windblown sand be so similar? What are the sources of the decameter radio emissions on Jupiter, each less than 100 kilometers across, fixed on the Jovian surface, which intermittently radiate to space?

Mariner 9 observations imply that the winds on Mars at least occasionally exceed half the local speed of sound. Are the winds ever much larger? What is the nature of a transonic meteorology? There are pyramids on Mars about three kilometers across at the base and one kilometer high. They are unlikely to have been constructed by Martian pharaohs. The rate of sandblasting by wind-transported grains on Mars is at least 10,000 times that on Earth because of the greater speeds necessary to move particles in the thinner Martian atmosphere. Could the facets of the Martian pyramids have been eroded by millions of years of such sandblasting from more than one prevailing wind direction?

The moons in the outer solar system are almost certainly not replicas of our own, rather dull satellite. Many of them have such low densities that they must be composed largely of methane, ammonia, or water ices. What will their surfaces look like close up? How will impact craters erode on an icy surface? Might there be volcanoes of solid ammonia with a lava of liquid NH_3 trickling down the sides? Why is Io, the innermost large satellite of Jupiter, enveloped in a cloud of gaseous sodium? How does Io help to modulate the synchrotron emission from the Jovian radiation belt in which it lives? Why is one side of Iapetus, a moon of Saturn, six times brighter than the other? Because of a particle-size difference? A chemical difference? How did such differences become established? Why on Iapetus and nowhere else in the solar system in so symmetrical a way?

The gravity of the solar system's largest moon, Titan, is so low and the temperature of its upper atmosphere sufficiently high that hydrogen should escape into space extremely rapidly in a process known as blow-off. But the spectroscopic evidence suggests that there is a substantial quantity of hydrogen on Titan. The atmosphere of Titan is a mystery. And if we go beyond the Saturnian system, we approach a region in the solar system about which we know almost nothing. Our feeble telescopes have not even reliably determined the periods of rotation of Uranus, Neptune, and Pluto, much less the character of their clouds and atmospheres, and the nature of their satellite systems. The poet Diane Ackerman of Cornell University writes: "Neptune / is / elusive as a dappled horse in fog. Pulpy? / Belted? Vapory? Frost-bitten? What we know / wouldn't / fill / a lemur's fist."

One of the most tantalizing issues that we are just beginning to approach seriously is the question of organic chemistry and biology elsewhere in the solar system. The Martian environment is by no means so hostile as to exclude life, nor do we know enough about the origin and evolution of life to guarantee its presence there or anywhere else. The question of organisms both large and small on Mars is entirely open, even after the Viking missions.

The hydrogen-rich atmospheres of places such as Jupiter, Saturn, Uranus, and Titan are in significant respects similar to the atmosphere of the early Earth at the time of the origin of life. From laboratory simulation experiments we know that organic molecules are produced in high yield under such conditions. In the atmospheres of Jupiter and Saturn the molecules will be convected to pyrolytic depths. But even there the steady-state concentration of organic molecules can be significant. In all simulation experiments the application of energy to such atmospheres produces a brownish polymeric material, which in many significant respects resembles the brownish coloring material in their clouds. Titan may be completely covered with a brownish, organic material. It is possible that the next few years will witness major and unexpected discoveries in the infant science of exobiology.

The principal means for the continued exploration of the solar system over the next decade or two will surely be unmanned planetary missions. Scientific space vehicles have now been launched successfully to all the planets known to the ancients. There is a range of unapproved proposed missions that have been studied in some detail. If most of these missions are actually implemented, it is clear that the present age of planetary exploration will continue brilliantly. But it is by no means clear that these splendid voyages of discovery will be continued, at least by the United States. Only one major planetary mission, the Galileo project to Jupiter, has been approved in the last seven years—and even it is in jeopardy.

Even a preliminary reconnaissance of the entire solar system out to Pluto and a more detailed exploration of a few planets by, for example, Mars rovers and Jupiter entry probes, will not solve the fundamental problem of solar-system origins; what we need is the discovery of other solar systems. Advances in ground-based and spaceborne techniques in the next two decades might be capable of detecting dozens of planetary systems orbiting nearby single stars. Recent observational studies of multiple-star systems by Helmut Abt and Saul Levy, both of Kitt Peak National Observatory, suggest that as many as one-third of the stars in the sky may have planetary companions. We do not know whether such other planetary systems will be like ours or built on very different principles.

We have entered, almost without noticing, an age of exploration and discovery unparalleled since the Renaissance. It seems to me that the practical benefits of comparative planetology for Earthbound sciences; the sense of adventure imparted by the exploration of other worlds to a society that has almost lost the opportunity for adventure; the philosophical implications of the search for a cosmic perspective—these are what will in the long run mark our time. Centuries hence, when our very real political and social problems may be as remote as the very real problems of the War of the Austrian Succession seem to us, our time may be remembered chiefly for one fact: this was the age when the inhabitants of the Earth first made contact with the cosmos around them.

PART III

THE ORIGIN OF THE EARTH AND THE LIFE UPON IT

Now we contract our field of view further and consider the creation of life on Earth. Again we begin by turning back to the Bible.

The events of the fifth and part of the sixth day of creation are described in these six verses. The animals are created, first those of the sea, then those of the air, and finally those of the land. They are described as living and moving. Motion is apparently considered inseparable from life, so that the rooted plants are seen as something quite different and unalive.

Notice that each type of creature is created "according to their kind." It is this that causes those who believe in the literal words of the Bible to suppose that their religion requires them to believe that all species were created separately and that biological evolution never took place. This, in turn, requires them to reject the clearest evidence to the contrary, making rationality the handmaiden of superstition.

GENESIS 1:20–25
NEW ENGLISH BIBLE

God said, "Let the waters teem with countless living creatures, and let birds fly above the earth across the vault of heaven." God then created the great sea-monsters and all living creatures that move and swarm in the waters, according to their kind, and every kind of bird; and God saw that it was good. So he blessed them and said, "Be fruitful and increase, fill the waters of the seas; and let the birds increase on land." Evening came, and morning came, a fifth day.

God said, "Let the earth bring forth living creatures, according to their kind: cattle, reptiles, and wild animals, all according to their kind." So it was; God made wild animals, cattle, and all reptiles, each according to its kind; and he saw that it was good.

Although the general thinking of scientists today is that life started on Earth more than 3 billion years ago, through the operation of some energy-source such as the Sun's ultraviolet light upon the small molecules of the primordial sea, making use of chance combinations in accordance with the laws of physics and chemistry, this thinking tends to be troublesome.

Can something as complicated and versatile as life arise by chance, except by the luckiest of lucky breaks? Might it have started only once in all the history of the Universe—perhaps elsewhere than on Earth—and might that one form of life have seeded forms of life elsewhere?

The physicist Francis Crick has worked out such a theory of life having originated on Earth through seeding. The astronomer Thomas Gold has suggested (half in jest, perhaps) that some cosmic explorers on primordial Earth may have left their garbage behind and thus contaminated Earth with life, accidentally. The astronomer Fred Hoyle maintains that such seeding continues to this day; that a primitive form of life has its beginning in interstellar gas clouds and in comets. The passage of comets in Earth's proximity may seed Earth with viruses that lead to the occasional pandemics such as the Black Death and the 1918 Spanish influenza.

None of these suggestions is taken seriously by science as a whole, but Arthur C. Clarke has turned to this theme more than once. It forms the basis of his popular book and motion picture 2001: A Space Odyssey, *for instance, and this story sounds as though it may be a prologue to that motion picture.*

EXPERIMENT
ARTHUR C. CLARKE

Call it the Star Gate.

For 3 million years, it had circled Saturn, waiting for a moment of destiny that might never come. In its making, a moon had been shattered, and the debris of its creation orbited still.

Now the long wait was ending. On yet another world, intelligence had been born and was escaping from its planetary cradle. An ancient experiment was about to reach its climax.

Those who had begun that experiment, so long ago, had not been men—or even remotely human. But they were flesh and blood, and when they looked out across the deeps of space, they had felt awe, and wonder, and loneliness. As soon as they possessed the power, they set forth for the stars.

In their explorations, they encountered life in many forms, and watched the workings of evolution on a thousand worlds. They saw how often the first faint sparks of intelligence flickered and died in the cosmic night.

And because, in all the galaxy, they had found nothing more precious than Mind, they encouraged its dawning everywhere. They became farmers in the fields of stars; they sowed and sometimes they reaped.

And sometimes, dispassionately, they had to weed.

The great dinosaurs had long since perished when the survey ship entered the Solar System after a voyage that had already lasted a thousand years. It swept past the frozen outer planets, paused briefly above the deserts of dying Mars, and presently looked down on Earth.

Spread out beneath them, the explorers saw a world swarming with life. For years they studied, collected, cataloged. When they had learned all that they could, they began to modify. They tinkered with the destiny of many species, on land and in the ocean. But which of their experiments would succeed they could not know for at least a million years.

They were patient, but they were not yet immortal. There was so much to do in this universe of a hundred billion suns, and other worlds were calling. So they set out once more into the abyss, knowing that they would never come this way again.

Nor was there any need. The servants they had left behind would do the rest.

On Earth, the glaciers came and went, while above them the changeless Moon still carried its secret. With a yet slower rhythm than the polar ice, the tides of civilization ebbed and flowed across the galaxy. Strange and beautiful and terrible empires rose and fell, and passed on their knowledge to their successors. Earth was not forgotten, but another visit would serve little purpose. It was one of a million silent worlds, few of which would ever speak.

And now, out among the stars, evolution was driving toward new goals. The first explorers of Earth had long since come to the limits of flesh and blood; as soon as their machines were better than their bodies, it was time to move. First their brains, and then their thoughts alone, they transferred into shining new homes of metal and of plastic.

In these, they roamed among the stars. They no longer built spaceships. They *were* spaceships.

But the age of the Machine-entities swiftly passed. In their ceaseless experimenting, they had learned to store knowledge in the structure of space itself, and to preserve their thoughts for eternity in frozen lattices of light. They could become creatures of radiation, free at last from the tyranny of matter.

Into pure energy, therefore, they presently transformed themselves; and on a thousand worlds, the empty shells they had discarded twitched for a while in a mindless dance of death, then crumbled into rust.

Now they were lords of the galaxy, and beyond the reach of time. They could rove at will among the stars, and sink like a subtle mist through the very interstices of space. But despite their godlike powers, they had not wholly forgotten their origin, in the warm slime of a vanished sea.

And they still watched over the experiments their ancestors had started, so long ago.

Origin of life on Earth through seeding might not perhaps require intelligent design. Or, if we think of Hoyle's notion, it might not consist of accidental contamination through near-contact.

Back in 1907, the Swedish chemist Svante Arrhenius suggested that microscopic spores might be launched in space—not deliberately, but just through the vagaries of the wind, and the buffeting of air-molecules. Such spores might be wafted or butted high into the upper atmosphere and one out of many billion might make its way into outer space and then be swept away from the nearby star by its light-pressure. (We now know that each star has a "stellar wind" of charged particles sweeping out from itself in all directions and that this would do the job more efficiently.)

Such spores could endure in space for a long time, perhaps. The low temperature in the interstellar spaces would not harm them; would indeed keep them in the kind of deep freeze that would preserve the spark of life. Nor would they lose water or other necessary components through the impervious spore-shell.

The one thing that Arrhenius did not count upon was the hard radiation in space; from ultraviolet to gamma rays, to say nothing of the universal hail of cosmic rays. None of these things were known in 1907. It is that which may make any such accidental interstellar seeding impractical and certainly no signs of space spores have yet been detected.

Nevertheless, one could imagine them reaching the solar system and progressing inward from planet to planet to allow the origin of life on Earth, or even of a second coming of life after the original had been in operation for billions of years.

SEEDS OF THE DUSK
RAYMOND Z. GALLUN

I

It was a spore, microscopic in size. Its hard shell—resistant to the utter dryness of interplanetary space—harbored a tiny bit of plant protoplasm. That protoplasm, chilled almost to absolute zero, possessed no vital pulsation now—only a grim potentiality, a savage capacity for revival, that was a challenge to fate itself.

For years the spore had been drifting and bobbing erratically between the paths of Earth and Mars, along with billions of other spores of the same kind. Now the gravity of the Sun drew it a few million miles closer to Earth's orbit, now powerful magnetic radiations from solar vortices forced it back toward the world of its origin.

It seemed entirely a plaything of chance. And, of course, up to a point it was. But back of its erratic, unconscious wanderings, there was intelligence that had done its best to take advantage of the law of averages.

The desire for rebirth and survival was the dominant urge of this intelligence. For this was during the latter days, when Earth itself was showing definite signs of senility, and Mars was near as dead as the Moon.

Strange, intricate spore-pods, conceived as a man might conceive a new invention, but put into concrete form by a process of minutely exact growth control, had burst explosively toward a black, spacial sky. In dusty clouds the spores had been hurled upward into the vacuum thinness that had once been an extensive atmosphere. Most of them had, of course, dropped back to the red, arid soil; but a comparative few, buffeted by feeble air currents, and measured numerically in billions, had found their way from the utterly tenuous upper reaches of Mars's gaseous envelope into the empty ether of the void.

With elements of a conscious purpose added, the thing that was taking place was a demonstration of the ancient Arrhenius Spore Theory, which, countless ages ago, had explained the propagation of life from world to world.

The huge, wonderful parent growths were left behind, to continue a hopeless fight for survival on a burnt-out world. During succeeding summer seasons they would hurl more spores into the interplanetary abyss. But soon they themselves would be only brown, mummied relics—one with the other relics of Mars; the gray, carven monoliths; the strange, hemispherical dwellings, dotted with openings arranged like the cells of a honeycomb. Habitations of an intelligent animal folk, long perished, who had never had use for halls or rooms, as such things are known to men on earth.

The era of utter death would come to Mars, when nothing would move on its surface except the shadows shifting across dusty deserts, and the molecules of sand and rock vibrating with a little warmth from the hot, though shrunken, Sun. Death—complete death! But the growths which were the last civilized beings of

Mars had not originated there. Once they had been on the satellites of Jupiter, too. And before that—well, perhaps even the race memory of their kind had lost the record of those dim, distant ages. Always they had waited their chance, and when the time came—when a world was physically suited for their development—they had acted.

A single spore was enough to supply the desired foothold on a planet. Almost inevitably—since chance is, in fundamentals, a mathematical element depending on time and numbers and repetition—that single spore reached the upper atmosphere of Earth.

For months, it bobbed erratically in tenuous, electrified gases. It might have been shot into space again. Upward and downward it wandered; but with gravity to tug at its insignificant mass, probability favored its ultimate descent to the harsh surface.

It found a resting place, at last, in a frozen desert gully. Around the gully were fantastic, sugar-loaf mounds. Nearby was one thin, ruined spire of blue porcelain—an empty reminder of a gentler era, long gone.

The location thus given to it seemed hardly favorable in its aspect. For this was the northern hemisphere, locked now in the grip of a deadly winter. The air, depleted through the ages, as was the planet's water supply, was arid and thin. The temperature, though not as rigorous and deadening as that of interplanetary space, ranged far below zero. Mars in this age was near dead; Earth was a dying world.

But perhaps this condition, in itself, was almost favorable. The spore belonged to a kind of life developed to meet the challenge of a generally much less friendly environment than that of even this latter-day Earth.

There was snow in that desert gully—maybe a quarter-inch depth of it. The rays of the Sun—white and dwarfed after so many eons of converting its substance into energy—did not melt any of that snow even at noon. But this did not matter. The life principle within the spore detected favorable conditions for its germination, just as, in spring, the vital principle of earthly seeds had done for almost incalculable ages.

By a process parallel to that of simple fermentation, a tiny amount of heat was generated within the spore. A few crystals of snow around it turned to moisture, a minute quantity of which the alien speck of life absorbed. Roots finer than spiderweb grew, groping into the snow. At night they were frozen solid, but during the day they resumed their brave activity.

The spore expanded, but did not burst. For its shell was a protecting armor which must be made to increase in size gradually without rupture. Within it, intricate chemical processes were taking place. Chlorophyll there was absorbing sunshine and carbon dioxide and water. Starch and cellulose and free oxygen were being produced.

So far, these processes were quite like those of common terrestrial flora. But there were differences. For one thing, the oxygen was not liberated to float in the atmosphere. It had been ages since such lavish waste had been possible on Mars, whose thin air had contained but a small quantity of oxygen in its triatomic form, ozone, even when Earth was young.

The alien thing stored its oxygen, compressing the gas into the tiny compartments in its hard, porous, outer shell. The reason was simple. Oxygen, combining with starch in a slow, fermentive combustion, could produce heat to ward off the cold that would otherwise stop growth.

The spore had become a plant now. First, it was no bigger than a pinhead. Then it increased its size to the dimensions of a small marble, its fuzzy, green-brown shape firmly anchored to the soil itself by its long, fibrous roots. Like any terrestrial growth, it was an intricate chemical laboratory, where transformations took place that were not easy to comprehend completely.

And now, perhaps, the thing was beginning to feel the first glimmerings of a consciousness, like a human child rising out of the blurred, unremembering fog of birth. Strange, oily nodules, scattered throughout its tissues, connected by means of a complex network of delicate, white threads, which had the functions of a nervous system, were developing and growing—giving to the spore plant from Mars the equivalent of a brain. Here was a sentient vegetable in the formative stage.

A sentient vegetable? Without intelligence it is likely that the ancestors of this nameless invader from across the void would long ago have lost their battle for survival.

What senses were given to this strange mind, by means of which it could be aware of its environment? Undoubtedly it possessed faculties of sense that could detect things in a way that was as far beyond ordinary human conception as vision is to those individuals who have been born blind. But in a more simple manner it must have been able to feel heat and cold and to hear sounds, the latter perhaps by the sensitivity of its fine, cilialike spines. And certainly it could see in a way comparable to that of a man.

For, scattered over the round body of the plant, and embedded deep in horny hollows in its shell, were little organs, lensed with a clear vegetable substance. These organs were eyes, developed, perhaps, from far more primitive light-sensitive cells, such as many forms of terrestrial flora possess.

But during those early months, the spore plant saw little that could be interpreted as a threat, swiftly to be fulfilled. Winter ruled, and the native life of this desolate region was at a standstill.

There was little motion except that of keen, cutting winds, shifting dust, and occasional gusts of fine, dry snow. The white, shrunken Sun rose in the east, to creep with protracted slowness across the sky, shedding but the barest trace of warmth. Night came, beautiful and purple and mysterious, yet bleak as the crystalline spirit of an easy death.

Through the ages, Earth's rate of rotation had been much decreased by the tidal drag of solar and lunar gravities. The attraction of the Moon was now much increased, since the satellite was nearer to Terra than it had been in former times. Because of the decreased rate of rotation, the days and nights were correspondingly lengthened.

All the world around the spore plant was a realm of bleak, unpeopled desolation. Only once, while the winter lasted, did anything happen to break the stark monotony. One evening, at moonrise, a slender metal car flew across the sky with the speed of a bullet. A thin propelling streamer of fire trailed in its wake, and the pale moonglow was reflected from its prow. A shrill, mechanical scream made the rarefied atmosphere vibrate, as the craft approached to a point above the desert gully, passed, and hurtled away, to leave behind it only a startling silence and an aching memory.

For the spore plant did remember. Doubtless there was a touch of fear in that memory, for fear is a universal emotion, closely connected with the law of self-preservation, which is ingrained in the texture of all life, regardless of its nature or origin.

Men. Or rather, the cold, cruel, cunning little beings who were the children of men. The Itorloo, they called themselves. The invader could not have known their form as yet, or the name of the creatures from which they were descended. But it could guess something of their powers from the flying machine they had built. Inherited memory must have played a part in giving the queer thing from across the void this dim comprehension. On other worlds its ancestors had encountered animal folk possessing a similar science. And the spore plant was surely aware that here on Earth the builders of this speeding craft were its most deadly enemies.

The Itorloo, however, inhabiting their vast underground cities, had no knowledge that their planet had received an alien visitation —one which might have deadly potentialities. And in this failure to know, the little spore plant, hidden in a gully where no Itorloo foot had been set in a thousand years, was safe.

Now there was nothing for it to do but grow and prepare to reproduce its kind, to be watchful for lesser enemies, and to develop its own peculiar powers.

It is not to be supposed that it must always lack, by its very nature, an understanding of physics and chemistry and biological science. It possessed no test tubes, or delicate instruments, as such things were understood by men. But it was gifted with something—call it an introspective sense—which enabled it to study in minute detail every single chemical and physical process that went on within its own substance. It could feel not only the juices coursing sluggishly through its tissues, but it could feel, too, in a kind of atomic pattern, the change of water and carbon dioxide into starch and free oxygen.

Gift a man with the same power that the invader's kind had acquired, perhaps by eons of practice and directed will—that of feeling vividly even the division of cells, and the nature of the protoplasm in his own tissues—and it is not hard to believe that he would soon delve out even the ultimate secret of life. And in the secret of life there must be involved almost every conceivable phase of practical science.

The spore plant proceeded with its marvelous self-education, part of which must have been only recalling to mind the intricate impressions of inherited memories.

Meanwhile it studied carefully its bleak surroundings, prompted not only by fear, but by curiosity as well. To work effectively, it needed understanding of its environment. Intelligence it possessed beyond question; still it was hampered by many limitations. It was a plant, and plants have not an animal's capacity for quick action, either of offense or defense. Here, forever, the entity from across the void was at a vast disadvantage, in this place of pitiless competition. In spite of all its powers, it might now have easily been destroyed.

The delicate, ruined tower of blue porcelain, looming up from the brink of the gully—The invader, scrutinizing it carefully for hours and days, soon knew every chink and crack and fanciful arabesque on its visible side. It was only a ruin, beautiful and mysterious alike by sunshine and moonlight, and when adorned with a fine sifting of snow. But the invader, lost on a strange world, could not be sure of its harmlessness.

Close to the tower were those rude, high, sugar-loaf mounds, betraying a sinister cast. They were of hard-packed earth, dotted with many tiny openings. But in the cold, arid winter, there was no sign of life about them now.

All through those long, arctic months, the spore plant continued to develop, and to grow toward the reproductive stage. And it was making preparations, too, combining the knowledge acquired by its observations with keen guesswork, and with a science apart from the manual fabrication of metal and other substances.

II

A milder season came at last. The Sun's rays were a little warmer now. Some of the snow melted, moistening the ground enough to germinate earthly seeds. Shoots sprang up, soon to develop leaves and grotesque, devilish-looking flowers.

In the mounds beside the blue tower a slow awakening took place. Millions of little, hard, reddish bodies became animated once more, ready to battle grim Nature for sustenance. The ages had done little to the ants, except to increase their fierceness and cunning. Almost any organic substances could serve them as food, and their tastes showed but little discrimination between one dainty and another. And it was inevitable, of course, that presently they should find the spore plant.

Nor were they the latter's only enemies, even in this desert region. Of the others, Kaw and his black-feathered brood were the most potent makers of trouble. Not because they would attempt active offense themselves, but because they were able to spread news far and wide.

Kaw wheeled alone now, high in the sunlight, his ebon wings outstretched, his cruel, observant little eyes studying the desolate terrain below. Buried in the sand, away from the cold, he and his mate and their companions had slept through the winter. Now Kaw was fiercely hungry. He could eat ants if he had to, but there should be better food available at this time of year.

Once, his keen eyes spied gray movement far below. As if his poised and graceful flight was altered by the release of a trigger, Kaw dived plummetlike and silent toward the ground.

His attack was more simple and direct than usual. But it was successful. His reward was a large, long-tailed rodent, as clever as himself. The creature uttered squeaks of terror as meaningful as human cries for help. In a moment, however, Kaw split its intelligently rounded cranium with a determined blow from his strong, pointed beak. Bloody brains were devoured with indelicate gusto, to be followed swiftly by the less tasty flesh of the victim. If Kaw had ever heard of table manners, he didn't bother with them. Kaw was intensely practical.

His crop full, Kaw was now free to exercise the mischievous curiosity which he had inherited from his ancient forebears. They who had, in the long-gone time when Earth was young, uprooted many a young corn shoot, and had yammered derisively from distant treetops when any irate farmer had gone after them with a gun.

With a clownish skip of his black, scaly feet, and a show-offish swerve of his dusty ebon wings, Kaw took to the air once more. Upward he soared, his white-lidded eyes directed again toward the ground, seeking something interesting to occupy his attention and energies.

Thus, presently, he saw a brownish puff that looked like smoke or dust in the gully beside the ruined blue tower at the pinnacle of which he and his mate were wont to build their nest in summer. Sound came then—a dull, ringing pop. The dusty cloud expanded swiftly upward, widening and thinning until its opacity was dissipated into the clearness of the atmosphere.

Kaw was really startled. That this was so was evinced by the fact that he did not voice his harsh, rasping cry, as he would have done had a lesser occurrence caught his attention. He turned back at first, and began to retreat, his mind recognizing only one possibility in what had occurred. Only the Itorloo, the Children of Men, as far as he knew, could produce explosions like that. And the Itorloo were cruel and dangerous.

However, Kaw did not go far in his withdrawal. Presently—since there were no further alarming developments—he was circling back toward the source of the cloud and the noise. But for many minutes he kept what he considered a safe distance, while he tried to determine the nature of the strange, bulging, grayish-green thing down there in the gully.

A closer approach, he decided finally, was best made from the ground. And so he descended, alighting several hundred yards distant from the narrow pocket in the desert.

Thence he proceeded to walk cautiously forward, taking advantage of the cover of the rocks and dunes, his feathers gleaming with a dusty rainbow sheen, his large head bobbing with the motion of his advance like any fowl's. His manner was part laughably ludicrous, part scared, and part determined.

And then, peering from behind a large boulder, he saw what he had come to see. It was a bulging, slightly flattened sphere, perhaps a yard across. From it projected flat, oval things of a gray-green color, like the leaves of a cactus. And from these, in turn, grew clublike protuberances of a hard, horny texture—spore-pods. One of them was blasted open, doubtless by the pressure of gas accumulated within it. These spore-pods were probably not as complexly or powerfully designed as those used by the parent growths on Mars, for they were intended for a simpler purpose. The entire plant bristled with sharp spines, and was furred with slender hairs, gleaming like little silver wires.

Around the growth, thousands of ant bodies lay dead, and from its vicinity other thousands of living were retreating. Kaw eyed these evidences critically, guessing with wits as keen as those of a man of old their sinister significance. He knew, too, that presently other spore-pods would burst with loud, disturbing noises.

Kaw felt a twinge of dread. Evolution, working through a pro-cess of natural selection—and, in these times of hardship and pitiless competition, putting a premium on intelligence—had given to his kind a brain power far transcending that of his ances-tors. He could observe, and could interpret his observations with the same practical comprehension which a primitive human being might display. But, like those primitives, he had developed, too, a capacity to feel superstitious awe.

That gray-green thing of mystery had a fantastic cast which failed to identify it with—well—with naturalness. Kaw was no bot-anist, certainly; still he could recognize the object as a plant of some kind. But those little, bright eye-lenses suggested an un-imaginable scrutiny. And those spines, silvery in sheen, suggested ghoulish animation, the existence of which Kaw could sense as a nameless and menacing unease.

He could guess, then, or imagine—or even know, perhaps—that here was an intruder who might well make itself felt with far-reaching consequences in the future. Kaw was aware of the simple fact that most of the vegetation he was acquainted with grew from seeds or the equivalent. And he was capable of concluding that this flattened spheroid reproduced itself in a manner not markedly unfamiliar. That is, if one was to accept the evidence of the spore-pods. Billions of spores, scattering with the wind! What would be the result?

Kaw would not have been so troubled were it not for those crumpled thousands of ant bodies, and the enigma of their death. It was clear that the ants had come to feed on the invader—but they had perished. How? By some virulent plant poison, perhaps?

The conclusions which intelligence provides can produce fear where fear would otherwise be impossible. Kaw's impulse was to seek safety in instant departure, but horror and curiosity fascinated him. Another deeper, more reasoned urge commanded him. When a man smells smoke in his house at night, he does not run away; he investigates. And so it was with Kaw.

He hopped forward cautiously toward the invader. A foot from its rough, curving side he halted. There, warily, as if about to attack a poisonous lizard, he steeled himself. Lightly and swiftly his beak shot forward. It touched the tip of a sharp spine.

The result left Kaw dazed. It was as though he had received a stunning blow on the head. A tingling, constricting sensation shot through his body, and he was down, flopping in the dust.

Electricity. Kaw had never heard of such a thing. Electricity generated chemically in the form of the invader, by a process analogous to that by which, in dim antiquity, it had been generated in the bodies of electric eels and other similar creatures.

However, there was a broad difference here between the subject and the analogy. Electric eels had never understood the nature of their power, for they were as unresponsible for it as they were unresponsible for the shape of the flesh in which they had been cast. The spore plant, on the other hand, comprehended minutely. Its electric organs had been minutely preplanned and conceived before one living cell of their structure had been caused to grow on another. And these organs were not inherited, but were designed to meet the more immediate needs of self-protection. During the winter, the invader, studying its surroundings, had guessed well.

Slowly Kaw's brain cleared. He heard an ominous buzzing, and knew that it issued from the plant. But what he did not know was that, like the electric organs, the thing's vocal equipment was invented for possible use in its new environment. For days, since the coming of spring, the invader had been listening to sounds of various kinds, and had recognized their importance on Earth.

Now Kaw had but one thought, and that was to get away. Still dazed and groggy, he leaped into the air. From behind him, in his hurried departure, he heard a dull plop. More billions of spores, mixing with the wind, to be borne far and wide.

But now, out of his excitement, Kaw drew a reasoned and fairly definite purpose. He had a fair idea of what he was going to do, even though the course of action he had in mind might involve him with the greatest of his enemies. Yet, when it came to a choice, he would take the known in preference to the unknown.

He soared upward toward the bright blue of the heavens. The porcelain tower, the ant hills, and the low mounds which marked the entrances to the rodent colonies slipped swiftly behind. As if the whole drab landscape were made to move on an endless belt.

Kaw was looking for his mate, and for the thirty-odd, black-winged individuals who formed his tribe. Singly and in small groups, he contacted and collected them. Loud, raucous cries, each with a definite verbal meaning, were exchanged. Menace was on the Earth—bizarre, nameless menace. Excitement grew to fever pitch.

Dusk, beautiful and soft and forbidding, found the bird clan assembled in a chamber high-placed in a tremendous edifice many miles from where Kaw had made his discovery. The building belonged to the same gentle culture which had produced the blue porcelain tower. The floor of the chamber was doubtless richly mosaiced. But these were relics of departed splendor now thickly masked with dust and filth.

From the walls, however, painted landscapes of ethereal beauty, and the faces of a happy humankind of long ago peeped through the gathering shadows. They were like ghosts, a little awed at what had happened to the world to which they had once belonged. Those gentle folk had dwelt in a kindlier climate which was now stripped forever from the face of the Earth. And they had been wiped out by creatures who were human, too, but of a different, crueler race.

Through delicately carven screens of pierced marble, far up on the sides of the chamber's vast, brooding rotunda, the fading light of day gleamed, like a rose glow through the lacework of fairies.

But this palace of old, dedicated to laughter and fun and luxury, and to the soaring dreams of the fine arts, was now only a chill, dusty gathering place for a clan of black-winged, gruesome harpies.

They chuckled and chattered and cawed, like the crows of dead eras. But these sounds, echoing eerily beneath cloistered arches, dim and abhorrent in the advancing gloom of night, differed from that antique yammering. It constituted real, intelligent conversation.

Kaw, perched high on a fancifully wrought railing of bronze, green with the patina of age, urged his companions with loud cries, and with soft, pleading notes. In his own way, he had some of the qualities of a master orator. But, as all through an afternoon of similar arguing, he was getting nowhere. His tribe was afraid. And so it was becoming more and more apparent that he must undertake his mission alone. Even Teka, his mate, would not accompany him.

At last Kaw ruffled his neck feathers, and shook his head violently in an avian gesture of disgust. He leaped from his perch and shot through a glassless window with an angry scream that was like the curse of a black ghoul.

It was the first time that he had ever undertaken a long journey at night. But in his own judgment, necessity was such that no delay could be tolerated.

The stars were sharp and clear, the air chill and frosty. The ground was dotted sparsely with faint glimmerings from the chimneys of the crude furnaces which, during the colder nights of spring and fall, warmed the underground rodent colonies.

After a time the Moon rose, huge and yellow, like the eye of a monster. In that bloom and silence, Kaw found it easy to feel the creeping and imperceptible, yet avalanching, growth of horror. He could not be sure, of course, that he was right in his guess that the mission he had undertaken was grimly important. But his savage intuition was keen.

The Itorloo—the Children of Men—he must see them, and tell them what he knew. Kaw was aware that the Itorloo had no love for any but themselves. But they were more powerful than the winds and the movements of the Sun and Moon themselves. They would find a swift means to defeat the silent danger.

And so, till the gray dawn, Kaw flew on and on, covering many hundreds of miles, until he saw a low dome of metal, capping a hill. The soft half-light of early morning sharpened its outlines to those of a beautiful, ebon silhouette, peaceful and yet forbidding. Beneath it, as Kaw knew, was a shaft leading down to the wondrous underworld of the Itorloo, as intriguing to his mind as a shadowland of magic.

Fear tightened its constricting web around Kaw's heart—but retreat was something that must not be. There was too much at stake ever to permit a moment of hesitation.

Kaw swung into a wide arc, circling the dome. His long wings, delicately poised for a soaring glide, did not flap now, but dipped and rose to capture and make use of the lifting power of every vagrant wisp of breeze. And from his lungs issued a loud, raucous cry.

"Itorloo!" he screamed. "Itorloo!"

The word, except for its odd, parrotlike intonation, was pronounced in an entirely human manner. Kaw, in common with his crow ancestors, possessed an aptitude for mimicry of the speech of men.

Tensely he waited for a sign, as he swung lower and nearer to the dome.

III

Zar felt irritable. He did not like the lonely surface vigil and the routine astronomical checkings that constituted his duty. All night he'd sat there at his desk with signal lights winking around him, helping surface watchers at the other stations check the position of a new meteor swarm by means of crossing beams of probe rays.

Angles, distances, numbers! Zar was disgusted. Why didn't the construction crews hurry? The whole race could have been moved to Venus long ago, and might just as well have been. For as far as Zar could see, there was no real reason to retain a hold on the burnt-out Earth. The native Venusians should have been crushed a century back. There wasn't any reason why this pleasant task shouldn't have been accomplished then—no reason except stupid, official inertia!

The sound of a shrill bird cry, throbbing from the pickup diaphragm on the wall, did not add any sweetening potion to Zar's humor. At first he paid no attention; but the insistent screaming of the name of his kind—"Itorloo! Itorloo!"—at length aroused him to angry action.

His broad, withered face, brown and hideous and goblinlike, twisted itself into an ugly grimace. He bounded up from his chair, and seized a small, pistol-like weapon.

A moment later he was out on the sandy slopes of the hill, looking up at the black shape that swooped and darted timidly, close to his head. On impulse Zar raised his weapon, no thought of compassion in his mind.

But Kaw screamed again: "Itorloo! Loaaah!"

In Zar's language, "Loaaah!" meant "Danger!" very emphatically. Zar's hand, bent on execution, was stayed for the moment at least. His shrewd little eyes narrowed, and from his lips there issued yammering sounds which constituted an understandable travesty of the speech of Kaw's kind.

"Speak your own tongue, creature!" he ordered sharply. "I can understand!"

Still swooping and darting nervously, Kaw screamed forth his story, describing in quaint manner the thing he had seen, employing comparisions such as any primitive savage would use. In this way the invader was like a boulder, in that way it was like a thorn cactus, and in other ways it resembled the instruments of death which the Itorloo employed. In all ways it was strange, and unlike anything ever seen before.

And Zar listened with fresh and calculated attention, getting from this bird creature the information he required to locate the strange miracle. Kaw was accurate and clear enough in giving his directions.

Zar might have forgotten his inherent ruthlessness where his feathered informer was concerned, had not Kaw become a trifle too insistent in his exhortations to action. He lingered too long and screamed too loudly.

Irritated, Zar raised his weapon. Kaw swept away at once, but there was no chance for him to get out of range. Invisible energy shot toward him. Black feathers were torn loose, and floated aflame in the morning breeze. Kaw gave a shrill shriek of agony and reproach. Erratically he wavered to the ground.

Zar did not even glance toward him, but retraced his way leisurely into the surface dome. An hour later, however, having received permission from his superiors, he had journeyed across those hundreds of miles to the gully beside the blue porcelain tower. And there he bent over the form of the invader. Zar was somewhat awed. He had never been to Mars. For two hundred thousand years or more, no creature from Earth had ever visited that planet. The Itorloo were too practical to attempt such a useless venture, and their more recent predecessors had lacked some of the adventurous incentive required for so great and hazardous a journey.

But Zar had perused old records, belonging to an era half a million years gone by. He knew that this gray-green thing was at least like the flora of ancient Mars. Into his mind, matter-of-fact for the most part, came the glimmerings of mighty romance, accentuating within him a consciousness of nameless dread, and of grand interplanetary distances.

Spines. Bulging, hard-shelled, pulpy leaves that stored oxygen under pressure. Chlorophyll that absorbed sunshine and made starch, just as in an ordinary Earthly plant. Only the chlorophyll of this growth was beneath a thick, translucent shell, which altered the quality of the light it could reflect. That was why astronomers in the preinterplanetary era had doubted the existence of vegetation on Mars. Green plants of Terra, when photographed with infrared light, looked silvery, like things of frost. But—because of their shells—Martian vegetation could not betray its presence in the same manner.

Zar shuddered, though the morning air was not chill by his standards. The little gleaming orbs of the invader seemed to scrutinize him critically and coldly, and with a vast wisdom. Zar saw the shattered spore-pods, knowing that their contents now floated in the air, like dust—floated and settled—presenting a subtle menace whose tool was the unexpected, and against which, because of the myriad numbers of the widely scattered spores, only the most drastic methods could prevail.

Belatedly, then, anger came. Zar drew a knife from his belt. Half in fury and half in experiment, he struck the invader, chipping off a piece of its shell. He felt a sharp electric shock, though by no means strong enough to kill a creature of his size. From the wound he made in the plant, oxygen sizzled softly. But the invader offered no further defense. For the present it had reached the end of its resources.

Zar bounded back. His devilish little weapon flamed then, for a full two minutes. When he finally released pressure on its trigger, there was only a great, smoldering, glowing hole in the ground where the ghoulish thing from across space had stood.

Such was Zar's and the entire Itorloo race's answer to the intruder. Swift destruction! Zar chuckled wickedly. And there were ways to rid Earth of the treacherous menace of the plant intelligences of Mars entirely, even though they would take time.

Besides there was Venus, the world of promise. Soon half of the Itorloo race would be transported there. The others certainly could be accommodated if it became necessary.

Necessary? Zar laughed. He must be getting jittery. What had the Itorloo to fear from those inert, vegetable things? Now he aimed his weapon toward the blue tower, and squeezed the trigger. Weakened tiles crumbled and fell down with a hollow, desolate rattle that seemed to mock Zar's ruthlessness.

Suddenly he felt sheepish. To every intelligent being there is a finer side that prompts and criticizes. And for a moment Zar saw himself and his people a little more as they really were.

Unlike the lesser creatures, the Children of Men had not advanced very much mentally. The ups and downs of history had not favored them. War had reversed the benefits of natural selection, destroying those individuals of the species best suited to carry it on to greater glory. Zar knew this, and perhaps his senseless assault upon the ruined building was but a subconscious gesture of resentment toward the people of long ago who had been kinder and wiser and happier.

Zar regretted his recent act of destroying the spore plant. It should have been preserved for study. But now—well—what was done could not be changed.

He entered his swift, gleaming rocket car. When he closed its cabin door behind him, it seemed that he was shutting out a horde of mocking, menacing ghosts.

In a short while he was back at the surface station. Relieved there of his duty by another little brown man, he descended the huge cylindrical shaft which dropped a mile to the region that was like the realm of the Cyclops. Thrumming sounds, winking lights, shrill shouts of the workers, blasts of incandescent flame, and the colossal majesty of gigantic machines, toiling tirelessly.

In a vast, pillared plaza the keels of spaceships were being laid —spaceships for the migration and the conquest. In perhaps a year—a brief enough time for so enormous a task—they would soar away from Earth, armed to the teeth. There would be thousands of the craft then, for all over the world, in dozens of similar underground places, they were in process of construction.

Zar's vague fears were dissipated in thoughts of conquest to come. The Venus folk annihilated in withering clouds of flame. The glory of the Itorloo carried on and on—

IV

Kaw was not dead. That this was so was almost a miracle, made possible, perhaps, by a savage, indomitable will to live. In his small bird body there was a fierce, burning courage that compensated for many of his faults.

For hours he lay there on the desert sand, a pathetic and crumpled bundle of tattered feathers, motionless except for his labored breathing, and the blinking of his hate-filled eyes. Blood dripped slowly from the hideous, seared wound on his breast, and his whole body ached with a vast, dull anguish.

Toward sundown, however, he managed to hobble and flutter forward a few rods. Here he buried himself shallowly in the sand, where his chilled body would be protected from the nocturnal cold.

For three days he remained thus interred. He was too weak and sick to leave his burrow. Bitterness toward Zar and the other cruel Itorloo, he did not feel. Kaw had lived too long in this harsh region to expect favors. But a black fury stormed within him, nevertheless —a black fury as agonizing as physical pain. He wanted revenge. No, he needed revenge as much as he needed the breath of life. He did not know that Itorloo plans directed against the intruding spores from Mars were already underway, and that—as a byproduct—they would destroy his own kind, and all primitive life on the surface of the Earth.

Kaw left his hiding place on the fourth day. Luck favored him, for he found a bit of carrion—part of the dead body of an antelopelike creature.

Somehow, through succeeding weeks and days, he managed

to keep alive. The mending of his injured flesh was slow indeed, for the burnt wound was unclean. But he started toward home, hopping along at first, then flying a little, a hundred yards at a time. Tedium and pain were endless. But the fiendish light of what must seem forever fruitless hatred, never faded in those wicked, white-lidded eyes. Frequently Kaw's long, black beak snapped in a vicious expression of boundless determination.

Weeks of long days became a month, and then two months. Starved to a black-clad skeleton, and hopeless of ever being fit to hunt again, Kaw tottered into a deep gorge one evening. Utterly spent, he sank to the ground here, his brain far too weary to take note of any subtle unusualness which the deepening shadows half masked.

He scarcely saw the rounded things scattered here. Had he noticed them, his blurred vision would have named them small boulders and nothing more. Fury, directed at the Itorloo, had made him almost forget the spore plants. He did not know that this was to be a place of magic. Chance and the vagrant winds had made it so. A hundred spores, out of many millions, had lodged here. Conditions had been just right for their swift development. It was warm, but not too warm. And there was moisture too. Distantly Kaw heard the trickle of water. He wanted to get to it, but his feebleness prevented him.

He must have slept, then, for a long time. It seemed that he awoke at the sound of an odd buzzing, which may have possessed hypnotic properties. He felt as weak and stiff as before, but he was soothed and peaceful now, in spite of his thirst and hunger.

He looked about. The gorge was deep and shadowy. A still twilight pervaded it, though sunshine gilded its bulging, irregular lips far above. These details he took in in a moment.

He looked, then, at the grotesque shapes around him—things which, in the deeper darkness, he had thought to be only boulders. But now he saw that they were spore plants, rough, eerie, brooding, with their little, lensed light-sensitive organs agleam.

The excitement of terror seized him, and he wanted to flee, as from a deadly enemy. But this urge did not last long. The hypnotic buzz, which issued from the diaphragmic vocal organs of the plants, soothed and soothed and soothed, until Kaw felt very relaxed.

There were dead ants around him, doubtless the victims of electrocution. Since no better food was within reach, Kaw hopped here and there, eating greedily.

After that he hobbled to the brackish spring that dripped from the wall, and drank. Next he dropped to the ground, his fresh drowsiness characterized by sleepy mutterings about himself, his people, and the all-wise Itorloo. And it seemed, presently, that the buzzing of the invaders changed in character at last, seeming to repeat his own mutterings clumsily, like a child learning to talk.

"Kaw! Itorloo!" And other words and phrases belonging to the speech of the crow clans.

It was the beginning of things miraculous and wonderful for Kaw, the black-feathered rascal. Many suns rose and set, but somehow he felt no urge to wander farther toward his home region. He did not know the Lethean fascination of simple hypnotism. True, he sallied afield farther and farther, as his increasing strength permitted. He hunted now, eating bugs and beetles for the most part. But always he returned to the gorge, there to listen to the weird growths, buzzing, chattering, speaking to him in his own tongue. In them there seemed somehow to be a vague suggestion of the benignance of some strange, universal justice, in spite of their horror.

And night and day, rocket cars, streamlined and gleaming, swept over the desert. Now and then beams of energy were unleashed from them, whipping the sand into hot flame, destroying the invading spore plants that had struck root here and there. Only the law of chance kept them away from the gorge, as doubtless it allowed them to miss other hiding places of alien life. For the wilderness was wide.

But this phase of the Itorloo battle against the invading spore plants was only a makeshift preliminary, intended to keep the intruders in check. Only the Itorloo themselves knew about the generators now being constructed far underground—generators which, with unseen emanations, could wipe out every speck of living protoplasm on the exposed crust of the planet. Theirs was a monumental task, and a slow one. But they meant to be rid, once and for all, of the subtle threat which had come perhaps to challenge their dominion of the Earth. Kaw and his kind, the rodents, the ants, and all the other simple People of the Dusk of Terra's Greatness, were seemingly doomed.

Kaw's hatred of the Children of Men was undimmed, more justly than he was aware. Thus it was easy for him to listen when he was commanded: "Get an Itorloo! Bring him here! Alone! On foot!"

Zar was the logical individual to produce, for he was the nearest, the most readily available. But summer was almost gone before Kaw encountered the right opportunity, though he watched with care at all times.

Evening, with Venus and the Moon glowing softly in the sky. Kaw was perched on a hilltop, close to the great surface dome, watching as he had often watched before. Out of its cylindrical hangar, Zar's flier darted, and then swung in a slow arc. Presently it headed at a leisurely pace into the northwest. For once its direction was right, and it was not traveling too fast for Kaw to keep pace with it. Clearly its pilot was engaged in a rambling pleasure jaunt, which had no definite objective.

Kaw, pleased and excited, fell in behind at a safe distance. There he remained until the craft was near the gorge. Now there was danger, but if things were done right—

He flapped his wings violently to catch up with his mechanical quarry. He screamed loudly: "Itorloo! Itorloo! Descend! Descend! I am Kaw, who informed you of the unknown long ago! I would show you more! More! More!" All of this in shrill, avian chatterings.

Kaw's trickery was naïvely simple. But Zar heard, above the noise of his rocket blasts. Suspicion? He felt it, of course. There was no creature in this era who accepted such an invitation without question. Yet he was well armed. In his own judgment he should be quite safe. Curiosity led him on.

He shut off his rocket motors, and uttered the bird jargon, questioning irritably: "Where? What is it, black trickster?"

Kaw skittered about defensively. "Descend!" he repeated. "Descend to the ground. The thing that bears you cannot take you where we must go!"

The argument continued for some little time, primitive with matching curiosity and suspicion.

And meanwhile, in the gloomy gorge cut in vague geologic times by some gushing stream, entities waited patiently. Sap flowed in their tissues, as in the tissues of any other vegetation, but the fine hairs on their forms detected sounds, and their light-sensitive cells served as eyes. Within their forms were organs equivalent to human nerve and brain. They did not use tools or metals, but worked in another way, dictated by their vast disadvantages when compared to animal intelligences. Yet they had their advantages, too.

Now they waited, dim as bulking shadows. They detected the excited cries of Kaw, who was their instrument. And perhaps they grew a little more tense, like a hunter in a blind, when he hears the quacking of ducks through a fog.

There was a grating of pebbles and a little brown man, clad in a silvery tunic, stepped cautiously into view. There was a weapon clutched in his slender hand. He paused, as if suddenly awed and fearful. But no opportunity to retreat was given him.

A spore-pod exploded with a loud plop in the confined space.

A mass of living dust filled the gorge, like a dense, opaque cloud, choking blinding. Zar squeezed the trigger of his weapon impulsively. Several of the invaders were blasted out of existence. Stones clattered down from where the unaimed beam of energy struck the wall.

Panic seized the little man, causing him to take one strangling breath. In a few moments he was down, writhing helpless on the ground. Choked by the finely divided stuff, his consciousness seemed to drop into a black hole of infinity. He, Zar, seemed about to pay for his misdeeds. With a mad fury he heard the derisive screams of Kaw, who had tricked him. But he could not curse in return, and presently his thoughts vanished away to nothing.

Awareness of being alive came back to him very slowly and painfully. At first he felt as though he had pneumonia: fever, suffocation, utter vagueness of mind. Had the spores germinated within his lungs, he would surely have died. But they did not, there; conditions were too moist and warm for them. Gradually he coughed them up.

He felt cold with a bitter, aching chill, for the weather had changed with the lateness of the season. Fine snow sifted down into the gorge from clouds that were thin and pearly and sun-gilded. Each tiny crystal of ice glittered with a thousand prismatic hues as it slowly descended. And the silence was deathly, bearing a burden of almost tangible desolation. In that burden there seemed to crowd all the antique history of a world—history whose grand movement shaded gradually toward stark, eternal death.

Zar wanted to flee this awful place that had become like part of another planet. He jerked his body as if to scramble feebly to his feet. He found then that he was restrained by cordlike tendrils, hard as horn, and warm with a faint, fermentive, animallike heat. Like the beat of a nameless pulse, tiny shocks of electricity tingled his flesh in a regular rhythm.

It was clear to Zar that while he had been inert the tendrils had fastened themselves slowly around him, in a way that was half like the closing of an ancient Venus's-flytrap, carnivorous plant of old, and half like the simple creeping of a vine on a wall.

Those constricting bonds were tightening now. Zar could feel the tiny thorns with which they were equipped biting into his flesh. He screamed in horror and pain. His cries echoed hollowly in the cold gorge. The snow, slowly sifting, and the silence, both seemed to mock—by their calm, pitiless lack of concern—the plight in which he found himself.

And then a voice, chattering faintly in the language of Kaw the Crow: "Be still. Peace. Peace. Peace. Peace. Peace—"

Gradually the sleepy tone quieted Zar, even though he was aware that whatever the invaders might do to him could bring him no good.

Plants with voices. Almost human voices! Some sort of tympanic organs, hidden, perhaps, in some of those pulpy leaves, Zar judged. From the records of the old explorations of Mars, he knew a little about these intruders, and their scheme of life. Organs, with the functions of mechanical contrivances, conceived and grown as they were needed! An alien science, adapted to the abilities and limitations of vegetative intelligences—intelligences that had never controlled the mining and smelting and shaping of metal!

Zar, tight in the clutch of those weird monstrosities, realized some of their power. Strangely it did not affect the hypnotic calm that wrapped him.

Mars. These wondrous people of the dusk of worlds had survived all animal life on the Red Planet. They had spanned Mars in a vast, irregularly formed network, growing along dry river beds, and the arms of vanished seas. They had not been mere individuals, for they had cooperated to form a civilization of a weird, bizarre sort. Great, hollow roots, buried beneath the ground, had drawn water from melting polar snows. Those roots had been like water conduits. A rhythmic pulsation within them had pumped the water across thousands of miles of desert, providing each plant along the way with moisture, even on that dying and almost dehydrated world. The canals of Mars! Yes, a great irrigation system, a great engineering feat—but out of the scope of Itorloo methods entirely.

And through the living texture of those immense joining roots, too, had doubtless flowed the impulses of thoughts and commands—the essence of leadership and security. Even now, when Mars was all but dead, its final civilization must still be trying to fight on.

Strange, wonderful times those old explorers had seen. Cold sunlight on bizarre ruins, left by extinct animal folk. Thin air and arctic weather, worse than that of Earth in the present age. Death everywhere, except for those vegetative beings grouped in immense, spiny, ribbonlike stretches. Dim shapes at night under hurtling Phobos, the nearer moon, and Deimos, her leisurely sister. Zar did not know just how it had happened, but he had heard that only a few of those human adventurers had escaped from the people of Mars with their lives.

Zar's thoughts rambled on in a detached way that was odd for him. Perhaps Nature had a plan that she used over and over again. On Terra the great reptiles of the Mesozoic period had died out to be replaced by mammals. Men and the Children of Men had become supreme at last.

Succession after succession, according to some well-ordered scheme? In the desolate quiet of falling snow, tempered only by the muted murmur of the frigid wind, it was easy for Zar to fall prey to such a concept, particularly since he was held powerless in the grasp of the invaders. Tendrils, thorny, stinging tendrils, which must have been grown purposely to receive an Itorloo captive! Zar could realize, then, a little of the fantastic introspective sense which gave these beings a direct contact with the physical secrets of their forms. And in consequence a knowledge of chemistry and biology that was clearer than anything that an Itorloo might be expected to attain along similar lines.

Zar wanted to shriek, but his awe and his weakness strangled him beyond more than the utterance of a gasping sigh.

Then the mighty spirit of his kind reasserted itself. Zar was aware that most probably he himself would presently perish; but the Itorloo, his kind, his real concern, could never lose! Not with all the mighty forces at their command! To suppose that they could be defeated by the sluggish intruders was against reason! In a matter of months—when the preparations for the vast purification process had been completed—Earth would be free of those intruders once more. Zar's brown face contracted into a leer of defiance that had a touch of real greatness. Brutality, force, cunning, and the capacity for quick action—those were the tools of the Itorloo, but they had strength, too. Zar was no fool—no shortsighted individual who leaps to hasty, optimistic conclusions—but in a contest between the Itorloo and the invaders there could be but a single outcome by any standard within Zar's reach.

In this belief, he was comforted, and his luck, presently, after long hours of suffering, seemed far better than he had any reason to hope for. The hard, thorny tendrils unquestionably were relaxing from about him a very little. He could not guess why, and in consequence he suspected subtle treachery. But he could find no reason to suppose that some hidden motive was responsible.

All his avid energies were concentrated, now, on escape. He concluded that perhaps the cold had forced the slight vegetable relaxation, and he proceeded to make the best possible use of his chances. Sometime during the night his straining hands reached the hilt of his knife. Not long afterward Zar clutched his blast gun.

Zar limped stiffly to his flier, cursing luridly; while behind him in the gorge, red firelight flickered, and wisps of smoke lanced into the frigid wind.

Zar wished that Kaw was somewhere in sight, to receive his wrath, too. The ebon rascal had vanished.

Winter deepened during succeeding days. The Itorloo in their buried cities felt none of its rigors, however.

Zar had submitted to a physical examination after his weird adventure, and had been pronounced fit. And of all his people he seemed to toil the most conscientiously.

The Venus project. Soon the Children of Men would be masters of that youthful, sunward planet. The green plains and jungles, and the blue skies of Venus. Soon! Soon! Soon! Zar was full of dreams of adventure and brutal pleasure.

Periodically the rocket craft of the Itorloo sallied forth from the cities to stamp out the fresh growth of the invaders. The oxygen-impregnated substance of their forms flamed in desert gullies, and along the rims of shriveled salt seas, where the spore plants were trying to renew their civilization. Most of them did not get a chance, even, to approach maturity. But because even one mature survivor could pollute the Earth with billions of spores, impossible to destroy otherwise, the purification process must be carried through.

Spring again, and then midsummer. The spaceships were almost ready to leap Venus-ward on the great adventure. The generators, meant to spread life-destroying emanations over the crust and atmosphere above, stood finished and gleaming in the white-domed caverns that housed them.

Zar looked at the magnificent, glittering array in the spaceship construction chamber of his native community with pride and satisfaction.

"Tomorrow," he said to a companion, a fierce light in his eyes.

The other nodded, the white glare of the atomic welding furnaces lighting up his features, and betraying there a wolfish grin of pleasure.

"Tomorrow," Zar repeated, an odd sort of vagueness in his tone.

V

Kaw had long ago rejoined his tribe. Life, during those recent months, had been little different from what had been usual in the crow clans for thousands of years. For purposes of safety, Kaw had led his flock into a desert fastness where patrolling Itorloo fliers were seldom seen, and where only a few spore plants had yet appeared.

His first intimation that all was not well was a haunting feeling of unease, which came upon him quite suddenly one day just before noon. His body burned and prickled uncomfortably, and he felt restless. Other than these dim evidences, there was nothing to betray the invisible hand of death.

Emanations, originating in the generators of the Itorloo, far underground. But Kaw was no physicist. He knew only that he and his fellows were vaguely disturbed.

With Teka, his mate, and several of their companions, he soared high into the sky. There, for a time, he felt better. Far overhead, near the Sun's bright disk, he glimpsed the incandescent streamers of Itorloo vessels, distant in space. And presently, with little attention, he saw those vessels—there were five in the group—turn back toward Earth.

The advance in the strength of the deadly emanations was slow. Vast masses of rock, covering the upper crust of the planet in a thin shell, had to develop a kind of resonance to them before they could reach their maximum power.

By nightfall Kaw felt only slightly more uncomfortable. By the following dawn, however, he was definitely droopy and listless. The gradual, worldwide process of purification advanced, directed at the invaders, but promising destruction to the less favored native life of Earth, too.

Four days. Huddled in a pathetic group in a ruined structure of antiquity, Kaw's tribe waited. Their features were dull and ruffled, and they shivered as if with cold. Some of them uttered low, sleepy twitterings of anguish.

That evening from a battered window embrasure, Kaw watched the pale moon rise. He was too weak to stand, but rested slumped forward on his breast. His eyes were rheumy and heavy-lidded, but they still held a savage glitter of defiance, which perhaps would burn in them even after they had ceased to live and see. And Kaw's clouded mind could still hazard a guess as to the identity of the author of his woes. Brave but impotent, he could still scream a hoarse challenge inspired by a courage as deathless as the ages.

"Itorloo! Itorloo—!"

Sometime before the first group of spaceships, headed for Venus, had been recalled to Earth, Zar, assigned to the second group, which had not yet entered the launching tubes, collapsed against his instrument panels.

His affliction had come with a suddenness that was utterly abrupt. Recovering from his swoon, he found himself lying on a narrow pallet in the hospital quarters of the city. His vision was swimming and fogged, and he felt hot and cold by turns.

But he could see the silvery tunicked figure of the physician standing close to him.

"What is wrong?" he stammered. "What is it that has happened to me? A short time ago I was well!"

"Much is wrong," the physician returned quietly. "And you have not really been well for a long time. A germ disease—a type of thing which we thought our sanitation had stamped out millennia ago—has been ravaging your brain and nerves for months! Only its insidiousness prevented it from being discovered earlier. During its incipient stages the poisons of it seem actually to stimulate mental and physical activity, giving a treacherous impression of robust health. And we know, certainly, that this disease is extremely contagious. It does not reveal itself easily, but I and others have examined many apparently healthy individuals with great care. In each there is the telltale evidence that the disease is not only present, but far advanced. Hundreds have collapsed as you have. More, surely, will follow. It is my belief that the entire race has been afflicted. And the plague has a fatal look. Panic has broken out. There is a threatened failure of power and food supplies. Perhaps an antitoxin can be found—but there is so little time."

Half delirious, Zar could still grasp the meaning of the physician's words, and could understand the origin of the disease.

He began to mutter with seeming incoherence: "The changing Earth. Reptiles. Mammals. Men—Succession. Nature—"

His voice took on a fiercer tone. "Fight, Itorloc!" he screamed. "Fight!"

Cruel he was, as were all his people, but he had pluck. Suddenly he arose to a sitting posture on his bed. His eyes flamed. If his act represented the final dramatic gesture of all the hoary race of man, still it was magnificent. Nor were any tears to be shed, for extinction meant only a task completed.

"Fight!" he shouted again, as if addressing a limitless multitude. "Fight, Itorloo! Study! Learn! Work! It is the only hope! Keep power flowing in the purification generators if you can. The old records of the explorations of Mars—those plants! Their approach to problems is different from our own. No metals. No machines as we know them. But in hidden compartments in their tissues it was easy for them to create the bacteria of death! They *invented* those bacteria, and grew them, breaking them away from their own substance. Some way, when I was a captive, I was infected. The thorns on the tendrils that held me! I was the carrier! Find an antitoxin to fight the plague, Itorloo! Work—"

VI

One year. Two. Three. The sunshine was brilliant, the air almost warm. The rusty desert hills in the distance were the same. Ancient ruins brooded in the stillness, as they had for so long. On the slopes ant hordes were busy. Rodent colonies showed similar evidence of population. In the sky, Kaw and his companions wheeled and turned lazily.

This was the same Earth, with several changes. Bulbous, spiny things peopled the gorges, and were probing out across the desert, slowly building—with hollow, connecting roots—the water pipes of a tremendous irrigation system. Like that of Mars, and like that of Ganymede, moon of Jupiter, in former ages. Saline remnants of seas and polar snows could alike provide the needed moisture.

Thoughts traveled swiftly along connecting roots. Little orbs and wicked spines gleamed. The invaders were at peace now. Only the Itorloo could have threatened their massed might. There was no danger in the lesser native life.

The subterranean cities of the former rulers of Earth were inhabited only by corpses and by intruding ants, who, like the other fauna of this planet, were immune to the plague, which had been directed and designed for the Itorloo alone. The last race of men was now one with the reptiles of the Mesozoic. But all was peace.

Kaw screamed out his contentment in loud, lazy cries, as he circled in the clear air. He seldom thought of the past anymore. If the new masters were not truly benignant, they were indifferent. They left him alone. Kaw, creature of Earth's dusk, was happy.

The great surface dome where Zar, the Itorloo, had once kept watch, was already surrounded by crowded growths. The plants had achieved a great, but an empty, victory. For Earth was a dying planet. Within the dome an astronomical telescope gleamed dully, collecting dust. Often Zar had directed it toward Venus, goal of shattered Itorloo dreams.

But who knew? Out of the void to Ganymede the invaders had come. Across space to Mars. Riding light to Earth. Perhaps when the time came—when Venus was growing old—

I have spoken in earlier headnotes of the old notion of "creationism" being altered into something apparently new by the false use of the adjective "scientific." The New York Times asked me to write an article on the subject for their Sunday magazine, and I was glad to oblige. We include that article here.

One result of the publication of the article was a sudden increase in the number of angry letters I received. Some were from people who excoriated me in imperfect English. A few (almost always women) wrote gentle letters of distress. The former I ignored. The latter received polite answers in which I explained that I could not change my mind except under the pressure of scientific evidence.

THE THREAT OF CREATIONISM
ISAAC ASIMOV

Scientists thought it was settled.

The universe, they had decided, is about 20 billion years old, and Earth itself is 4.5 billion years old. Simple forms of life came into being more than three billion years ago, having formed spontaneously from nonliving matter. They grew more complex through slow evolutionary processes and the first hominid ancestors of humanity appeared more than four million years ago. Homo sapiens itself—the present human species, people like you and me—has walked the earth for at least 50,000 years.

But apparently it isn't settled. There are Americans who believe that the earth is only about 6,000 years old; that human beings and all other species were brought into existence by a divine Creator as eternally separate varieties of beings, and that there has been no evolutionary process.

They are creationists—they call themselves "scientific" creationists—and they are a growing power in the land, demanding that schools be forced to teach their views. State legislatures, mindful of votes, are beginning to succumb to the pressure. In perhaps fifteen states, bills have been introduced, putting forth the creationist point of view, and in others, strong movements are gaining momentum. In Arkansas, a law requiring that the teaching of creationism receive equal time was passed this spring and was scheduled to go into effect in September 1982, though the Amer-

177

ican Civil Liberties Union has filed suit on behalf of a group of clergymen, teachers, and parents to overturn it, and was successful. And a California father named Kelly Segraves, the director of the Creation-Science Research Center, sued to have taught in public-school science classes that there are other theories of creation besides evolution, and that one of them was the Biblical version. The suit came to trial in March 1981, and the judge ruled that educators must distribute a policy statement to schools and textbook publishers explaining that the theory of evolution should not be seen as "the ultimate cause of origins." Even in New York, the Board of Education delayed making a final decision on whether schools will be required to include the teaching of creationism in their curriculums.

The Reverend Jerry Falwell, the head of the Moral Majority, who supports the creationist view from his television pulpit, claims that he has 17 million to 25 million viewers (though Arbitron places the figure at a much more modest 1.6 million). But there are sixty-six electronic ministries which have a total audience of about 20 million. And in parts of the country where the Fundamentalists predominate—the so-called Bible Belt—creationists are in the majority.

They make up a fervid and dedicated group, convinced beyond argument of both their rightness and righteousness. Faced with an apathetic and falsely secure majority, smaller groups have used intense pressure and forceful campaigning—as the creationists do —and have succeeded in disrupting and taking over whole societies.

Yet, though creationists seem to accept the literal truth of the Biblical story of creation, this does not mean that all religious people are creationists. There are millions of Catholics, Protestants, and Jews who think of the Bible as a source of spiritual truth and accept much of it as symbolically rather than literally true. They do not consider the Bible to be a textbook of science, even in intent, and have no problem teaching evolution in their secular institutions.

To those who are trained in science, creationism seems like a bad dream, a sudden reliving of a nightmare, a renewed march of an army of the night risen to challenge free thought and enlightenment.

The scientific evidence for the age of the earth and for the evolutionary development of life seems overwhelming to scientists. How can anyone question it? What are the arguments the creationists use? What is the "science" that makes their views "scientific"? Here are some of them:

- The argument from analogy.

A watch implies a watchmaker, say the creationists. If you were to find a beautifully intricate watch in the desert, far from habitation, you would be sure that it had been fashioned by human hands and somehow left there. It would pass the bounds of credibility that it had simply formed, spontaneously, from the sands of the desert.

By analogy, then, if you consider humanity, life, earth, and the universe, all infinitely more intricate than a watch, you can believe far less easily that it "just happened." It, too, like the watch, must have been fashioned, but by more-than-human hands—in short by a divine Creator.

This argument seems unanswerable, and it has been used (even though not often explicitly expressed) ever since the dawn of consciousness. To have explained to prescientific human beings that the wind and the rain and the sun follow the laws of nature and do so blindly and without a guiding hand would have been utterly unconvincing to them. In fact, it might well have gotten you stoned to death as a blasphemer.

There are many aspects of the universe that still cannot be explained satisfactorily by science; but ignorance implies only ignorance that may someday be conquered. To surrender to ignorance and call it God has always been premature, and it remains premature today.

In short, the complexity of the universe—and one's inability to explain it in full—is not in itself an argument for a Creator.

- The argument from general consent.

Some creationists point out that belief in a Creator is general among all peoples and all cultures. Surely this unanimous craving hints at a great truth. There would be no unanimous belief in a lie.

General belief, however, is not really surprising. Nearly every people on earth that considers the existence of the world assumes it to have been created by a god or gods. And each group invents full details for the story. No two creation tales are alike. The Greeks, the Norsemen, the Japanese, the Hindus, the American Indians, and so on and so on all have their own creation myths, and all of these are recognized by Americans of Judeo-Christian heritage as "just myths."

The ancient Hebrews also had a creation tale—two of them, in fact. There is a primitive Adam-and-Eve-in-Paradise story, with man created first, then animals, then woman. There is also a poetic tale of God fashioning the universe in six days, with animals preceding man, and man and woman created together.

These Hebrew myths are not inherently more credible than any of the others, but they are our myths. General consent, of course, proves nothing: there can be a unanimous belief in something that isn't so. The universal opinion over thousands of years that the earth was flat never flattened its spherical shape by one inch.

•   The argument by belittlement.

Creationists frequently stress the fact that evolution is "only a theory," giving the impression that a theory is an idle guess. A scientist, one gathers, arising one morning with nothing particular to do, decides that perhaps the moon is made of Roquefort cheese and instantly advances the Roquefort-cheese theory.

A theory (as the word is used by scientists) is a detailed description of some facet of the universe's workings that is based on long observation and, where possible, experiment. It is the result of careful reasoning from those observations and experiments and has survived the critical study of scientists generally.

For example, we have the description of the cellular nature of living organisms (the "cell theory"); of objects attracting each other according to a fixed rule (the "theory of gravitation"); of energy behaving in discrete bits (the "quantum theory"); of light traveling through a vacuum at a fixed measurable velocity (the "theory of relativity"), and so on.

All are theories; all are firmly founded; all are accepted as valid descriptions of this or that aspect of the universe. They are neither guesses nor speculations. And no theory is better founded, more closely examined, more critically argued, and more thoroughly accepted, than the theory of evolution. If it is "only" a theory, that is all it has to be.

Creationism, on the other hand, is not a theory. There is no evidence, in the scientific sense, that supports it. Creationism, or at least the particular variety accepted by many Americans, is an expression of early Middle Eastern legend. It is fairly described as "only a myth."

•   The argument from imperfection.

Creationists, in recent years, have stressed the "scientific" background of their beliefs. They point out that there are scientists who base their creationist beliefs on a careful study of geology, paleontology, and biology and produce "textbooks" that embody those beliefs.

Virtually the whole scientific corpus of creationism, however, consists of the pointing out of imperfections in the evolutionary view. The creationists insist, for example, that evolutionists cannot show true transition states between species in the fossil evidence; that age determinations through radioactive breakdown are uncertain; that alternate interpretations of this or that piece of evidence are possible, and so on.

Because the evolutionary view is not perfect and is not agreed upon in every detail by all scientists, creationists argue that evolution is false and that scientists, in supporting evolution, are basing their views on blind faith and dogmatism.

To an extent, the creationists are right here: The details of evolution are not perfectly known. Scientists have been adjusting and modifying Charles Darwin's suggestions since he advanced his theory of the origin of species through natural selection back in 1859. After all, much has been learned about the fossil record and about physiology, microbiology, biochemistry, ethology, and various other branches of life science in the last 125 years, and it is to be expected that we can improve on Darwin. In fact, we have improved on him.

Nor is the process finished. It can never be, as long as human beings continue to question and to strive for better answers.

The details of evolutionary theory are in dispute precisely because scientists are not devotees of blind faith and dogmatism. They do not accept even as great a thinker as Darwin without question, nor do they accept any idea, new or old, without thorough argument. Even after accepting an idea, they stand ready to overrule it, if appropriate new evidence arrives. If, however, we grant that a theory is imperfect and that details remain in dispute, does that disprove the theory as a whole?

Consider. I drive a car, and you drive a car. I do not know exactly how an engine works. Perhaps you do not either. And it may be that our hazy and approximate ideas of the workings of an automobile are in conflict. Must we then conclude from this disagreement that an automobile does not run, or that it does not exist? Or, if our senses force us to conclude that an automobile does exist and run, does that mean it is pulled by an invisible horse, since our engine theory is imperfect?

However much scientists argue their differing beliefs in details of evolutionary theory, or in the interpretation of the necessary imperfect fossil record, they firmly accept the evolutionary process itself.

• The argument from distorted science.

Creationists have learned enough scientific terminology to use it in their attempts to disprove evolution. They do this in numerous ways, but the most common example, at least in the mail I receive, is the repeated assertion that the second law of thermodynamics demonstrates the evolutionary process to be impossible.

In kindergarten terms, the second law of thermodynamics says that all spontaneous change is in the direction of increasing disorder, that is, in a "downhill" direction. There can be no spontaneous buildup of the complex from the simple, therefore, because that would be moving "uphill." According to the creationist argument, since, by the evolutionary process, complex forms of life evolve from simple forms, that process defies the second law, so creationism must be true.

Such an argument implies that this clearly visible fallacy is somehow invisible to scientists, who must therefore be flying in the face of the second law through sheer perversity.

Scientists, however, do know about the second law and they are not blind. It's just that an argument based on kindergarten terms is suitable only for kindergartens.

To lift the argument a notch above the kindergarten level, the second law of thermodynamics applies to a "closed system"—that is, to a system that does not gain energy from without, or lose energy to the outside. The only truly closed system we know of is the universe as a whole.

Within a closed system, there are subsystems that can gain complexity spontaneously, provided there is a greater loss of complexity in another interlocking subsystem. The overall change then is a complexity loss in line with the dictates of the second law.

Evolution can proceed and build up the complex from the simple, thus moving uphill, without violating the second law, as long as another interlocking part of the system—the sun, which delivers energy to the earth continuously—moves downhill (as it does) at a much faster rate than evolution moves uphill.

If the sun were to cease shining, evolution would stop and so, eventually, would life.

Unfortunately, the second law is a subtle concept which most people are not accustomed to dealing with, and it is not easy to see the fallacy in the creationist distortion.

There are many other "scientific" arguments used by creationists, some taking quite clever advantage of present areas of dispute in evolutionary theory, but every one of them is as disingenuous as the second-law argument.

The "scientific" arguments are organized into special creationist textbooks, which have all the surface appearance of the real thing, and which school systems are being heavily pressured to accept. They are written by people who have not made any mark as scientists, and, while they discuss geology, paleontology, and biology with correct scientific terminology, they are devoted almost entirely to raising doubts over the legitimacy of the evidence and reasoning underlying evolutionary thinking on the assumption that this leaves creationism as the only possible alternative.

Evidence actually in favor of creationism is not presented, of course, because none exists other than the word of the Bible, which it is current creationist strategy not to use.

• The argument from irrelevance.

Some creationists put all matters of scientific evidence to one side and consider all such things irrelevant. The Creator, they say, brought life and the earth and the entire universe into being 6,000 years ago or so, complete with all the evidence for an eons-long evolutionary development. The fossil record, the decaying radioactivity, the receding galaxies were all created as they are, and the evidence they present is an illusion.

Of course, this argument is itself irrelevant, for it can neither be proved nor disproved. It is not an argument, actually, but a statement. I can say that the entire universe was created two minutes ago, complete with all its history books describing a nonexistent past in detail, and with every living person equipped with a full memory: you, for instance, in the process of reading this article in midstream with a memory of what you had read in the beginning—which you had not really read.

What kind of a Creator would produce a universe containing so intricate an illusion? It would mean that the Creator formed a universe that contained human beings whom He had endowed with the faculty of curiosity and the ability to reason. He supplied those human beings with an enormous amount of subtle and cleverly consistent evidence designed to mislead them and cause them to be convinced that the universe was created 20 billion years ago and developed by evolutionary processes that included the creation and development of life on Earth.

Why?

Does the Creator take pleasure in fooling us? Does it amuse Him to watch us go wrong? Is it part of a test to see if human beings will deny their senses and their reason in order to cling to myth? Can it be that the Creator is a cruel and malicious prankster, with a vicious and adolescent sense of humor?

• The argument from authority.

The Bible says that God created the world in six days, and the Bible is the inspired word of God. To the average creationist this is all that counts. All other arguments are merely a tedious way of countering the propaganda of all those wicked humanists, agnostics, and atheists who are not satisfied with the clear word of the Lord.

The creationist leaders do not actually use that argument because that would make their argument a religious one, and they would not be able to use it in fighting a secular school system. They have to borrow the clothing of science, no matter how badly it fits, and call themselves "scientific" creationists. They also speak only of the "Creator," and never mention that this Creator is the God of the Bible.

We cannot, however, take this sheep's clothing seriously. However much the creationist leaders might hammer away at their "scientific" and "philosophical" points, they would be helpless and a laughingstock if that were all they had.

It is religion that recruits their squadrons. Tens of millions of Americans, who neither know nor understand the actual arguments for—or even against—evolution, march in the army of the night with their Bibles held high. And they are a strong and frightening force, impervious to, and immunized against, the feeble lance of mere reason.

Even if I am right and the evolutionists' case is very strong, have not creationists, whatever the emptiness of their case, a right to be heard?

If their case is empty, isn't it perfectly safe to discuss it since the emptiness would then be apparent?

Why, then, are evolutionists so reluctant to have creationism taught in the public schools on an equal basis with evolutionary theory? Can it be that the evolutionists are not as confident of their case as they pretend? Are they afraid to allow youngsters a clear choice?

First, the creationists are somewhat less than honest in their demand for equal time. It is not their views that are repressed: schools are by no means the only place in which the dispute between creationism and evolutionary theory is played out.

There are the churches, for instance, which are a much more serious influence on most Americans than the schools are. To be sure, many churches are quite liberal, have made their peace with science and find it easy to live with scientific advance—even with evolution. But many of the less modish and citified churches are bastions of creationism.

The influence of the church is naturally felt in the home, in the newspapers, and in all of surrounding society. It makes itself felt in the nation as a whole, even in religiously liberal areas, in thousands of subtle ways: in the nature of holiday observance, in expressions of patriotic fervor, even in total irrelevancies. In 1968, for example, a team of astronauts circling the moon were instructed to read the first few verses of Genesis as though NASA felt it had to placate the public lest they rage against the violation of the firmament. At the present time, even the current President of the United States has expressed his creationist sympathies.

It is only in school that American youngsters in general are ever likely to hear any reasoned exposition of the evolutionary viewpoint. They might find such a viewpoint in books, magazines, newspapers, or even, on occasion, on television. But church and family can easily censor printed matter or television. Only the school is beyond their control.

But only just barely beyond. Even though schools are now allowed to teach evolution, teachers are beginning to be apologetic about it, knowing full well their jobs are at the mercy of school boards upon which creationists are a stronger and stronger influence.

Then, too, in schools, students are not required to believe what they learn about evolution—merely to parrot it back on tests. If they fail to do so, their punishment is nothing more than the loss of a few points on a test or two.

In the creationist churches, however, the congregation is required to believe. Impressionable youngsters, taught that they will go to hell if they listen to the evolutionary doctrine, are not likely to listen in comfort or to believe if they do.

Therefore, creationists, who control the church and the society they live in and who face the public school as the only place where evolution is even briefly mentioned in a possibly favorable way, find they cannot stand even so minuscule a competition and demand "equal time."

Do you suppose their devotion to "fairness" is such that they will give equal time to evolution in their churches?

Second, the real danger is the manner in which creationists want their "equal time."

In the scientific world, there is free and open competition of ideas, and even a scientist whose suggestions are not accepted is nevertheless free to continue to argue his case.

In this free and open competition of ideas, creationism has clearly lost. It has been losing in fact, since the time of Copernicus four and a half centuries ago. But creationists, placing myth above reason, refuse to accept the decision and are now calling on the government to force their views on the schools in lieu of the free expression of ideas. Teachers must be forced to present creationism as though it has equal intellectual respectability with evolutionary doctrine.

What a precedent this sets.

If the government can mobilize its policemen and its prisons to make certain that teachers give creationism equal time, they can next use force to make sure that teachers declare creationism the victor so that evolution will be evicted from the classroom altogether.

We will have established the full groundwork, in other words, for legally enforced ignorance and for totalitarian thought control.

And what if the creationists win? They might, you know, for there are millions who, faced with the choice between science and their interpretation of the Bible, will choose the Bible and reject science, regardless of the evidence.

This is not entirely because of a traditional and unthinking reverence for the literal words of the Bible; there is also a pervasive uneasiness—even an actual fear—of science that will drive even those who care little for Fundamentalism into the arms of the creationists. For one thing, science is uncertain. Theories are subject to revision; observations are open to a variety of interpretations, and scientists quarrel among themselves. This is disillusioning for those untrained in the scientific method, who thus turn to the rigid certainty of the Bible instead. There is something comfortable about a view that allows for no deviation and that spares you the painful necessity of having to think.

Second, science is complex and chilling. The mathematical language of science is understood by very few. The vistas it presents are scary—an enormous universe ruled by chance and impersonal rules, empty and uncaring, ungraspable and vertiginous. How comfortable to turn instead to a small world, only a few thousand years old, and under God's personal and immediate care; a world in which you are His peculiar concern and where He will not consign you to hell if you are careful to follow every word of the Bible as interpreted for you by your television preacher.

Third, science is dangerous. There is no question but that poison gas, genetic engineering, and nuclear weapons and power stations are terrifying. It may be that civilization is falling apart and the world we know is coming to an end. In that case, why not turn to religion and look forward to the Day of Judgment, in which you and your fellow believers will be lifted into eternal bliss and have the added joy of watching the scoffers and disbelievers writhe forever in torment.

So why might they not win?

There are numerous cases of societies in which the armies of the night have ridden triumphantly over minorities in order to establish a powerful orthodoxy which dictates official thought. Invariably, the triumphant ride is toward long-range disaster.

Spain dominated Europe and the world in the sixteenth century, but in Spain orthodoxy came first, and all divergence of opinion was ruthlessly suppressed. The result was that Spain settled back into blankness and did not share in the scientific, technological, and commercial ferment that bubbled up in other nations of Western Europe. Spain remained an intellectual backwater for centuries.

In the late seventeenth century, France in the name of orthodoxy revoked the Edict of Nantes and drove out many thousands of Huguenots, who added their intellectual vigor to lands of refuge such as Great Britain, the Netherlands, and Prussia, while France was permanently weakened.

In more recent times, Germany hounded out the Jewish scientists of Europe. They arrived in the United States and contributed immeasurably to scientific advancement here, while Germany lost so heavily that there is no telling how long it will take it to regain its former scientific eminence. The Soviet Union, in its fascination with Lysenko, destroyed its geneticists, and set back its biological sciences for decades. China, during the Cultural Revolution, turned against Western science and is still laboring to overcome the devastation that resulted.

Are we now, with all these examples before us, to ride backward into the past under the same tattered banner of orthodoxy? With creationism in the saddle, American science will wither. We will raise a generation of ignoramuses ill-equipped to run the industry of tomorrow, much less to generate the new advances of the days after tomorrow.

We will inevitably recede into the backwater of civilization and those nations that retain open scientific thought will take over the leadership of the world and the cutting edge of human advancement.

I don't suppose that the creationists really plan the decline of the United States, but their loudly expressed patriotism is as simple-minded as their "science." If they succeed, they will, in their folly, achieve the opposite of what they say they wish.

Of all the pseudosciences, the most successful, and the most ancient (and some people think that time is in itself enough to sanctify) is astrology.

It seems reasonable to many people to suppose that the astronomical bodies have some influence upon us. After all, the Sun warms us and the Moon causes tides; therefore, if Jupiter is in Libra, that means it is safe for us, on February 16, to invest our money in stocks, provided we were born in October. (Is the reasoning incomplete? Tell that to the astrologers.)

Others may think that it is not a matter of physical influence of the heavenly objects upon ourselves. Rather, it seems to be that God has created a heavenly cryptogram which, when deciphered by knowledgeable people, will tell us when to invest in stocks or when to avoid risking an argument with friends. (I should think that creating the Universe in six days would be child's play, compared to that of constructing such a cryptogram.)

Still others don't give it any thought at all. They are simply nervous concerning the future (as anyone should be) and totally unconfident of their own ability to take wise action (undoubtedly with justice) so that they will gratefully take the advice of anyone who claims to know what they ought to do.

Nevertheless, there is a strange influence that the stars have on us, and on the very creation of the Earth and of life, but no astrologer has ever worked it out or dreamed it existed. That was left to the real scientists, as Sagan explains.

THE COSMIC CONNECTION
CARL SAGAN

From earliest times, human beings have pondered their place in the universe. They have wondered whether they are in some sense connected with the awesome and immense cosmos in which the Earth is embedded.

Many thousands of years ago a pseudoscience called astrology was invented. The positions of the planets at the birth of a child were supposed to play a major role in determining his or her future. The planets, moving points of light, were thought, in some mysterious sense, to be gods. In his vanity, Man imagined the universe designed for his benefit and organized for his use.

Perhaps the planets were identified with gods because their motions seemed irregular. The word *planet* is Greek for "wanderer." The unpredictable behavior of the gods in many legends may have corresponded well with the apparently unpredictable motions of the planets. The argument may have been: Gods don't follow rules; planets don't follow rules; planets are gods.

When the ancient priestly astrological caste discovered that the motions of the planets were not irregular but predictable, they seem to have kept this information to themselves. No use unnecessarily worrying the populace, undermining religious belief, and eroding the supports of political power. Moreover, the Sun was the source of life. The Moon, through the tides, dominated agriculture —especially in river basins like the Indus, the Nile, the Yangtze, and the Tigris-Euphrates. How reasonable that these lesser lights, the planets, should have a subtler but no less definite influence on human life!

The search for a connection, a hooking-up between people and the universe, has not diminished since the dawn of astrology. The same human needs exist despite the advances of science.

We now know that the planets are worlds more or less like our own. We know that their light and gravity have negligible influence on a newborn babe. We know that there are enormous numbers of other objects—asteroids, comets, pulsars, quasars, exploding galaxies, black holes, and the rest—objects not known to the ancient speculators who invented astrology. The universe is immensely grander than they could have imagined.

Astrology has not attempted to keep pace with the times. Even the calculations of planetary motions and positions performed by most astrologers are usually inaccurate.

No study shows a statistically significant success rate in predicting through their horoscopes the futures or the personality traits of newborn children. There is no field of radioastrology or X-ray astrology or gamma-ray astrology, taking account of the energetic new astronomical sources discovered in recent years.

Nevertheless, astrology remains immensely popular everywhere. There are at least ten times more astrologers than astronomers. A large number, perhaps a majority, of newspapers in the United States have daily columns on astrology.

Many bright and socially committed young people have more than a passing interest in astrology. It satisfies an almost unspoken need to feel a significance for human beings in a vast and awesome cosmos, to believe that we are in some way hooked up with the universe—an ideal of many drug and religious experiences, the *samadhi* of some Eastern religions.

The great insights of modern astronomy have shown that, in some senses quite different from those imagined by the earlier astrologers, we *are* connected up with the universe.

The first scientists and philosophers—Aristotle, for example—imagined that the heavens were made of a different sort of material than the Earth, a special kind of celestial stuff, pure and undefiled. We now know that this is not the case. Pieces of the asteroid belt called meteorites; samples of the Moon returned by Apollo astronauts and Soviet unmanned spacecraft; the solar wind, which expands outward past our planet from the Sun; and the cosmic rays, which are probably generated from exploding stars and their remnants—all show the presence of the same atoms we know here on Earth. Astronomical spectroscopy is able to determine the chemical composition of collection of stars billions of light-years away. The entire universe is made of familiar stuff. The same atoms and molecules occur at enormous distances from Earth as occur here within our Solar System.

These studies have yielded a remarkable conclusion. Not only is the universe made everywhere of the same atoms, but the atoms, roughly speaking, are present everywhere in approximately the same proportions.

Almost all the stuff of the stars and the interstellar matter between the stars is hydrogen and helium, the two simplest atoms. All other atoms are impurities, trace constituents. This is also true for the massive outer planets of our Solar System, like Jupiter. But it is not true for the comparatively tiny hunks of rock and metal in the inner part of the Solar System, like our planet Earth. This is because the small terrestrial planets have gravities too weak to hold their original hydrogen and helium atmospheres, which have slowly leaked away to space.

The next most abundant atoms in the universe turn out to be oxygen, carbon, nitrogen, and neon. These are atoms everyone has heard of. Why are the cosmically most abundant elements those that are reasonably common on Earth, rather than, say, yttrium or praseodymium?

The theory of the evolution of stars is sufficiently advanced that astronomers are able to understand the various kinds of stars and their relations—how a star is born from the interstellar gas and dust, how it shines and evolves by thermonuclear reactions in its hot interior, and how it dies. These thermonuclear reactions are of the same sort as the reactions that underlie thermonuclear weapons (hydrogen bombs): the conversion of four atoms of hydrogen into one of helium.

But in the later stages of stellar evolution, higher temperatures are reached in the insides of stars, and elements heavier than helium are generated by thermonuclear processes. Nuclear astrophysics indicates that the most abundant atoms produced in such hot red giant stars are precisely the most abundant atoms on Earth and elsewhere in the universe. The heavy atoms generated in the insides of red giants are spewed out into the interstellar medium, by slow leakage from the star's atmosphere like our own solar wind, or by mighty stellar explosions, some of which can make a star a billion times brighter than our Sun.

Recent infrared spectroscopy of hot stars has discovered that they are blowing off silicates into space—rock powder spewed out into the interstellar medium. Carbon stars probably expel graphite particles into surrounding cosmic space. Other stars shed ice. In their early histories, stars like the Sun probably propelled large quantities of organic compounds into interstellar space; indeed, simple organic molecules are found by radio astronomical methods to be filling the space between the stars. The brightest planetary nebula known (a planetary nebula is an expanding cloud usually surrounding an exploding star called a nova) seems to contain particles of magnesium carbonate: dolomite, the stuff of the European mountains of the same name, expelled by a star into interstellar space.

These heavy atoms—carbon, nitrogen, oxygen, silicon, and the rest—then float about in the interstellar medium until, at some later time, a local gravitational condensation occurs and a new sun and new planets are formed. This second-generation solar system is enriched in heavy elements.

The fate of individual human beings may not now be connected in a deep way with the rest of the universe, but the matter out of which each of us is made is intimately tied to processes that occurred immense intervals of time and enormous distances in space away from us. Our Sun is a second- or third-generation star. All of the rocky and metallic material we stand on, the iron in our blood, the calcium in our teeth, the carbon in our genes were produced billions of years ago in the interior of a red giant star. We are made of star-stuff.

Our atomic and molecular connection with the rest of the universe is a real and unfanciful cosmic hookup. As we explore our surroundings by telescope and space vehicle, other hookups may emerge. There may be a network of intercommunicating extraterrestrial civilizations to which we may link up tomorrow, for all we know. The undelivered promise of astrology—that the stars impel our individual characters—will not be satisfied by modern astronomy. But the deep human need to seek and understand our connection with the universe is a goal well within our grasp.

PART IV

THE ORIGIN OF HUMANKIND

Now we concentrate on the creation of humanity.

The passage of the Bible here included contains two different accounts of the creation of human beings. The conclusion of Genesis 1 describes it in the same austere fashion that characterizes the chapter generally. It is part of what is known as the "P document."

Beginning with Genesis 2:5, the story of creation is retold in what is known as the "J document." Even the name of the deity is different: "God" in the P document, and "Lord God" in the J document.

The J document is more anecdotal. There is no mention of the inanimate Universe except for the absence of rain. First man is created, then the plant world, then the animal world, last of all woman. In the P document, the order is the plant world, the animal world, and then humanity, both sexes at the same time.

Why the double tale? The second one—the Adam and Eve story—was undoubtedly a popular folktale. The first was devised by the priests during the Babylonian exile, for Genesis 1 is a clear adaptation of the Babylonian creation myth—with the polytheism and the less edifying portions omitted. The Babylonians were, at that time, the most scientifically advanced people in the west, so that Genesis 1 is a very early attempt to reconcile religion and science.

Since the second version was too popular to omit, and the first one too scientific, the Biblical editors included both and considered them equally inspired, just as creationists want schools to teach both the scientific account of evolution and the folktales of creationism and to consider them equally scientific.

GENESIS 1:26–31 AND GENESIS 2:1–25
NEW ENGLISH BIBLE

Then God said, "Let us make man in our image and likeness to rule the fish in the sea, the birds of heaven, the cattle, all wild animals on earth, and all reptiles that crawl upon the earth." So God created man in his own image; in the image of God he created him; male and female he created them. God blessed them and said to them, "Be fruitful and increase, fill the earth and subdue it, rule over the fish in the sea, the birds of heaven, and every living thing that moves upon the earth." God also said, "I give you all plants that bear seed everywhere on earth, and every tree bearing fruit which yields seed: they shall be yours for food. All green plants I give for food to the wild animals, to all the birds of heaven, and to all reptiles on earth, every living creature." So it was; and God saw all that he had made, and it was very good. Evening came, and morning came, a sixth day.

Thus heaven and earth were completed with all their mighty throng. On the sixth day God completed all the work he had been doing, and on the seventh day he ceased from all his work. God blessed the seventh day and made it holy, because on that day he ceased from all the work he had set himself to do.

This is the story of the making of heaven and earth when they were created.

When the Lord God made Earth and Heaven, there was neither shrub nor plant growing wild upon the earth. because the Lord God had sent no rain on the earth; nor was there any man to till the ground. A flood used to rise out of the earth and water all the surface of the ground. Then the Lord God formed a man from the dust of the ground and breathed into his nostrils the breath of life. Thus the man became a living creature. Then the Lord God planted a garden in Eden away to the east, and there he put the man whom he had formed. The Lord God made trees spring from the ground, all trees pleasant to look at and good for food; and in the middle of the garden he set the tree of life and the tree of the knowledge of good and evil.

There was a river flowing from Eden to water the garden, and when it left the garden it branched into four streams. The name of the first is Pishon; that is the river which encircles all the land of Havilah, where the gold is. The gold of that land is good; bdellium and cornelians are also to be found there. The name of the second river is Gihon; this is the one which encircles all the land of Cush. The name of the third is Tigris; this is the river that runs east of Asshur. The fourth river is the Euphrates.

The Lord God took the man and put him in the garden of Eden to till it and care for it. He told the man, "You may eat from every tree in the garden, but not from the tree of the knowledge of good and evil; for on the day that you eat from it, you will certainly die." Then the Lord God said, "It is not good for the man to be alone. I will provide a partner for him." So God formed out of the ground all the wild animals and all the birds of heaven. He brought them to the man to see what he would call them, and whatever the man called each living creature, that was its name. Thus the man gave names to all cattle, to the birds of heaven, and to every wild animal; but for the man himself no partner had yet been found. And so the Lord God put the man into a trance, and while he slept, he took one of his ribs and closed the flesh over the place. The Lord God then built up the rib, which he had taken out of the man, into a woman. He brought her to the man, and the man said:

> "Now this, at last—
> bone from my bones,
> flesh from my flesh—
> this shall be called woman,
> for from man was this taken."

That is why a man leaves his father and mother and is united to his wife, and the two become one flesh. Now they were both naked, the man and his wife, but they had no feeling of shame toward one another.

Human beings are clearly related to other animals—anatomically, physiologically, biochemically. They fit into the careful and methodical classification of all species. They are so close to chimpanzees from the standpoint of the intimate biochemistry of the genes that far from finding a wide difference, we are puzzled by the lack of difference. The genes of human beings and chimpanzees are so similar in structure that we can only wonder at why we are so clearly separate. How large a final difference a small starting difference makes, we can only conclude.

This alone makes it utterly unlikely that human beings, alone of all species upon this planet, had their start somewhere else. Nothing that developed on another planet, by the sheer chance of genetic development, would just happen to fit into the classification scheme on Earth. Nor would human beings and chimpanzees be so alike, if one species originated on Earth and one elsewhere.

And yet, just as children very commonly imagine themselves to be noble-born and to have been changed in the cradle, human beings are sometimes tempted to imagine that they are born of a highly developed species elsewhere and have nothing in common with the animals of Earth. The second dream is even less conceivable than the first. It is at least conceivable that you were changed in the cradle; it is not conceivable that humanity is extraterrestrial in origin.

Still, science-fiction writers are allowed to speculate, and Eric Frank Russell can do so very convincingly.

FIRST PERSON SINGULAR
ERIC FRANK RUSSELL

1. NEW PLANET

The new planet could be seen as a dark disk surrounded by a glowing nimbus. Its halo was created by the small red sun burning far behind it. There were other spheres in this same locality, some with many satellites and one—a glorious sight—with multicolored rings. Sensed by the instruments, although not from this angle evident to the eyes, was a dangerous belt of rocks rushing aimlessly through the void and forming the reef of the stars.

Quivering and red-tailed, the long particle-scarred spaceship had tilted high above the reef and was now heading for the nimbus. There was another smaller paler halo close to the objective, sharing its orbit, indicative of an almost airless moon.

Seated behind the bow observation port, Captain Rafel twisted around as Edham came into the cabin. He said, "I summoned you forward, thinking you might like first view. It has just expanded sufficiently for straight vision." He pointed into the sparkling darkness. "There it is."

Taking a seat beside the commander, Selected Granor Edham looked at the thin circle shining upon the backdrop of creation. The picture was unsatisfactory in that it told little. All the same it meant enough. It was a dim, ghostly lamp marking the end of his trail.

It represented the purpose for which he had been chosen and, for all he knew, the specific function for which he had been conceived and born. That faraway light, pale, wan, and beckoning, surrounded the hidden fact of fate. It marked the site of death or glory. It was the cradle—or the grave.

His young, strong, and decidedly stubborn features did not change expression while his gaze remained leveled forward. Rafel was watching him and he was aware of the scrutiny but this had nothing to do with his grim phlegmaticism. Either he was peculiarly insensitive or had superb control of his emotions, for he gave Rafel nothing to go by. His face remained set, just a little cold, a little forbidding, and his eyes were steady, unwinking.

Rafel said quietly, "We'll be there in about two hundred tempors by the clock." He waited for comment, watching, watching. There was no remark, not even the quirk of an eyebrow. The other's countenance might have been carved in rock. Rafel went on, his manner verging upon the paternal, "You speak but seldom. Once I saw you smile and that I shall always remember. I have never heard you laugh."

"I do my laughing inside myself."

"But not often," pursued Rafel. "Not as frequently as others do."

"Not all are the same," Edham observed.

"Of course not. There are differences. So long as we can lay claim to be individuals there must be differences. Therefore some laugh and some weep."

In the same even unaccentuated tones, Edham asked, "Have you wept?"

Rafel leaned back in his air-cushioned seat and eyed the stars. He had thin aquiline features and the large luminous optics of the highly intelligent. The eyes were upon the stars without seeing them.

"Six times or perhaps seven. Please do not ask me when, where, or why."

"I have not the slightest desire to do so. One cannot seize part of another man's heart." For the first time Edham showed hint of expression, no more than a narrowing of the eyes, a slight hardening of the jaw muscles. "But if ever the time comes to weep for me it would be well to remember something."

"Such as?"

"I shall be laughing."

Rafel said soberly, "I hope you will, I hope you will." He hesitated, continued. "No one sees himself truly pictured in the mirror of another's mind. Sometimes one is given to wonder how one looks.

"Has one the faults and virtues of which he is conscious or do his fellows see some faults as virtues, some virtues as faults? Do others see additional faculties not apparent to their possessor? I am the captain of my ship but what sort of a captain am I to my crew—good, bad, or indifferent?"

"It is of little consequence. The shape is set."

"Bear with me. I am leading up to something. Do you mind if I put a personal question?"

"I mind nothing," said Edham. "Would I be where I am, going where I'm going, if I had cares, susceptibilities?"

"You are treading my conversational path a little ahead of me," Rafel told him. "What I would like to ask you is this—have you ever suspected yourself of unsociability?"

"I do not suspect it—I know it." Edham turned his head, looked straight at him. "During and since childhood I have not mixed quite as others have mixed and such mixing as I have done has been done self-consciously. Sometimes I have wondered whether it is an inferiority complex or sheer unsociability.

"I console myself with the thought that I am not antisocial. I like and enjoy my fellows—providing there are not too many at one time. I have never liked crowds." His dark gray orbs studied Rafel. "Why do you ask?"

The other gave him a slow smile. "You console yourself because you think your character at fault or suspect that others consider it faulty. Is it a true flaw?" He waved his hand at the enveloping cosmos. "In the big cities, perhaps. Out here, no! Out here it is a virtue."

Edham said nothing.

"You are a Selected Granor," Rafel pointed out. "A chosen son born under the sun called Di. Selection is not based on idle whims. It is a careful sifting from the mass of Di's children, a sorting out of the hardy pioneering types, the ones who may be restless, out-of-place, unsocial in the cities.

"But on the loneliest frontiers—*ah!*" He spread expressive hands. "There, they come into their own. They are independent, self-reliant, they do not mourn for the comfort of the crowd."

Edham offered no remark.

"In the College of Granors is a great obelisk bearing eighteen hundred honored names," Rafel mused reminiscently. "I have read them as doubtless you have read them. Every man jack was much like you."

"That is gratifying." Edham offered it with glum humor as if he were laughing inside of himself. His gray eyes met Rafel's again. "Because every man jack is dead."

The nimbus had grown to sky-filling size and had resolved itself to an atmosphere heavily clouded. There was a blaze of crimson light and an awful roaring and a frantic scattering of thunderheads as the spaceship came cautiously through the blanket. A huge saucerlike object, flat in its center, thin at the edge, the ship lowered amid a spume of fire.

Jungle below sent up trunks and fronds and greenly reaching arms. Steam came from it and vegetable warmth and cloying odors mingled with the stench of noisome things rotting in the dark. Living shapes came up with the vapor and the smells, flying, fluttering, flapping away, some dexterously, some with the ungainly awkwardness of creations ill-conceived, some with shrill screechings or harsh cries.

Other entities that could not fly, landbound and raging, slunk or blundered through the undergrowth and howled their hatred at each other and at the monster in the air.

For a little while the vessel hung half a mile above hell, uncountable miles below heaven. The superheated clouds it had thrust aside had now swung back together, closing the gap and sending down a torrent of warm rain.

The downpour made an angry rattle on the spaceship's topside and venturis bellowed and the jungle screamed. More clouds in the distance, black and bloated, were drifting to the aid of their fellows, rumbling from time to time and casting vivid shafts across the sky.

Planetary Surveyor Jolin was in the underbelly blister when Edham joined him. Together they looked down upon the wetness and the tangled green.

"You can blame me for this," said Jolin. "I pronounced it possible. Every time I declare a planet to be possible the decision fidgets within my conscience."

"That is natural," Edham soothed. "Since you will not live long enough to see the end result you must feel the weight of uncertainty. But why worry? No man can do more than his best."

"I have seen failures," Jolin observed moodily. "That is the curse of it. Failures can and do become apparent swiftly enough to damn my judgment. The successes are long-term ones, so long that they will be known only to my grandsons' grandsons."

"It is frustrating," agreed Edham. "What a pity that we have never achieved that time-travel which Kalteniel is so fond of depicting in his visi-scrolls. You could then go forward many centuries and see precisely where you have done well, where you have erred."

"Kalteniel irks me now and again." Jolin shook his head in mild condemnation. "Take his supposedly more plausible stories of space-travel. He dumps people here, dumps them there, keeps them alive in spite of every adverse circumstance, makes them perform all sorts of antics as if the fundamental problem of existence were no problem at all. Life isn't so resilient. It's precarious. It is balanced by margins incredibly fine. If it were otherwise you and I would have different jobs."

Edham offered no comment.

"We are life-forms delicately held within ten million tiny and elusive circumstances," Jolin went on. "One small item, one seemingly insignificant feature, can create the bias that kills. On one otherwise innocent world it is the existence in its atmosphere of an exceedingly minute trace of gas with accumulative properties.

"On another it is an unsuspected undetected virus in the water." He glanced at the other. "A few Di-born plants grew erratically but clung to life on Theta Ten. Far more would not. They lacked only a vague trace of copper in the soil."

"Who can measure the unknown?" said Edham.

"And the same is true in reverse." Jolin nodded toward the jungle. "In the Di-system some of those plants might flourish, others might contrive to exist by changing form to suit slightly different conditions, but many might wither and die for lack of one titanium atom in each ten thousand molecules of soil—or for lack of something else equally dispersed."

"I have been told all this," Edham reminded. "I do not fear the death of metabolic imbalance. By all accounts it comes insidiously, without pain." Cold-eyed, he studied the world beneath.

"But I do dislike the notion of involuntary change. Admittedly one survives when gradually altered by Nature to fit the new framework but one cannot be sure of the manner of one's change or the picture it presents in the end. There are so many possibilities, some of them repulsive."

"Yes." Jolin admitted it solemnly. "It is that I would find the most repugnant—alteration out of recognition. It is death which is not death. It is severance from one's own kind plus the torment of being something strange and new amid older unchanged life-forms that hate the strange and new. It is utter loneliness." He shuddered without shame. "I could not bear it."

"I could," said Edham, "if absolutely necessary." He paused, added in the same flat voice. "For a while."

Rafel changed the subject by appearing at the blister. "That is a fair sample down below. Most of the planet is the same. It spawns ferociously." He cupped his chin in his hand, regarded the tangle of life for a while, then said, "We cannot sit down in any old place. We'll search the world and make a landing in the most attractive spot."

Edham said, "Or the least unattractive."

He did not smile when Rafel looked at him as if striving to discern what lay behind the mask. He was accustomed to the long penetrating gaze of those large eyes. As always it was an attempted estimating—and none can weigh the soul. So he met Rafel's questing orbs with a tantalizing blankness that provided inward amusement for himself but did not irritate the other.

"Perhaps you are right," conceded Rafel. He shrugged and went away.

Presently the venturis lengthened their blasts to a multitude of fire-spears. The jungle leaves swayed and cowered while unseen forms beneath them sent up a cacophony of noise.

The ship soared a mile higher, moved forward. The clouds stabbed it with hot forks.

2. SPHERE OF WRATH

Paralleling the equator on a route where the subtropics merged into the temperate zone, the Disian vessel traveled at sedate pace. There was no need for great speed, no urgency. Accurate observation of the land was the prime purpose; it was not possible to find sanctuary at high velocity. So the ship roamed on, circumnavigating the world four times while its crew watched and waited for a haven of gentleness in this domain of savagery.

It was a sphere of wrath, hot, violent, and seething with the sperm of a million things, great and small. Its clouds hung black and belly-bloated. Its trees climbed upon the bodies of their forbears as they fought hugely toward the blanketed sun.

Its animal forms were drinkers of blood, eaters of meat, feeders upon all other kinds, upon their own kind and upon their own young. They battled and copulated with an appalling frenzy, howling in labor, screaming in death, and giving up their offal.

There was a horrid, pseudolife even beneath the earth. In certain places the surface crawled and rolled and heaved while great fissures opened and steam burst forth. A river bent down into a hole and was spewed out boiling.

Topless mountains volleyed meteor-streams that curved through the clouds and fired the jungle. The quivering surface emitted tremendous groans and the river hissed deafeningly and the mountains cannonaded again and again and again.

The atmosphere was heavy, thick, moist, and somehow enervating and invigorating at one and the same time. It was invisibly striated with smells—the odors of wood-rot, wet leaves, sulfur, steam, crushed funguses, burning bark, cooling lava, and decay.

To search all this for a resting place was to seek a lesser hell and that they found on the fourth time around. There was a raised valley between rounded hills with slow-moving yellow rivers flowing at either side. The valley was broad and large—the hills silent, without inward fires. No steam arose from vents in the solidly founded ground.

The trees, shrubs, vines, and creepers were all present together with the hot-blooded things that hunted beneath them. The same smells came up, the same noises. But purely by contrast with other parts of the world the valley seemed a little more sheltered, a little more stable, a little less racked with the strains of competing life.

Lowering his vessel, Captain Rafel took it along the valley with assault-beams blazing at full intensity. Every living thing beneath promptly resolved itself to an ash so fine that much hung suspended while some slowly settled.

The trees and the tangles beneath the trees and the monsters who lurked in the tangles all became ash. From one end of the valley to the other, all ash. From hill-base to hill-base, nothing but thin unsoiled stalks of ash quavering like newborn ghosts. The very ground was sterilized to a depth of twenty feet.

They ripped a cloud and rain came down and laid the reluctant dust. Over a smaller central area of the valley they beam-baked the mud so formed and converted it to the hard cake of an emergency landing place. On this the ship sat, touching soil lightly, letting its weight be felt gradually and forming an earthly cup in which to rest.

The crew emerged, six hundred strong. They knew exactly what to do and needed no orders. It was a familiar task—they had planted a Granor many times before.

Dragging out their machines, the wall-builders began to cut huge stone blocks from the hills, to move them along and around the valley, to mount them one upon another and fuse them together. Heavily armed, the guard squads patrolled beyond them near the burned rim of the jungle and kept hostile shapes at bay. Well inside the walls the prefab-erectors busied themselves assembling the sections of a small, compact house.

The biological party divided itself, extracted from the ship's cargo space a load of Disian seeds, tubers, cuttings, shoots, and baby plants. These they unwrapped with loving care and proceeded to set in the alien earth according to a scheme conceived long in the past and executed time and time again in places spread across half creation's span.

Rafel hung around, watching. The wall arose and a raucous antagonism beyond the wall was quieted with a distant blast and the momentary shine of a beam. The house swung together, every addition making it more like a house. A quadruple row of tiny green growths already stretched from his feet to the base of the eastward wall. More plants, larger and darker, were being set beyond them.

"This performance, I presume, has the boredom of repetition," suggested Edham, joining him.

"Not at all. I look at today—but I see tomorrow." He glanced at the other, his eyes bright, luminous. "What do *you* see?"

Edham thought a moment, said, "I am given to visualize a few lines from that ancient saga called *The Granor of Theta Ten.* Doubtless they are familiar to you." He carried on and recited them, speaking with a peculiar lack of emotion that somehow lent point to the words.

> "They labor'd without rest or cease
> To make the land more fair,
> And builded him a place of peace
> Five thousand cubits square."

"The verse is appropriate," said Rafel. "It cannot be otherwise since the technique has remained the same."

"But not the tomorrows?"

"Not the tomorrows," Rafel admitted with some reluctance. "Nature will not have us everywhere."

"Nor have us exactly as we are."

"Sometimes." Rafel felt that he was being pushed where he had no desire to go. "And sometimes not." He counterpushed with a proposal. "Come with me and explore beyond the walls."

"It is a useful idea," said Edham, betraying no hint of humor. "One should know one's neighbors."

Getting two pairs of scout-wings from the ship they struggled into the harness, each tightening the other's buckles. The wings swept white and gleaming from their shoulders as they switched on the tiny propulsors and soared. There was a certain trickiness in using this personal mode of flight, each user's pleasure being proportionate to his own dexterity.

Crossing the northward wall, already man-height and still growing, they floated wide-winged above the jungle's trees. Their closer approach made visible many things formerly hidden though others lurked lower and remained unseen. There were great worms in some treetops, sinuous, sliding, many-colored creatures that writhed up the trunks and lay along the branches and stared with beady unblinking eyes. There were other entities, barrel-bodied, beetle-browed, that swung from limb to limb and yelled at the winged forms above.

"A-a-ah! *A-a-ah!*"

And from faraway came the answering call of their fellows, red-eyed and toothy, "A-a-ah!"

At one point where a rocky outcrop made a space of barrenness in the warring vegetation, there slumbered an eater too gigantic to be eaten. It was a slate-gray monstrosity, stupidly evil of face, massive of body, with a high serration running along its back. Its balloonlike belly shrank and filled as it breathed and its tail curved away through tree-gap after tree-gap. With tiny eyes closed it snored in a manner that shook the shrubs before its nose.

Rafel had swooped daringly close to get a better look at the slumberer and as he curved upward on wide-set wings, coming low over a tree, a many-hued worm stabbed half its length at him from where it lay concealed in the foliage.

So much swifter was his own reaction that he had time only to glimpse the soft elastic mouth and darting tongue before his beam sliced the thing in three. The parts fell near to the slate-gray sleeper and continued to jerk around with raw ends. The sleeper opened one eye, stared with dull disinterest at the squirming pieces, grunted deep down, and closed the eye again.

"That," remarked Rafel, unruffled, "is another item for my collection of cosmic incongruities—ambition in a worm."

Edham said, "Sometimes I wonder whether anyone else has us similarly rated."

"When we meet them—if ever we meet them—we shall not try to get them down our gullets," promised Rafel.

"What else shall we do?"

"We will allow *them* to swallow *us.*" Rafel gave him a sly smile. "We have never found any difficulty in permitting the unavoidable."

"Neither shall I." He did not smile back. "In a way I shall have complete control of this world—I shall sit upon it and permit everything." Edham deftly tilted against a side-current, swung straight. "Let us view this river."

The westward waterway over which they skimmed was the broader of the two at either side of the valley. Slow-moving and sullen, its depths were yellow and full of life. Small shapes occasionally leaped from its undersurface to escape larger pursuers and now and again the big ones jumped amid a shower of drops to avoid the monstrous. Logs floated downstream past other half-submerged things that strove to look like logs.

A black hook-beaked flyer fell from the clouds, coming silently on broad leathery surfaces, and plunged at Rafel while he was studying a log that had reptilian eyes. Edham sliced its head off in midair. The body shot straight to the water but did not touch it.

Great jaws came out of the river and caught it at the last moment, then sank from sight. A few lazy bubbles arose. The log which had drawn Rafel's attention split at one end and yawned, exposing many teeth.

"Here life is a phase—death an incident," Edham commented. "What a world!"

"To face alone," added Rafel.

Edham laughed without showing it.

3. SANCTUARY

The encampment was complete in every detail on the fortieth day. Its walls stood a hundred cubits high by ten cubits thick, solid, jointless, four-square, without a break except for one armorplate door in the center of the side that faced south. The living house was finished and equipped.

The instrument shed stood near it, the toolshed adjoined it, and the transparent house for incubating plants was right behind. Apart from that occupied by the spaceship, the rest of the area within the walls was a parade ground for Disian plants in companies and battalions.

Rafel had a schematic diagram spread across the table inside the house and his long slender forefinger shifted from point to point as he spoke.

"As you know your main task will be to keep check on all this. Every plant-section must be covered not less than once in five days. Every stage of growth must be carefully noted. Any departure from the norm must be recorded in the fullest possible detail. Any failure to develop must likewise be entered.

"Take special note of comparative rates of progress for they are important. If the hard-fruited trees do well while the soft-fruiting bushes do not, we want to know in what way they differ, item by item, for such information is invaluable."

"I have had all this at the training college," Edham remarked. "We may never know why some Di-plants flourish in alien conditions while others do not, but it is sufficient to learn which can survive."

"Exactly," agreed Rafel. "Where enough of them cling to existence, so can we. It is essential to know in advance how many can live and of what kinds. That is real knowledge." He mused a little while over the graph. "I find it galling that we are reduced to animal status by one dismal fact—that any world can resist our settlement by resisting our digestive juices."

"Kalteniel has the problem solved. His characters are never guilty of any animal function. Would that I were one of them."

"That brings me to the most emphatic point," Rafel's great eyes looked straight and steadily into his. "This also is something you've had before, had it until you're sick of it, but before I go it must be said again. That is the strictest rule of Granor-planting— the Granor must not be left without being told again. Until such time as we return you will subsist solely upon foods of Di-origin."

"I know, I know."

"The stores we leave will last far beyond your fifth harvest—if there *are* any harvests. You are free to eke out your preserved supplies with fresh stuff grown within these walls—if any does grow." His voice grew sharp, authoritative. "But of the foods native to this world you must not eat!"

His long schooling at the College of Granors made itself felt as Edham squared his shoulders and obediently echoed, "Of native fruits I must not eat."

"Remember that—always remember," Rafel emphasized. "The food natural to this earth may be quite innocuous. Possibly you might wax fat upon it, more so than upon Di-foods. If so we are lucky indeed. But the time for testing the matter is not yet.

"Be satisfied that already you are breathing alien air of unknown potentialities, that you are continually subjected to the rays of an alien sun with hidden powers, that you remain within alien gravitational and magnetic fields—and the total long-term effects of all these are pure guesswork until such time as you have eliminated the guesses.

"So do not be venturesome or impatient. Remember that

enough is enough and rest content with the hazards already imposed upon you."

"Do you suspect me of excessive zeal?" asked Edham.

"I have no suspicions—but I do have memories."

"Of what?"

"Of many things." He hesitated, went on. "My mind holds vivid pictures I would give much to forget. For example, I see the Granor of the unnamed world near Arka. He suffered unanticipated disaster to his stores, became hungry and thirsty long before our return. And when we came back—"

"Go on," urged Edham.

"I remember his lonely distorted shape crawling into the dark as our ship lifted and cut him off forever from his kind. What he had was terrible, incurable, and contagious. So he crept humbly into the dark and waited for the deeper darkness of the end. His name is upon the obelisk."

"Where mine will never be," capped Edham. "I shall live and grow fat out of sheer spite."

Rafel said severely, "There is nothing funny about it. There is nothing funny."

"I am not jesting. I am trying only to reassure you."

At that moment Jolin came along to bid farewell and Rafel said to him, "*He* is attempting to comfort *me.*"

"It would be more logical if I were the subject of his solicitude," returned Jolin morbidly. "The weight upon his spirit is equaled by the weight upon my mind."

"Did you choose that unnamed world near Arka?" Edham asked him.

"No, thank the broad heavens! That one was not my mistake."

"Neither will this one be."

"Now he's comforting *you.*" Rafel spread his hands to indicate helplessness. "What can one do with a person who insists on giving what he is supposed to receive?"

Gazing at the sky Edham suggested, "Leave him to his fearsome task of lazing around and permitting the unavoidable."

Jolin swallowed, said uneasily, "It's not going to be quite that." Then he changed his mind, hurriedly finished. "Farewell!" He shook hands and went, his features worried.

"He's somewhat sensitive for a planetary surveyor," opined Edham, gazing after him.

"He has seen too much," Rafel corrected. "As I have done." He, too, shook hands, returned to the ship, paused in its open lock to wag a warning finger and utter a final, "Remember!"

The lock closed. Edham backed well away from the venturis.

Presently the tubes spouted fire and dust flew around and a great wave of warmth went through the walled area. Voices beyond the walls set up a chorus of hoots and screams.

Slowly the vessel rose, teetering and repeatedly correcting its plane until it had gained stabilizing speed. The lone watcher stood there while it was reduced to a tiny shining circle entering a cloud. It vanished into a black belly. He sighed and sat upon a handy rock.

"I am the Granor of the Green World, a seed of Di planted to discover just what happens to me. I am the lowliest tool of a superagronomy, the test-piece, the fleshly nurseling among a million vegetable ones. If I live here my kind will live here. If I change my kind will change. If I die my kind will die. For better or for worse I am the Granor of the Green World."

Beyond the walls, "A-a-ah! *A-a-ah!*"

Of course the first night was the worst. The felon caged for life can hear and sometimes see evidence of the workaday world outside. The shipwrecked survivor upon a deserted island can scan the horizon hopefully, week by week, tempor by tempor. But one with an entire planet to himself knows an isolation that cannot be more complete. The Granor is alone, utterly alone.

He lay on his air-cushioned bunk within the prefabricated house while the world's gloom thickened toward midnight and sleep refused to come. His mind insisted upon busying itself with calculations of tempors and velocities which would enable it to place the approximate position of the departing vessel.

His eyes kept opening to stare at the pearls of condensation shining on the ceiling. He could have cleared these away at one turn of a handy switch but he had not noticed them because he was looking at an imaginary spaceship. All the time his ears were straining to catch outside noises, of which there were plenty.

There had been a peculiar hush when the hidden sun went down and twilight came and coldness flowed in. The daytime noises had subsided—the night howlers had been slow to appear. Now, as the earth turned farther around from the warmth, the hairy things that shouted, "A-a-ah!" were silent and other creatures with different voices built up their own characteristic din.

For almost a quarter tempor two of them—huge and invisible —fought with shrill screams and much flapping of batwings right over his roof. In the end one landed upon the roof, gasped and bubbled awhile, made many scratching scrabbling sounds before it took off and vanished into the dark. It left an acrid smell as of strange blood.

Eastward, just outside the wall, a pair of unknown shapes of unknown tonnage battled tremendously, emitting piercing whistles at intervals and causing the faintest of tremors in the ground. Edham pressed a hand on the floor to sense the quivers, slight but discernible.

To cap the rest the wind built itself up to a loud moan that sounded as if the world itself were registering its agony. Distant trees thrashed and great limbs broke loose and tattered objects flew through the air.

The moan went up a hundred cycles where the airstream hit the wall, dropped lower as it sped across the planted area. Clouds rushed close-packed across the sky, seeming to be held in space while the earth rotated independently.

As the tempors crept nearer to morning Edham dozed without really sleeping. He had fragmentary dreams of the great city of Dise upon the planet also called Dise beneath the sun named Di. At no time had he scorned the city, yet he had failed to enjoy it as others had enjoyed it.

Now he wanted it. They had warned him at the college that it is natural to desire lost things when it is too late. He must conquer the yearning—but he wanted the city.

Dawn found him heavy-eyed and restless. The hurricane had gone, the heatmeter's hand already had begun to move along its scale, and the same bellowers were back with their sounds. Taking the top package from the nearest pile in his ground-level stockroom he opened it, ate a four-course breakfast.

The torn wrappings lay across his knees while he ate and he could see the lettering—*Sunup Meal 1.* The sight did not please him despite his long training. This irritation was no more than evidence of an incongruity which for centuries had bedeviled the worthy tutors at the College of Granors, namely, that trainees are selected as natural pioneers—and men who are natural pioneers do not take kindly to regimentation.

Thus he scowled at the lettering because he knew that when the correct tempor chimed he would open *Noon Meal 1* and later *Sundown Meal 1* and tomorrow *Sunup Meal 2.*

He was being fed prepared fodder at prescribed times exactly like an exhibit in the zoo.

Finishing, he got mild satisfaction out of burning the wrappings with their offending inscription. He went out to inspect the Di-nursery, hoping for work. Already there was a little for him to do. Limbs and pieces of bark and strips of frond and thousands of leaves ripped from outer trees lay scattered all over the place.

Patiently he gathered this rubbish into the bare circle where the ship had squatted and beamed it to ash. That filled in his morning and after the noon meal he spent a couple of tempors tending plants that had suffered slight damage overnight.

A short time before sunset he got out his wings, had an awkward job with the harness, which was not easy to fit singlehanded. The tiny propulsor drove him to the top of the wall, where he strolled along its broad flat crest with pinions folded and gleaming.

The toothy ones in the jungle snarled and gibbered in anger at the unearthly sight.

At a point near the corner where the wall right-angled northward a local objector waddled out of its hiding place, came right to the base of the impassable rampart, and stood directly below him. Staring upward with red eyes that burned beneath projecting brows, it drummed resoundingly upon its chest, made deep grunting sounds, and drooled saliva.

Its attitude was challenging, an unmistakable invitation to come down and settle once for all the question of who was the superior life-form. Edham answered it by pausing in his walk, giving glare for glare, and laughing inside of himself until the creature foamed with fury.

At the height of its rage he calmly spread his wings, glided within the walls and out of its sight.

4. LONELY VIGIL

There was little sleep that night either. He made a fitting end to an imperfect day by consuming *Sundown Meal 1*, recited his brief notes into his autorecorder, had a short time with a pictorialized story taken from his small library, then composed himself upon his bunk.

Soon the rain came. It sounded as if someone high above were throwing away an unwanted ocean. He had never heard anything like it. The skies thundered and the ground thundered and the jungle bent over. There was alarm in his mind comparable to the noise in his ears for he had visions of tender sucklings being bombarded out of existence.

Kalteniel would have countered this menace by shielding the whole area under a force-screen. A Granor has no such means available since he must rely upon what exists in reality rather than in the imagination.

Disian science had produced effective power-beams, which could perform work or be concentrated destructively, but there was no known way in which to spread a beam without loss of power to the point of impotence. In grim fact there was nothing to discipline the torrent but the pumps.

His restlessness soon turned to action. Getting a transparent waterproof sheath from a nearby hook he pulled it over himself like an upended sack, went out with his powerful handlight shining through the protecting material. The rain battered at him furiously and ran over the sheath in such a heavy stream that it blurred his vision.

Despite this he made his way to the instrument shed wherein were his power plant and the pumps which were connected with the area's irrigation system. The squat heavy atomic engine needed no starting for it was built to run continuously until due for replacement in several years' time. He put the six pumps into operation one by one, letting the engine take up the load in stages.

Very soon their joint output meter registered eight aquabulks per millitempor, an accurate indication of the great quantity pouring from the clouds. He remained in the shed for part of the night, nursing the pumps, watching the meters, and listening to the downpour.

When eventually outside sounds were replaced by an amazing calm and the output meter showed a drop, he stopped the pumps, returned to the house, voiced a complaint into his autorecorder before lying down on his bunk.

"I can switch from the house everything switchable excepting the pumps. This world being what it is, remote control of those would be a convenience."

That was telling them. At some future time on some similar planet a Granor would be able to cope with a flood at the touch of a hand. They might even arrange it for *him* the trip after next—if he were still living at that time. If he were still . . . Slumber stepped in and drove the speculation from his mind.

Three weeks of backbreaking toil were needed to make good the damage. He finished with sore fingers and a crick in the spine. Had all the growths suffered he could not have coped in time to save them. But the bulbs and tubers had squatted undisturbed while the baby trees had survived the overnight ordeal.

Only the smallest, most delicate surface plants had been washed out and the major part of these he had been able to restore. Perhaps 10 percent were beyond rescue. At least there had been no further disaster while the job was in hand.

With the midday task complete, he bathed, gave his aching back some radiant heat treatment, consumed *Noon Meal 22*, dictated his notes to the autorecorder.

"Sectors ten to eighteen have been reset. The loss numbers about one in ten. All other sectors remain rooted. The six end rows in sector nine are turning from green to yellow and their leaves show first signs of shriveling.

"The whole of the trees in twenty-four to forty are advancing at above normal rate, appear healthy and vigorous and seem likely to grow much larger than their usual size. There is nothing to report about remaining sectors."

Gazing absently at the mouthpiece into which he had spoken, he thought awhile, added, "I have examined myself in the mirror and see nothing unusual except that I look physically tired. To date my sleep has been inadequate. My weight has gone down by one-twentieth. Doubtless these things will correct themselves in due course."

The listening machine got no more than that, the bare facts. At the college his brevity often had been deplored. They liked garrulous Granors who filled in the picture with a wealth of detail. It did not matter that the babblers were compounding an unnatural situation by talking to themselves, using spool after spool of recording tape to hear their own voices.

According to the tutors, much information of great value had been sorted out from such seemingly inconsequential chatter. Edham did not feel that he had yet got to the self-conversational stage or that he would ever get to it. So far as he was concerned, when the time came to pray for a voice it must be another's voice, different, new.

A full day of lounging in the library, watching selections from pictorialized books, served to refresh him and take away the aches. The Disian breed recovers swiftly, is resilient. That is to say, the fleshly Disians.

The vegetable ones varied for no known reason. Thus the yellowing plants in sector nine turned yellower and slowly released their frail hold on life while the burgeoning *bodhi* trees in twenty-four to forty continued to progress at rates almost detectable between successive sundowns.

He took samples of the dying ones, dissecting them, subjecting thin slivers of cross section to microscopic inspection, analyzing the roots and the dirt in which they had been buried.

Either the cause of the casualties was something too minute and elusive to identify with what he had available—or more probably it was beyond identification in the light of present-day knowledge. It might well be seated in improperly understood plant-psychology, the mysterious reasons why one growth made itself at home while another died rather than endure the strangeness.

What little he did discover went into the notes. Characteristically all hazard and speculation were left out. The bare facts as usual. On the day the last member of the six rows was definitely dead and all the growths in sector twelve began to show first signs of surrendering the battle, he recorded the matter impassively.

Two months later, after he had beamed to dust the faded remnants of sector twelve, he sickened himself. The temperature of his blood arose, he perspired profusely, felt weak and muddle-minded. His digestive system went haywire.

Frequent doses of the likeliest drugs had no effect. The disease put him on his back, too exhausted to weed the acres or carry out inspections, make notes or do anything else than let it run its course—to recovery or to the end.

Between spells of delirium he listened for outer disaster, wondering whether—if necessity proved dire enough—he could lift and thumb his attack-beam or crawl to the pumps. Experimentally he made two attempts to begin the crawl, failed both times.

He was many five-day reports overdue when eventually the illness relaxed its hold. The rain had come almost every night and sometimes by day but never in a menacing torrent. The plants still stood undisturbed. He was alive though thin and weak. There was much for which to be thankful.

The autorecorder got a curt uncomplaining description of his sickness, its symptoms, its progress. He did not bother to emphasize that he was breathing alien air, drinking distilled alien water but eating Disian food, that therefore the food was not to blame.

Let the machine's future listeners draw their own conclusions—that was their job. His was to be the subject of the operation and tell how it felt, stage by stage, even though the knife sank deep. The Granor is a seed of his race. It is helpful to plant a seed that can talk, even though laconically.

In the third year, when the *bodhi* trees fruited tremendously and became smothered with their typical golden balls of succulence, the *ahbodhi* trees produced a lesser load of distorted discolored objects that were repulsively sour to the taste.

The two kinds were related, different varieties of the same species, yet one had spawned and the other miscarried. One had mastered circumstances, the other been mastered by them—almost like people.

Edham got a thought out of that, a dark suspicion. He did not record it because it was not yet a self-evident fact. But the notion kept circling tentatively in his mind, without hardening. It gained strength nearer the year's end when ten allied breeds of bushes produced crops as eatable as any on their home territory—but at different dates, in different sizes, shapes, and colors.

All tasted the same. All gave the same responses to his perhaps inadequate analysis. All provided a welcome freshness for his digestive juices and nourished him to the same extent. Yet all were different.

"If I live my kind can live. If I live my kind will settle here, build new cities, a new world. They will have natural increase—but will that increase be natural? Will their children be the same?"

No answer—no way of telling. It was entirely his own mystery, as unsatisfactory and frustrating as Jolin's sad puzzle. So he held it in restraint without putting it aside, and gladly ate of such of the crop as was eatable. He had consumed *Sunup Meal 1100* already and was more than eager for a change of diet.

"I am now going out of count with the packaged food," he recorded, "by reason of using part of the crop. There are yet no signs of anything seeding apart from the usual influx of local weeds. The crop has to be protected not only from these but also from periodic attacks of flying things, occurring always during daylight tempors, never at night.

"So far I have killed about four hundred raiders and lost little. There has been nothing to show why night-time flyers are not similarly attracted. I have examined myself and appear the same except that my color remains heightened."

Propagation eventually followed the same course as the fruiting, delays where there had been delays, intervals matching intervals, differences where there had been differences. Something in the rays of the concealed sun or the soil or the rain or the air was creating new varieties and thrusting a subtle wedge between existing ones to force them further apart.

Nevertheless he noted every item, patiently set the seed, drove off the winged monsters whose bellies yearned for the grains as much as for the fruits. Aware by training that what he had eaten of this, his first crop, though of Di-origin, was alien grown, he watched himself more frequently for secondary effects. There were none visible and when one did come it caught him unknowing, unsuspicious.

He was winged for one of his boredom-breaking strolls around the wall and a pleasant exchange of insults with his neighbors when a black thing came down from the sky, intent on plunder. Many a seed was being coddled by the ash of such a visitor but this time he did not wait for it to land before dissolving it in smoke.

A sudden unfamiliar feeling swept irresistibly over him. His veins swelled, his eyes blazed, he spread his wings and bulleted upward to meet it. The creature died halfway down from a cloud and as he beamed it he heard a yell of triumph in his own voice.

Sitting on top of the wall, pinions folded, the midjoints pointing high above his shoulders, legs dangling down on the jungle side, he pondered the phenomenon. It was unwonted bellicosity. That any Disian can display belligerence was not in itself surprising. No kind can settle a thousand worlds without taking the offensive whenever the occasion demanded it. The point was that he had displayed uncontrolled animosity at the drop of a meal wrapper without real need to do so. It was lack of self-discipline. It was unreason.

The subject stewed in his mind a full tempor, during which he gave grave consideration to the possible state of his liver, his gall bladder, his kidneys or, alternatively, the subtler effect upon his mentality of three years of isolation.

Before he had finished his speculations the chest-drummer or its twin brother shambled out of the jungle shadows, stood directly below him, glared up red-eyed and roared its hate. On other days when this had happened he'd contented himself with an answering mock-glare guaranteed to make the creature put over an interesting exhibition of animal frenzy. This time his own eyes blazed. He bent forward—and spat upon it.

5. THE SOUND OF A VOICE

For a considerable time afterward he was broody, introspective, frequently consulted the mirror. There was no physical change that he could pin down as more than imaginary. The hair on his head seemed thicker, more wiry, harder to subdue. His eyes held a constant hint of aggressiveness—or so he fancied. He could not be sure.

Sheer self-discipline kept him away from the walls while he concentrated upon the plants, his progress reports, and the potentially alterable phenomenon of his own body. On four occasions he bit his lips as he beamed a flying raider, coolly, carefully, with determined disregard of that part of him which screamed for closer battle.

Nothing of this went into the autorecorder, not a jot, not a hint. All the transformations he could perceive were duly noted but not those only half seen or dimly suspected.

With the end of winter and the coming of spring the rising tide of his blood swamped his restraint. Day after day, tempor after tempor, he had paced his enclosure from one end to the other, to and fro, to and fro, like a caged animal. The skies retained their everlasting gray but the fresher air was cool and warm by turns. Putting on his wings he soared to the wall, strolled along its crest.

A slate-colored colossus, resembling that monstrous sleeper of long ago, was standing close to the base on the southern side and rubbing its back against the stone to scrape off unseeable parasites. The process created loud rasping sounds and sent up an odor of pungent hide.

Standing directly above it and looking down into the smell, Edham felt his mouth open of its own accord and he bawled an ugly name at it. The monster ceased its scratching, looked stupidly around in every direction but upward. He called it again. It discovered him, focused eyes incongruously small in so tremendous a head.

Releasing an angry snort of such power that Edham felt the wind of it many cubits above, the thing reared itself against the wall, tried to claw him down, found him out of reach by more than a man-length. It gave another snort of imbecilic disappointment, fell back to ground with a rousing thud. Its stench was strong, acrid.

For the first time since his almost forgotten trip with Rafel the winged Edham left the enclosure. With no thought of rules and regulations and temporarily forgetful of past training he spread his pinions and dived off the wall—outward. His bold swoop carried him straight across the other's serrated back, his feet touching it in passing. It twisted with twenty-ton clumsiness, clawed at him, and missed. Behemoth swiping a wasp.

Edham landed lightly in thick grass. His opponent snuffled eagerly and charged. He soared again at the very last instant, his eyes afire. The thing tossed its head as its own momentum carried it beneath him, touched a foot. He beamed away the tip of its tail as it passed. The jungle was full of spectators, howling and hooting at the pair of them. The treetops quivered and gave forth noises.

Coming down into the grass once more he whirled around in readiness for another charge. His lungs were big, his breath came fast, and some strange appetite within him was satiating itself upon he knew not what.

The slate-gray nightmare had lumbered around in a small circle, snuffling all the while. Finding him, it fixed tiny eyes upon him, expanded its nostrils to keep his scent and launched itself forward. The ponderous beat of its oncoming feet resounded far through the ground and vibrated up the trees to where the hidden audience stank and gibbered.

With wings folded Edham waited for the creature to be almost upon him. He remained stock still until he could see the wetness upon a huge misshapen tooth. Then he sprang aside. Too much tonnage carried the other on, unable to swerve. He rayed away another section of its tail.

By now the peculiar hunger within him had gone. He opened

wings to soar, found himself anchored. A weirdly patterned worm in the undergrowth had coiled itself around one ankle. It had beady unblinking eyes that watched him fixedly as coil after coil came slithering through the grass.

The slate-gray monster came back thunderously, cheered on by the crowd. Edham chopped the worm at random, arose sluggishly with the severed portion still clinging as if unconscious of its loss. The slate-gray monster was almost upon him.

For an awful moment he thought he was not going to make it. Power poured through the propulsor and his wings swept wide while the beady-eyed thing clung raw-ended and tried to summon its missing length.

Dragging it with him he went up, frantically shaking his leg. It dropped off barely in time to save him and sudden release of the burden caused him to shoot skyward almost from under the twenty-tonner's nose.

This close escape eased the peculiar gnawing inside him. Gaining the wall he sat on its top, drew long relieved breaths and perspired. There were queer disconnected thoughts running through his mind, the inconsequential notions of an uneasy sleep.

"Life is beautiful because of death, like light in the darkness. To battle is to live and to live is to be not-dead. I must fight or be dead. I must live. A Granor must live."

He looked down upon his recent opponent, now snorting around defeatedly and echoed in bemused manner. "A Granor? What is a Granor?"

Then he stood up and yelled at the jungle, "I am Man! Look, I am Man!"

The ship's return was like the occurrence of a major miracle. True, after most of six years it should have been expected or at least hoped for. But six years can be six tempors or as many centuries, according to the circumstances. By the time it came back it was to Edham little more than the figment of a half-forgotten dream.

He stiffened with incredulity when the clouds were blown apart and the vessel appeared. A multitude of emotions electrified his being while he watched the shining thing come down. A conflicting mixture of surly resentment and ecstatic anticipation took hold of him as though somehow he had become two individuals in one body, each reacting in its own way. The vision of the ship had precipitated a sort of spiritual schizophrenia.

Rafel was first out. His big luminous eyes alive with pleasure, he seized Edham's hand, winced at the power of its grasp.

"Here we are, not merely up to time, but early." His hands went to either side of the other's shoulders, patting them, estimating their width. "My, but you look splendid! You're bigger, broader, heavier, and it's all muscle. This place must suit you. Jolin will be overjoyed."

"Jolin," murmured Edham, looking around.

"He's not with us this trip," Rafel went on. "No point in him judging the same planet twice. He has gone with Razudiel to look over a new system beyond Neo-Dise."

"So?" said Edham, staring at the ship.

"Well, aren't you pleased to see us?" Rafel regarded him more carefully. "You never did say much but now you seem almost speechless." His smile followed quickly, full of sympathy. "I guess you're a little overwhelmed by company and the sound of a voice."

"The sound of a voice," repeated Edham, speaking as if from far away.

Taking his arm, Rafel led him toward the ship. "The first part of your task—the stage of silence—is ended. The worst is over. The next will be shorter and sweeter—if the medicos pass you."

"If," said Edham.

"There seems little likelihood that they won't," encouraged Rafel. "I have never seen a Granor looking in such excellent trim."

"I am not fattening myself for the kill," Edham assured him. "And what is more I am laughing." He nodded toward the wall. "As I have laughed at them, loud, long, and often." He paused, licking his lips, added with strange satisfaction, "They do not like my laughing."

Sobering, Rafel became thoughtful as he took Edham into the ship, handed him over to the medicos.

There were six of these examiners, tall, coldly professional, white-coated. Stripping him they went over him cell by cell, made him breathe down a tube so that the contents of his lungs bubbled into an inverted bottle, took blood samples from various parts of him, took hair and nail clippings, even a skin section.

They rayed him, studied his insides upon a fluorescent screen from four different angles, discussed his spleen in incomprehensible jargon. They photographed the lining of his stomach with a button camera at the end of a flexible tube, used a powerful light beam and a magnaglass to examine his tongue, throat, and epiglottis. They asked a hundred questions.

"You have a seed molar. Did the first one expel itself in normal manner or did you have to extract it?"

"When did you first observe the appearance of body hair?"

"Did you make a note of it in your autorecorder?"

"Did it appear simultaneously in all places where now evident, or did it start in one place and spread from there?"

He asked, "Does hair matter?"

"Most certainly."

"Why?"

They became evasive. "Hair upon the body is not a normal feature of our kind—and every change matters."

"So I *have* changed?"

The chief examiner said, "Look, everyone alters from birth to death."

"As *I* have?"

"This is a routine investigation and not a debate," reminded the examiner. "Leave it to us to decide which physical phenomena are significant and which are not."

Edham said, "Don't bellow at me."

"I am not bellowing. I spoke in perfectly ordinary tones." He gestured to an assistant. "Have a look at his ears."

They went over the ears, presently put down upon a form the words, *Aural sense preternaturally sharpened.*

A bit later, "How did you acquire those scars on the calf muscle of your right leg?"

He stared down at the leg, twisting himself to see the marks. "Fighting a wild thing. It clawed me."

They were tempted to ask why he had not beamed it before it got that near but refrained. Such questions were for the psychoanalysts.

In due time the latter had their turn and put it to him, "Is your hand-projector still energized and efficient?"

"Yes."

"Why didn't you use it?"

"I please myself. I am an individual."

"We have not the slightest desire to challenge your rights as such," soothed the other. "We are merely interested in your reasons for doing whatever you saw fit to do. We cannot and would not force you to give an explanation."

"You'd have a hot time trying," assured Edham, involuntarily tightening his fist.

The expert was very observant. Calmly he regarded the fist, estimated the degree of muscular contraction, the amount of mental tension behind it. Edham forced the hand to open, the fingers to relax. The other was not deceived.

"Have you been beyond the walls?"

"Yes."

"Have you actually landed outside the walls?"

"Yes."

"Often?"

"Yes."

"Knowing that it was contrary to instructions?"

"Yes."

"And dangerous?"

Edham said nothing.

The expert wrote down a couple of little squiggles meaning, *Co-operative with reluctance—but truthful,* before he went off on another tack.

"Members of the crew are checking over the state of the plantation and condition of the ramparts. Beyond the wall they have found a bloodthirsty-looking creature, thick-furred, with striped markings. It is dead. It appears to have expired recently, in mid-spring, claws extended, mouth open."

He stared at Edham, who remained silent. He placed an object on his desk. "It was pierced by four of those."

The object was a long slender arrow.

"It is well-made," commented the expert. "Skillfully constructed with a needle-sharp metal head. The bow from which it came must have been powerful."

"It was," Edham acknowledged indifferently.

"Did you shoot this creature from the wall top or were you in the outside grass?"

"The grass."

"A bow, a bow and arrows," commented the other, poking the pointed and feathered shaft away from him. "He uses a primitive type of weapon in lieu of a modern beam-projector." His gaze lifted, he surveyed Edham curiously. "It would be nice to learn the logic on which such a preference is based."

Edham said, "The targets are just as primitive. They struggle with what they've got, what they can make themselves."

"I see." The leading questioner glanced at his silently listening fellows, returned his attention to Edham. "You cannot manufacture a projector which needs all the craft of an experienced armorer—but you can make a bow. You derive satisfaction from that?"

"Yes."

"Why?"

Both his fists hardened and whitened as Edham leaned forward and snapped, "I am Man!"

"That will be all," said the other.

6. THE REDHEAD

Edham never saw the reports. Written conclusions invariably are withheld from the Granor. His only clue lay in the length of the deliberations and the frequent summoning of Rafel, who looked a mite more solemn at each successive visit. It was evident that there was some difference of opinion, some profound uncertainty which made the question of triumph or failure highly debatable.

Eventually he would know their decision from what they did with him. If he had changed in manner not to their liking but had nothing contagious, they would put a black mark against the planet and take him home.

If he were afflicted with something unwanted, incurable, and uncontrollable, they would abandon him along with his accursed world and add his name to those upon the obelisk. But if failure were not yet certain and success a possibility, no matter how remote, they would push him into the second stage of his task.

It was four days before he knew. In that time the crew had attended to all repairs, overhauled the engine and pumps, installed a remote control for the latter, supplied fresh spools for his autorecorder, recharged his beam, supplied new wings and propulsion, landed a huge load of packaged meals, all duly numbered. They did not touch the plants. The living would go on living —the dead stay dead.

There were eight females with the crew. Moving around together in a lithe colorful bunch, they explored the house, the instrument shed, the plantation. In single file they trotted along the wall-top, chattering like birds, laughing in lilting tones and exclaiming from time to time over the few exotic flowers visible in the jungle.

All were young, strong, well-shaped. All studied Edham with clear frank eyes at every opportunity, weighing him up, estimating him. For his part he tried to avoid them. Their presence was closely linked with his fate. He was acutely conscious of the fact and embarrassed by the uncertainty of his position.

In the late afternoon of the fourth day Rafel came to him. "The conference is over. I am more than glad to hear the end of it. Yours has been a difficult case."

"I know I am hairy."

Rafel did not smile. He went on, "They say you have changed and in all probability will continue to do so. The purely physical features of it are innocuous. They are nothing to worry about, nothing to fear. Indeed, some of them are advantageous."

"Come to the worst," Edham suggested impatiently.

"It is the psychological shift that has them bothered. They detect an abnormal combativeness which, in theory, could grow until it becomes completely irrational."

"This life of mine is abnormal. What do they expect? The dullness of a routine worker in Dise?"

"All your troubles and trials have been taken into account," said Rafel. "After considering everything—even the impetuosity of the pioneer, even boredom—they find more bellicosity than can be explained, more than is natural or necessary. It is the little extra you have absorbed from this bellicose world. You may continue to absorb it. At saturation point—if you live to reach it—where will you be?"

"Sitting around and *not* permitting everything," Edham answered. "And laughing."

Letting it pass Rafel continued. "Anyway, the second stage of this planet-probing task is shorter, less trying. You should come to no great harm if we carry on awhile. Besides, we would deserve to lose a world if we let go of it at the first setback." He looked straight at Edham. "Do you want to be taken home while the going is still good?"

Edham said in level tones, "To return voluntarily would be to return in disgrace, to be pointed out as the Granor who came back screaming. Do you think I would enjoy that? How would you like a bust on the nose?"

"There you go again!" said Rafel, shrugging good-humoredly. "Well, the die is cast. It is for you to go through the second stage."

"With whom?"

"Of the eight Companions who have seen you and looked over this place, six have volunteered."

"Two don't like me, eh?"

"Not necessarily," denied Rafel. "For some reason which is beyond my mere male mind there are always two who want to see the next place. No matter how many Companions I take out, invariably I return with two—eagerly awaiting yet another world."

"Feminine curiosity," ventured Edham.

"The six have taken first pick as is the right of their sex. It is now your turn."

"Which six?"

Rafel nodded toward somewhere behind the other's back. "They are over there. The pair of transgalactic tourists are in the ship."

Without looking around Edham said, "If the tall, slender one with the flaming hair is among them—"

"The redhead. So be it. You have chosen your Companion as

she has chosen you." Rafel eyed the sky. "I will perform the ceremony of association this evening if you are agreeable. We will depart at the fourth tempor of tomorrow."

With the morning they were summoned to the vessel, the Granor and his Companion.

Rafel began with, "We are ready to boost. Is there anything you desire, anything you wish to ask before we go?"

"No," replied Edham.

"Are you satisfied with each other?" He smiled as he read the answer in their faces. "We shall return in about three and a half years. I hope then to find evidence in favor of systematic settlement.

"If so, a time may come when more Disians share your world, building it to greatness." His gaze shifted from one face to the other. "You will have much honor."

"Darn the honor," said Edham. "Give me the fun."

Trying to frown his disapproval, Rafel found it far from easy. He switched the subject. "Any alterations in yourselves will be the results of or adjustment to local conditions. Comparatively speaking it will be slow, insidious. It cannot have the swiftness and extremism of radical mutation." He stopped, rubbed his forehead while he sought around for further words.

"Meaning our children?" Edham prompted.

Rafel seized upon it gratefully. "We could learn more of real significance from your children than we can ever learn from you. Apart from other yet undetected peculiarities this planet has a deal of radioactivity. What does it mean to our kind? What might it do?" He spread helpless hands. "We don't know."

"All in good time," offered Edham.

"Your children are very much to be desired—by us," Rafel went on. "Nevertheless I advise you not to have any unless desired by you."

The redhead put it tartly. "The Ancient College of Granors' Companions is not a consortium for the stupid and—"

Hurriedly, Rafel countered her. "I am reminding you that Dise imposes no duty upon you in this particular respect. You are completely free to please yourselves "

"That goes for me, too," she said, blandly shoving him off balance.

Recovering, he stood up, made his voice serious. "Except in one respect—you will eat nothing native to this world. It is strictly forbidden. When the time comes to try subsisting on local products, you will be informed."

"Boxed-up meals." She sighed regretfully. "Enriched, concentrated, reduced, fastened down, and caged. I took a tedious course on them—*How to Make Packaged Food Interesting.* Oh, well." She patted her flaming hair, tucked a curl behind her ear. "There are other interests."

Eyeing her somewhat askance Rafel avoided the subject, held out his hand.

The two stood side by side watching the ship go up. It shrank as before, was swallowed up by a cloud, was gone.

"And that is that," remarked Edham, sensing the loss and yet glad of it.

"What now, Flabby?" she inquired.

I think that for a start—" His voice petered out, his eyes suddenly burned at her. "What was that you called me?"

She repeated it with annoying gusto, a smile on her oval face, and she turned slightly sidewise. A growl sounded low in his chest. He pounced at her, hands out, fingers wide. She was away like the wind, hair streaming.

It was a full and arduous tempor before he cornered her by the southern wall. The laughter of their struggle brought answering howls and screams from the other side of the ramparts.

More imaginative treatment of meals plus the comfort of her presence transformed the area into a haven of peace and satisfaction—for a time. Edham lazed around, ignored the jungle, enjoyed his newfound domesticity.

The girl had a seemingly endless capacity for keeping him amused, occupying his attention, diverting his energies from former paths. When his spell of idleness wore off she found him numerous tasks and when she came to the end of those she invented new ones. He performed them all with the casual uncomplaining air of one who has known the weight of time on his hands.

Now and again she tantalized him, apparently on sheer impulse born of some feminine quirk. Invariably he failed to notice that such occasions were carefully chosen.

Thus, for example, there was that moment he stood at the west end, close by the wall, looking longingly at the top and sensing once more the urge to go out and do battle and shout with triumph until exhausted. His eyes were shining, his chest was out, brown-skinned with hairs upon it.

She came silently behind him, noting every detail, and said, "See here, Rugbust, I—" Then she turned and fled for her life, long slender legs moving with the grace of a ballet dancer's.

Three jumps behind her he collided with the door of the instrument shed as she slammed it against him. He could hear her squealing with excitement. Scrambling onto the roof, his muscles bulged as he began to tear up a sheet and make a gap big enough to drop through. She came out and immediately he realized that he'd been fooled. Her wings had been hidden within. She emerged on white pinions, soared gracefully, waggled pink toes just beyond leaping distance from his head.

Perforce he had to go back to the house, don his own wings. It was near nightfall before he got her at tremendous height in the base of a cloud. By then he was tired and hungry, precisely as she had calculated.

None of this went into the autorecorder. The blithe waste of propulsor-power was part of the mating game and there were no dutiful confessions for the ears of others.

They did not have a real difference until a hundred days later when he came in for the noon meal and found flowers upon the table. He glowered at the blooms, then at her.

"Where did you get these?"

"In the jungle." The reply was made with disturbing matter-of-factness as she placed a steaming dish upon the table and seated herself.

"So you have been outside the walls without my knowledge while my attention was diverted elsewhere?"

"Of course."

"There are dangerous creatures in the jungle."

"I know it."

He was chewing his bottom lip and glowering at her now. "You could be torn to pieces."

"So could you." Her eyes came up, faintly accusing and at the same time expressing the resignation of one who has tried in vain to control a mischievous child.

"I know how to look after myself."

"So do I."

"Hah!" he exclaimed. *"Hah!"*

She snapped at him. "All right, Fungus-front, go out and see for yourself. It's just over the south wall."

Giving her a look he went out, investigated, came back, and said, "You killed it while you had both feet on the ground. You beamed it face to face."

"That's me," she admitted. "Man to man!"

"It wasn't a man. Neither are you."

Putting shapely elbows on the table she rested her chin in one hand and made her voice sugar-sweet. "What I like about you is your swift grasp of things."

"Then how about this?" he retorted, making a quick grab across the table, fingers crooked for a coil of thick red hair.

The snatch missed solely because the table jumped. The floor jumped with it. The house performed a brief jig. A dull cavernous rumbling sounded from east to west. The stony ramparts quivered along their full length. The rumble ended in a faraway crack.

"What was that?" she asked, sitting erect, wide-eyed, startled.

"A quake." He leaned back, stared at his grabbing hand while he cooled off. "They come once in a while. Elsewhere they're more frequent and much more violent. Elsewhere they're really something!"

She thought it over for a while, said suddenly, "Do you believe in precognition?"

"It is a subject that has been argued for a thousand years and will be for another thousand. I have no opinion about it." He studied her curiously. "Why do you ask?"

"To take unnecessary risks is against the rules. Yet despite that, despite your training, despite my attempts to divert you, the jungle calls you—until you obey." Her long fingers toyed with each other nervously.

"So last evening, when you thought yourself unobserved, you went outside with your bow. And this morning I went outside for flowers—the flowers you have never brought me."

He flinched at that and began, "I would gladly bring them if you did not criticize the getting and—"

"You misunderstand me. I am not criticizing you. Not anymore." The hands folded. "You see I feel as you do—*I* yearn to go outside."

"*You* do?"

"The desire grows, encouraged by your bad example." Her gaze upon him was thoughtful, speculative. "Do you suppose that something may be impelling us to get accustomed to the jungle—while there is time?"

It made him vaguely uneasy.

"Instinct is a peculiar thing," she went on. "It comes to animals and birds as a mixture of precognition and ancestral memory and helps them survive." The steadiness of her gaze unsettled him as she finished, "Why do *you* crave the green hell?"

"I get restless."

"Why?"

"Kind of have the fidgets sometimes."

"Why?"

"Oh, heck!" he said, giving it up.

"Take me with you next time you go out," she pleaded. "Two together are safer than one—and I get such a wonderful feeling of freedom beyond the walls."

It was his turn to come back with, "Why?"

"Because I know that this world will take us only on its own terms. Not on ours but on its own. We must be ready."

"My luck," he commented, making a mock-frown at the ceiling. "Just my luck. I need a Companion who is pink and soft and warm and understanding. I pick one and what do I get? A seer! A long-legged second-sighter! A prophet of disaster! A red witch!"

"Think of the remarkable children we could have," she jibed. "With your hair and my magical powers. Furry demons."

"Be quiet," he ordered. His shoulders hunched to rid themselves of a cold little shiver. There are jokes—and there are jokes.

7. REJECTED

Disaster came in the midsummer of Edham's eighth year and his Companion's second. There was no warning, no preliminary sounding of some deep note of doom. Indeed at first there was nothing to show that an experiment was being ended in order that a new one might begin. All that happened was that the sun shone.

It was the first time they had seen the sun from this planet's surface. Up to date there had been only the great blanket of cloud overhead, darkening or glowing and pouring heat by day, deepening the nights and hiding the stars. Always the fierce primary had been concealed.

Now the clouds broke widely, revealing a bronze-blue sky in which the sun burned with awful vim and sent down stinging rays. Edham studied it through a dark glass, saw a great spot upon its tormented surface. The visual radioscope in his instrument shed picked up a mass of flickering shadows and swiftly changing checkered patterns indicative of violent disturbances across all bands.

By day and by night the heat was terrific. At first it did not bother the red-haired Companion. She came from Ultra-Dise, a planet far hotter than Dise itself, and thus was well fitted to endure the blaze. But as the sun burned on, week upon week, she began to wilt along with the barely surviving plants, along with the wilting jungle.

In the seventh week the last tortured Disian plant gave up its eight-year-old battle and lay in the hot dust. Smoke from fires in the dehydrated jungle drifted over the walled area, brought with it a stench of burning flesh and hide. A small quake came, followed by another and another while still the orb flamed in the sky and the shrinking rivers steamed.

With the death of the last *bodhi* tree the Companion's uncomplaining endurance ended. She posed taut but tired in the hot shadow of the instrument shed, looked across the barren area shimmering with heatwaves.

"There is that deep cave we found in the mountainside far across the river. It is cool, comfortable, and has water at its back. I think it might have been better had we moved there when first we discovered it."

"A Granor does not desert his post for the sake of comfort." He wiped his forehead with the back of a hairy hand, kept his eyes away from the blazing thing in the sky.

"I know, I know. I am with you while there is duty to be done." She surveyed the dust of their hopes. "There is now no post to desert—nothing but four walls. The alien sun has eaten everything. Are we going to let it consume us, too?"

"We should hang on and wait for Rafel," he said.

"What—for at least another year and a half? Of what use to Rafel are whitened bones?"

"We have enough food."

"One cannot live on food alone. One must have water and sleep. One *must* have sleep." She eyed him slantwise. "How much have you slept?"

"Little. It is too hot. We must suffer until the clouds come back."

"Not me," she declared flatly. "What is left to merit the suffering? Nothing! Tonight I shall slumber peacefully in the cool of the cave even if I sleep alone, even if it is my last sleep on this world." With that she went for her wings.

He remained, pondering gloomily. After a while he put on his wings and followed her—as she had known he would.

They were asleep in the cave ten nights afterward when the great quake that shook their mountain range flattened the distant plantation's south wall, blocked the west river, created a great, shallow stinking lake which lapped close to the remaining ramparts. Thirsty monsters, half crazed by heat, made the lake their drinking place, the broken area their stamping ground.

Throughout the following week Edham battled more savage life-forms than he had tackled in any one year. Under the merciless sun he swooped down wide-winged, beamed them away from the house, rescued packages of food and took them to the cave. He made trips by night, expecting less opposition, but they were there in even greater numbers, red-toothed and eager for him.

Thus the food stocks were laboriously reduced in loads pitifully small. The cost approximated one killing per package plus the risk of his own violent ending. The area swarmed with ferocious forms as did every place within easy reach of water. The world screamed for water and, having got it, wanted flesh.

On something over his one-hundredth trip he returned to the cave so borne down by his burden that he barely escaped the brown scalded tops of trees from which menacing worms had long vanished. At that point his propulsor expired. Too-frequent usage and heavy overloading had dried up the power source. The wings were useless.

Food is more important than flight. Using his Companion's equipment he continued the trips, transported to the cave more than half the stock of the distant house before the second propulsor failed. They were landbound. They were at one with the animals, the things that crept through the shadows and could never reach the sky.

It seemed a major blow to Edham since the remaining stores now were ten days' march away with every step disputed. To his Companion it was a secret relief. Now she had him close by and did not have to scan the skies at every flight, praying for his safe return.

Both beam projectors continued to function long after clouds had reappeared to hide the sun and right through the raging winter. One petered out with the spring—the other eighty days later. They turned to bows, fought the reviving jungle, consumed its fruits, ate of its flesh, grew heavy yet more agile.

They quaffed the undistilled water which seeped from the rock at the back of the cave and they did not fall ill, they did not die. Neither the water nor the food nor the past torment of that violent sun made them diseased or misshapen.

No change was apparent to them except that the longer they knew the jungle the more it seemed like home, for they did not realize that they had developed a swift, abiding fury equal to its own.

Eternal hope kept them from being completely absorbed by this world. No matter how powerfully surged the passions it induced within them they held fast to respective memories of Dise and Ultra-Dise and to the dream of being found on Rafel's return.

Yet, strangely, along with the desire to be discovered lurked another frequently repressed wish that neither mentioned to the other and that they denied even to themselves—the hope that discovery would not mean removal. This world had not yet taken them body and soul but it was establishing by insidious means a claim that grew stronger tempor by tempor, day by day.

"I have found golden grain to the east, Bristle-body. I don't know how or why the animals have missed it. Big, beautiful heads of grain."

"Probably it isn't fit to eat."

"I tried it on myself a week ago."

"You—" His deeply tanned face went taut. "You might have died."

"So might you this morning when you fought that beast which we did not need for meat."

"It was interested in the cave. I permit nothing near the cave." He bunched a fist. "I am Man!"

"Then you can make me a stone grinder," she said. "If I had a grinder I could make flour and bread and cakes."

"*Cakes!*" he spat. "In this place."

"You'll see," she promised, not the least bit disturbed by his attitude. "Fruit cakes and meat patties. Real food!"

"Forbidden food."

"What else is there?"

"The packages I took such pains to get."

"They will not last. Eventually we shall have to subsist only on what this world has to offer and chance what it does to us. We might as well start now. I'm not afraid."

"Not afraid but impetuous."

She studied his heavily muscular body, clad in the colorful skin of some animal he had slaughtered, shifted her gaze to the powerful bow grasped in his right hand, and said, "Listen to who's talking."

"I will make a grinder and you can have your cakes," he agreed, conscious of unspoken accusations. "And may the stars preserve us!"

"From what? From this world's fruits? We have been eating them already and flesh as well. Can *more* fruit do any worse?"

"If their dangerous properties are accumulative we can step over the margin between enough and too much. Besides you and I might gorge ourselves to the limit of our capacity without ill effect upon ourselves but—but—"

"Our children?"

"Yes."

She took a step toward him. "Do you wish for children?"

"Do you?" he countered.

"Of course."

"No matter what they may be like—or *not* like?"

"They would still be ours," she pointed out.

"Unrecognizably perhaps."

"I would always know my own—and I am not afraid."

"But as I have already said you are impetuous," he gave back more gently. "Wouldn't it be better first to wait for the vessel and learn our fate?"

"Perhaps," she admitted, relaxing.

She watched him as he tightened his bow, watched him stride down the path from the cave and enter between the trees. Something far back in the trees screamed its anger at his coming while she still watched.

"*A-a-ah!*"

The great vessel from Dise—it was like some misty figment of a bygone dream. A phantom of the past, hoped for yet feared.

A thing of dreams it seemed when at last it did come down. Deep in their cave at dead of night they heard a whine come through the sky and resolve itself to the thunderous roar of hot venturis.

They ran to the cave's mouth, saw a ring of crimson spears floating over the distant plantation. The spears shortened, went out. Thunder ceased. For a moment they gazed at each other like people who have seen the impossible come to pass.

Edham got the tiny signal generator which he had rescued from the house, drew out its telescopic antenna, cranked the handle bemusedly. Somewhere over there, far away in the dark, loops were swinging to get his bearing. But his thoughts were not of that. They were of the threatening upheaval to his way of life.

Winged members of the crew arrived and took them high above the trees, back to the ship. There was huge excitement and much congratulating before they were passed along to the examiners.

The poking and prying was much longer, more tedious than before and almost unbearably irritating, but the decision came more quickly.

Rafel summoned them before him. "The plantation has ceased to exist through no fault of yours. All Di-growths have long gone, this world having proved too much for them." His tones were solemn, regretful. "In the circumstances we must reject this planet. It is unsuitable for settlement." Then he added, "But I can comfort Jolin by telling him that he was not entirely wrong."

Edham said, "How do you mean?"

"I said this planet *is* of no use to us. Someday it may be. We have tried it too early, many centuries too early."

"So it seems," commented Edham, dryly. "If we two can survive among the beasts, so can others."

Rafel shot back at him, "In what shape?"

There was no effective answer, no answer at all. Edham fidgeted with the sheer impotence of it, stared back at him, said nothing.

"I have the examiners' report here," Rafel went on, eyeing the written scroll. "I am not permitted to give it to you in detail but I can state the conclusions. They say you may stay here or return to Dise—at your own choice."

Silent up to that moment, the redhead shrewdly noted his forced impassiveness, asked, "Suppose we elect to go back, what then?"

With great reluctance, Rafel told her, "There must be no issue of your association."

"So that's the snag. Always a Companion but never a mother."

"I am sorry. Truly I am sorry. The basic law must be obeyed even when it thwarts the rights of individuals, and that law says Disians remain Disians now and forevermore. The law says un-Disians are non-Disians except when scientifically produced under proper control. Much as I would like to do so, for your sake it is beyond the power of a mere ship's commander to modify a basic law and—"

"I prefer to stay," she interrupted. Her air was too positive, too decided to permit argument.

Rafel's gaze moved inquiringly to Edham, who responded with, "Since you reject it this world is ours, entirely ours, every stick and stone of it ours! Who would surrender a world for the comfort of Dise?"

"You sadden me," said Rafel. He sighed resignedly. "So be it. I shall put a red mark against this planet to indicate that it is not condemned for all time, that it may be suitable in the future." With slight emphasis, looking at Edham, he repeated, "The distant future."

"I know what you mean," Edham assured. "And I do not care. A Granor does not care—can you believe that?"

"Most certainly. To be a Granor one must not care—much."

"Anyway I've a feeling about this," chipped in the Companion, blithely exercising her feminine precognition. "In the distant future to which you refer the next visit may be from *here*. What of the law of Dise then?"

"They will permit the unavoidable," remarked Edham, giving Rafel no time to reply.

Frowning a little Rafel shrugged it off. "We shall give you new wings, new beam projectors, anything else you may require. They will last awhile and be of some help. More than that I cannot do. When those things are exhausted there will be no further help and you will have to continue as best you can."

"We have managed without them. We can do so again."

"I know. I shall make a full report on it. Your names will be honored in your respective colleges and you will be remembered."

"While we hasten to forget," remarked Edham.

It embarrassed Rafel. He covered up by saying, "May the eternal stars be with you," and went away.

In due time Edham watched the ship go up and noted with only a hint of surprise that the finality of its departure created no emotion within him. There were queer insubstantial tentacles holding him to the dirt of this restless world, alienating him from that other world of his youth. His psychic shape had changed invisibly.

It was geohypnosis, the cunning fascination of a sphere.

The ship went through the clouds. In silence they used their new wings to transport equipment to the cave. The task was easier this time for the great vessel's blasting arrival and fiery departure had driven every hostile form from the vicinity.

Three-walled, open-ended, and dead beneath the twilight sky, the area that once had been a place of hope held them musing a little while on their final trip. In the days when it flourished and was thought of as a sometime-city the woman had blessed it with its future name. To please her he had carved it upon the wall now broken by one belly-heave of a world not yet ready for names or walls.

He was gazing set-faced at the shattered name when she asked, "What is the matter?"

"I am laughing."

She grasped his hand. "Come—come with me."

So together they fled from Para-Dise and set forth into the land and begat many children, all of their own shape but none truly of their kind.

The first was a murderer.

The second, his victim.

The fifth had a yellow skin and tilted eyes.

Only the tenth had red hair.

The twelfth was born black.

But the seed of this seed subdued and mastered the stormy world which some call Terra.

The Neanderthals have generally received a very bad press. The first skull was discovered in 1857 in Neanderthal, Germany (hence its name). This was before Darwin's book had launched the modern evolutionary view of human development, and religious preconceptions made it difficult to assume it was really the skull of an ancient man. Some thought it was the remains of a Russian soldier (Westerners were willing to believe Russians were half-human), others the result of a normal human being suffering from a bone disease.

However, more skulls and bones were found and it was clear that Neanderthals were not quite like modern human beings, and that they lived much longer ago than Adam and Eve were supposed to have. They were rather short, had heavy eyebrow ridges, a backward-sloping forehead, no chin. Other old skeletons were found in Cro-Magnon, France. They were clearly of human beings resembling those of today. In fact, they were rather taller on the average.

At that point, a certain racism entered in. Neanderthal man and Cro-Magnon man both lived in Europe at the same time, and Neanderthal man no longer exists. There must have been war and the Neanderthals were wiped out; clearly they were the inferior race since, for one thing, they were not us.

Consequently, when the skulls were drawn as they might appear when clothed in flesh, the Neanderthals were shown with stubble and slack jaws, as though they were idiots. The Cro-Magnons were shown clean-shaven (fat chance!), with high, creased brows, and thoughtful appearances, as though they were philosophers.

And generally, fictional comparisons were heavily weighted against the Neanderthals as in the Wells story that follows. It did my heart good to read the contemporary best-seller Clan of the Cave Bear, *by Jean Auel, (Crown Publishers, Inc., 1980) simply as a corrective.*

THE GRISLY FOLK
H. G. WELLS

"Can these bones live?"

Could anything be more dead, more mute and inexpressive to the inexpert eye than the ocherous fragments of bone and the fractured lumps of flint that constitute the first traces of something human in the world? We see them in the museum cases, sorted out in accordance with principles we do not understand, labeled with strange names. Chellean, Mousterian, Solutrian, and the like, taken mostly from the places Chelles, La Moustier, Solutre, and so forth where the first specimens were found. Most of us stare through the glass at them, wonder vaguely for a moment at that half-savage, half-animal past of our race, and pass on. "Primitive man," we say. "Flint implements. The mammoth used to chase him." Few of us realize yet how much the subtle indefatigable cross-examination of the scientific worker has been extracting from the evidence of these rusty and obstinate witnesses during the last few years.

One of the most startling results of this recent work is the gradual realization that great quantities of these flint implements and some of the earlier fragments of bone that used to be ascribed to humanity are the vestiges of creatures, very manlike in many respects, but not, strictly speaking, belonging to the human species. Scientific men call these vanished races man *(Homo)*, just as they call lions and tigers cats *(Felis)*, but there are the soundest reasons for believing that these earlier so-called men were not of our blood, not our ancestors, but a strange and vanished animal, like us, akin to us, but different from us, as the mammoth was like, and akin to, and yet different from, the elephant. Flint and bone implements are found in deposits of very considerable antiquity; some in our museums may be a million years old or more, but the traces of really human creatures, mentally and anatomically like ourselves, do not go back much earlier than twenty or thirty thousand years ago. True men appeared in Europe then, and we do not know whence they came. These other tool-using, fire-making animals, the things that were like men and yet were not men, passed away before the faces of the true men.

Scientific authorities already distinguish four species of these pseudomen, and it is probable that we shall learn from time to time of other species. One strange breed made the implements called Chellean. These are chiefly sole-shaped blades of stone found in deposits of perhaps 300,000 or 400,000 years ago. Chellean implements are to be seen in any great museum. They are huge implements, *four or five times as big as those made by any known race of true men,* and they are not ill made. Certainly some creature with an intelligent brain made them. Big clumsy hands must have gripped and used these rocky chunks. But so far only one small fragment of a skeleton of this age has been found, a very massive chinless lower jawbone, with teeth rather *more* specialized than those of men today. We can only guess what strange foreshadowing of the human form once ate with that jaw, and struck at its enemies with those big but not unhandy flint blades. It may have been a tremendous fellow, probably much bigger in the body than a man. It may have been able to take bears by the scruff and the saber-toothed lion by the throat. We do not know. We have just these great stone blades and that bit of a massive jaw and—the liberty to wonder.

Most fascinating riddle of all these riddles of the ages of ice and hardship, before the coming of the true men, is the riddle of the Mousterian men, because they were perhaps still living in the world when the true men came wandering into Europe. They lived much later than those unknown Chellean giants. They lived thirty or forty thousand years ago—a yesterday compared with the Chellean time. These Mousterians are also called Neanderthalers. Until quite recently it was supposed that they were true men like ourselves. But now we begin to realize that they were different, so different that it is impossible that they can be very close relations of ours. They walked or shambled along with a peculiar slouch, they could not turn their heads up to the sky, and their teeth were very different from those of true men. One oddity about them is that in one or two points they were less like apes than we are. The dog tooth, the third tooth from the middle, which is so big in the gorilla, and which in man is pointed and still quite distinct from the other teeth, is not distinct at all in the Neanderthaler. He had a very even row of teeth, and his cheek teeth also were very unlike ours, and less like the apes' than ours. He had more face and less brow than true men, but that is not because he had a lesser brain; his brain was as big as a modern man's but it was different, bigger behind and smaller in front, so that probably he thought and behaved differently from us. Perhaps he had a better memory and less reasoning power than real men, or perhaps he had more nervous energy and less intelligence. He had no chin, and the way his jawbones come together below make it very doubtful if he could have used any such sounds in speech as we employ. Probably he did not talk at all. He could not hold a pin between his finger and thumb. The more we learn about this beast-man the stranger he becomes to us and the less like the Australoid savage he was once supposed to be.

And as we realize the want of any close relationship between this ugly, strong, ungainly, manlike animal and mankind, the less likely it becomes that he had a naked skin and hair like ours and the more probable that he was different, and perhaps bristly or hairy in some queer inhuman fashion like the hairy elephant and the woolly rhinoceros who were his contemporaries. Like them he lived in a bleak land on the edge of the snows and glaciers that were even then receding northward. Hairy or grisly, with a big face like a mask, great brow ridges, and no forehead, clutching an enormous flint, and running like a baboon with his head forward and not, like a man, with his head up, he must have been a fearsome creature for our forefathers to come upon.

Almost certainly they met, these grisly men and the true men. The true man must have come into the habitat of the Neanderthaler, and the two must have met and fought. Someday we may come upon the evidences of this warfare.

Western Europe, which is the only part of the world that has yet been searched with any thoroughness for the remains of early men, was slowly growing warmer age by age; the glaciers that had once covered half the continent were receding, and wide stretches of summer pasture and thin woods of pine and birch were spreading slowly over the once icy land. South Europe then was like northern Labrador today. A few hardy beasts held out amidst the snows, the bears hibernated. With the spring grass and foliage came great herds of reindeer, wild horses, mammoth, elephant, and rhinoceros, drifting northward from the slopes of the great warm valley that is now filled up with water—the Mediterranean Sea. It was in those days before the ocean waters broke into the Mediterranean that the swallows and a multitude of other birds acquired the habit of coming north, a habit that nowadays impels them to brave the passage of the perilous seas that flow over and hide the lost secrets of the ancient Mediterranean valleys. The grisly men rejoiced at the return of life, came out of the caves in which they had lurked during the winter, and took their toll of the beasts.

These grisly men must have been almost solitary creatures.

The winter food was too scanty for communities. A male may have gone with a female or so; perhaps they parted in the winter and came together in the summer; when his sons grew big enough to annoy him, the grisly man killed them or drove them off. If he killed them he may have eaten them. If they escaped him they may have returned to kill him. The grisly folk may have had long unreasoning memories and very set purposes.

The true men came into Europe, we know not whence, out of the South. When they appeared in Europe their hands were as clever as ours; they could draw pictures we still admire, they could paint and carve; the implements they made were smaller than the Mousterian ones, far smaller than the Chellean, but better made and more various. They wore no clothes worth speaking of, but they painted themselves and probably they talked. And they came in little bands. They were already more social than the Neanderthaler; they had laws and self-restraints; their minds had traveled a long way along that path of adaptation and self-suppression which has led to the intricate mind of man today with its concealed wishes, its confusions, and laughter and the fantasies and reveries and dreams. They were already held together, these men, and kept in order by the strange limitations of tabu.

They were still savages, very prone to violence and convulsive in their lusts and desires; but to the best of their poor ability they obeyed laws and customs already immemorably ancient, and they feared the penalties of wrongdoing. We can understand something of what was going on in their minds, those of us who can remember the fears, desires, fancies, and superstitions of our childhood. Their moral struggles were ours—in cruder forms. They were our kind. But the grisly folk we cannot begin to understand. We cannot conceive in our different minds the strange ideas that chased one another through those queerly shaped brains. As well might we try to dream and feel as a gorilla dreams and feels.

We can understand how the true men drifted northward from the lost lands of the Mediterranean valley into the high Spanish valleys and the south and center of France, and so on to what is now England—for there was no Channel then between England and France—and eastward to the Rhineland and over the broad wilderness which is now the North Sea, and the German plain. They would leave the snowy wilderness of the Alps, far higher then and covered with great glaciers, away on their right. These people drifted northward for the very good reason that their kind was multiplying and food diminishing. They would be oppressed by feuds and wars. They had no settled home; they were accustomed to drift with the seasons, every now and then some band would be pushed by hunger and fear a little farther northward into the unknown.

We can imagine the appearance of a little group of these wanderers, our ancestors, coming over some grassy crest into these northern lands. The time would be late spring or early summer, and they would probably be following up some grazing beasts, a reindeer herd or horses.

By a score of different means our anthropologists have been able to reconstruct the particulars of the appearance and habits of these early pilgrim fathers of mankind.

They would not be a very numerous band, because if they were there would be no reason why they should have been driven northward out of their former roving grounds. Two or three older men of thirty or so, eight or ten women and girls with a few young children, a few lads between fourteen and twenty, might make up the whole community. They would be a brownish brown-eyed people with wavy dark hair; the fairness of the European and the straight blue-black hair of the Chinaman had still to be evolved in the world. The older men would probably lead the band, the women and children would keep apart from the youths and men, fenced off by complex and definite tabus from any close companionship. The leaders would be tracking the herd they were following. Tracking was then the supreme accomplishment of mankind. By signs and traces that would be invisible to any modern civilized eye, they would be reading the story of the previous day's trek of the herd of sturdy little horses ahead of them. They would be so expert that they would go on from one faint sign to another with as little delay as a dog who follows a scent.

The horses they were following were only a little way ahead— so the trackers read the signs—they were numerous and nothing had alarmed them. They were grazing and moving only very slowly. There were no traces of wild dog or other enemies to stampede them. Some elephants were also going north, and twice our human tribe had crossed the spoor of woolly rhinoceros roaming westward.

The tribe traveled light. They were mainly naked, but all of them were painted white and black and red and yellow ocher. At this distance of time it is difficult to see whether they were tattooed. Probably they were not. The babies and small children were carried by the women on their backs in slings or bags made of animal skins, and perhaps some or all of them wore mantles and loin bands of skin and had pouches and belts of leather. The men had stone-pointed spears, and carried sharpened flints in their hands.

There was no Old Man who was lord and master and father of this particular crowd. Weeks ago the Old Man had been charged and trampled to a jelly by a great bull in the swamp far away. Then two of the girls had been waylaid and carried off by the young men of another larger tribe. It was because of these losses that this remnant was now seeking new hunting grounds.

The landscape that spread before the eyes of this little band as they crested the hill was a bleaker, more desolate, and altogether unkempt version of the landscape of Western Europe today. About them was a grassy down athwart which a peewit flew with its melancholy cry. Before them stretched a great valley ridged with transverse purple hills over which the April cloud-shadows chased one another. Pinewoods and black heather showed where these hills became sandy, and the valleys were full of brown brushwood, and down their undrained troughs ran a bright green band of peaty swamps and long pools of weedy water. In the valley thickets many beasts lurked unseen, and where the winding streams had cut into the soil there were cliffs and caves. Far away along the northern slopes of the ridge that were now revealed, the wild ponies were to be seen grazing.

At a sign from the two leaders the little straggle of menfolk halted, and a woman who had been chattering in subdued tones to a little girl became silent. The brothers surveyed the wide prospect earnestly.

"Ugh!" said one abruptly and pointed.

"Ugh!" cried his brother.

The eyes of the whole tribe swung round to the pointing finger.

The group became one rigid stare.

Every soul of them stood still, astonishment had turned them into a tense group of statuettes.

Far away down the slope with his body in profile and his head turned toward them, frozen by an equal amazement, stood a hunched gray figure, bigger but shorter than a man. He had been creeping up behind a fold in the ground to peer at the ponies, and suddenly he had turned his eyes and seen the tribe. His head projected like a baboon's. In his hand he carried what seemed to the menfolk a great rock.

For a little while this animal scrutiny held discoverers and discovered motionless. Then some of the women and children began to stir and line out to see the strange creature better. "Man!" said an old crone of forty. *"Man!"* At the movement of the women the grisly man turned, ran clumsily for a score of yards or so toward a thicket of birch and budding thorn. Then he halted again for a moment to look at the newcomers, waved an arm strangely, and then dashed into cover.

The shadows of the thicket swallowed him up, and by hiding him seemed to make him enormous. It identified itself with him, and watched them with his eyes. Its tree stems became long silvery limbs, and a fallen trunk crouched and stared.

It was still early in the morning, and the leaders of the tribe had hoped to come up with the wild ponies as the day advanced and perhaps cut one off and drive it into difficulties among the bushes and swampy places below, and wound it and follow it up and kill it. Then they would have made a feast, and somewhere down in the valley they would have found water and dry bracken for litter and a fire before night. It had seemed a pleasant and hopeful morning to them until this moment. Now they were disconcerted. This gray figure was as if the sunny morning had suddenly made a horrible and inexplicable grimace.

The whole expedition stood gazing for a time, and then the two leaders exchanged a few words. Waugh, the elder, pointed. Click, his brother, nodded his head. They would go on, but instead of slanting down the slopes toward the thickets they would keep round the ridge.

"Come," said Waugh, and the little band began to move again. But now it marched in silence. When presently a little boy began a question his mother silenced him by a threat. Everybody kept glancing at the thickets below.

Presently a girl cried out sharply and pointed. All started and stopped short.

There was the grisly thing again. It was running across an open space, running almost on all fours, in joltering leaps. It was hunch-backed and very big and low, a gray hairy wolflike monster. At times its long arms nearly touched the ground. It was nearer than it had been before. It vanished amidst the bushes again. It seemed to throw itself down among some red dead bracken. . . .

Waugh and Click took counsel.

A mile away was the head of the valley where the thickets had their beginning. Beyond stretched the woldy hills, bare of cover. The horses were grazing up toward the sun, and away to the north the backs of a herd of woolly rhinoceros were now visible on a crest—just the ridges of their backs showing like a string of black beads.

If the tribe struck across those grassy spaces, then the lurking prowler would have either to stay behind or come into the open. If he came into the open the dozen youths and men of the tribe would know how to deal with him.

So they struck across the grass. The little band worked round to the head of the valley, and there the menfolk stayed at the crest while the women and children pushed on ahead across the open.

For a time the watchers remained motionless, and then Waugh

was moved to gestures of defiance. Click was not to be outdone. There were shouts at the hidden watcher, and then one lad, who was something of a clown, after certain grimaces and unpleasant gestures, obliged with an excellent imitation of the gray thing's lumbering run. At that, scare gave place to hilarity.

In those days laughter was a social embrace. Men could laugh, but there was no laughter in the grisly preman who watched and wondered in the shadow. He marveled. The men rolled about and guffawed and slapped their thighs and one another. Tears ran down their faces.

Never a sign came from the thickets.

"Yahah," said the menfolk. "Yahah! Bzzzz. Yahah! Yah!"

They forgot altogether how frightened they had been.

And when Waugh thought the women and children had gone on a sufficient distance, he gave the word for the men to follow them.

In some such fashion it was that men, our ancestors, had their first glimpse of the premen of the wilderness of Western Europe. . . .

The two breeds were soon to come to closer quarters.

The newcomers were pushing their way into the country of these grisly men. Presently came other glimpses of lurking semi-human shapes and gray forms that ran in the twilight. In the morning Click found long narrow footprints round the camp. . . .

Then one day one of the children, eating those little green thornbuds that rustic English children speak of as bread and cheese, ventured too far from the others. There was a squeal and a scuffle and a thud, and something gray and hairy made off through the thickets carrying its victim, with Waugh and three of the younger men in hot pursuit. They chased the enemy into a dark gully, very much overgrown. This time it was not a solitary Neanderthaler they had to deal with. Out of the bushes a big male came at them to cover the retreat of his mate, and hurled a rock that bowled over the youth it hit like a ninepin, so that thereafter he limped always. But Waugh with his throwing spear got the gray monster in the shoulder, and he halted snarling.

No further sound came from the stolen child.

The female showed herself for a moment up the gully, snarling, bloodstained, and horrible, and the menfolk stood about afraid to continue their pursuit, and yet not caring to desist from it. One of them was already hobbling off with his hand to his knee.

How did that first fight go?

Perhaps it went against the men of our race. Perhaps the big Neanderthaler male, his mane and beard bristling horribly, came down the gully with a thunderous roar, with a great rock in either hand. We do not know whether he threw these big disks of flint or whether he smote with them. Perhaps it was then that Waugh was killed in the act of running away. Perhaps it was bleak disaster then for the little tribe. Short of two of its members it presently made off over the hills as fast as it could go, keeping together for safety, and leaving the wounded youth far behind to limp along its tracks in lonely terror.

Let us suppose that he got back to the tribe at last—after nightmare hours.

Now that Waugh had gone, Click would become Old Man and he made the tribe camp that night and build their fire on the high ridges among the heather far away from the thickets in which the grisly folk might be lurking.

The grisly folk thought we know not how about the menfolk, and the men thought about the grisly folk in such ways as we can understand; they imagined how their enemies might act in this fashion or that, and schemed to circumvent them. It may have been Click who had the first dim idea of getting at the gorge in which the Neanderthalers had their lair, from above. For as we have said, the Neanderthaler did not look up. Then the menfolk could roll a great rock upon him or pelt him with burning brands and set the dry bracken alight.

One likes to think of a victory for the human side. This Click we have conjured up had run in panic from the first onset of the grisly male, but as he brooded by the fire that night he heard again in imagination the cry of the lost girl, and he was filled with rage. In his sleep the grisly male came to him and Click fought in his dreams and started awake stiff with fury. There was a fascination for him in the gorge in which Waugh had been killed. He was compelled to go back and look again for the grisly beasts, to waylay them in their tracks, and watch them from an ambush. He perceived that the Neanderthalers could not climb as easily as the menfolk could climb, nor hear so quickly, nor dodge with the same unexpectedness. These grisly men were to be dealt with as the bears were dealt with, the bears before whom you run and scatter, and then come at again from behind.

But one may doubt if the first human group to come into the grisly land was clever enough to solve the problems of the new warfare. Maybe they turned southward again to the gentler regions from which they had come, and were killed by or mingled with their own brethren again. Maybe they perished altogether in that new land of the grisly folk into which they had intruded. Yet the truth may be that they even held their own and increased. If they died there were others of their kind to follow them and achieve a better fate.

That was the beginning of a nightmare age for the little children of the human tribe. They knew they were watched.

Their steps were dogged. The legends of ogres and man-eating giants that haunt the childhood of the world may descend to us from those ancient days of fear. And for the Neanderthalers it was the beginning of an incessant war that could end only in extermination.

The Neanderthalers, albeit not so erect and tall as men, were the heavier, stronger creatures, but they were stupid, and they went alone or in twos and threes; the menfolk were swifter, quicker-witted, and more social—when they fought they fought in combination. They lined out and surrounded and pestered and pelted their antagonists from every side. They fought the men of that grisly race as dogs might fight a bear. They shouted to one another what each should do, and the Neanderthaler had no speech; he did not understand. They moved too quickly for him and fought too cunningly.

Many and obstinate were the duels and battles these two sorts of men fought for this world in that bleak age of the windy steppes, thirty or forty thousand years ago. The two races were intolerable to each other. They both wanted the caves and the banks by the rivers where the big flints were got. They fought over the dead mammoths that had been bogged in the marshes and over the reindeer stags that had been killed in the rutting season. When a human tribe found signs of the grisly folk near their cave and squatting place, they had perforce to track them down and kill them; their own safety and the safety of their little ones was only to be secured by that killing. The Neanderthalers thought the little children of men fair game and pleasant eating.

How long the grisly folk lived on in that chill world of pines and silver birch between the steppes and the glaciers, after the true menfolk came, we do not know. For ages they may have held out, growing more cunning and dangerous as they became rare. The true men hunted them down by their spoor and by their tracks, and watched for the smoke of their fires, and made food scarce for them.

Great paladins arose in that forgotten world, men who stood forth and smote the gray man-beast face to face and slew him. They made long spears of wood, hardened by fire at the tips; they raised shields of skin against his mighty blows. They struck at him with stones on cords, and slung them at him with slings. And it was not simply men who withstood the grisly beast but women.

They stood over their children; they stood by their men against this eerie thing that was like and yet not like mankind. Unless the savants read all the signs awry, it was the women who were the makers of the larger tribes into which human families were already growing in those ancient times. It was the woman's subtle, love-guided wits which protected her sons from the fierce anger of the Old Man, and taught them to avoid his jealousy and wrath, and persuaded him to tolerate them and so have their help against the grisly enemy. It was woman, says Atkinson, in the beginning of things human, who taught the primary tabus, that a son must go aside out of the way of his stepmother, and get himself a wife from another tribe, so as to keep the peace within the family. She came between the fratricides, and was the first peacemaker. Human societies in their beginnings were her work, done against the greater solitariness, the lonely fierceness of the adult male. Through her, men learned the primary cooperation of sonship and brotherhood. The grisly folk had not learned even the rudest elements of cooperation, and mankind had already spelled out the alphabet of a unit that may someday comprehend the whole earth. The menfolk kept together by the dozen and by the score. By ones and twos and threes therefore the grisly folk were beset and slain, until there were no more of them left in the world.

Generation after generation, age after age, that long struggle for existence went on between these men who were not quite men and the men, our ancestors, who came out of the south into Western Europe. Thousands of fights and hunts, sudden murders, and headlong escapes there were amidst the caves and thickets of that chill and windy world between the last age of glaciers and our own warmer time. Until at length the last poor grisly was brought to bay and faced the spears of his pursuers in anger and despair.

What leapings of the heart were there not throughout that long warfare! What moments of terror and triumph! What acts of devotion and desperate wonders of courage! And the strain of the victors was our strain; we are lineally identical with those sun-brown painted beings who ran and fought and helped one another, the blood in our veins glowed in those fights and chilled in those fears of the forgotten past. For it was forgotten. Except perhaps for some vague terrors in our dreaming life and for some lurking element of tradition in the legends and warnings of the nursery, it has gone altogether out of the memory of our race. But nothing is ever completely lost. Seventy or eighty years ago a few curious savants began to suspect that there were hidden memories in certain big chipped flints and scraps of bone they found in ancient gravels. Much more recently others have begun to find hints of remote strange experiences in the dreams and odd kinks in modern minds. By degrees these dry bones begin to live again.

This restoration of the past is one of the most astonishing adventures of the human mind. As humanity follows the gropings of scientific men among these ancient vestiges, it is like a man who turns over the yellow pages of some long-forgotten diary, some engagement book of his adolescence. His dead youth lives again. Once more the old excitements stir him, the old happiness returns. But the old passions that once burned only warm him now, and the old fears and distresses signify nothing.

A day may come when these recovered memories may grow as vivid as if we in our own persons had been there and shared the thrill and the fear of those primordial days; a day may come when the great beasts of the past will leap to life again in our imaginations, when we shall walk again in vanished scenes, stretch painted limbs we thought were dust, and feel again the sunshine of a million years ago.

In an earlier headnote, I pointed out that human beings could not have arisen elsewhere and been transported to the Earth because human beings are too like the apes. Another reason is that hominid fossils—prehuman—have been discovered.

Well, then, is it possible that human beings and their hominid precursors and their ape cousins all arose elsewhere and were grafted onto an Earth that held all the other life-forms and that that is why we are so unusual?

No, the relationship doesn't stop with the apes. The apes as a whole are closely related to monkeys which are closely related to lemurs which are closely related to tree shrews which are closely related to insectivores which are closely related to mammals generally which are clearly vertebrates and part of the phylum Chordata. The relationship is too intricate. If human beings developed elsewhere, then all of life on Earth developed elsewhere, for it is a seamless web, and it all belongs together.

But at least Chad Oliver, an anthropologist, wasn't trapped by the very first step.

Incidentally, the doctrine that alien intelligences are superdestructive is a highly dramatic component of some kinds of science fiction. I think it is a matter of psychological projection, for there are very few species that kill for any reason other than fear or hunger, and of those few, Homo sapiens is by far the worst. We are a species that, apparently, enjoys killing. If, therefore, there is any supervillain in the universe it is, on the basis of evidence so far, likely to be us.

TRANSFUSION
CHAD OLIVER

THE MACHINE STOPPED.

There was no sound at all now, and the green light on the control panel blinked like a mocking eye. With the easy precision born of long routine, Ben Hazard did what had to be done. He did it automatically, without real interest, for there was no longer any hope.

He punched a figure into the recorder: 377.

He computed the year, using the Gottwald-Hazard Correlation, and added that to the record: 254,000 B.C.

He completed the form with the name of the site: Choukoutien.

Then, with a lack of anticipation that eloquently reminded him that this was the three hundred seventy-seventh check instead of the first, Ben Hazard took a long preliminary look through the viewer. He saw nothing that interested him.

Careful as always before leaving the Bucket, he punched in the usual datum: Viewer Scan Negative.

He unlocked the hatch at the top of the Bucket and climbed out of the metallic gray sphere. It was not raining, for a change, and the sun was warm and golden in a clean blue sky.

Ben Hazard stretched his tired muscles and rested his eyes on the fresh green of the tangled plants that grew along the banks of the lazy stream to his right. The grass in the little meadow looked cool and inviting, and there were birds singing in the trees. He was impressed as always by how little this corner of the world had changed in fifty years. It was very much as it had been a thousand years ago, or two thousand, or three. . . .

It was just a small corner of nowhere, lost in the mists of time, waiting for the gray sheets of ice to come again.

It was just a little stream, bubbling along and minding its own business, and a lonely limestone hill scarred with the dark staring eyes of rock shelters and cave entrances.

There was nothing different about it.

It took Man to change things in a hurry, and Man wasn't home.

That was the problem.

Ben took the six wide-angle photographs of the terrain that he always took. There were no animals within camera range this trip. He clambered through the thick brown brush at the base of the limestone hill and climbed up the rough rocks to the cave entrance. It was still open, and he knew its location by heart.

He well remembered the thrill he had felt the first time he had entered this cave. His heart had hammered in his chest and his throat had been so dry that he couldn't swallow. His mind had been ablaze with memories and hopes and fears, and it had been the most exciting moment of his life.

Now, only the fear remained—and it was a new kind of fear, the fear of what he *wouldn't* find.

His light blazed ahead of him as he picked his way along the winding passage of the cave. He disturbed a cloud of indignant bats, but there was no other sign of life. He reached the central cavern, dark and hushed and hidden under the earth, and flashed his light around carefully.

There was nothing new.

He recognized the familiar bones of wolf, bear, tiger, and camel. He photographed them again, and did manage to find the remains of an ostrich that he had not seen before. He took two pictures of that.

He spent half an hour poking around in the cavern, checking all of the meticulously recorded sites, and then made his way back to the sunlit entrance.

The despair welled up in him, greater than before. Bad news, even when it is expected, is hard to take when it is confirmed. And there was no longer any real doubt.

Man wasn't home.

Ben Hazard wasn't puzzled any longer. He was scared and worried. He couldn't pass the buck to anyone else this time. He had come back to see for himself, and he had seen.

Imagine a man who built a superb computer, a computer that could finally answer the toughest problems in his field. Suppose the ultimate in computers, and the ultimate in coded tapes; a machine—however hypothetical—that was never wrong. Just for kicks, suppose that the man feeds in an easy one: *What is two plus three?*

If the computer answers *six,* then the man is in trouble. Of course, the machine might be multiplying rather than adding—

But if the computer answers *zero* or *insufficient data,* what then?

Ben Hazard slowly walked back to the Bucket, climbed inside, and locked the hatch.

He filed his films under the proper code number.

He pushed in the familiar datum: Field Reconnaissance Negative.

He sat down before the control board and got ready.

He was completely alone in the small metallic sphere; he could see every inch of it. He *knew* that he was alone. And yet, as he had before, he had the odd impression that there was someone with him, someone looking over his shoulder. . . .

Ben Hazard had never been one to vault into the saddle and gallop off in all directions. He was a trained scientist, schooled to patience. He did not understand the soundless voice that kept whispering in his mind: *Hurry, hurry, hurry—*

"Boy," he said aloud, "you've been in solitary too long."

He pulled himself together and reached for the controls. He was determined to run out the string—twenty-three checks to go now—but he already knew the answer.

Man wasn't home.

When Ben Hazard returned to his original year of departure, which was 1982, he stepped out of the Bucket at New Mexico Station—for the machine, of necessity, moved in space as well as time. As a matter of fact, the spatial movement of the Bucket was one of the things that made it tough to do an intensive periodic survey of any single spot on the Earth's surface; it was hard to hold the Bucket on target.

According to his own reckoning and in terms of physiological time, he had spent some forty days in his check of Choukoutien in the Middle Pleistocene. Viewed from the other end at New Mexico Station, he had been gone only five days.

The first man he saw was the big M.P. corporal.

"I'll need your prints and papers, sir," the M.P. said.

"Dammit, Ames." Ben handed over the papers and stuck his thumbs in the scanner. "Don't you know me by now?"

"Orders, sir."

Ben managed a tired smile. After all, the military implications of time-travel were staggering, and care was essential. If you could move back in time only a few years and see what the other side had done, then you could counter their plans in the present. Since the old tribal squabbles were still going full blast, Gottwald had had to pull a million strings in order to get his hands on some of the available Buckets.

"Sorry, Ames. You look pretty good to me after a month or so of old camel bones."

"Nice to have you back, Dr. Hazard," the M.P. said neutrally.

After he had been duly identified as Benjamin Wright Hazard, Professor of Anthropology at Harvard and Senior Scientist on the Joint Smithsonian-Harvard-Berkeley Temporal Research Project, he was allowed to proceed. Ben crossed the crowded floor of the room they called Grand Central Station and paused a moment to see how the chimps were getting along.

There were two of them, Charles Darwin and Cleopatra, in separate cages. The apes had been the first time travelers, and were still used occasionally in testing new Buckets. Cleopatra scratched herself and hooted what might have been a greeting, but Charles Darwin was busy with a problem. He was trying to fit two sticks together so he could knock down a banana that was hanging just out of reach. He was obviously irritated, but he was no quitter.

"I know just how you feel, Charles," Ben said.

Charles Darwin pursed his mobile lips and redoubled his efforts.

What they won't do for one lousy banana.

Ben looked around for Nate York, who was working with the chimps, and spotted him talking to a technician and keeping track of his experiment out of the corner of his eye. Ben waved and went on to the elevator.

He rode up to the fourth floor and walked into Ed Stone's office. Ed was seated at his desk and he looked very industrious as he studied the dry white skull in front of him. The skull, however, was just a paperweight; Ed had used it for years.

He stood up, grinned, and stuck out his hand. "Sure glad you're back, Ben. Any luck?"

Ben shook hands and straddled a chair. He pulled out his pipe, filled it from a battered red can, and lit it gratefully. It felt good to be back with Ed. A man doesn't find too many other men he can really talk to in his lifetime, and Ed was definitely Number One. Since they were old friends, they spoke a private language.

"He was out to lunch," Ben said.

"For twenty thousand years?"

"Sinanthropus has always been famous for his dietary eccentricities."

Ed nodded to show that he caught the rather specialized joke —Sinanthropus had been a cannibal—and then leaned forward, his elbows on the desk. "You satisfied now?"

"Absolutely."

"No margin for error?" Ed insisted.

"None. I didn't really doubt Thompson's report, but I wanted to make certain. Sinanthropus isn't there. Period."

"That tears it then. We're up the creek for sure."

"Without a paddle."

"Without even a canoe." Ben puffed on his pipe. "Blast it, Ed, where *are* they?"

"You tell me. Since you left, Gottwald and I have gotten exactly nowhere. The way it looks right now, man hasn't got any ancestors —and that's crazy."

It's more than crazy, Ben thought. It's frightening. When you stop to think about it, man is a lot more than just an individual. Through his children, he extends on into the future. Through his ancestors, he stretches back far into the past. It is immortality of a sort. And when you chop off one end—

"I'm scared," he said. "I don't mind admitting it. There's an answer somewhere, and we've got to find it."

"I know how you feel, Ben. If this thing means what it seems to mean, then all science is just so much hot air. There's no cause and effect, no evidence, no reason. Man isn't what he thinks he is at all. We're just frightened animals sitting in a cave gaping at the darkness outside. Don't think I don't feel it, too. But what are we going to *do?*"

Ben stood up and knocked out his pipe. "Right now, I'm going home and hit the sack; I'm dead. Then the three of us—you and I and Gottwald—are going to sit down and hash this thing out. Then we'll at least know where we are."

"Will we?"

"We'd better."

He walked to the elevator and rode down to the ground floor of New Mexico Station. He had to identify himself twice more before he finally emerged into the glare of the desert sunlight. The situation struck him as the height of irony; here they were worried about spies and fancy feuds, when all the time—

What?

He climbed into his car and started for home. The summer day was bright and hot, but he felt as though he were driving down an endless tunnel of darkness, an infinite black cave to nowhere.

The voice whispered in his brain: *Hurry, hurry—*

His home was a lonely one, lonely with a special kind of emptiness. All his homes seemed deserted now that Anne was gone, but he liked this one better than most.

It was built of adobe with heavy exposed roof beams, cool in the summer and warm in winter. The Mexican tile floor was artfully broken up by lovely Navaho rugs—the rare Two Gray Hills kind in subdued and intricate grays and blacks and whites. He had brought many of his books with him from Boston and their familiar jackets lined the walls.

Ben was used to loneliness, but memories died hard. The plane crash that had taken Anne from him had left an emptiness in his heart. Sometimes, late in the evening, he thought he heard her footsteps in the kitchen. Often, when the telephone rang, he waited for her to answer it.

Twenty years of marriage are hard to forget.

Ben took a hot shower, shaved, and cooked himself a steak from the freezer. Then he poured a healthy jolt of Scotch over two ice cubes and sat down in the big armchair, propping his feet on the padded bench. He was still tired, but he felt more like a human being.

His eyes wandered to his books. There was usually something relaxing about old books and long-read titles, something reassuring. It had always been that way for him, but not any longer.

The titles jeered at him: *Mankind So Far, Up from the Ape, History of the Primates, Fossil Men. The Story of Man, Human Origins, The Fossil Evidence for Human Evolution, History of the Vertebrates. . . .*

Little man, what now?

"We seem to have made a slight mistake, as the chemist remarked when his lab blew up," Ben said aloud.

Yes, but where could they have gone wrong?

Take Sinanthropus, for example. The remains of forty different Sinanthropus individuals had been excavated from the site of Choukoutien in China by Black and Weidenreich, two excellent men. There was plenty of material and it had been thoroughly studied. Scientists knew when Sinanthropus had lived in the Middle Pleistocene, where he lived, and how he lived. They even had the hearths where he cooked his food, the tools he used, the animals he killed. They knew what he looked like. They knew how he was related to his cousin, Pithecanthropus erectus, and to modern men. There was a cast of his skull in every anthropology museum in the world, a picture of him in every textbook.

There was nothing mysterious about Sam Sinanthropus. He was one of the regulars.

Ben and Gottwald had nailed the date to the wall at 250,000 B.C. After Thompson's incredible report, Ben himself had gone back in time to search for Sinanthropus. Just to make certain, he had checked through twenty thousand years.

Nobody home.

Sinanthropus wasn't there.

That was bad enough.

But *all* the early human and prehuman fossils were missing.

There *were* no men back in the Pleistocene.

No Australopithecus, no Pithecanthropus, no Neanderthal, no nothing.

It was impossible.

At first, Ben had figured that there must be an error somewhere in the dating of the fossils. After all, a geologist's casual "Middle Pleistocene" isn't much of a target, and radiocarbon dating was no good that far back. But the Gottwald-Hazard Correlation had removed that possibility.

The fossil men simply were not there.

They had disappeared. Or they had never been there. Or—

Ben got up and poured himself another drink. He needed it.

When the Winfield-Homans equations had cracked the time barrier and Ben had been invited by old Franz Gottwald to take part in the Temporal Research Project, Ben had leaped at the opportunity. It was a scientist's dream come true.

He could actually go back and *see* the long-vanished ancestors of the human species. He could listen to them talk, watch their kids, see them make their tools, hear their songs. No more sweating with a few broken bones. No more puzzling over flint artifacts. No more digging in ancient firepits.

He had felt like a man about to sit down to a Gargantuan feast.

Unhappily, it had been the cook's night out. There was nothing to eat.

Every scientist knows in his heart that his best theories are only educated guesses. There is a special Hall of Fame reserved for thundering blunders: that flat Earth, the medical humors, the unicorn.

Yes, and don't forget Piltdown Man.

Every scientist expects to revise his theories in the light of new knowledge. That's what science means. But he doesn't expect to find out that it's *all* wrong. He doesn't expect his Manhattan Project to show conclusively that uranium doesn't actually exist.

Ben finished his drink. He leaned back and closed his eyes. There had to be an answer somewhere—or somewhen. *Had* to be. A world of total ignorance is a world of terror; anything can happen.

Where was Man?

And why?

He went to bed and dreamed of darkness and ancient fears. He dreamed that he lived in a strange and alien world, a world of fire and blackness and living shadows—

When he woke up the next morning, he wasn't at all sure that he had been dreaming.

Among them, an impartial observer would have agreed, the three men in the conference room at New Mexico Station knew just about all there was to know concerning early forms of man. At the moment, in Ben's opinion, they might as well have been the supreme experts on the Ptolemaic theory of epicycles.

They were three very different men.

Ben Hazard was tall and lean and craggy-featured, as though the winds of life had weathered him down to the tough, naked rock that would yield no further. His blue eyes had an ageless quality about them, the agelessness of deep seas and high mountains, but they retained an alert and restless curiosity that had changed little from the eyes of an Ohio farm boy who had long ago wondered at the magic of the rain and filled his father's old cigar boxes with strange stones that carried the imprints of plants and shells from the dawn of time.

Ed Stone looked like part of what he was: a Texan, burned by the sun, his narrow gray eyes quiet and steady. He was not a big man, and his soft speech and deliberate movement gave him a deceptive air of lassitude. Ed was an easy man to underestimate; he wasted no time on frills or pretense, but there was a razor-sharp brain in his skull. He was younger than Ben, not yet forty, but Ben trusted his judgment more than he did his own.

Franz Gottwald, old only in years, was more than a man now; he was an institution. They called him the dean of American anthropology, but not to his white-bearded face; Franz had small respect for deans. They stood when he walked into meetings, and Franz took it as his due—he had earned it, but it concerned him no more than the make of the car he drove. Ben and Ed had both studied under Franz, and they still deferred to him, but the relationship was a warm one. Franz had been born in Germany—he never spoke about his life before he had come to the United States at the age of thirty—and his voice was still flavored by a slight accent that generations of graduate students had tried to mimic without much success. He was the Grand Old Man.

"Well?" asked Dr. Gottwald when Ben had finished his report. "What is the next step, gentlemen?"

Ed Stone tapped on the polished table with a yellow pencil that showed distinct traces of gnawing. "We've got to accept the facts and go on from there. We know what the situation is, and we think that we haven't made any whopping mistakes. In a nutshell, man has vanished from his own past. What we need is an explanation, and the way to get it is to find some relatively sane hypothesis that we can *test*, not just kick around. Agreed?"

"Very scientific, Edward," Gottwald said, stroking his neat white beard.

"O.K.," Ben said. "Let's work from what we know. Those skeletons *were* in place in Africa, in China, in Europe, in Java—they had to be there because that's where they were originally dug up. The bones are real, I've held them in my hands, and they're still in place in the museums. No amount of twaddle about alternate time-tracks and congruent universes is going to change that. Furthermore, unless Franz and I are the prize dopes of all time, the dating of those fossils is accurate in terms of geology and the associated flora and fauna and whatnot. The Buckets work; there's no question about that. So why can't we find the men who left the skeletons, or even the bones themselves in their original sites?"

"That's a question with only one possible answer," Ed said.

"Check. Paradoxes aside—and there are no paradoxes if you have enough accurate information—the facts have to speak for themselves. *We don't find them because they are not there.* Next question: Where the devil are they?"

Ed leaned forward, chewing on his pencil. "If we forget about their geological context, none of those fossils are more than a few hundred years old. I mean, that's when they were found. Even Neanderthal only goes back to around 1856 or thereabouts. Science itself is an amazingly recent phenomenon. So—"

"You mean Piltdown?" Gottwald suggested, smiling.

"Maybe."

Ben filled his pipe and lit it. "I've thought about that, too. I guess all of us have. If one fossil man was a fake, why not all of them? But it won't hold water, and you know it. For one thing, it would have required a worldwide conspiracy, which is nonsense. For another—sheer manpower aside—the knowledge that would have been required to fake all those fossils simply did not exist at the time they were discovered. Piltdown wouldn't have lasted five minutes with fluorine dating and decent X-rays, and no one can sell me on the idea that men like Weidenreich and Von Koenigswald and Dart were fakers. Anyhow, that idea would leave us with a problem tougher than the one we're trying to solve—where did man come from if he had no past, no ancestors? I vote we exorcise that particular ghost."

"Keep going," Gottwald said.

Ed took it up. "Facts, Ben. Leave the theories for later. If neither the bones nor the men were present back in the Pleistocene where they belong, but the bones were present to be discovered later, then they *have* to appear somewhere in between. Our problem right now is *when*."

Ben took his pipe out of his mouth and gestured with it, excited now. "We can handle that one. Dammit, *all* of our data can't be haywire. Look: for most of his presumed existence, close to a million years, man was a rare animal—all the bones of all the fossil men ever discovered wouldn't fill up this room we're sitting in; all the crucial ones would fit in a broom closet. O.K.? But by Neolithic times, with agricultural villages, there were men everywhere, even here in the New World. That record is clear. So those fossils *had* to be in place by around eight thousand years ago. All we have to do—"

"Is to work back the other way," Ed finished, standing up. "By God, that's it! We can send teams back through history, checking at short intervals, until we *see* how it started. As long as the bones are where they should be, fine. When they disappear—and they have to disappear, because we know they're not there earlier—we'll reverse our field and check it hour by hour if necessary. Then we'll know what happened. After that, we can kick the theories around until we're green in the face."

"It'll work," Ben said, feeling like a man walking out of a heavy fog. "It won't be easy, but it can be done. Only—"

"Only what?" Gottwald asked.

"Only I wonder what we'll find. I'm a little afraid of what we're going to see."

"One thing sure," Ed said.

"Yes?"

"This old world of ours will never be the same. Too bad—I kind of liked it the way it was."

Gottwald nodded, stroking his beard.

For months, Ben Hazard virtually lived within the whitewashed walls of New Mexico Station. He felt oddly like a man fighting a rattlesnake with his fists at some busy intersection, while all about him people hurried by without a glance, intent on their own affairs.

What went on in New Mexico Station was, of course, classified information. In Ben's opinion, this meant that there had been a ludicrous reversion to the techniques of magic. Facts were stamped with the sacred symbol of CLASSIFIED, thereby presumably robbing them of their power. Nevertheless, the world outside didn't know what the score was, and probably didn't care, while inside the Station—

History flickered by, a wonderful and terrible film.

Man was its hero and its villain—but for how long?

The teams went back, careful to do nothing and to touch nothing. The teams left Grand Central and pushed back, probing, searching. . . .

Back past the Roman legions and the temples of Athens, back beyond the pyramids of Egypt and the marvels of Ur, back through the sunbaked villages of the first farmers, back into the dark shadows of prehistory—

And the teams found nothing.

At every site they could reach without revealing their presence, the bones of the early men were right where they should have been, waiting patiently to be unearthed.

Back past 8,000 B.C.

Back past 10,000.

Back past 15,000—

And then, when the teams reached 25,000 B.C., it happened. Quite suddenly, in regions as far removed from one another as France and Java, the bones disappeared.

And not just the bones.

Man himself was gone.

The world, in some ways, was as it had been—or was to be. The gray waves still tossed on the mighty seas, the forests were cool and green under clean blue skies, the sparkling sheets of snow and ice still gleamed beneath a golden sun.

The Earth was the same, but it was a strangely empty world without men. A desolate and somehow fearful world, hushed by long silences and stroked coldly by the restless winds. . . .

"That's it," Ben said. "Whatever it was, we know when it happened—somewhere between twenty-three and twenty-five thousand at the end of the Upper Paleolithic. I'm going back there."

"*We're* going back there," Ed corrected him. "If I sit this one out I'll be ready for the giggle factory."

Ben smiled, not trying to hide his relief. "I think I could use some company this trip."

"It's a funny feeling, Ben."

"Yes." Ben Hazard glanced toward the waiting Buckets. "I've seen a lot of things in my life, but I never thought I'd see the Beginning."

The machine stopped and the green light winked.

Ed checked the viewer while Ben punched data into the recorder.

"Nothing yet," Ed said. "It's raining."

"Swell." Ben unlocked the hatch and the two men climbed out. The sky above them was cold and gray. An icy rain was pouring down from heavy, low-hanging clouds. There was no thunder. Apart from the steady hiss of the rain, France in the year 24,571 B.C. was as silent as a tomb. "Let's get this thing covered up."

They hauled out the plastic cover, camouflaged to blend with the landscape, and draped it over the metallic gray sphere. They had been checking for eighteen days without results, but they were taking no chances.

They crossed the narrow valley through sheets of rain, their boots sinking into the soaked ground with every step. They climbed up the rocks to the gaping black hole of the cave entrance and worked their way in under the rock ledge, out of the rain. They switched on their lights, got down on their hands and knees, and went over every inch of the dry area just back of the rock overhang.

Nothing.

The gray rain pelted the hillside and became a torrent of water that splashed out over the cave entrance in a hissing silver waterfall. It was a little warmer in the cave, but dark and singularly uninviting.

"Here we go again," Ed muttered. "I know this blasted cave better than my own backyard."

"I'd like to see that backyard of yours about now. We could smoke up some chickens in the barbecue pit and sample some of Betty's tequila sours."

"Right now I'd just settle for the tequila. If we can't figure this thing out any other way we might just as well start looking in the old bottle."

"Heigh-ho," Ben sighed, staring at the waiting cave. "Enter one dwarf and one gnome, while thousands cheer."

"I don't hear a thing."

Ed took the lead and they picked and crawled their way back through the narrow passages of the cave, their lights throwing grotesque black shadows that danced eerily on the spires and pillars of ancient dripping stone. Ben sensed the weight of the great rocks above him and his chest felt constricted. It was hard to breathe, hard to keep going.

"Whatever I am in my next incarnation," he said, "I hope it isn't a mole."

"You won't even make the mammals," Ed assured him.

They came out into a long, twisted vault. It was deep in the cave, far from the hidden skies and insulated from the pounding of the rain. They flashed their lights over the walls, across the dry gray ceiling, into the ageless silence.

Nothing.

No cave paintings.

It was as though man had never been, and never was to be.

"I'm beginning to wonder whether *I'm* real," Ed said.

"Wait a minute." Ben turned back toward the cave entrance, his body rigid. "Did you hear something?"

Ed held his breath and listened. "Yeah. There it is again."

It was faint and remote as it came to them in the subterranean vault, but there was no mistaking it.

A sound of thunder, powerful beyond belief.

Steady, now.

Coming closer.

And there had been no thunder in that cold, hissing rain. . . .

"Come on." Ben ran across the cavern and got down on his hands and knees to crawl back through the twisting passage that led to the world outside. "There's something out there."

"What is it?"

Ben didn't stop. He clawed at the rocks until his hands were bloody. "I think the lunch hour's over," he panted. "I think Man's coming home."

Like two frightened savages, they crouched in the cave entrance and looked out across the rain-swept valley. The solid stone vibrated under their feet and the cold gray sky was shattered by blasting roars.

One thing was certain: that was no natural thunder.

"We've got to get out of here," Ben yelled. "We've got to hide before—"

"Where? The Bucket?"

"That's the best bet. It's almost invisible in this rain, and we can see through the viewer."

"Right. Run for it!"

They scrambled down among the slick rocks and ran across the wet grass and mud of the valley floor. It was cold and the rain pelted their faces in icy gray sheets. The deafening roar grew even louder, falling down from the leaden sky.

Fumbling in their haste, they jerked up a corner of the plastic cover so that the viewer could operate. Then they squirmed and wriggled under the plastic, dropped through the hatch, and sealed the lock. They dripped all over the time sphere but there was no time to bother about it. Even inside the Bucket they could feel the ocean of sound around them.

Ben cut in the recorder. "Start the cameras."

"Done."

"Hang on—"

The shattering roar reached an earsplitting crescendo. Suddenly, there was something to see.

Light.

Searing white flame stabbing down from the gray skies.

They saw it: gargantuan, lovely, huge beyond reason.

Before their eyes, like a vast metal fish from an unknown and terrible sea, the spaceship landed in the rain-soaked valley of Paleolithic France.

The long silence came again.

Fists clenched, Ben Hazard watched the *Creation*.

The great ship towered in the rain, so enormous that it was hard to imagine that it had ever moved. It might have been there always, but it was totally alien, out of place in its setting of hills and earth and sodden grasses.

Circular ports opened in the vast ship like half a hundred awakening eyes. Bright warm yellow light splashed out through the rain. Men—strangely dressed in dark, close-fitting tunics—floated out of the ship and down to the ground on columns of the yellow light.

The men were human, no different physically from Ben or Ed.

Equipment of some sort drifted down the shafts of light: strange spider-legged machines, self-propelled crates that gleamed in the light, shielded stands that might have been for maps or charts, metallic robots that were twice the size of a man.

It was still raining, but the men ignored it. The yellow light deflected the rain—Ben could see water dripping down the yellow columns as though solid tubes had been punched through the air —and the rain was also diverted from the men and their equipment.

The men from the ship moved quickly, hardly pausing to glance around them. They fanned out and went to work with the precision of trained specialists who knew exactly what they were doing.

Incredible as it was, Ben thought that he knew what they were doing too.

The spider-legged machines stayed on the valley floor, pulsing. Most of the men, together with three of the robots and the bulk of the self-propelled crates, made their way up to the cave Ben and Ed had just left and vanished inside.

"Want to bet on what's in those crates?" Ben whispered.

"Haven't the faintest idea, but two bits says you spell it b-o-n-e-s."

The great ship waited, the streams of yellow light still spilling out into the rain. Five men pored over the shielded stands, looking for all the world like engineers surveying a site. Others worked over the spider-legged machines, setting up tubes of the yellow light that ran from the machines to the rocky hills. Two of the robots, as far as Ben could see, were simply stacking rocks into piles.

After three hours, when it was already growing dark, the men came back out of the cave. The robots and the crates were reloaded through the ship's ports and the uniformed men themselves boarded the ship again.

Night fell. Ben stretched to ease his cramped muscles, but he didn't take his eyes from the viewer for a second.

The rain died down to a gentle patter and then stopped entirely. The overcast lifted and slender white clouds sailed through the wind-swept sky. The moon rose, fat and silver, its radiance dimming the burning stars.

The impossible ship, towering so complacently beneath the moon of Earth, was a skyscraper of light. It literally hummed with activity. Ben would have given a lot to know what was going on inside that ship, but there was no way to find out.

The pulsing spider-legged machines clicked and buzzed in the cold of the valley night. Rocks were conveyed along tubes of the yellow light to the machines, which were stamping something out by the hundreds of thousands. Something . . .

Artifacts?

The long, uncanny night ended. Ben and Ed watched in utter

fascination, their fears almost forgotten, sleep never even considered.

Dawn streaked the eastern sky, touching the clouds with fingers of rose and gold. A light breeze rustled the wet, heavy grasses. Water still dripped from the rocks.

The uniformed men came back out of the ship, riding down on the columns of yellow light. The robots gathered up some immense logs and stacked them near the mouth of the cave. They treated the wood with some substance to dry it, then ignited a blazing fire.

Squads of men moved over the valley floor, erasing all traces of their presence. One of them got quite close to the Bucket and Ben felt a sudden numbing chill. What would happen if they were seen? He was no longer worried about himself. But what about all the men who were to live on the Earth? Or—

The squad moved away.

Just as the red sun lifted behind the hills, while the log fire still blazed by the cave, the ship landed the last of its strange cargo.

Human beings.

Ben felt the sweat grow clammy in the palms of his hands.

They floated down the shafts of yellow light, shepherded by the uniformed men. There were one hundred of them by actual count, fifty men and fifty women. There were no children. They were a tall, robust people, dressed in animal skins. They shivered in the cold and seemed dazed and uncomprehending. They had to be led by the hand, and several had to be carried by the robots.

The uniformed men took them across the wet valley, a safe distance away from the ship. They huddled together like sheep, clasping one another in sexless innocence. Their eyes turned from the fire to the ship, understanding neither. Like flowers, they lifted their heads to the warmth of the sun.

It was a scene beyond age; it had always been. There were the rows of uniformed men, standing rigidly at attention. And there were the clustered men in animal skins, waiting without hope, without regret.

An officer—Ben thought of him that way, though his uniform was no different from the others—stepped forward and made what seemed to be a speech. At any rate, he talked for a long time, nearly an hour. It was clear that the dazed people did not understand a word of what he was saying, and that, too, was older than time.

It's a ceremony, Ben thought. *It must be some kind of ritual. I hadn't expected that.*

When it was over, the officer stood for a long minute looking at the huddle of people. Ben tried to read his expression in the viewer, but it was impossible. It might have been regret. It might have been hope. It might have been only curiosity.

It might have been anything.

Then, at a signal, the uniformed men turned and abandoned the others. They walked back to their waiting ship and the columns of yellow light took them inside. The ports closed.

Ten minutes later, the ship came to life.

White flame flared beneath its jets and the earth trembled. The terrible roar came again. The people who had been left behind fell to the ground, covering their ears with their hands. The great ship lifted slowly into the blue sky, then faster and faster—

It was gone, and only the sound remained, the sound of thunder. . . .

In time, that, too, was gone.

Ben watched his own ancestors with an almost hypnotic fascination. They did not move.

Get up, get up—

The skin-clad people stood up shakily after what seemed to be hours. They stared blankly at one another. As though driven by some vague instinct that spoke through their shock, they turned and looked at the blazing fire that burned by the mouth of the cave.

Slowly, one by one, they pulled themselves over the rocks to the fire. They stood before it, seeking a warmth they could not understand.

The sun climbed higher into the sky, flooding the rain-clean world with golden light.

The people stood for a long time by the cave entrance, watching the fire burn down. They did nothing and said nothing.

Hurry, hurry. The voice spoke again in Ben's brain. He shook his head. Was he thinking about those dazed people out there, or was someone thinking about *him?*

Gradually, some of them seemed to recover their senses. They began to move about purposefully—still slowly, still uncertainly, like men coming out from under an anesthetic. One man picked up a fresh log and threw it on the fire. Another crouched down and fingered a chipped piece of flint he found on a rock. Two women stepped behind the fire and started into the dark cave.

Ben turned away from the viewer, his unshaven face haggard. "Meet Cro-Magnon," he said, waving his hand.

Ed lit a cigarette, his first in eighteen hours. His hand was shaking. "Meet everybody, you mean. Those jokers planted the other boys—Neanderthal and whatnot—back in the cave before they landed the living ones."

"We came out of that ship too, Ed."

"I know—but where did the *ship* come from? And why?"

Ben took a last long look at the people huddled around the fire. He didn't feel like talking. He was too tired to think. None of it made any sense.

What kind of people could *do* a thing like that?

And if they hadn't—

"Let's go home," Ed said quietly.

They went out and removed the plastic cover, and then set the controls for New Mexico Station in a world that was no longer their own.

Old Franz Gottwald sat behind his desk. His white suit was freshly pressed and his hair was neatly combed. He stroked his beard in the old familiar gesture, and only the gleam in his eyes revealed the excitement within him.

"It has always been my belief, gentlemen, that there is no substitute for solid thinking based on verified facts. There is a time for action and there is a time for thought. I need hardly remind you that action without thought is pointless; it is the act of an animal, the contraction of an earthworm. We have the facts we need. You have been back for three days, but the thinking is yet to be done."

"We've been beating our brains out," Ben protested.

"That may be, Ben, but a man can beat his brains out with a club. It is not thinking."

"*You* try thinking," Ed said, grinding out a cigarette.

Gottwald smiled. "You are too old to have your thinking done for you, Edward. I have given you all I can give. It is your turn now."

Ben sat back in his chair and lit his pipe. He took his time doing it, trying to clear his mind. He had to forget those frightened people huddled around a fire in the mists of time, had to forget the emotions he had felt when the great ship had left them behind. Gottwald was right, as always.

The time had come for thought.

"O.K.," he said. "We all know the facts. Where do we go from here?"

"I would suggest to you, gentlemen, that we will get no answers until we begin to ask the right questions. That is elementary, if I may borrow from Mr. Holmes."

"You want questions?" Ed laughed shortly. "Here's one, and it's a dilly. 'There's a hole in all this big enough to drive the American Anthropological Association through in a fleet of trucks.' What about the apes?"

Ben nodded. "You quoted Conan Doyle, Franz, so I'll borrow a line from another Englishman, Darwin's pal Huxley. 'Bone for bone, organ for organ, man's body is repeated in the body of the ape.' Hell, we all know that. There are differences, sure, but the apes are closer to men than they are to monkeys. If man didn't evolve on Earth—"

"You've answered your own question, Ben."

"Of course!" Ed fished out another cigarette. "If man didn't evolve on Earth, then neither did the apes. That ship—or some ship—brought them both. But that's impossible."

"Impossible?" Franz asked.

"Maybe not," Ben said slowly. "After all, there are only four living genera of apes—two in Africa and two in Asia. We could even leave out the gibbon; he's a pretty primitive customer. It *could* have been done."

"Not for all the primates," Ed insisted. "Not for all the monkeys and lemurs and tarsiers, not for all the fossil primate bones. It would have made Noah's ark look like a rowboat."

"I would venture the suggestion that your image is not very apt," Gottwald said. "That ship *was* big enough to make any of our ships look like rowboats."

"Never mind," Ben said, determined not to get sidetracked. "It doesn't matter. Let's assume that the apes were seeded, just as the men were. The other primates could have evolved here without outside interference, just as the other animals did. That isn't the real problem."

"I wonder," Ed said. "Could that ship have come out of *time* as well as space? After all, if we have time-travel they must have it. They could do anything—"

"Bunk," Gottwald snorted. "Don't let yourself get carried away, Edward. Anything is *not* possible. A scientific law is a scientific law, no matter who is working with it, or where, or when. We know from the Winfield-Homans equations that it is impossible to go back into time and alter it in any way, just as it is impossible to go into the future which does not yet exist. There are no paradoxes in time-travel. Let's not make this thing harder than it is by charging off into all the blind alleys we can think of. Ben was on the right track. What is the real problem here?"

Ben sighed. He saw the problem all too clearly. "It boils down to this, I think. *Why* did they plant those fossils—and probably the apes too? I can think of fifty reasons why they might have seeded men like themselves on a barren planet—population pressure and so forth—but why go to all the trouble of planting a false evolutionary picture for them to dig up later?"

"Maybe it isn't false," Ed said slowly.

Franz Gottwald smiled. "Now you're *thinking,* Edward."

"Sorry, Ed. I don't follow you. You saw them plant those bones. If that isn't a prime example of salting a site, then what the devil is it?"

"Don't shoot, pal. I was trying to say that the fossils could have been planted and *still* tell a true story. Maybe I'm just an old codger set in his ways, but I can't believe that human evolution is a myth. And there's a clincher, Ben: Why bother with the apes if there is no relationship?"

"I still don't see—"

"He means," Gottwald said patiently, "that the fossil sequence is a true one—*someplace else.*"

Ed nodded. "Exactly. The evolutionary series is the genuine article, but man developed on their world rather than on ours. When they seeded men on Earth, they also provided them with a kind of history book—if they could read it."

Ben chewed on his pipe. It made sense, to the extent that anything made sense anymore. "I'll buy that. But where does it leave us?"

"Still up that well-known creek. Every answer we get just leads back to the same old question. *Why* did they leave us a history book?"

"Answer that one," Gottwald said, "and you win the gold cigar."

Ben got to his feet. His head felt as though it were stuffed with dusty cotton.

"Where are you going?"

"I'm going fishing. As long as I'm up the creek I might as well do something useful. I'll see you later."

"I hope you catch something," Ed said.

"So do I," Ben Hazard said grimly.

The car hummed sleepily across the monotonous flatlands of New Mexico, passed through the gently rolling country that rested the eye, and climbed into the cool mountains where the pines grew tall and the grass was a thick dark green in the meadows.

Ben loved the mountains. As he grew older, they meant more and more to him. The happiest times of his life had been spent up next to the sky, where the air was crisp and the streams ran clear. He needed the mountains, and he always returned to them when the pressure was too much to bear.

He turned off the main road and jolted over a gravel trail; paved roads and good fishing were mutually exclusive, like cities and sanity. He noted with approval that the clouds were draping the mountain peaks, shadowing the land below. When the sun was too bright the fish could see a man coming.

He took a deep breath, savoring the tonic of the air.

Relax, that's the ticket.

He checked to see that no interloper had discovered his favorite stretch of water, then parked his car by the side of Mill Creek, a gliding stream of crystal-clean water that tumbled icily out of the mountains and snaked its lazy way through the long green valley. He grinned like a kid with his first cane pole.

Ben pulled on his waders, assembled his rod with practiced skill, and tied on his two pet flies: a Gray Hackle Yellow and a Royal Coachman. He hung his net over one shoulder and his trout basket over the other, lit his pipe, and waded out into the cold water of Mill Creek.

He felt wonderful. He hooked a nice brook trout within five minutes, taking him from a swirl of dark water shadowed by the bank of the stream. He felt the knots and the tensions flow out of him like melting snow, and that was the first step.

He *had* to relax. There was no other way.

Consider the plight of a baseball player in a bad slump. He gives it all he has, tries twice as hard as usual, but everything he does backfires. His hits don't fall in, he misses the easy grounders. He lies awake at night and worries.

"Relax, Mac," his manager tells him. "All you gotta do is *relax*. Take it easy."

Sure, but how?

It was the same with a tough scientific problem. Ben had long ago discovered that persistent and orderly logic could take him only so far. There came a time when no amount of forced thinking would get the job done.

The fresh insights and the new slants seldom came to him when he went after them, no matter how hard he tried. In fact, the more he sweated over a problem the more stubbornly recalcitrant his mind became. The big ideas, and the good ones, came to him in a flash of almost intuitive understanding—a flash that was conditioned by what he knew, of course, but a flash that did not come directly from the conscious mind.

The trick was to let the conscious mind get out of the way, let the message get through—

In Ben's case, go fishing.

It took him two hours, seven trout, and part of a banana to get the answer he sought.

He had taken a long, cool drink from the stream, cleaned his fish, and was sitting down on a rock to eat the lunch he had packed when the idea came.

He had peeled a banana and taken one bite of it when his mind was triggered by a single, innocuous word:

Banana.

Not just any old banana, of course. A specific one, used for a specific purpose.

Remember?

Charles Darwin and Cleopatra, two chimpanzees in their cages. Charles Darwin pushing his ape brain to the limit to fit two sticks together. Why?

To get a banana.

One lousy banana.

That was well enough, but there was more. Darwin might get his banana, and that was all he cared about. But who had placed the sticks in the cage, who had supplied the banana?

And why?

That was an easy one. It was so simple a child could have figured it out. Someone had given Charles Darwin two sticks and a banana for just one reason: to see whether or not he could solve the problem.

In a nutshell, a scientific experiment.

Now, consider another Charles Darwin, another problem.

Or consider Ben Hazard.

What is the toughest problem a man can tackle? Howells pointed it out many years ago. Of all the animals, man is the only one who wonders where he has come from and where he is going. All the other questions are petty compared to that one. It pushes the human brain to the limit. . . .

Ben stood up, his lunch forgotten.

It was all so obvious.

Men had been seeded on the Earth, and a problem had been planted with them—a real problem, one capable of yielding to a true solution. A dazed huddle of human beings had been abandoned by a fire in the mouth of a cave, lost in the morning of a strange new world. Then they had been left strictly alone; there was no evidence that they had been helped in any way since that time.

Why?

To see what they could do.

To see how long it would take them to solve the problem.

In a nutshell, a scientific experiment.

Ben picked up his rod and started back toward the car.

There was one more thing, one more inevitable characteristic of a scientific experiment. No scientist merely sets up his experiment and then goes off and forgets about it, even if he is the absolute ultimate in absentminded professors.

No.

He has to stick around to see how it all comes out. He has to observe, take notes.

It was monstrous.

The whole history of man on Earth. . . .

Ben climbed into his car, started the engine.

There's more. Face up to it.

Suppose that you had set up a fantastic planetary experiment with human beings. Suppose that you—or one of your descendants, for human generations are slow—came back to check on your experiment. What would you do, what would you be?

A garage mechanic?

A shoe salesman?

A pool-room shark?

Hardly. You'd have to be in a position to know what was going on. You'd have to work in a field where you could find out the score.

In a word, you'd be an anthropologist.

There's still more. Take it to the end of the line.

Now, suppose that man on Earth cracked the time barrier. Suppose a Temporal Research Project was set up. Wouldn't you be in on it, right at the top?

Sure.

You wouldn't miss it for anything.

Well, who fit the description? It couldn't be Ed; Ben had known him most of his life, known his folks and his wife and his kids, visited the Texas town that had been his home.

It wasn't Ben.

That left Franz Gottwald.

Franz, who had come from Germany and never talked about his past. Franz, with the strangely alien accent. Franz, who had no family. Franz, who had contributed nothing to the project but shrewd, prodding questions . . .

Franz.

The Grand Old Man.

Ben drove with his hands clenched on the wheel and his lips pressed into a thin, hard line. Night had fallen by the time he got out of the mountains, and he drove across an enchanted desert beneath the magic of the stars. The headlights of his car lanced into the night, stabbing, stabbing—

He passed the great New Mexico rocket base, from which men had hurled their missiles to the moon and beyond. There had been talk of a manned shot to Mars. . . .

How far would the experimenters let them go?

Ben lit a cigarette, not wanting to fool with his pipe in the car. He was filled with a cold anger he had never known before.

He had solved the problem.

Very well.

It was time to collect his banana.

It was after midnight when Ben got home.

He stuck his fish in the freezer, took a shower, and sat down in his comfortable armchair to collect his thoughts. He promptly discovered yet another fundamental truth about human beings: when they get tired enough, they sleep.

He woke up with a start and looked at his watch. It was five o'clock in the morning.

Ben shaved and was surprised to find that he was hungry. He cooked himself some bacon and scrambled eggs, drank three cups of instant coffee, and felt ready for anything.

Even Franz.

He got into his car and drove through the still-sleeping town to Gottwald's house. It looked safe and familiar in the pale morning light. As a matter of fact, it looked a lot like his own house, since both had been supplied by the government.

The government had given *Gottwald* a house to live in.

That, he thought, was a laugh.

He got out of his car, walked up to the door, and rang the bell. Franz never got to the office before nine, and his car was still in the garage.

His ring was greeted by total silence.

He tried again, holding his finger on the bell. He rang it long enough to wake the dead.

Ben tried the door. It was unlocked. He took a deep breath and stepped inside. The house was neat and clean. The familiar books were on the shelves in the living room. It was like stepping into his own home.

"Franz! It's me, Ben."

No answer.

Ben strode over to the bedroom, opened the door, and looked inside. The bed was tidily made, and Franz wasn't in it. Ben walked through the whole house, even peering inside the closets, before he was satisifed.

Franz wasn't home.

Fine. A scientist keeps records, doesn't he?

Ben proceeded to ransack the house. He looked in dresser drawers, on closet shelves, even in the refrigerator. He found nothing unusual. Then he tried the obvious.

He opened Gottwald's desk and looked inside.

The first thing he saw was a letter addressed to himself. There it was, a white envelope with his name typed on it: *Dr. Benjamin Wright Hazard.*

Not to be opened until Christmas?

Ben took the letter, ripped it open, and took out a single sheet of paper. He started to read it, then groped for a chair and sat down.

The letter was neatly typed. It said:

My Dear Ben:

I have always believed that a scientist must be capable of making predictions. This is not always an easy matter when you are dealing with human beings, but I have known you for a long, long time.

Obviously, you are searching my home, or you would not be reading this note. Obviously, if you are searching my home, you know part of the truth.

If you would like to know the rest of the story, the procedure is simple. Look behind the picture of the sand painting in my bedroom. You will find a button there. Press the button for exactly five seconds. Then walk out into my patio and stand directly in front of the barbecue pit.

Trust me, Ben. I am not a cannibal.

The letter was signed with Gottwald's scrawled signature.

Ben got up and walked into the bedroom. He looked behind the picture that was hanging over the dresser. There was a small red button.

Press the button for exactly five seconds.

And then—what?

Ben replaced the picture. The whole thing was a trifle too reminiscent of a feeble-minded practical joke. Press the button and get a shock. Press the button and get squirted with water. Press the button and blow up the house—

No. That was absurd.

Wasn't it?

He hesitated. He could call Ed, but then Ed would insist on coming over right away—and Ed had a wife and kids. He could call the police, but the story he had to tell would have sounded absolutely barmy. He had no proof. He might as well recite "Gunga Din."

He went back to Gottwald's desk, found some paper, and typed a letter. He outlined the theory he had formed and wrote down exactly what he was going to do. He put the letter into an envelope, addressed the envelope to Ed, stamped it, and went outside and dropped it in the mailbox on the corner.

He went back into the house.

This time he did not hesitate—not for a second.

He punched the button behind the picture for exactly five seconds. Nothing happened. He went out into the patio and stood directly in front of the barbecue pit.

The wall around the patio hid the outside world, but the blue sky overhead was the same as ever. He saw nothing, heard nothing.

"Snipe hunt," he said aloud.

Then, with breathtaking suddenness, something *did* happen.

There was an abrupt stillness in the air, a total cessation of sound. It was as though invisible glass walls had slipped silently into place and sealed off the world around him.

There was no perceptible transition. One moment the cone of yellow light was not there, and the next it was. It surrounded him: taut, living, seething with an energy that prickled his skin.

He knew that yellow light.

He had seen it once before, in the dawn of time. . . .

Ben held his breath; he couldn't help it. He felt strangely weightless, buoyant, a cork in a nameless sea—

His feet left the ground.

"Good God," Ben said.

He was lifted into the yellow light, absorbed in it. He could see perfectly, and it didn't help his stomach any. He could see the town below him—there was Gottwald's patio, the barbecue pit, the adobe house. He began to regret the bacon and eggs he had eaten.

He forced himself to breathe again. The air was warm and tasteless. He rose into the sky, fighting down panic.

Think of it as an elevator. It's just a way of getting from one place to another. I can see out, but of course nothing is visible from the outside. . . .

But then how did I see the yellow light before?

This must be different. They couldn't risk being seen—

Relax!

But he kept going higher, and faster.

The Earth was far away.

It was an uncanny feeling—not exactly unpleasant, but he didn't care for the view. It was like falling through the sky. It was impossible to avoid the idea that he was falling, that he was going to hit something. . . .

The blue of the sky faded into black, and he saw the stars.

Where am I going, where are they taking me?

There!

Look up, look up—

There it was, at the end of the tunnel of yellow light.

It blotted out the stars.

It was huge even against the immense backdrop of space itself. It stunned his mind with its size, that sleeping metal beast, but he recognized it.

It was the same ship that had landed the first men on Earth.

Dark now, dark and vast and lonely—but the same ship.

The shaft of yellow light pulled him inside; there was no air lock. As suddenly as it had come, the light was gone.

Ben stumbled and almost fell. The gravity seemed normal, but the light had supported him for so long that it took his legs a moment to adjust themselves.

He stood in a cool green room. It was utterly silent.

Ben swallowed hard.

He crossed the room to a metal door. The door opened before he reached it. There was only blackness beyond, blackness and the total silence of the dead.

Ben Hazard tried to fight down the numbing conviction that the ship was empty.

There is an almost palpable air of desolation about long-deserted things, about empty houses and derelict ships and crumbling ruins. There is a special kind of silence about a place that has once known life and knows it no longer. There is a type of death that hovers over things that have not been *used* for a long, long time.

That was the way the ship felt.

Ben could see only the small green room in which he stood and the corridor of darkness outside the door. It could have been only a tiny fraction of the great ship, only one room in a vast city in the sky. But he *knew* that the men who had once lived in the ship were gone. He knew it with a certainty that his mind could not question.

It was a ghost ship.

He knew it was.

That was why his heart almost stopped when he heard the footsteps moving toward him through the silence.

Heavy steps.

Metallic steps.

Ben backed away from the door. He tried to close it but it would not shut. He saw a white light coming at him through the dark tunnel. The light was higher than a man—

Metallic steps?

Ben got a grip on himself and waited. *You fool, you knew they had robots. You saw them. Robots don't die, do they?*

Do they kill?

He saw it now, saw its outline behind the light. Twice the size of a man, its metal body gleaming.

It had no face.

The robot filled the doorway and stopped. Ben could hear it now: a soft whirring noise that somehow reminded him of distant winds. He told himself that it was just a machine, just an animated hunk of metal, and his mind accepted the analysis. But it is one thing to know what a robot is, and it is quite another to find yourself in the same room with one.

"Well?" Ben said. He had to say something.

The robot was evidently under no such compulsion. It said nothing and did nothing. It simply stood there.

"You speak English, of course?" Ben said, recalling the line from an idiotic story he had once read.

If the robot spoke anything, it wasn't English.

After a long, uncomfortable minute, the robot turned around and walked into the dark corridor, its light flashing ahead of it. It took four steps, stopped, and looked back over its shoulder.

There was just one thing to do, and one way to go.

Ben nodded and stepped through the doorway after the robot.

He followed the giant metallic man along what seemed to be miles of featureless passageways. Ben heard no voices, saw no lights, met no living things.

He felt no fear now; he was beyond that. He knew that he was in a state of shock where nothing could get through to him, nothing could hurt him. He felt only a kind of sadness, the sadness a man knows when he walks through the tunnels of a pyramid or passes a graveyard on a lonely night.

The ship that men had built was so vast, so silent, so empty. . . .

A door opened ahead of them.

Light spilled out into the corridor.

Ben followed the robot into a large, comfortable room. The room was old, old and worn, but it was alive. It was warm and vital and human because there were two people in it. Ben had never before been quite so glad to see anyone.

One of the persons was an elderly woman he had never met before.

The other was Franz Gottwald.

"Hello, Ben," he said, smiling. "I don't believe you've met my wife."

Ben didn't know whether he was coming into a nightmare or coming out of one, but his manners were automatic.

"I'm very pleased to meet you," he said, and meant it.

The room had a subtle strangeness about it that once more reminded Ben of a dream. It was not merely the expected strangeness of design of a new kind of room, a room lost in the lonely miles of a silent spaceship; it was an out-of-phase oddness that at first he could not identify.

Then he caught it. There were alien things in the room: furniture that was planned for human beings but produced by a totally different culture pattern, carvings that were grotesque to his eyes, rugs that glowed in curiously wrong figures. But there were also familiar, everyday items from the world he knew: a prosaic reading lamp, a coffee pot bubbling on a table, some potted plants, a framed painting by Covarrubias. The mixture was a trifle jarring, but it did have a reassuring air of homeliness.

How strange the mind is. At a time like this, it concentrates on a room.

"Sit down, sit down," Franz said. "Coffee?"

"Thank you." Ben tried a chair and found it comfortable.

The woman he persisted in thinking of as Mrs. Gottwald—though that was certainly not her actual name—poured out a cup and handed it to him. Her lined, delicate face seemed radiant with happiness, but there were tears in her eyes.

"I speak the language too a little," she said hesitantly. "We are so proud of you, so happy—"

Ben took a sip of the coffee to cover his embarrassment. He didn't know what he had expected, but certainly not *this.*

"Don't say anything more, Arnin," Franz said sharply. "We must be very careful."

"That robot of yours," Ben said. "Couldn't you send him out for oiling or something?"

Franz nodded. "I forgot how weird he must seem to you. Please forgive me. I would have greeted you myself, but I am growing old and it is a long walk." He spoke to the robot in a language Ben had never heard, and the robot left the room.

Ben relaxed a little. "Do you two live up here all alone?"

An insane question. But what can I do, what can I say?

Old Franz seated himself next to Ben. He still wore his white suit. He seemed tired, more tired than Ben had ever seen him, but there was a kind of hope in his eyes, a hope that was almost a prayer.

"Ben," he said slowly, "it is hard for me to talk to you—now. I can imagine how you must feel after what you have been through. But you must trust me a little longer. Just forget where you are, Ben—a spaceship is just a ship. Imagine that we are back at the Station, imagine that we are talking as we have talked so many times before. You must think clearly. This is important, my boy, more important than you can know. I want you to tell me what you have discovered—I want to know what led you here. Omit nothing, and choose your words with care. Be as specific and precise as you can. Will you do this one last thing for me? When you have finished, I think I will be able to answer all your questions."

Ben had to smile. *"Be as specific and precise as you can."* How many times had he heard Franz use that very phrase on examinations?

He reached for his pipe. For a moment he had a wild, irrational fear that he had forgotten it—that would have been the last straw, somehow—but it was there. He filled it and lit it gratefully.

"It's your party, Franz. I'll tell you what I know."

"Proceed, Ben—and be careful."

Mrs. Gottwald—Arnin?—sat very still, waiting.

The ship was terribly silent around them.

Ben took his time and told Franz what he knew and what he believed. He left nothing out and made no attempt to soften his words.

When he was finished, Gottwald's wife was crying openly.

Franz, amazingly, looked like a man who had suddenly been relieved of a sentence of death.

"Well?" Ben asked.

Gottwald stood up and stroked his white beard. "You must think I am some kind of a monster," he said, smiling.

Ben shrugged. "I don't know."

Mrs. Gottwald dried her eyes. "Tell him," she said. "You can tell him now."

Gottwald nodded. "I am proud of you, Ben, very proud."

"I was right?"

"You were right in the only thing that matters. The fossils *were* a test, and you have passed that test with flying colors. Of course, you had some help from Edward—"

"I'll give him part of the banana."

Gottwald's smile vanished. "Yes. Yes, I daresay you will. But I am vain enough to want to clear up one slight error in your reconstruction. I do not care for the role of monster, and mad scientists have always seemed rather dull to me."

"The truth is the truth."

"A redundancy, Ben. But never mind. I must tell you that what has happened on Earth was *not* a mere scientific experiment. I must also tell you that I am not only a scientist who has come back, as you put it, to see how the chimpanzees are doing. In fact, I didn't come back at all. We—my people—never left. I was born right here in this ship, in orbit around the Earth. It has always been here."

"For twenty-five thousand years?"

"For twenty-five thousand years."

"But what have you been doing?"

"We've been waiting for you, Ben. You almost did not get here in time. My wife and I are the only ones left."

"Waiting for *me?* But—"

Gottwald held up his hand. "No, not this way. I can show you better than I can tell you: If my people had lived—my other people, I should say, for I have lived on the Earth most of my life—there would have been an impressive ceremony. That can never be now. But I can show you the history lesson we prepared. Will you come with me? It is not far."

The old man turned and walked toward the door, his wife leaning on his arm.

"So long," she whispered. "We have waited so long."

Ben got up and followed them into the corridor.

In a large assembly room filled with empty seats, somewhere in the great deserted ship, Ben saw the history of Man.

It was more than a film, although a screen was used. Ben lived the history, felt it, was a part of it.

It was not a story of what King Glotz did to King Goop; the proud names of conventional history fade into insignificance when the perspective is broad enough. It was a story of Man, of all men.

It was Gottwald's story—and Ben's.

Ben lived it.

Millions of years ago, on a world that circled a sun so far away that the astronomers of Earth had no name for it and not even a number, a new animal called Man appeared. His evolution had been a freakish thing, a million-to-one shot, and it was not likely to be repeated.

Man, the first animal to substitute cultural growth for physical change, was an immediate success. His tools and his weapons grew ever more efficient. On his home world, Man was a patient animal—but he was Man.

He was restless, curious. One world could not hold him. He built his first primitive spaceships and set out to explore the great dark sea around him. He established colonies and bases on a few of the worlds of his star system. He looked outward, out along the infinite corridors of the universe, and it was not in him to stop.

He tinkered and worked and experimented.

He found the faster-than-light drive.

He pushed on through the terrible emptiness of interstellar space. He touched strange worlds and stranger suns—

And he found that Man was not alone.

There were ships greater than his, and Beings—

Man discovered the Enemy.

It was not a case of misunderstanding, not a failure of diplomacy, not an accident born of fear or greed or stupidity. Man was a civilized animal. He was careful, reasonable, prepared to do whatever was ethically right.

He had no chance.

The Enemy—pounced. That was the only word for it. They were hunters, destroyers, killers. They were motivated by a savage hunger for destruction that Man had never known. They took many shapes, many forms.

Ben saw them.

He saw them rip ships apart, gut them with an utter ferocity that was beyond understanding. He saw them tear human beings to shreds, and eat them, and worse—

Ben screamed.

The Beings were more different from Man than the fish that swim in the sea, and yet . . .

Ben recognized them. He knew them.

They were there, all of them.

Literally, the Beings of nightmares.

The monsters that had troubled the dark sleeps of Earth, the things that crawled through myths, the Enemy who lived on the black side of the mind. The dragons, the serpents, the faces carved on masks, the Beings shaped in stones dug up in rotting jungles—

The Enemy.

We on Earth have not completely forgotten. We remember, despite the shocks that cleansed our minds. We remember, we remember. We have seen them in the darkness that lives always beyond the fires, we have heard them in the thunder that booms in the long, long night.

We remember.

It was not a war. A war, after all, is a specific kind of contest with rules of a sort. There were no rules. It was not a drive for conquest, not an attempt at exploitation. It was something new, something totally alien.

It was destruction.

It was extermination.

It was a fight between two different kinds of life, as senseless as a bolt of lightning that forked into the massive body of a screaming dinosaur.

Man wasn't ready.

He fell back, fighting where he could.

The Enemy followed.

Whether he liked it or not, Man was in a fight to the finish.

He fought for his life. He pushed himself to the utmost, tried everything he could think of, fought with everything he had. He exhausted his ingenuity. The Enemy countered his every move.

There was a limit.

Man could not go on.

Ben leaned forward, his fists clenched on his chair. He was a product of his culture. He read the books, saw the tri-di plays. He expected a happy ending.

There wasn't one.

Man lost.

He was utterly routed.

He had time for one last throw of the dice, one last desperate try for survival. He did his best.

He worked out the Plan.

It wasn't enough to run away, to find a remote planet and hide. It wasn't enough just to gain time.

Man faced the facts. He had met the Enemy and he had lost. He had tried everything he knew, and it hadn't been good enough. One day, no matter how far he ran, he would meet the Enemy again.

What could he do?

Man lives by his culture, his way of life. The potential for any culture is great, but it is not limitless. Culture has a way of putting blinders on its bearers; it leads them down certain paths and ignores others. Technological complexity is fine, but it is impotent without the one necessary ingredient:

Ideas.

Man needed new ideas, radically new concepts.

He needed a whole new way of thinking.

Transplanting the existing culture would not do the job. It would simply go on producing variants of the ideas that had already been tried.

Man didn't need transplanting.

He needed a transfusion, a transfusion of ideas.

He needed a brand-new culture with fresh solutions to old problems.

There is only one way to get a really different culture pattern: grow it from scratch.

Sow the seeds and get out.

Man put the Plan into effect.

With the last of his resources, he outfitted four fugitive ships and sent them out into the wastes of the seas between the stars.

"We don't know what happened to the other three ships," Franz Gottwald said quietly when the projection was over. "No ship knew the destination of any other ship. They went in different directions, each searching for remote, hidden worlds that might become new homes for men. There is no way of knowing what became of the others; I think it highly unlikely that any of them survived."

"Then Earth is all there is?"

"That is what we believe, Ben—we have to go ahead on that assumption. You know most of the rest of the story. This ship slipped through the Enemy and found the Earth. We landed human beings who were so conditioned that they could remember little or nothing, for they had to begin all over again. We planted the fossils and the apes as a test, just as you supposed."

"But why? There was no need for such a stunt—"

Gottwald smiled. "It wasn't a stunt, my boy. It was the key to everything. You see, we had to warn the men of Earth about what they had to face. More than that, once their cultures had developed along their own lines, we had to share what we had with them. I need hardly remind you that this ship is technologically many thousands of years ahead of anything the Earth has produced. But we couldn't turn the ship over to them until we were *certain* they were ready. You don't give atomic bombs to babies. The men of Earth had to *prove* that they could handle the toughest problem we could dream up. You solved it, Ben."

"I didn't do it alone."

"No, of course not. I can tell you now that my people—my other people—never did invent time-travel. That was a totally unexpected means of tackling the problem; we never could have done it. It is the most hopeful thing that has happened."

"But what became of the men and women who stayed here on the ship?"

Franz shook his head. "Twenty-five thousand years is a long, long time, Ben. We were a defeated people. We worked hard; we were not idle. For one thing, we prepared dictionaries for every major language on Earth so that all the data in our libraries will be available to you. But man does not live well inside a ship. Each generation we became fewer; children were very scarce."

"It's like the old enigma of the cities, isn't it?"

"Exactly. No city in human history has ever reproduced its population. Urban births are always lower than rural ones. All cities have always drawn their personnel from the surrounding countryside. The ship was sealed up; we had no rural areas. It was only a matter of time before we were all gone. My wife and I were the last ones, Ben—and we had no children."

"We were so afraid," Mrs. Gottwald said. "So afraid that you would not come before it was too late. . . ."

"What would you have done?"

Franz shrugged wearily. "That is one decision I was spared. I did cheat a little, my boy. I was careful to give you no help, but I did plant some projectors near you that kept you stirred up. They broadcast frequencies that . . . ah . . . stimulate the mind, keep it in a state of urgency. Perhaps you noticed them?"

Ben nodded. He remembered the voice that spoke in his skull: *Hurry, hurry—*

"Franz, what will happen now?"

Gottwald stroked his beard, his eyes very tired. "I can't tell you that. I don't know the answer. I have studied the men of Earth for most of my life, and I still don't know. You are a tough people, Ben, tougher than we ever were. You have fought many battles, and your history is a proud one. But I cannot read the future. I have done my best, and the rest is up to you."

"It's a terrible responsibility."

"Yes, for you and for others like you it will be a crushing burden. But it will be a long fight; we will not live to see more than the beginning of it. It will take centuries for the men of Earth to learn all that is in this ship. It's an odd thing, Ben—I have never seen the Enemy face to face. You will probably never see them. But what we do now will determine whether mankind lives or dies."

"It's too much for one man."

"Yes." Gottwald smiled, remembering. "It is."

"I don't know where to begin."

"We will wait for Edward—he will be here tomorrow, unless I don't know him at all—and then the three of us will sit down together for one last time. We will think it out. I am very tired, Ben; my wife and I have lived past our time. It is hard to be old, and to have no children. I always thought of you and Edward as my sons; I hope you do not find this too maudlin."

Ben searched for words and couldn't find any.

Franz put his arm around his wife. "Sometimes, when the job was too big for me, when I felt myself giving up, I would walk up into the old control room of this ship. My wife and I have stood there many times. Would you like to see it?"

"I need it, Franz."

"Yes. So do I. Come along."

They walked for what seemed to be miles through the dark passages of the empty ship, then rode a series of elevators up to the control room.

Franz switched on the lights.

"The ship is not dead, you know," he said. "It is only the people who are gone. The computers still maintain the ship's orbit, and the defensive screens still make it invulnerable to detection—you wouldn't have seen it if you had not been coming up the light tube, and there is no way the ship can be tracked from Earth. What do you think of the control room?"

Ben stared at it. It was a large chamber, acres in extent, but it was strangely empty. There were panels of switches and a few small machines, but the control room was mostly empty space.

"It's not what I expected," he said, hiding his disappointment.

Franz smiled. "When machinery is efficient you don't need a lot of it. There is no need for flashing lights and sparks of electricity. What you see here gets the job done."

Ben felt a sudden depression. He had badly needed a lift, and he didn't see it here. "If you'll forgive me for saying so, Franz, it isn't very inspiring. I suppose it is different for you—"

Gottwald answered him by throwing a switch.

Two immense screens flared into life, covering the whole front of the control room.

Ben caught his breath.

One of the screens showed the globe of the Earth far below, blue and green and necklaced with silver clouds.

The other showed the stars.

The stars were alive, so close he could almost touch them with his hand. They turned like radiant beacons in the cold sea of space. They whispered to him, called to him—

Ben knew then that the men of Earth had remembered something more than monsters and nightmares, something more than the fears and terrors that crept through the great dark night.

Not all the dreams had been nightmares.

Through all the years and all the sorrows, Man had never forgotten.

I remember. I remember.

I have seen you through all the centuries of nights. I have looked up to see you, I have lifted my head to pray, I have known wonder—

I remember.

Ben looked again at the sleeping Earth.

He sensed that old Franz and his wife had drawn back into the shadows.

He stood up straight, squaring his shoulders.

Then Ben Hazard turned once more and looked out into the blazing heritage of the stars.

I remember, I remember—

It has been long, but you, too, have not forgotten.

Wait for us.

We'll be back.

I spoke in an earlier headnote of the slow, painful ascent of humanity up from its hominid ancestry. Could this have been short-circuited if there were some way of bringing technological advance back in time?

There is unfortunately a certain resistance to change and besides an advanced technology all hangs together. Suppose you take a television set to ancient Greece. Even if you could explain how it works, how would you make the solid-state devices, the picture tube, the wires, given the technology of that day? In fact, how could you make it serve as anything but a lump of complicated material without any television stations to send out images?

What if you brought something simpler—a stainless-steel knife? And given the technology of that day, how would you make stainless steel?

Suppose you were simply a doctor with modern medical technology at your fingertips. What could you do if you found yourself among Homo erectus? *Thomas in this story is remarkably convincing.*

THE DOCTOR
THEODORE L. THOMAS

When Gant first opened his eyes he thought for an instant he was back in his home in Pennsylvania. He sat up suddenly and looked wildly around in the dark of the cave, and then he remembered where he was. The noise he made frightened his wife and his son, Dun, and they rolled to their feet, crouched, ready to leap. Gant grunted reassuringly at them and climbed off the moss-packed platform he had built for a bed. The barest glimmerings of dawn filtered into the cave, and the remnants of the fire glowed at the mouth. Gant went to the fire and poked it and put some chips on it and blew on them. It had been a long time since he had had such a vivid memory of his old life half a million years away. He looked at the wall of the cave, at the place where he kept his calendar, painfully scratched into the rock. It had been ten years ago today when he had stepped into the molybdenum-steel cylinder in the Bancroft Building at Pennsylvania State University. What was it he had said? "Sure, I'll try it. You ought to have a medical doctor in it on the first trial run. You physicists could not learn anything about the physiological effects of time travel. Besides, this will make history, and I want to be in on it."

Gant stepped over the fire and listened carefully at the mouth of the cave, near the log barrier. Outside he heard the sound of rustling brush and heavy breathing, and he knew he could not leave now. He drank some water from a gourd and ate some dried bison with his wife and son. They all ate quietly.

Dawn came, and he stepped to the mouth of the cave and listened. The great animal had left. He waved to his wife and Dun, dragged aside the barrier, and went out.

He went along the face of the cliff, staying away from the heavy underbrush at its foot. He would go into it when he returned, and he would look for food.

In the marsh that lay beyond the underbrush was one of the many monuments to his failures. In the rocks and tree stumps there, he had tried to grow penicillium molds on the sweet juices of some of the berries that abounded in the region. He had crushed the berries and placed the juices in a hundred different kinds of receptacles. For three years he had tried to raise the green mold, but all he ever produced was a slimy gray mass that quickly rotted when the sun struck it.

He hefted the heavy stone ax in his right hand. As he approached the cave he was looking for, he grunted loudly and then went in. The people inside held their weapons in their hands, and he was glad he had called ahead. He ignored them and went to a back corner to see the little girl.

She sat on the bare stone, leaning against the rock with her mouth open, staring dully at him as he came up to her, her eyes black against the thick blond hair that grew on her face. Gant whirled at the others and snarled at them, and snatched a bearhide from the bed of the man and carried it to the girl. He wrapped her in it and then felt the part of her forehead where there was no hair. It was burning hot, must be about 105 degrees, possibly a little more. He put her down on the rock and thumped her chest and heard the solid, hard sound of filled lungs. It was full-blown pneumonia, no longer any doubt. She gasped for breath, and there was no breath. Gant picked her up again and held her. He sat with her for over an hour, changing her position frequently in his arms, trying to make her comfortable as she gasped. He held a handful of wet leaves to her forehead to try to cool her burning face, but it did not seem to help. She went into convulsions at the end.

He laid the body on a rock ledge and pulled the mother over to see it. The mother bent and touched the girl gently on the face and then straightened and looked at Gant helplessly. He picked up the body and walked out of the cave and down into the woods. It took several hours to dig a hole deep enough with a stick.

He hunted on the way back to the caves, and he killed a short, heavy-bodied animal that hung upside down from the lower branches of a tree. It emitted a foul odor as he killed it, but it would make a good meal. He found a large rock outcropping with a tiny spring coming out from under it. A mass of newly sprouted shoots grew in the soggy ground. He picked them all, and headed back to his cave. His wife and Dun were there and their faces brightened when they saw what he brought. His wife immediately laid out the animal and skinned it with a fragment of sharp, shiny rock. Dun watched her intently, leaning over while it cooked to smell the fragrant smoke. Gant looked at the short, thick hairy woman tending the cooking, and he looked at the boy. He could easily see himself in the thin-limbed boy. Both his wife and his son had the heavy brows and the jutting jaw of the cave people. But Dun's body was lean and his eyes were blue and sparkling, and he often sat close to Gant and tried to go with him when he went out of the cave. And once, when the lightning blazed and the thunder roared, Gant had seen the boy standing at the mouth of the cave staring at the sky in puzzlement, not fear, and Gant had put a hand on his shoulder and tried to find the words that told of electrical discharges and the roar of air rushing into a void, but there were no words.

The meat was done and the shoots were softened, and the three of them squatted at the fire and reached for the food. Outside the cave they heard the sound of movement in the gravel, and Gant leaped for his club while his wife and Dun retreated to the rear of the cave. Two men appeared, one supporting the other, both empty-handed. Gant waited until he could see that one of them was injured; he could not place his right foot on the ground. Then Gant came forward and helped the injured man to a sitting position at the mouth of the cave. He leaned over to inspect the foot. The region just above the ankle was discolored and badly swollen, and the foot was at a slight angle to the rest of the leg. Both the fibula and the tibia seemed to be broken, and Gant stood up and looked around for splints. The man would probably die; there was no one to take care of him during the weeks needed for his leg to heal, no one to hunt for him and give him food and put up with his almost complete inactivity.

Gant found two chips from logs and two short branches and some strips from a cured hide. He knelt in front of the man and carefully held his hands near the swollen leg so the man could see he was going to touch it.

The man's great muscles were knotted in pain and his face was gray beneath the hair. Gant waved the second man around to one side where he could keep an eye on him, and then he took the broken leg and began to apply tension. The injured man stood it for a moment and then roared in pain and instinctively lashed out with his good leg. Gant ducked the kick, but he could not duck the blow from the second man. It hit him on the side of the head and knocked him out of the mouth of the cave. He rolled to his feet and came back in. The second man stood protectively in front of the injured man, but Gant pushed him aside and knelt down again. The foot was straight, so Gant placed the chips and branches on the leg and bound them in place with the leather thongs. Weak and helpless, the injured man did not resist. Gant stood up and showed the second man how to carry the injured man. He helped them on their way.

When they left, Gant returned to his food. It was cold, but he was content. For the first time they had come to him. They were learning. He hurt his teeth on the hard meat and he gagged on the spongy shoots, but he squatted in his cave and he smiled. There had been a time long ago when he had thought that these people would be grateful to him for his work, that he would become known by some such name as The Healer. Yet here he was, years later, happy that at last one of them had come to him with an injury. Yet Gant knew them too well by now to be misled. These people did not have even the concept of medical treatment, and the day would probably come when one of them would kill him as he worked.

He sighed, picked up his club, and went out of the cave. A mile away was a man with a long gash in the calf of his left leg. Gant had cleaned it and packed it with moss and tied it tight with a hide strip. It was time to check the wound, so he walked the mile carefully, on the lookout for the large creatures that roamed the forests. The man was chipping rock in front of his cave, and he nodded his head and waved and showed his teeth in a friendly gesture when he saw Gant. Gant showed his teeth in turn and looked at the leg. He saw that the man had removed the moss and bandage, and had rubbed the great wound with dung. Gant bent to inspect the wound and immediately smelled the foul smell of corruption. Near the top of the wound, just beneath the knee, was a mass of black, wet tissues. Gangrene. Gant straightened and looked around at some of the others near the cave. He went to them and tried to make them understand what he wanted to do, but they did not pay much attention. Gant returned and looked down on the wounded man, noting that his movements were still quick and coordinated, and that he was as powerfully built as the rest of them. Gant shook his head; he could not perform the amputation unaided, and there was no help to be had. He tried again to show them that the man would die unless they helped him, but it was no use. He left.

He walked along the foot of the cliffs, looking in on the caves. In one he found a woman with a swollen jaw, in pain. She let him look in her mouth, and he saw a rotted molar. He sat down with her and with gestures tried to explain that it would be painful at first if he removed the tooth, but that it would soon be better. The woman seemed to understand. Gant took up a fresh branch and scraped a rounded point on one end. He picked up a rock twice the size of his fist, and placed the woman in a sitting position with her head resting on his thigh. He placed the end of the stick low on the gum to make sure he got the root. Carefully he raised the rock, knowing he would have but one try. He smashed the rock down and felt the tooth give way and saw the blood spout from her mouth. She screamed and leaped to her feet and turned on Gant, but he jumped away. Then something struck him from behind and he found himself pinned to the ground with two men sitting on him. They growled at him and one picked up a rock and the stick and smashed a front tooth from Gant's mouth. Then they threw him out of the cave. He rolled down through the gravel and came up short against a bush. He leaped to his feet and charged back into the cave. One of the men swung a club at him, but he ducked and slammed the rock against the side of the man's head. The other ran. Gant went over to the woman, picking as he went a half-handful of moss from the wall of the cave. He stood in front of her and packed some of the moss in the wound in his front jaw, and leaned over to show her the bleeding had stopped. He held out the moss to her, and she quickly took some and put it in the proper place in her jaw. She nodded to him and patted his arm and rubbed the blood out of the hair on her chin. He left the cave, without looking at the unconscious man.

Someday they would kill him. His jaw throbbed as he walked along the gravel shelf and headed for home. There would be no more stops today, and so he threaded his way along the foot of the cliff. He heard sounds of activity in several of the caves, and in one of the largest of them he heard excited voices yelling. He stopped, but his jaw hurt too much to go in. The noise increased and Gant thought they might be carving up a large kill. He was always on the lookout for meat, so he changed his mind and went back in. Inside was a boy about the age of Dun, lying on his back, gasping for air. His face had a bluish tinge, and at each intake of air his muscles tensed and his back arched with the effort to breathe. Gant pushed to his side and forced his mouth open. The throat and uvula were greatly swollen, the air passage almost shut. He quickly examined the boy, but there was no sign of injury or disease. Gant was puzzled, but then he concluded the boy must have chewed or eaten a substance to which he was sensitive. He looked at the throat again. The swelling was continuing. The boy's jutting jaws made mouth-to-mouth resuscitation impossible. A tracheotomy was indicated. He went over to the fire and smashed one piece of flint chopping stone on another, and quickly picked over the pieces. He chose a short, sharp fragment against the skin just beneath the larynx, squeezed his thumb and forefinger on the fragment to measure a distance a little over half an inch from the point, and then thrust down and into the boy's throat until his thumb and forefinger just touched the skin. Behind him he heard a struggle, and he looked up in time to see several people restrain a woman with an ax. He watched to see that they kept her out of the cave and away from him before he turned back to the boy. By gently turning the piece of flint he made an opening in the windpipe. He turned the boy on his side to prevent the tiny trickle of blood from running into the opening. The result was dramatic. The boy's struggles stopped, and the rush of air around the piece of flint sounded loud in the still of the cave. The boy lay back and relaxed and breathed deeply, and even the people in the cave could tell he was now much better. They gathered around and watched silently, and Gant could see the interest in their faces. The boy's mother had not come back.

For half an hour Gant sat holding the flint in the necessary position. The boy stirred restlessly a time or two, but Gant quieted him. The people drifted back to their activities in the cave, and Gant sat and tended his patient.

He leaned over the boy. He could hear the air beginning to pass through his throat once again. In another fifteen minutes the boy's throat was open enough, and Gant withdrew the flint in one swift movement. The boy began to sit up, but Gant held him down and pressed the wound closed. It stayed closed, and Gant got up. No one paid any attention when he left.

He went along the gravel shelf, ignoring the sounds of life that came out of the caves as he went by. He rounded a boulder and saw his own cave ahead.

The log barrier was displaced and he could hear snarls and grunts as he ran into the semidarkness inside. Two bodies writhed on the floor of the cave. He ran closer and saw that his wife and another woman were struggling there, raking each other's skin with thick, sharp nails, groping for each other's jugular vein with long, yellow teeth. Gant drove his heel into the side of the woman's body, just above the kidney. The air exploded from her lungs and she went limp. He twisted a hand in her hair and yanked her limp body away from his wife's teeth and ran for the entrance of the cave, dragging her after him. Outside, he threw the limp body down the slope. He turned and caught his wife as she came charging out. She fought him, trying to get to the woman down the slope, and it was only because she was no longer trying to kill that he was able to force her back into the cave.

Inside, she quickly stopped fighting him. She went and knelt over something lying at the foot of his bed. He rubbed his sore jaw and went over to see what it was. He stared down in the dim light of the cave. It was Dun, and he was dead. His head had been crushed. Gant cried out and leaned against the wall. He knelt and hugged Dun's warm body to him, pushing his wife aside. He pressed his face into the boy's neck and thought of the years that he had planned to spend in teaching Dun the healing arts. He felt a heavy pat on his shoulder and looked up. His wife was there, awkwardly patting him on the shoulder, trying to comfort him. Then he remembered the woman who had killed his son.

He ran out of the cave and looked down the slope. She was not there, but he caught a flash of movement down the gravel shelf and he could see her staggering toward her cave. He began to run after her, but stopped. His anger was gone, and he felt no emotion save a terrible emptiness. He turned and went back into the cave for Dun's body. In the forest he slowly dug a deep hole. He felt numb as he dug, but when it was done and he had rolled a large stone on top of the grave, he kneeled down near it, held his face in his hands and cried. Afterward, he followed the stream bed to a flat table of solid rock. At the edge of the rock table, where the wall of rock began to rise to the cliffs above, half hidden in the shrub pine, was a mass of twisted metal wreckage. He looked down on it and thought again of that day ten years ago. Here, on the site of Pennsylvania State University, at College Park, Pennsylvania, was where he started and where he ended. But a difference of half a million years lay between the start and the end.

Once tears had come to his eyes when he looked at the wreckage, but no longer. There was work to do here and he was the only one who could do it. He nodded and turned to climb to his cave. There were cold meat and shoots there, and a wife, and perhaps there could be another son. And this day, for the first time, an injured man had come to see him.

Here is another attempt to portray a Neanderthal, and, I think, a fairer one than Wells managed. Remember, we now consider Neanderthal man a subspecies of us. They are Homo sapiens neanderthalensis and we are Homo sapiens sapiens. They may not have been very different from us, either physically or mentally.

For one thing, their brains were actually larger than ours, though the shape was somewhat different. For another, they almost certainly intermarried with us, so that many human beings now alive may carry genes inherited from the Neanderthals. (My wife claims proudly that she has an ancient strain of Neanderthal nobility in her gene pool, and she is a highly intelligent and lovable psychiatrist.)

In any case, here is my Neanderthal story, written long before I met my wife.

THE UGLY LITTLE BOY
ISAAC ASIMOV

Edith Fellowes smoothed her working smock as she always did before opening the elaborately locked door and stepping across the invisible dividing line between the *is* and the *is not.* She carried her notebook and her pen although she no longer took notes except when she felt the absolute need for some report.

• This time, she also carried a suitcase. ("Games for the boy," she had said, smiling to the guard—who had long since stopped even thinking of questioning her and who waved her on.)

And, as always, the ugly little boy knew that she had entered and came running to her, crying, "Miss Fellowes— Miss Fellowes—" in his soft, slurring way.

"Timmie," she said, and passed her hand over the shaggy, brown hair on his misshapen little head. "What's wrong?"

He said, "Will Jerry be back to play again? I'm sorry about what happened."

"Never mind that now, Timmie. Is that why you've been crying?"

He looked away. "Not just about that, Miss Fellowes. I dreamed again."

293

"The same dream?" Miss Fellowes's lips set. Of course, the Jerry affair would bring back the dream.

He nodded. His too large teeth showed as he tried to smile and the lips of his forward-thrusting mouth stretched wide. "When will I be big enough to go out there, Miss Fellowes?"

"Soon," she said softly, feeling her heart break. "Soon."

Miss Fellowes let him take her hand and enjoyed the warm touch of the thick dry skin of his palm. He led her through the three rooms that made up the whole of Stasis Section One—comfortable enough, yes, but an eternal prison for the ugly little boy all the seven (was it seven?) years of his life.

He led her to the one window, looking out onto a scrubby woodland section of the world of *is* (now hidden by night), where a fence and painted instructions allowed no men to wander without permission.

He pressed his nose against the window. "Out there, Miss Fellowes?"

"Better places. Nicer places," she said sadly as she looked at his poor little imprisoned face outlined in profile against the window. The forehead retreated flatly and his hair lay down in tufts upon it. The back of his skull bulged and seemed to make the head overheavy so that it sagged and bent forward, forcing the whole body into a stoop. Already, bony ridges were beginning to bulge the skin above his eyes. His wide mouth thrust forward more prominently than did his wide and flattened nose and he had no chin to speak of, only a jawbone that curved smoothly down and back. He was small for his years and his stumpy legs were bowed.

He was a very ugly little boy and Edith Fellowes loved him dearly.

Her own face was behind his line of vision, so she allowed her lips the luxury of a tremor.

They would *not* kill him. She would do anything to prevent it. Anything. She opened the suitcase and began taking out the clothes it contained.

Edith Fellowes had crossed the threshold of Stasis, Inc., for the first time just a little over three years before. She hadn't, at that time, the slightest idea as to what Stasis meant or what the place did. No one did then, except those who worked there. In fact, it was only the day after she arrived that the news broke upon the world.

At the time, it was just that they had advertised for a woman with knowledge of physiology, experience with clinical chemistry, and a love for children. Edith Fellowes had been a nurse in a maternity ward and believed she fulfilled those qualifications.

Gerald Hoskins, whose nameplate on the desk included a Ph.D. after the name, scratched his cheek with his thumb and looked at her steadily.

Miss Fellowes automatically stiffened and felt her face (with its slightly asymmetric nose and its a-trifle-too-heavy eyebrows) twitch.

He's no dreamboat himself, she thought resentfully. He's getting fat and bald and he's got a sullen mouth. But the salary mentioned had been considerably higher than she had expected, so she waited.

Hoskins said, "Now, do you really love children?"

"I wouldn't say I did if I didn't."

"Or do you just love pretty children? Nice chubby children with cute little button noses and gurgly ways?"

Miss Fellowes said, "Children are children, Dr. Hoskins, and the ones that aren't pretty are just the ones who may happen to need help most."

"Then suppose we take you on—"

"You mean you're offering me the job now?"

He smiled briefly, and for a moment, his broad face had an absentminded charm about it. He said, "I make quick decisions. So far the offer is tentative, however. I may make as quick a decision to let you go. Are you ready to take the chance?"

Miss Fellowes clutched at her purse and calculated just as swiftly as she could, then ignored calculations and followed impulse. "All right."

"Fine. We're going to form the Stasis tonight and I think you had better be there to take over at once. That will be at eight P.M. and I'd appreciate it if you could be here at seven-thirty."

"But what—"

"Fine. Fine. That will be all now." On signal, a smiling secretary came in to usher her out.

Miss Fellowes stared back at Dr. Hoskins's closed door for a moment. What was Stasis? What had this large barn of a building —with its badged employees, its makeshift corridors, and its unmistakable air of engineering—to do with children?

She wondered if she should go back that evening or stay away and teach that arrogant man a lesson. But she knew she would be back if only out of sheer frustration. She would have to find out about the children.

She came back at seven-thirty and did not have to announce herself. One after another, men and women seemed to know her and to know her function. She found herself all but placed on skids as she was moved inward.

Dr. Hoskins was there, but he only looked at her distantly and murmured, "Miss Fellowes."

He did not even suggest that she take a seat, but she drew one calmly up to the railing and sat down.

They were on a balcony, looking down into a large pit filled with instruments that looked like a cross between the control panel of a spaceship and the working face of a computer. On one side were partitions that seemed to make up an unceilinged apartment, a giant dollhouse into the rooms of which she could look from above.

She could see an electronic cooker and a freeze-space unit in one room and a washroom arrangement off another. And surely the object she made out in another room could only be part of a bed, a small bed.

Hoskins was speaking to another man and, with Miss Fellowes, they made up the total occupancy of the balcony. Hoskins did not offer to introduce the other man, and Miss Fellowes eyed him surreptitiously. He was thin and quite fine-looking in a middle-aged way. He had a small mustache and keen eyes that seemed to busy themselves with everything.

He was saying, "I won't pretend for one moment that I understand all this, Dr. Hoskins; I mean, except as a layman, a reasonably intelligent layman, may be expected to understand it. Still, if there's one part I understand less than another, it's this matter of selectivity. You can only reach out so far; that seems sensible; things get dimmer the further you go; it takes more energy. But then, you can only reach out so near. That's the puzzling part."

"I can make it seem less paradoxical, Deveney, if you will allow me to use an analogy."

(Miss Fellowes placed the new man the moment she heard his name, and despite herself was impressed. This was obviously Candide Deveney, the science writer of the Telenews, who was notoriously at the scene of every major scientific breakthrough. She even recognized his face as one she saw on the news-plate when the landing on Mars had been announced. So Dr. Hoskins must have something important here.)

"By all means use an analogy," said Deveney ruefully, "if you think it will help."

"Well, then, you can't read a book with ordinary-size print if it is held six feet from your eyes, but you can read it if you hold it one foot from your eyes. So far, the closer the better. If you bring the book to within one inch of your eyes, however, you've lost it again. There is such a thing as being too close, you see."

"Hmmm," said Deveney.

"Or take another example. Your right shoulder is about thirty inches from the tip of your right forefinger and you can place your right forefinger on your right shoulder. Your right elbow is only half the distance from the tip of your right forefinger; it should by all ordinary logic be easier to reach, and yet you cannot place your right finger on your right elbow. Again, there is such a thing as being too close."

Deveney said, "May I use these analogies in my story?"

"Well, of course. Only too glad. I've been waiting long enough for someone like you to have a story. I'll give you anything else you want. It is time, finally, that we want the world looking over our shoulder. They'll see something."

(Miss Fellowes found herself admiring his calm certainty despite herself. There was strength there.)

Deveney said, "How far out will you reach?"

"Forty thousand years."

Miss Fellowes drew in her breath sharply.

Years?

There was tension in the air. The men at the controls scarcely moved. One man at a microphone spoke into it in a soft monotone, in short phrases that made no sense to Miss Fellowes.

Deveney, leaning over the balcony railing with an intent stare, said, "Will we see anything, Dr. Hoskins?"

"What? No. Nothing till the job is done. We detect indirectly, something on the principle of radar, except that we use mesons rather than radiation. Mesons reach backward under the proper conditions. Some are reflected and we must analyze the reflections."

"That sounds difficult."

Hoskins smiled again, briefly as always. "It is the end product of fifty years of research; forty years of it before I entered the field. . . . Yes, it's difficult."

The man at the microphone raised one hand.

Hoskins said, "We've had the fix on one particular moment in time for weeks; breaking it, remaking it after calculating our own movements in time; making certain that we could handle time-flow with sufficient precision. This must work now."

But his forehead glistened.

Edith Fellowes found herself out of her seat and at the balcony railing, but there was nothing to see.

The man at the microphone said quietly, "Now."

There was a space of silence sufficient for one breath and then the sound of a terrified little boy's scream from the dollhouse rooms. Terror! Piercing terror!

Miss Fellowes's head twisted in the direction of the cry. A child was involved. She had forgotten.

And Hoskins's fist pounded on the railing and he said in a tight voice, trembling with triumph, "*Did* it."

Miss Fellowes was urged down the short, spiral flight of steps by the hard press of Hoskins's palm between her shoulder blades. He did not speak to her.

The men who had been at the controls were standing about now, smiling, smoking, watching the three as they entered on the main floor. A very soft buzz sounded from the direction of the doll-house.

Hoskins said to Deveney, "It's perfectly safe to enter Stasis. I've done it a thousand times. There's a queer sensation which is momentary and means nothing."

He stepped through an open door in mute demonstration, and Deveney, smiling stiffly and drawing an obviously deep breath, followed him.

Hoskins said, "Miss Fellowes! Please!" He crooked his forefinger impatiently.

Miss Fellowes nodded and stepped stiffly through. It was as though a ripple went through her, an internal tickle.

But once inside all seemed normal. There was the smell of the fresh wood of the dollhouse and—of—of soil somehow.

There was silence now, no voice at least, but there was the dry shuffling of feet, a scrabbling as of a hand over wood—then a low moan.

"Where is it?" asked Miss Fellowes in distress. Didn't these fool men *care?*

The boy was in the bedroom; at least in the room with the bed in it.

It was standing naked, with its small, dirt-smeared chest heaving raggedly. A bushel of dirt and coarse grass spread over the floor at his bare brown feet. The smell of soil came from it and a touch of something fetid.

Hoskins followed her horrified glance and said with annoyance, "You can't pluck a boy cleanly out of time, Miss Fellowes. We had to take some of the surroundings with it for safety. Or would you have preferred to have it arrive here minus a leg or with only half a head?"

"*Please!*" said Miss Fellowes, in an agony of revulsion. "Are we just to stand here? The poor child is frightened. And it's *filthy.*"

She was quite correct. It was smeared with encrusted dirt

and grease and had a scratch on its thigh that looked red and sore.

As Hoskins approached him, the boy, who seemed to be something over three years in age, hunched low and backed away rapidly. He lifted his upper lip and snarled in a hissing fashion like a cat. With a rapid gesture, Hoskins seized both the child's arms and lifted him, writhing and screaming, from the floor.

Miss Fellowes said, "Hold him, now. He needs a warm bath first. He needs to be cleaned. Have you the equipment? If so, have it brought here, and I'll need to have help in handling him just at first. Then, too, for heaven's sake, have all this trash and filth removed."

She was giving the orders now and she felt perfectly good about that. And because now she was an efficient nurse, rather than a confused spectator, she looked at the child with a clinical eye—and hesitated for one shocked moment. She saw past the dirt and shrieking, past the thrashing of limbs and useless twisting. She saw the boy himself.

It was the ugliest little boy she had ever seen. It was horribly ugly from misshapen head to bandy legs.

She got the boy cleaned with three men helping her and with others milling about in their efforts to clean the room. She worked in silence and with a sense of outrage, annoyed by the continued strugglings and outcries of the boy and by the undignified drenchings of soapy water to which she was subjected.

Dr. Hoskins had hinted that the child would not be pretty, but that was far from stating that it would be repulsively deformed. And there was a stench about the boy that soap and water was only alleviating little by little.

She had the strong desire to thrust the boy, soaped as he was, into Hoskins's arms and walk out; but there was the pride of profession. She had accepted an assignment after all. And there would be the look in his eyes. A cold look that would read: Only pretty children, Miss Fellowes?

He was standing apart from them, watching coolly from a distance with a half-smile on his face when he caught her eye, as though amused at her outrage.

She decided she would wait a while before quitting. To do so now would only demean her.

Then, when the boy was a bearable pink and smelled of scented soap, she felt better anyway. His cries changed to whimpers of exhaustion as he watched carefully, eyes moving in quick frightened suspicion from one to another of those in the room. His cleanness accentuated his thin nakedness as he shivered with cold after his bath.

Miss Fellowes said sharply, "Bring me a nightgown for the child!"

A nightgown appeared at once. It was as though everything were ready and yet nothing were ready unless she gave orders; as though they were deliberately leaving this in her charge without help, to test her.

The newsman, Deveney, approached and said, "I'll hold him, Miss. You won't get it on yourself."

"Thank you," said Miss Fellowes. And it was a battle indeed, but the nightgown went on, and when the boy made as though to rip it off, she slapped his hand sharply.

The boy reddened, but did not cry. He stared at her and the splayed fingers of one hand moved slowly across the flannel of the nightgown, feeling the strangeness of it.

Miss Fellowes thought desperately: Well, what next?

Everyone seemed in suspended animation, waiting for her— even the ugly little boy.

Miss Fellowes said sharply, "Have you provided food? Milk?"

They had. A mobile unit was wheeled in, with its refrigeration compartment containing three quarts of milk, with a warming unit and a supply of fortifications in the form of vitamin drops, copper-cobalt-iron syrup and others she had no time to be concerned with. There was a variety of canned self-warming junior foods.

She used milk, simply milk, to begin with. The radar unit heated the milk to a set temperature in a matter of ten seconds and clicked off, and she put some in a saucer. She had a certainty about the boy's savagery. He wouldn't know how to handle a cup.

Miss Fellowes nodded and said to the boy, "Drink. Drink." She made a gesture as though to raise the milk to her mouth. The boy's eyes followed but he made no move.

Suddenly, the nurse resorted to direct measures. She seized the boy's upper arm in one hand and dipped the other in the milk. She dashed the milk across his lips, so that it dripped down cheeks and receding chin.

For a moment, the child uttered a high-pitched cry, then his tongue moved over his wetted lips. Miss Fellowes stepped back.

The boy approached the saucer, bent toward it, then looked up and behind sharply as though expecting a crouching enemy; bent again and licked at the milk eagerly, like a cat. He made a slurping noise. He did not use his hands to lift the saucer.

Miss Fellowes allowed a bit of the revulsion she felt to show on her face. She couldn't help it.

Deveney caught that, perhaps. He said, "Does the nurse know, Dr. Hoskins?"

"Know what?" demanded Miss Fellowes.

Deveney hesitated, but Hoskins (again that look of detached amusement on his face) said, "Well, tell her."

Deveney addressed Miss Fellowes. "You may not suspect it, Miss, but you happen to be the first civilized woman in history ever to be taking care of a Neanderthal youngster."

She turned on Hoskins with a kind of controlled ferocity. "You might have told me, Doctor."

"Why? What difference does it make?"

"You said a child."

"Isn't that a child? Have you ever had a puppy or a kitten, Miss Fellowes? Are those closer to the human? If that were a baby chimpanzee, would you be repelled? You're a nurse, Miss Fellowes. Your record places you in a maternity ward for three years. Have you ever refused to take care of a deformed infant?"

Miss Fellowes felt her case slipping away. She said, with much less decision, "You might have told me."

"And you would have refused the position? Well, do you refuse it now?" He gazed at her coolly, while Deveney watched from the other side of the room, and the Neanderthal child, having finished the milk and licked the plate, looked up at her with a wet face and wide, longing eyes.

The boy pointed to the milk and suddenly burst out in a short series of sounds repeated over and over; sounds made up of gutturals and elaborate tongue-clickings.

Miss Fellowes said, in surprise, "Why, he talks."

"Of course," said Hoskins. "*Homo neanderthalensis* is not a truly separate species, but rather a subspecies of *Homo sapiens.* Why shouldn't he talk? He's probably asking for more milk."

Automatically, Miss Fellowes reached for the bottle of milk, but Hoskins seized her wrist. "Now, Miss Fellowes, before we go any further, are you staying on the job?"

Miss Fellowes shook free in annoyance, "Won't you feed him if I don't? I'll stay with him—for a while."

She poured the milk.

Hoskins said, "We are going to leave you with the boy, Miss Fellowes. This is the only door to Stasis Number One and it is elaborately locked and guarded. I'll want you to learn the details of the lock which will, of course, be keyed to your fingerprints as they are already keyed to mine. The spaces overhead" (he looked upward to the open ceilings of the dollhouse) "are also guarded and we will be warned if anything untoward takes place in here."

Miss Fellowes said indignantly, "You mean I'll be under view." She thought suddenly of her own survey of the room interiors from the balcony.

"No, no," said Hoskins seriously, "your privacy will be respected completely. The view will consist of electronic symbolism only, which only a computer will deal with. Now you will stay with him tonight, Miss Fellowes, and every night until further notice. You will be relieved during the day according to some schedule you will find convenient. We will allow you to arrange that."

Miss Fellowes looked about the dollhouse with a puzzled expression. "But why all this, Dr. Hoskins? Is the boy dangerous?"

"It's a matter of energy, Miss Fellowes. He must never be allowed to leave these rooms. Never. Not for an instant. Not for any reason. Not to save his life. Not even to save *your* life, Miss Fellowes. Is that clear?"

Miss Fellowes raised her chin. "I understand the orders, Dr. Hoskins, and the nursing profession is accustomed to placing its duties ahead of self-preservation."

"Good. You can always signal if you need anyone." And the two men left.

Miss Fellowes turned to the boy. He was watching her and there was still milk in the saucer. Laboriously, she tried to show him how to lift the saucer and place it to his lips. He resisted, but let her touch him without crying out.

Always, his frightened eyes were on her, watching, watching for the one false move. She found herself soothing him, trying to move her hand very slowly toward his hair, letting him see it every inch of the way, see there was no harm in it.

And she succeeded in stroking his hair for an instant.

She said, "I'm going to have to show you how to use the bathroom. Do you think you can learn?"

She spoke quietly, kindly, knowing he would not understand the words but hoping he would respond to the calmness of the tone.

The boy launched into a clicking phrase again.

She said, "May I take your hand?"

She held out hers and the boy looked at it. She left it outstretched and waited. The boy's own hand crept forward toward hers.

"That's right," she said.

It approached within an inch of hers and then the boy's courage failed him. He snatched it back.

"Well," said Miss Fellowes calmly, "we'll try again later. Would you like to sit down here?" She patted the mattress of the bed.

The hours passed slowly and progress was minute. She did not succeed either with bathroom or with the bed. In fact, after the child had given unmistakable signs of sleepiness he lay down on the bare ground and then, with a quick movement, rolled beneath the bed.

She bent to look at him and his eyes gleamed out at her as he tongue-clicked at her.

"All right," she said, "if you feel safer there, you sleep there."

She closed the door to the bedroom and retired to the cot that had been placed for her use in the largest room. At her insistence, a makeshift canopy had been stretched over it. She thought: Those stupid men will have to place a mirror in this room and a larger chest of drawers and a separate washroom if they expect me to spend nights here.

It was difficult to sleep. She found herself straining to hear possible sounds in the next room. He couldn't get out, could he? The walls were sheer and impossibly high but suppose the child could climb like a monkey? Well, Hoskins said there were observational devices watching through the ceiling.

Suddenly she thought: Can he be dangerous? Physically dangerous?

Surely, Hoskins couldn't have meant that. Surely, he would not have left her here alone, if—

She tried to laugh at herself. He was only a three- or four-year-old child. Still, she had not succeeded in cutting his nails. If he should attack her with nails and teeth while she slept—

Her breath came quickly. Oh, ridiculous, and yet—

She listened with painful attentiveness, and this time she heard the sound.

The boy was crying.

Not shrieking in fear or anger; not yelling or screaming. It was crying softly, and the cry was the heartbroken sobbing of a lonely, lonely child.

For the first time, Miss Fellowes thought with a pang: Poor thing!

Of course, it was a child; what did the shape of its head matter? It was a child that had been orphaned as no child had ever been orphaned before. Not only its mother and father were gone, but all its species. Snatched callously out of time, it was now the only creature of its kind in the world. The last. The only.

She felt pity for it strengthen, and with it shame at her own callousness. Tucking her own nightgown carefully about her calves (incongruously, she thought: Tomorrow I'll have to bring in a bathrobe) she got out of bed and went into the boy's room.

"Little boy," she called out in a whisper. "Little boy."

She was about to reach under the bed, but she thought of a possible bite and did not. Instead, she turned on the night light and moved the bed.

The poor thing was huddled in the corner, knees up against his chin, looking up at her with blurred and apprehensive eyes.

In the dim light, she was not aware of his repulsiveness.

"Poor boy," she said, "poor boy." She felt him stiffen as she stroked his hair, then relax. "Poor boy. May I hold you?"

She sat down on the floor next to him and slowly and rhythmically stroked his hair, his cheek, his arm. Softly, she began to sing a slow and gentle song.

He lifted his head at last, staring at her mouth in the dimness, as though wondering at the sound.

She maneuvered him closer while he listened to her. Slowly, she pressed gently against the side of his head, until it rested on her shoulder. She put her arm under his thighs and with a smooth and unhurried motion lifted him into her lap.

She continued singing, the same simple verse over and over, while she rocked back and forth, back and forth.

He stopped crying, and after a while the smooth burr of his breathing showed he was asleep.

With infinite care, she pushed his bed back against the wall and laid him down. She covered him and stared down. His face looked so peaceful and little-boy as he slept. It didn't matter so much that it was so ugly. Really.

She began to tiptoe out, then thought: If he wakes up?

She came back, battled irresolutely with herself, then sighed and slowly got into bed with the child.

It was too small for her. She was cramped and uneasy at the lack of canopy, but the child's hand crept into hers and, somehow, she fell asleep in that position.

She awoke with a start and a wild impulse to scream. The latter she just managed to suppress into a gurgle. The boy was looking at her, wide-eyed. It took her a long moment to remember getting into bed with him, and now, slowly, without unfixing her eyes from his, she stretched one leg carefully and let it touch the floor, then the other one.

She cast a quick and apprehensive glance toward the open ceiling, then tensed her muscles for quick disengagement.

But at that moment, the boy's stubby fingers reached out and touched her lips. He said something.

She shrank at the touch. He was terribly ugly in the light of day.

The boy spoke again. He opened his own mouth and gestured with his hand as though something were coming out.

Miss Fellowes guessed at the meaning and said tremulously, "Do you want me to sing?"

The boy said nothing but stared at her mouth.

In a voice slightly off key with tension, Miss Fellowes began the little song she had sung the night before and the ugly little boy smiled. He swayed clumsily in rough time to the music and made a little gurgly sound that might have been the beginnings of a laugh.

Miss Fellowes sighed inwardly. Music hath charms to soothe the savage breast. It might help—

She said, "You wait. Let me get myself fixed up. It will just take a minute. Then I'll make breakfast for you."

She worked rapidly, conscious of the lack of ceiling at all times. The boy remained in bed, watching her when she was in view. She smiled at him at those times and waved. At the end, he waved back, and she found herself being charmed by that.

Finally, she said, "Would you like oatmeal with milk?" It took a moment to prepare, and then she beckoned to him.

Whether he understood the gesture or followed the aroma, Miss Fellowes did not know, but he got out of bed.

She tried to show him how to use a spoon but he shrank away from it in fright. (Time enough, she thought.) She compromised on insisting that he lift the bowl in his hands. He did it clumsily enough and it was incredibly messy but most of it did get into him.

She tried the drinking milk in a glass this time, and the little boy whined when he found the opening too small for him to get his face into conveniently. She held his hand, forcing it around the glass, making him tip it, forcing his mouth to the rim.

Again a mess but again most went into him, and she was used to messes.

The washroom, to her surprise and relief, was a less frustrating matter. He understood what it was she expected him to do.

She found herself patting his head, saying, "Good boy. Smart boy."

And to Miss Fellowes's exceeding pleasure, the boy smiled at that.

She thought: When he smiles, he's quite bearable. Really.

Later in the day, the gentlemen of the press arrived.

She held the boy in her arms and he clung to her wildly while across the open door they set cameras to work. The commotion frightened the boy and he began to cry, but it was ten minutes before Miss Fellowes was allowed to retreat and put the boy in the next room.

She emerged again, flushed with indignation, walked out of the apartment (for the first time in eighteen hours) and closed the door behind her. "I think you've had enough. It will take me a while to quiet him. Go away."

"Sure, sure," said the gentleman from the *Times-Herald*. "But is that really a Neanderthal kid or is this some kind of gag?"

"I assure you," said Hoskins's voice, suddenly, from the background, "this is no gag. The child is authentic *Homo neanderthalensis.*"

"Is it a boy or a girl?"

"Boy," said Miss Fellowes briefly.

"Ape-boy," said the gentleman from the *News*. "That's what we've got here. Ape-boy. How does he act, Nurse?"

"He acts exactly like a little boy," snapped Miss Fellowes, annoyed into the defensive, "and he is not an ape-boy. His name is —is Timothy, Timmie—and he is perfectly normal in his behavior."

She had chosen the name Timothy at a venture. It was the first that had occurred to her.

"Timmie the Ape-boy," said the gentleman from the *News* and, as it turned out, Timmie the Ape-boy was the name under which the child became known to the world.

The gentleman from the *Globe* turned to Hoskins and said, "Doc, what do you expect to do with the ape-boy?"

Hoskins shrugged. "My original plan was completed when I proved it possible to bring him here. However, the anthropologists will be very interested, I imagine, and the physiologists. We have here, after all, a creature which is at the edge of being human. We should learn a great deal about ourselves and our ancestry from him."

"How long will you keep him?"

"Until such a time as we need the space more than we need him. Quite a while, perhaps."

The gentleman from the *News* said, "Can you bring it out into the open so we can set up subetheric equipment and put on a real show?"

"I'm sorry, but the child cannot be removed from Stasis."

"Exactly what is Stasis?"

"Ah." Hoskins permitted himself one of his short smiles. "That would take a great deal of explanation, gentlemen. In Stasis, time as we know it doesn't exist. Those rooms are inside an invisible bubble that is not exactly part of our Universe. That is why the child could be plucked out of time as it was."

"Well, wait now," said the gentleman from the *News* discontentedly, "what are you giving us? The nurse goes into the room and out of it."

"And so can any of you," said Hoskins matter-of-factly. "You would be moving parallel to the lines of temporal force and no great energy gain or loss would be involved. The child, however, was taken from the far past. It moved across the lines and gained temporal potential. To move it into the Universe and into our own time would absorb enough energy to burn out every line in the place and probably blank out all power in the city of Washington. We had to store trash brought with him on the premises and will have to remove it little by little."

The newsmen were writing down sentences busily as Hoskins spoke to them. They did not understand and they were sure their readers would not, but it sounded scientific and that was what counted.

The gentleman from the *Times-Herald* said, "Would you be available for an all-circuit interview tonight?"

"I think so," said Hoskins at once, and they all moved off.

Miss Fellowes looked after them. She understood all this about Stasis and temporal force as little as the newsmen but she managed to get this much. Timmie's imprisonment (she found herself suddenly thinking of the little boy as Timmie) was a real one and not one imposed by the arbitrary fiat of Hoskins. Apparently, it was impossible to let him out of Stasis at all, ever.

Poor child. Poor child.

She was suddenly aware of his crying and she hastened in to console him.

Miss Fellowes did not have a chance to see Hoskins on the all-circuit hookup, and though his interview was beamed to every part of the world and even to the outposts on the Moon, it did not penetrate the apartment in which Miss Fellowes and the ugly little boy lived.

But he was down the next morning, radiant and joyful.

Miss Fellowes said, "Did the interview go well?"

"Extremely. And how is—Timmie?"

Miss Fellowes found herself pleased at the use of the name. "Doing quite well. Now come out here, Timmie, the nice gentleman will not hurt you."

But Timmie stayed in the other room, with a lock of his matted hair showing behind the barrier of the door and, occasionally, the corner of an eye.

"Actually," said Miss Fellowes, "he is settling down amazingly. He is quite intelligent."

"Are you surprised?"

She hesitated just a moment, then said, "Yes, I am. I suppose I thought he was an ape-boy."

"Well, ape-boy or not, he's done a great deal for us. He's put Stasis, Inc., on the map. We're in, Miss Fellowes, we're in." It was as though he had to express his triumph to someone, even if only to Miss Fellowes.

"Oh?" She let him talk.

He put his hands in his pockets and said, "We've been working on a shoestring for ten years, scrounging funds a penny at a time wherever we could. We had to shoot the works on one big show. It was everything or nothing. And when I say the works, I mean it. This attempt to bring a Neanderthal took every cent we could borrow or steal, and some of it *was* stolen—funds for other projects, used for this one without permission. If that experiment hadn't succeeded, I'd have been through."

Miss Fellowes said abruptly, "Is that why there are no ceilings?"

"Eh?" Hoskins looked up.

"Was there no money for ceilings?"

"Oh. Well, that wasn't the only reason. We didn't really know in advance how old the Neanderthal might be exactly. We can detect only dimly in time, and he might have been large and savage. It was possible we might have had to deal with him from a distance, like a caged animal."

"But since that hasn't turned out to be so, I suppose you can build a ceiling now."

"Now, yes. We have plenty of money, now. Funds have been promised from every source. This is all wonderful, Miss Fellowes." His broad face gleamed with a smile that lasted and, when he left, even his back seemed to be smiling.

Miss Fellowes thought: He's quite a nice man when he's off guard and forgets about being scientific.

She wondered for an idle moment if he was married, then dismissed the thought in self-embarrassment.

"Timmie," she called. "Come here, Timmie."

In the months that passed, Miss Fellowes felt herself grow to be an integral part of Stasis, Inc. She was given a small office of her own with her name on the door, an office quite close to the dollhouse (as she never stopped calling Timmie's Stasis bubble). She was given a substantial raise. The dollhouse was covered by a ceiling; its furnishing were elaborated and improved; a second washroom was added—and even so, she gained an apartment of her own on the institute grounds and, on occasion, did not stay with Timmie during the night. An intercom was set up between the dollhouse and her apartment and Timmie learned how to use it.

Miss Fellowes got used to Timmie. She even grew less conscious of his ugliness. One day she found herself staring at an ordinary boy in the street and finding something bulgy and unattractive in his high domed forehead and jutting chin. She had to shake herself to break the spell.

It was more pleasant to grow used to Hoskins's occasional visits. It was obvious he welcomed escape from his increasingly harried role as head of Stasis, Inc., and that he took a sentimental interest in the child who had started it all, but it seemed to Miss Fellowes that he also enjoyed talking to her.

(She had learned some facts about Hoskins, too. He had invented the method of analyzing the reflection of the past-penetrating mesonic beam; he had invented the method of establishing Stasis; his coldness was only an effort to hide a kindly nature; and, oh yes, he *was* married.)

What Miss Fellowes could *not* get used to was the fact that she was engaged in a scientific experiment. Despite all she could do, she found herself getting personally involved to the point of quarreling with the physiologists.

On one occasion, Hoskins came down and found her in the midst of a hot urge to kill. They had no right; they had no *right*— Even if he *was* a Neanderthal, he still wasn't an animal.

She was staring after them in blind fury; staring out the open door and listening to Timmie's sobbing, when she noticed Hoskins standing before her. He might have been there for minutes.

He said, "May I come in?"

She nodded curtly, then hurried to Timmie, who clung to her, curling his little bandy legs—still thin, so thin—about her.

Hoskins watched, then said gravely, "He seems quite unhappy."

Miss Fellowes said, "I don't blame him. They're at him every day now with their blood samples and their probings. They keep him on synthetic diets that I wouldn't feed a pig."

"It's the sort of thing they can't try on a human, you know."

"And they can't try it on Timmie, either. Dr. Hoskins, I insist. You told me it was Timmie's coming that put Stasis, Inc., on the map. If you have any gratitude for that at all, you've *got* to keep them away from the poor thing at least until he's old enough to understand a little more. After he's had a bad session with them, he has nightmares, he can't sleep. Now I warn you" (she reached a sudden peak of fury), "I'm not letting them in here anymore."

(She realized that she had screamed that, but she couldn't help it.)

She said more quietly, "I know he's Neanderthal but there's a great deal we don't appreciate about Neanderthals. I've read up on them. They had a culture of their own. Some of the greatest human inventions arose in Neanderthal times. The domestication of animals, for instance; the wheel; various techniques in grinding stone. They even had spiritual yearnings. They buried their dead and buried possessions with the body, showing they believed in a life after death. It amounts to the fact that they invented religion. Doesn't that mean Timmie has a right to human treatment?"

She patted the little boy gently on his buttocks and sent him off into his playroom. As the door was opened, Hoskins smiled briefly at the display of toys that could be seen.

Miss Fellowes said defensively, "The poor child deserves his toys. It's all he has and he earns them with what he goes through."

"No, no. No objections, I assure you. I was just thinking how you've changed since the first day, when you were quite angry I had foisted a Neanderthal on you."

Miss Fellowes said in a low voice, "I suppose I didn't—" and faded off.

Hoskins changed the subject, "How old would you say he is, Miss Fellowes?"

She said, "I can't say, since we don't know how Neanderthals develop. In size, he'd only be three but Neanderthals are smaller generally and with all the tampering they do with him, he probably isn't growing. The way he's learning English, though, I'd say he was well over four."

"Really? I haven't noticed anything about learning English in the reports."

"He won't speak to anyone but me. For now, anyway. He's terribly afraid of others, and no wonder. But he can ask for an article of food; he can indicate any need practically; and he understands almost anything I say. Of course"—(she watched him shrewdly, trying to estimate if this was the time)—"his development may not continue."

"Why not?"

"Any child needs stimulation and this one lives a life of solitary confinement. I do what I can, but I'm not with him all the time and I'm not all he needs. What I mean, Dr. Hoskins, is that he needs another boy to play with."

Hoskins nodded slowly. "Unfortunately, there's only one of him, isn't there? Poor child."

Miss Fellowes warmed to him at once. She said, "You do like Timmie, don't you?" It was so nice to have someone else feel like that.

"Oh, yes," said Hoskins, and with his guard down, she could see the weariness in his eyes.

Miss Fellowes dropped her plans to push the matter at once. She said, with real concern, "You look worn out, Dr. Hoskins."

"Do I, Miss Fellowes? I'll have to practice looking more lifelike then."

"I suppose Stasis, Inc., is very busy and that keeps you very busy."

Hoskins shrugged. "You suppose right. It's a matter of animal, vegetable, and mineral in equal parts, Miss Fellowes. But then, I suppose you haven't ever seen our displays."

"Actually, I haven't. But it's not because I'm not interested. It's just that I've been so busy."

"Well, you're not all that busy right now," he said with impulsive decision. "I'll call for you tomorrow at eleven and give you a personal tour. How's that?"

She smiled happily. "I'd love it."

He nodded and smiled in his turn and left.

Miss Fellowes hummed at intervals for the rest of the day. Really—to think so was ridiculous, of course—but really, it was almost like—like making a date.

He was quite on time the next day, smiling and pleasant. She had replaced her nurse's uniform with a dress. One of conservative cut, to be sure, but she hadn't felt so feminine in years.

He complimented her on her appearance with staid formality and she accepted with equally formal grace. It was really a perfect prelude, she thought. And then the additional thought came, prelude to what?

She shut that off by hastening to say goodbye to Timmie and to assure him she would be back soon. She made sure he knew all about what and where lunch was.

Hoskins took her into the new wing, into which she had never yet gone. It still had the odor of newness about it and the sound of construction, softly heard, was indication enough that it was still being extended.

"Animal, vegetable, and mineral," said Hoskins, as he had the day before. "Animal right there; our most spectacular exhibits."

The space was divided into many rooms, each a separate Stasis bubble. Hoskins brought her to the view-glass of one and she looked in. What she saw impressed her first as a scaled, tailed chicken. Skittering on two thin legs it ran from wall to wall with its delicate birdlike head, surmounted by a bony keel like the comb of a rooster, looking this way and that. The paws on its small forelimbs clenched and unclenched constantly.

Hoskins said, "It's our dinosaur. We've had it for months. I don't know when we'll be able to let go of it."

"Dinosaur?"

"Did you expect a giant?"

She dimpled. "One does, I suppose. I know some of them are small."

"A small one is all we aimed for, believe me. Generally, it's under investigation, but this seems to be an open hour. Some interesting things have been discovered. For instance, it is not entirely cold-blooded. It has an imperfect method of maintaining internal temperatures higher than that of its environment. Unfortunately, it's a male. Ever since we brought it in we've been trying to get a fix on another that may be female, but we've had no luck yet."

"Why female?"

He looked at her quizzically. "So that we might have a fighting chance to obtain fertile eggs, and baby dinosaurs."

"Of course."

He led her to the trilobite section. "That's Professor Dwayne of Washington University," he said. "He's a nuclear chemist. If I recall correctly, he's taking an isotope ratio on the oxygen of the water."

"Why?"

"It's primeval water; at least half a billion years old. The isotope ratio gives the temperature of the ocean at that time. He himself happens to ignore the trilobites, but others are chiefly concerned in dissecting them. They're the lucky ones because all they need are scalpels and microscopes. Dwayne has to set up a mass spectrograph each time he conducts an experiment."

"Why's that? Can't he—"

"No, he can't. He can't take anything out of the room as far as can be helped."

There were samples of primordial plant life too and chunks of rock formations. Those were the vegetable and mineral. And every specimen had its investigator. It was like a museum; a museum brought to life and serving as a superactive center of research.

"And you have to supervise all of this, Dr. Hoskins?"

"Only indirectly, Miss Fellowes. I have subordinates, thank heaven. My own interest is entirely in the theoretical aspects of the matter: the nature of Time, the technique of mesonic intertemporal detection, and so on. I would exchange all this for a method of detecting objects closer in Time than ten thousand years ago. If we could get into historical times—"

He was interrupted by a commotion at one of the distant booths, a thin voice raised querulously. He frowned, muttered hastily, "Excuse me," and hastened off.

Miss Fellowes followed as best she could without actually running.

An elderly man, thinly bearded and red-faced, was saying, "I had vital aspects of my investigations to complete. Don't you understand that?"

A uniformed technician with the interwoven SI monogram (for Stasis, Inc.) on his lab coat, said, "Dr. Hoskins, it was arranged with Professor Ademewski at the beginning that the specimen could only remain here two weeks."

"I did not know then how long my investigations would take. I'm not a prophet," said Ademewski heatedly.

Dr. Hoskins said, "You understand, Professor, we have limited space; we must keep specimens rotating. That piece of chalcopyrite must go back; there are men waiting for the next specimen."

"Why can't I have it for myself, then? Let me take it out of there."

"You know you can't have it."

"A piece of chalcopyrite; a miserable five-kilogram piece? Why not?"

"We can't afford the energy expense!" said Hoskins brusquely. "You know that."

The technician interrupted. "The point is, Dr. Hoskins, that he tried to remove the rock against the rules and I almost punctured Stasis, not knowing he was in there."

There was a short silence and Dr. Hoskins turned on the investigator with a cold formality. "Is that so, Professor?"

Professor Ademewski coughed. "I saw no harm—"

Hoskins reached up to a hand-pull dangling just within reach, outside the specimen room in question. He pulled it.

Miss Fellowes, who had been peering in, looking at the totally undistinguished sample of rock that occasioned the dispute, drew in her breath sharply as its existence flickered out. The room was empty.

Hoskins said, "Professor, your permit to investigate matters in Stasis will be permanently voided. I am sorry."

"But wait—"

"I am sorry. You have violated one of the stringent rules."

"I will appeal to the International Association—"

"Appeal away. In a case like this, you will find I can't be over-ruled."

He turned away deliberately, leaving the professor still protest-ing and said to Miss Fellowes (his face still white with anger), "Would you care to have lunch with me, Miss Fellowes?"

He took her into the small administration alcove of the cafete-ria. He greeted others and introduced Miss Fellowes with complete ease, although she herself felt painfully self-conscious.

What must they think, she thought, and tried desperately to appear businesslike.

She said, "Do you have that kind of trouble often, Dr. Hoskins? I mean like you just had with the professor?" She took her fork in hand and began eating.

"No," said Hoskins forcefully. "That was the first time. Of course I'm always having to argue men out of removing specimens but this is the first time one actually tried to do it."

"I remember you once talked about the energy it would con-sume."

"That's right. Of course, we've tried to take it into account. Accidents will happen and so we've got special power sources de-signed to stand the drain of accidental removal from Stasis, but that doesn't mean we want to see a year's supply of energy gone in half a second—or can afford to without having our plans of expansion delayed for years. Besides, imagine the professor's being in the room while Stasis was about to be punctured."

"What would have happened to him if it had been?"

"Well, we've experimented with inanimate objects and with mice and they've disappeared. Presumably they've traveled back in time; carried along, so to speak, by the pull of the object simul-taneously snapping back into its natural time. For that reason, we have to anchor objects within Stasis that we don't want to move and that's a complicated procedure. The professor would not have been anchored and he would have gone back to the Pliocene at the moment we abstracted the rock—plus, of course, the two weeks it had remained here in the present."

"How dreadful it would have been."

"Not on account of the professor, I assure you. If he were fool enough to do what he did, it would serve him right. But imagine the effect it would have on the public if the fact came out. All people would need is to become aware of the dangers involved and funds could be choked off like that." He snapped his fingers and played moodily with his food.

Miss Fellowes said, "Couldn't you get him back? The way you got the rock in the first place?"

"No, because once an object is returned, the original fix is lost unless we deliberately plan to retain it and there was no reason to do that in this case. There never is. Finding the professor again would mean relocating a specific fix and that would be like dropping a line into the oceanic abyss for the purpose of dredging up a particular fish. My God, when I think of the precautions we take to prevent accidents, it makes me mad. We have every individual Stasis unit set up with its own puncturing device—we have to, since each unit has its separate fix and must be collapsible independently. The point is, though, none of the puncturing devices is ever activated until the last minute. And then we deliberately make activation impossible except by the pull of a rope carefully led outside the Stasis. The pull is a gross mechanical motion that requires strong effort, not something that is likely to be done accidentally."

Miss Fellowes said, "But doesn't it—change history to move something in and out of Time?"

Hoskins shrugged. "Theoretically, yes; actually, except in unusual cases, no. We move objects out of Stasis all the time. Air molecules. Bacteria. Dust. About ten percent of our energy consumption goes to make up microlosses of that nature. But moving even large objects in Time sets up changes that damp out. Take that chalcopyrite from the Pliocene. Because of its absence for two weeks some insect didn't find the shelter it might have found and is killed. That could initiate a whole series of changes, but the mathematics of Stasis indicates that this is a converging series. The amount of change diminishes with time and then things are as before."

"You mean, reality heals itself?"

"In a manner of speaking. Abstract a human from Time or send one back, and you make a larger wound. If the individual is an ordinary one, that wound still heals itself. Of course, there are a great many people who write to us each day and want us to bring Abraham Lincoln to the present, or Mohammed, or Lenin. *That* can't be done, of course. Even if we could find them, the change in reality in moving one of the history molders would be too great to be healed. There are ways of calculating when a change is likely to be too great and we avoid even approaching that limit."

Miss Fellowes said, "Then, Timmie—"

"No, he presents no problem in that direction. Reality is safe. But—" He gave her a quick, sharp glance, then went on, "But never mind. Yesterday you said Timmie needed companionship."

"Yes." Miss Fellowes smiled her delight. "I didn't think you paid that any attention."

"Of course I did. I'm fond of the child. I appreciate your feelings for him and I was concerned enough to want to explain to you. Now I have; you've seen what we do; you've gotten some insight into the difficulties involved; so you know why, with the best will in the world, we can't supply companionship for Timmie."

"You can't?" said Miss Fellowes, with sudden dismay.

"But I've just explained. We couldn't possibly expect to find another Neanderthal his age without incredible luck, and if we could, it wouldn't be fair to multiply risks by having another human being in Stasis."

Miss Fellowes put down her spoon and said energetically, "But, Dr. Hoskins, that is not at all what I meant. I don't want you to bring another Neanderthal into the present. I know that's impossible. But it isn't impossible to bring another child to play with Timmie."

Hoskins stared at her in concern. "A *human* child?"

"*Another* child," said Miss Fellowes, completely hostile now. "Timmie is human."

"I couldn't dream of such a thing."

"Why not? Why couldn't you? What is wrong with the notion? You pulled that child out of Time and made him an eternal prisoner. Don't you owe him something? Dr. Hoskins, if there is any man who, in this world, is that child's father in every sense but the biological, it is you. Why can't you do this little thing for him?"

Hoskins said, "His *father*?" He rose, somewhat unsteadily, to his feet. "Miss Fellowes, I think I'll take you back now, if you don't mind."

They returned to the dollhouse in a complete silence that neither broke.

It was a long time after that before she saw Hoskins again, except for an occasional glimpse in passing. She was sorry about that at times; then, at other times, when Timmie was more than usually woebegone or when he spent silent hours at the window with its prospect of little more than nothing, she thought, fiercely: Stupid man.

Timmie's speech grew better and more precise each day. It never entirely lost a certain soft slurriness that Miss Fellowes found rather endearing. In times of excitement, he fell back into tongue-clicking but those times were becoming fewer. He must be forgetting the days before he came into the present—except for dreams.

As he grew older, the physiologists grew less interested and the psychologists more so. Miss Fellowes was not sure that she did not like the new group even less than the first. The needles were gone; the injections and withdrawals of fluid; the special diets. But now Timmie was made to overcome barriers to reach food and water. He had to lift panels, move bars, reach for cords. And the mild electric shocks made him cry and drove Miss Fellowes to distraction.

She did not wish to appeal to Hoskins; she did not wish to have to go to him; for each time she thought of him, she thought of his face over the luncheon table that last time. Her eyes moistened and she thought: Stupid, *stupid* man.

And then one day Hoskins's voice sounded unexpectedly, calling into the dollhouse, "Miss Fellowes."

She came out coldly, smoothing her nurse's uniform, then stopped in confusion at finding herself in the presence of a pale woman, slender and of middle height. The woman's fair hair and complexion gave her an appearance of fragility. Standing behind her and clutching at her skirt was a round-faced, large-eyed child of four.

Hoskins said, "Dear, this is Miss Fellowes, the nurse in charge of the boy. Miss Fellowes, this is my wife."

(Was this his wife? She was not as Miss Fellowes had imagined her to be. But then, why not? A man like Hoskins would choose a weak thing to be his foil. If that was what he wanted—)

She forced a matter-of-fact greeting. "Good afternoon, Mrs. Hoskins. Is this your—your little boy?"

(*That* was a surprise. She had thought of Hoskins as a husband, but not as a father, except, of course—She suddenly caught Hoskins's grave eyes and flushed.)

Hoskins said, "Yes, this is my boy, Jerry. Say hello to Miss Fellowes, Jerry."

(Had he stressed the word "this" just a bit? Was he saying *this* was his son and not—)

Jerry receded a bit further into the folds of the maternal skirt and muttered his hello. Mrs. Hoskins's eyes were searching over Miss Fellowes's shoulders, peering into the room, looking for something.

Hoskins said, "Well, let's go in. Come, dear. There's a trifling discomfort at the threshold, but it passes."

Miss Fellowes said, "Do you want Jerry to come in, too?"

"Of course. He is to be Timmie's playmate. You said that Timmie needed a playmate. Or have you forgotten?"

"But—" She looked at him with a colossal, surprised wonder. "*Your* boy?"

He said peevishly, "Well, whose boy, then? Isn't this what you want? Come on in, dear. Come on in."

Mrs. Hoskins lifted Jerry into her arms with a distinct effort and, hesitantly, stepped over the threshold. Jerry squirmed as she did so, disliking the sensation.

Mrs. Hoskins said in a thin voice, "Is the creature here? I don't see him."

Miss Fellowes called, "Timmie. Come out."

Timmie peered around the edge of the door, staring up at the little boy who was visiting him. The muscles in Mrs. Hoskins's arms tensed visibly.

She said to her husband, "Gerald, are you sure it's safe?"

Miss Fellowes said at once, "If you mean is Timmie safe, why, of course he is. He's a gentle little boy."

"But he's a sa—savage."

(The ape-boy stories in the newspapers!) Miss Fellowes said emphatically, "He is not a savage. He is just as quiet and reasonable as you can possibly expect a five-and-a-half-year-old to be. It is very generous of you, Mrs. Hoskins, to agree to allow your boy to play with Timmie but please have no fears about it."

Mrs. Hoskins said with mild heat. "I'm not sure that I agree."

"We've had it out, dear," said Hoskins. "Let's not bring up the matter for new argument. Put Jerry down."

Mrs. Hoskins did so and the boy backed against her, staring at the pair of eyes which were staring back at him from the next room.

"Come here, Timmie," said Miss Fellowes. "Don't be afraid."

Slowly, Timmie stepped into the room. Hoskins bent to disengage Jerry's fingers from his mother's skirt. "Step back, dear. Give the children a chance."

The youngsters faced one another. Although the younger, Jerry was nevertheless an inch taller, and in the presence of his straightness and his high-held, well-proportioned head, Timmie's grotesqueries were suddenly almost as pronounced as they had been in the first days.

Miss Fellowes's lips quivered.

It was the little Neanderthal who spoke first, in childish treble. "What's your name?" And Timmie thrust his face suddenly forward as though to inspect the other's features more closely.

Startled, Jerry responded with a vigorous shove that sent Timmie tumbling. Both began crying loudly and Mrs. Hoskins snatched up her child, while Miss Fellowes, flushed with repressed anger, lifted Timmie and comforted him.

Mrs. Hoskins said, "They just instinctively don't like one another."

"No more instinctively," said her husband wearily, "than any two children dislike each other. Now put Jerry down and let him get used to the situation. In fact, we had better leave. Miss Fellowes can bring Jerry to my office after a while and I'll have him taken home."

The two children spent the next hour very aware of each other. Jerry cried for his mother, struck out at Miss Fellowes and, finally, allowed himself to be comforted with a lollipop. Timmie sucked at another, and at the end of an hour, Miss Fellowes had them playing with the same set of blocks, though at opposite ends of the room.

She found herself almost maudlinly grateful to Hoskins when she brought Jerry to him.

She searched for ways to thank him but his very formality was a rebuff. Perhaps he could not forgive her for making him feel like a cruel father. Perhaps the bringing of his own child was an attempt, after all, to prove himself both a kind father to Timmie and, also, not his father at all. Both at the same time!

So all she could say was, "Thank you. Thank you very much."

And all he could say was, "It's all right. Don't mention it."

It became a settled routine. Twice a week, Jerry was brought in for an hour's play, later extended to two hours' play. The children learned each other's names and ways and played together.

And yet, after the first rush of gratitude, Miss Fellowes found herself disliking Jerry. He was larger and heavier and in all things dominant, forcing Timmie into a completely secondary role. All that reconciled her to the situation was the fact that, despite difficulties, Timmie looked forward with more and more delight to the periodic appearances of his playfellow.

It was all he had, she mourned to herself.

And once, as she watched him, she thought: Hoskins's two children, one by his wife, and one by Stasis.

While she herself—

Heavens, she thought, putting her fists to her temples and feeling ashamed: I'm jealous!

"Miss Fellowes," said Timmie (carefully, she had never allowed him to call her anything else), "when will I go to school?"

She looked down at those eager brown eyes turned up to hers and passed her hand softly through his thick, curly hair. It was the most disheveled portion of his appearance, for she cut his hair herself while he sat restlessly under the scissors. She did not ask for professional help, for the very clumsiness of the cut served to mask the retreating forepart of the skull and the bulging hinder part.

She said, "Where did you hear about school?"

"Jerry goes to school. Kin-der-gar-ten." He said it carefully. "There are lots of places he goes. Outside. When can I go outside, Miss Fellowes?"

A small pain centered in Miss Fellowes's heart. Of course, she saw, there would be no way of avoiding the inevitability of Timmie's hearing more and more of the outer world he could never enter.

She said, with an attempt at gaiety, "Why, whatever would you do in kindergarten, Timmie?"

"Jerry says they play games, they have picture tapes. He says there are lots of children. He says—he says—" A thought, then a triumphant upholding of both small hands with the fingers splayed apart. "He says this many."

Miss Fellowes said, "Would you like picture tapes? I can get you picture tapes. Very nice ones. And music tapes, too."

So that Timmie was temporarily comforted.

He pored over the picture tapes in Jerry's absence and Miss Fellowes read to him out of ordinary books by the hour.

There was so much to explain in even the simplest story, so much that was outside the perspective of his three rooms. Timmie took to having his dreams more often now that the outside was being introduced to him.

They were always the same, about the outside. He tried haltingly to describe them to Miss Fellowes. In his dreams, he was outside, an empty outside, but very large, with children and queer indescribable objects half digested in his thought out of bookish descriptions half understood, or out of distant Neanderthal memories half recalled.

But the children and objects ignored him and though he was in the world, he was never part of it, but was as alone as though he were in his own room—and would wake up crying.

Miss Fellowes tried to laugh at the dreams, but there were nights in her own apartment when she cried, too.

One day, as Miss Fellowes read, Timmie put his hand under her chin and lifted it gently so that her eyes left the book and met his.

He said, "How do you know what to say, Miss Fellowes?"

She said, "You see these marks? They tell me what to say. These marks make words."

He stared at them long and curiously, taking the book out of her hands. "Some of these marks are the same."

She laughed with pleasure at this sign of his shrewdness and said, "So they are. Would you like to have me show you how to make the marks?"

"All right. That would be a nice game."

It did not occur to her that he could learn to read. Up to the very moment that he read a book to her, it did not occur to her that he could learn to read.

Then, weeks later, the enormity of what had been done struck her. Timmie sat in her lap, following word by word the printing in a child's book, reading to her. He was reading to her!

She struggled to her feet in amazement and said "Now, Timmie, I'll be back later. I want to see Dr. Hoskins "

Excited nearly to frenzy, it seemed to her she might have an answer to Timmie's unhappiness. If Timmie could not leave to enter the world, the world must be brought into those three rooms to Timmie—the whole world in books and film and sound. He must be educated to his full capacity. So much the world owed him.

She found Hoskins in a mood that was oddly analogous to her own; a kind of triumph and glory. His offices were unusually busy, and for a moment, she thought she would not get to see him, as she stood abashed in the anteroom.

But he saw her, and a smile spread over his broad face. "Miss Fellowes, come here."

He spoke rapidly into the intercom, then shut it off. "Have you heard? No, of course, you couldn't have. We've done it. We've actually done it. We have intertemporal detection at close range."

"You mean," she tried to detach her thought from her own good news for a moment, "that you can get a person from historical times into the present?"

"That's just what I mean. We have a fix on a fourteenth-century individual right now. Imagine. *Imagine!* If you could only know how glad I'll be to shift from the eternal concentration on the Mesozoic, replace the paleontologists with the historians—But there's something you wish to say to me, eh? Well, go ahead; go ahead. You find me in a good mood. Anything you want you can have."

Miss Fellowes smiled. "I'm glad. Because I wonder if we might not establish a system of instruction for Timmie?"

"Instruction? In what?"

"Well, in everything. A school. So that he might learn."

"But *can* he learn?"

"Certainly, he *is* learning. He can read. I've taught him so much myself."

Hoskins sat there, seeming suddenly depressed. "I don't know, Miss Fellowes."

She said, "You just said that anything I wanted—"

"I know and I should not have. You see, Miss Fellowes, I'm sure you must realize that we cannot maintain the Timmie experiment forever."

She stared at him with sudden horror, not really understanding what he had said. How did he mean "cannot maintain"? With an agonizing flash of recollection, she recalled Professor Ademewski and his mineral specimen that was taken away after two weeks. She said, "But you're talking about a boy. Not about a rock—"

Dr. Hoskins said uneasily, "Even a boy can't be given undue importance, Miss Fellowes. Now that we expect individuals out of historical time, we will need Stasis space, all we can get."

She didn't grasp it. "But you can't. Timmie—Timmie—"

"Now, Miss Fellowes, please don't upset yourself. Timmie won't go right away; perhaps not for months. Meanwhile we'll do what we can."

She was still staring at him.

"Let me get you something, Miss Fellowes."

"No," she whispered. "I don't need anything." She arose in a kind of nightmare and left.

Timmie, she thought, you will *not* die. You will *not* die.

It was all very well to hold tensely to the thought that Timmie must not die, but how was that to be arranged? In the first weeks, Miss Fellowes clung only to the hope that the attempt to bring forward a man from the fourteenth century would fail completely. Hoskins's theories might be wrong or his practice defective. Then things could go on as before.

Certainly that was not the hope of the rest of the world and, irrationally, Miss Fellowes hated the world for it. "Project Middle Ages" reached a climax of white-hot publicity. The press and the public had hungered for something like this. Stasis, Inc., had lacked the necessary sensation for a long time now. A new rock or another ancient fish failed to stir them. But *this* was *it*.

A historical human; an adult speaking a known language; someone who could open a new page of history to the scholar.

Zero-time was coming and this time it was not a question of three onlookers from a balcony. This time there would be a world-wide audience. This time the technicians of Stasis, Inc., would play their role before nearly all of mankind.

Miss Fellowes was herself all but savage with waiting. When young Jerry Hoskins showed up for his scheduled playtime with

Timmie, she scarcely recognized him. He was not the one she was waiting for.

(The secretary who brought him left hurriedly after the barest nod for Miss Fellowes. She was rushing for a good place from which to watch the climax of Project Middle Ages. And so ought Miss Fellowes with far better reason, she thought bitterly, if only that stupid girl would arrive.)

Jerry Hoskins sidled toward her, embarrassed. "Miss Fellowes?" He took the reproduction of a news strip out of his pocket.

"Yes? What is it, Jerry?"

"Is this a picture of Timmie?"

Miss Fellowes stared at him, then snatched the strip from Jerry's hand. The excitement of Project Middle Ages had brought about a pale revival of interest in Timmie on the part of the press.

Jerry watched her narrowly, then said, "It says Timmie is an ape-boy. What does that mean?"

Miss Fellowes caught the youngster's wrist and repressed the impulse to shake him. "Never say that, Jerry. Never, do you understand? It is a nasty word and you mustn't use it."

Jerry struggled out of her grip, frightened.

Miss Fellowes tore up the news strip with a vicious twist of the wrist. "Now go inside and play with Timmie. He's got a new book to show you."

And then, finally, the girl appeared. Miss Fellowes did not know her. None of the usual stand-ins she had used when business took her elsewhere was available now, not with Project Middle Ages at climax, but Hoskins's secretary had promised to find *someone* and this must be the girl.

Miss Fellowes tried to keep querulousness out of her voice. "Are you the girl assigned to Stasis Section One?"

"Yes, I'm Mandy Terris. You're Miss Fellowes, aren't you?"

"That's right."

"I'm sorry I'm late. There's just so much excitement."

"I know. Now, I want you—"

Mandy said. "You'll be watching, I suppose." Her thin, vacuously pretty face filled with envy.

"Never mind that. Now I want you to come inside and meet Timmie and Jerry. They will be playing for the next two hours so they'll be giving you no trouble. They've got milk handy and plenty of toys. In fact, it will be better if you leave them alone as much as possible. Now I'll show you where everything is located and—"

"Is it Timmie that's the ape-b—"

"Timmie is the Stasis subject," said Miss Fellowes firmly.

"I mean, he's the one who's not supposed to get out, is that right?"

"Yes. Now, come in. There isn't much time."

And when she finally left, Mandy Terris called after her shrilly, "I hope you get a good seat and, golly, I sure hope it works."

Miss Fellowes did not trust herself to make a reasonable response. She hurried on without looking back.

But the delay meant she did *not* get a good seat. She got no nearer than the wall-viewing-plate in the assembly hall. Bitterly, she regretted that. If she could have been on the spot; if she could somehow have reached out for some sensitive portion of the instrumentation; if she were in some way able to wreck the experiment—

She found the strength to beat down her madness. Simple destruction would have done no good. They would have rebuilt and reconstructed and made the effort again. And she would never be allowed to return to Timmie.

Nothing would help. Nothing but that the experiment itself fail; that it break down irretrievably.

So she waited through the countdown, watching every move on the giant screen, scanning the faces of the technicians as the focus shifted from one to the other, watching for the look of worry and uncertainty that would mark something going unexpectedly wrong; watching, watching—

There was no such look. The count reached zero, and very quietly, very unassumingly, the experiment succeeded!

In the new Stasis that had been established there stood a bearded, stoop-shouldered peasant of indeterminate age, in ragged dirty clothing and wooden shoes, staring in dull horror at the sudden mad change that had flung itself over him.

And while the world went mad with jubilation, Miss Fellowes stood frozen in sorrow, jostled and pushed, all but trampled; surrounded by triumph while bowed down with defeat.

And when the loudspeaker called her name with strident force, it sounded it three times before she responded.

"Miss Fellowes. Miss Fellowes. You are wanted in Stasis Section One immediately. Miss Fellowes. Miss Fell—"

"Let me through!" she cried breathlessly, while the loudspeaker continued its repetitions without pause. She forced her way through the crowds with wild energy, beating at it, striking out with closed fists, flailing, moving toward the door in a nightmare slowness.

Mandy Terris was in tears. "I don't know how it happened. I just went down to the edge of the corridor to watch a pocket-viewing-plate they had put up. Just for a minute. And then before I could move or do anything—" She cried out in sudden accusation, "You said they would make no trouble; you *said* to leave them alone—"

Miss Fellowes, disheveled and trembling uncontrollably, glared at her. "Where's Timmie?"

A nurse was swabbing the arm of a wailing Jerry with disinfectant and another was preparing an antitetanus shot. There was blood on Jerry's clothes.

"He bit me, Miss Fellowes," Jerry cried in rage. "He *bit* me."

But Miss Fellowes didn't even see him.

"What did you do with Timmie?" she cried out.

"I locked him in the bathroom," said Mandy. "I just threw the little monster in there and locked him in."

Miss Fellowes ran into the dollhouse. She fumbled at the bathroom door. It took an eternity to get it open and to find the ugly little boy cowering in the corner.

"Don't whip me, Miss Fellowes," he whispered. His eyes were red. His lips were quivering. "I didn't mean to do it."

"Oh, Timmie, who told you about whips?" She caught him to her, hugging him wildly.

He said tremulously, "She said, with a long rope. She said you would hit me and hit me."

"You won't be. She was wicked to say so. But what happened? What happened?"

"He called me an ape-boy. He said I wasn't a real boy. He said I was an animal." Timmie dissolved in a flood of tears. "He said he wasn't going to play with a monkey anymore. I said I wasn't a monkey; I *wasn't* a monkey. He said I was all funny-looking. He said I was horrible ugly. He kept saying and saying and I bit him."

They were both crying now. Miss Fellowes sobbed, "But it isn't true. You know that, Timmie. You're a real boy. You're a dear real boy and the best boy in the world. And no one, *no one* will ever take you away from me."

It was easy to make up her mind, now; easy to know what to do. Only it had to be done quickly. Hoskins wouldn't wait much longer, with his own son mangled—

No, it would have to be done this night, *this* night; with the place four-fifths asleep and the remaining fifth intellectually drunk over Project Middle Ages.

It would be an unusual time for her to return but not an unheard-of one. The guard knew her well and would not dream of questioning her. He would think nothing of her carrying a suitcase. She rehearsed the noncommittal phrase, "Games for the boy," and the calm smile.

Why shouldn't he believe that?

He did. When she entered the dollhouse again, Timmie was still awake, and she maintained a desperate normality to avoid frightening him. She talked about his dreams with him and listened to him ask wistfully after Jerry.

There would be few to see her afterward, none to question the bundle she would be carrying. Timmie would be very quiet and then it would be a *fait accompli.* It would be done and what would be the use of trying to undo it. They would leave her be. They would leave them both be.

She opened the suitcase, took out the overcoat, the woolen cap with the earflaps and the rest.

Timmie said, with the beginning of alarm, "Why are you putting all these clothes on me, Miss Fellowes?"

She said, "I am going to take you outside, Timmie. To where your dreams are."

"My dreams?" His face twisted in sudden yearning, yet fear was there, too.

"You won't be afraid. You'll be with me. You won't be afraid if you're with me, will you, Timmie?"

"No, Miss Fellowes." He buried his little misshapen head against her side, and under her enclosing arm she could feel his small heart thud.

It was midnight and she lifted him into her arms. She disconnected the alarm and opened the door softly.

And she screamed, for facing her across the open door was Hoskins!

There were two men with him and he stared at her, as astonished as she.

Miss Fellowes recovered first by a second and made a quick attempt to push past him; but even with the second's delay he had time. He caught her roughly and hurled her back against a chest of drawers. He waved the men in and confronted her, blocking the door.

"I didn't expect this. Are you completely insane?"

She had managed to interpose her shoulder so that it, rather than Timmie, had struck the chest. She said pleadingly, "What harm can it do if I take him, Dr. Hoskins? You can't put energy loss ahead of a human life?"

Firmly, Hoskins took Timmie out of her arms. "An energy loss this size would mean millions of dollars lost out of the pockets of investors. It would mean a terrible setback for Stasis, Inc. It would mean eventual publicity about a sentimental nurse destroying all that for the sake of an ape-boy."

"Ape-boy!" said Miss Fellowes, in helpless fury.

"That's what the reporters would call him," said Hoskins.

One of the men emerged now, looping a nylon rope through eyelets along the upper portion of the wall.

Miss Fellowes remembered the rope that Hoskins had pulled outside the room containing Professor Ademewski's rock specimen so long ago.

She cried out, "No!"

But Hoskins put Timmie down and gently removed the overcoat he was wearing. "You stay here, Timmie. Nothing will happen to you. We're just going outside for a moment. All right?"

Timmie, white and wordless, managed to nod.

Hoskins steered Miss Fellowes out of the dollhouse ahead of himself. For the moment, Miss Fellowes was beyond resistance. Dully, she noticed the hand-pull being adjusted outside the dollhouse.

"I'm sorry, Miss Fellowes," said Hoskins. "I would have spared you this. I planned it for the night so that you would know only when it was over."

She said in a weary whisper, "Because your son was hurt. Because he tormented this child into striking out at him."

"No. Believe me. I understand about the incident today and I know it was Jerry's fault. But the story has leaked out. It would have to with the press surrounding us on this day of all days. I can't risk having a distorted story about negligence and savage Neanderthalers, so-called, distract from the success of Project Middle Ages. Timmie has to go soon anyway; he might as well go now and give the sensationalists as small a peg as possible on which to hang their trash."

"It's not like sending a rock back. You'll be killing a human being."

"Not killing. There'll be no sensation. He'll simply be a Neanderthal boy in a Neanderthal world. He will no longer be a prisoner and alien. He will have a chance at a free life."

"What chance? He's only seven years old, used to being taken care of, fed, clothed, sheltered. He will be alone. His tribe may not be at the point where he left them now that four years have passed. And if they were, they would not recognize him. He will have to take care of himself. How will he know how?"

Hoskins shook his head in hopeless negative. "Lord, Miss Fellowes, do you think we haven't thought of that? Do you think we would have brought in a child if it weren't that it was the first successful fix of a human or near-human we made and that we did not dare to take the chance of unfixing him and finding another fix as good? Why do you suppose we kept Timmie as long as we did, if it were not for our reluctance to send a child back into the past. It's just"—his voice took on a desperate urgency—"that we can wait no longer. Timmie stands in the way of expansion! Timmie is a source of possible bad publicity; we are on the threshold of great things, and I'm sorry, Miss Fellowes, but we can't let Timmie block us. We cannot. We cannot. I'm sorry, Miss Fellowes."

"Well, then," said Miss Fellowes sadly. "Let me say goodbye. Give me five minutes to say goodbye. Spare me that much."

Hoskins hesitated. "Go ahead."

Timmie ran to her. For the last time he ran to her and for the last time Miss Fellowes clasped him in her arms.

For a moment, she hugged him blindly. She caught at a chair with the toe of one foot, moved it against the wall, sat down.

"Don't be afraid, Timmie."

"I'm not afraid if you're here, Miss Fellowes. Is that man mad at me, the man out there?"

"No, he isn't. He just doesn't understand about us. Timmie, do you know what a mother is?"

"Like Jerry's mother?"

"Did he tell you about his mother?"

"Sometimes. I think maybe a mother is a lady who takes care of you and who's very nice to you and who does good things."

"That's right. Have you ever wanted a mother, Timmie?"

Timmie pulled his head away from her so that he could look into her face. Slowly, he put his hand to her cheek and hair and stroked her, as long, long ago she had stroked him. He said, "Aren't you my mother?"

"Oh, Timmie."

"Are you angry because I asked?"

"No. Of course not."

"Because I know your name is Miss Fellowes, but—but sometimes, I call you 'Mother' inside. Is that all right?"

"Yes. Yes. It's all right. And I won't leave you anymore and nothing will hurt you. I'll be with you to care for you always. Call me Mother, so I can hear you."

"Mother," said Timmie contentedly, leaning his cheek against hers.

She rose, and, still holding him, stepped up on the chair. The sudden beginning of a shout from outside went unheard and, with her free hand, she yanked with all her weight at the cord where it hung suspended between two eyelets.

And Stasis was punctured and the room was empty.

AFTERTHOUGHT

Although the action of the woman in this story may be viewed as irrational, it may nevertheless have a deeper meaning. While the future society denies its kinship with the Neanderthal boy who has been brought forward in time, the nurse affirms that kinship. Society's denial is revealed in how it treats the boy; the affirmation of the nurse shows itself through her ethical choice, one no less right even though it might prove fatal. She may perish with the boy, but who is to say that this is inevitable? The moment at hand is all that matters, since a life is involved and the choice is hers to make; she cannot stand idle before immediate evil, even though her action may prove futile in the long run. It is this affirmation of human origins which makes this much-discussed story a rare work of science fiction.

Elsewhere, Asimov has written of his distaste for animal experimentation (even though he recognizes its necessity in relieving human misery), and that concern is reflected in this story. The boy is a kind of laboratory animal. Asimov's shining humanity here illuminates our kinship to all life.   GEORGE ZEBROWSKI

In an earlier headnote, I mentioned the growth of the human brain as "explosive" on the evolutionary scale. But, then, the human being is a social animal. In a sense, he is a domesticated animal. When we speak of domesticated animals, we usually speculate that the dog was the first animal to have been domesticated, and the goat was possibly next.

Wrong! The first animal domesticated by human beings was the human being. It seems to me that it takes more brains to have to deal with a bunch of peculiar, unpredictable human beings than to deal with an animal, plant, and mineral environment. The demands were a great force for natural selection in the only direction that could make it possible to live with human beings—a larger brain.

See how McKenna puts this thought into the following story.

MINE OWN WAYS
RICHARD McKENNA

Walter Cordice was plump and aging and he liked a quiet life. On what he'd thought was the last day of his last field job before retirement to New Zealand, he looked at his wife in the spy screen and was dismayed.

Life had not been at all quiet while he and Leo Brumm and Jim Andries had been building the hyperspace relay on Planet Robadur —they had their wives along and they'd had to live and work hidden under solid rock high on a high mountain. That was because the Robadurians were asymbolic and vulnerable to culture shock, and the Institute of Man, which had jurisdiction over hominid planets, forbade all contact with the natives. Even after they'd built her the lodge in a nearby peak, Martha was bored. Cordice had been glad when he and Andries had gone into Tau rapport with the communications relay unit.

That had been two months of peaceful isolation during which the unit's Tau circuits copied certain neural patterns in the men to make itself half sentient and capable of electronic telepathy. It was good and quiet. Now they were finished, ready to seal the station and take their pretaped escape capsule back to Earth; only anthropologists from the Institute of Man would ever visit Robadur again.

And Walter Cordice stood in the wrecked lodge and the picture on the illicit spy screen belted him with dismay.

Robadurians were not symbol users. They simply couldn't have raided the lodge. But the screen showed Martha and Willa Brumm and Allie Andries sitting bound to stakes at a forest edge. Martha's blue dress and tight red curls were unruffled. She sat with her stumpy legs extended primly together and her hard, plump pout said she was grimly not believing what she saw either.

Near a stream, across a green meadow starred yellow with flowers, naked and bearded Robadurians dug a pit with sharp sticks. Others piled dry branches. They were tall fellows, lump-muscled under sparse fur, with low foreheads and muzzle jaws. One, in a devil mask of twigs and feathers, seemed an overseer. Beside Martha, pert, dark little Allie Andries cried quietly. Willa was straining her white arms against the cords. They knew they were in trouble, all right.

Cordice turned from the screen, avoiding the eyes of Leo Brumm and Jim Andries. In their tan coveralls against the silver-and-scarlet decor they seemed as out of place as the dead Robadurian youth at their feet. Leo's chubby, pleasant face looked stricken. Jim Andries scowled. He was a big, loose-jointed man with bold angular features and black hair. They were young and junior and Cordice knew they were mutely demanding his decision.

Decision. He wouldn't retire at stat-8 now, he'd be lucky to keep stat-7. But he'd just come out of rapport and so far he was clear and the law was clear too, very clear: you minimized culture shock at whatever cost to yourself. But abandon *Martha?* He looked down at the Robadurian youth. The smooth ivory skin was free of blue hair except on the crushed skull. He felt his face burn.

"Our wives bathed him and shaved him and made him a pet?" His voice shook slightly. "Leo . . . Leo . . ."

"My fault, sir. I built 'em the spy screen and went to rescue the boy," Leo said. "I didn't want to disturb you and Jim in rapport." He was a chunky, blond young man and he was quite pale now. "They—well, I take all the blame, sir."

"The Institute of Man will fix blame," Cordice said.

My fault, he thought. For bringing Martha against my better judgment. But Leo's violation of the spy-screen ethic did lead directly to illicit contact and—*this mess!* Leo was young, they'd be lenient with him. All right, his fault. Cordice made his voice crisp.

"We minimize," he said. "Slag the lodge, get over and seal up the station, capsule home to Earth, and report this."

Jim really scowled. "I love my wife, Cordice, whatever you think of yours," he said. "I'm getting Allie out of there if I have to culture-shock those blue apes to death with a flame jet."

"You'll do what I say, Andries! You and your wife signed a pledge and a waiver, remember?" Cordice tried to stare him down. "The law says she's not worth risking the extinction of a whole species that may someday become human."

"Damn the law, she's worth it to me!" Jim said. "Cordice, those blue apes are human now. How else could they raid up here, kill this boy, carry off the women?" He spat. "We'll drop you to seal the station, keep your hands clean. Leo and I'll get the women."

Cordice dropped his eyes. Damn his insolence! Still . . . Leo could testify Andries forced it . . . he'd still be clear. . . .

"I'll go along, to ensure minimizing," he said. "Under protest —Leo, you're witness to that. But slag this lodge right now!"

Minutes later Leo hovered the flyer outside while Cordice played the flame jet on the rock face. Rock steamed, spilled away, fused, and sank into a bubbling, smoking cavity. Under it the dead youth, with his smooth, muscular limbs, was only a smear of carbon. Cordice felt better.

Half an hour later, lower on the same mountain, Leo hovered the flyer above the meadow. The Robadurians all ran wildly into the forest and Jim didn't need to use the flame jet. Leo grounded and the men piled out and Cordice felt his stomach relax. They ran toward the women. Allie Andries was smiling but Martha was shouting something from an angry face. As he stooped to untie Martha the blue horde came back out of the forest. They came yelling and leaping and slashing with wet, leafy branches and the sharp smell. . . .

Cordice came out of it sick with the awareness that he was tied to a stake like an animal and that it was his life, not his career, he had to save now. He feigned sleep and peered from eyecorners. Martha looked haggard and angry and he dreaded facing her. He couldn't see the others, except Allie Andries and she was smiling faintly—at Jim, no doubt.

Those two kids must escape, Cordice thought.

He must have been unconscious quite a while because sunset flamed in red and gold downvalley and the pit looked finished. It was elliptical, perhaps thirty feet long and three deep. Robadurians were still mounding black earth along the sides and others were piling brush into a circumscribed thicket, roughly triangular. They chattered, but Cordice knew it was only a mood-sharing noise. That was what made it so horrible. They were asymbolic, without speech and prior to good and evil, a natural force like falling water. He couldn't threaten, bribe, or even plead. Despite his snub nose and full lips he could present an impressive face—at home on Earth. But not to such as these.

Beside the pit the devil masker stood like a tall sentry. Abruptly he turned and strode toward Cordice, trailing his wooden spear. Cordice tensed and felt a scream shape itself in him. Then the devil towered lean and muscular above him. He had no little finger on his spear hand. Keen gray eyes peered down through feathers and twigs.

"Cordice, you fool, why did you bring the women?" the devil asked in fluent English. "Now all your lives are forfeit."

The scream collapsed in a grateful grasp. With speech Cordice felt armed again, almost free. But Martha spoke first.

"Men need women to inspire them and give them courage!" she said. "Walto! Tell him who you are! Make him let us go!"

Walto meant she was angry. In affection she called him *Wally Toes.* But as usual she was right. He firmed his jowls and turned a cool stat-7 stare on the devil mask.

"Look here, if you know our speech you must know we never land on a hominid planet," he said pleasantly. "There are plenty of other planets. For technical reasons we had to do a job here. It's done. We have stores and tools to leave behind." He laughed easily. "Take them and let us go. You'll never see another of us."

The devil shook his head. "It's not what we might see, it's what your women have already seen," he said. "They know a holy secret and the god Robadur demands your deaths."

Cordice paled but spoke smoothly. "I and Andries have been out of touch with the others for two months. I don't know any secret. While we were isolated Brumm built the women a spy screen and rescued that boy—"

"Who was forfeit to Robadur. Robadur eats his children."

"Arthur was being *tortured* when he broke free and ran," Martha said. "I saw *you* there!"

"On your strictly unethical spy screen."

"Why not? You're only brute animals!"

The devil pressed his spear to her throat. "Shut up or I'll spear you now!" he said. Martha's eyes blazed defiance.

"No! *Quiet,* Martha!" Cordice choked. His front collapsed. "Brumm did it all. Kill him and let us *go!*" He twisted in his bonds.

Leo spoke from behind. "Yes, I did it. Take me and let them go." His voice was high and shaky too.

"No! Oh, please no!" That was Willa, sobbing.

"Stop that!" Jim Andries roared. "All of us or none! Listen, you behind the feathers, I know your secret. You're a renegade playing god among the asymbolics. But we're here on clearance from the Institute of Man and they'll come looking for us. Your game's up. Let us go and you'll only be charged with causing culture shock."

The devil grounded his spear and cocked his head. Robadurians around the pit stood up to watch. Martha shrilled into the hush.

"My own brother is with the Institute of Man!"

"I told you shut up!" The devil slapped her with his spear butt. "I know your brother. Tom Brennan would kill you himself, to keep the secret."

"*What* secret, Featherface? That you're a god?" Jim asked.

"The secret that man created himself and what man has done, man can undo." the devil said. "I'm not Robadur, Andries, but I'm sealed to him from the Institute of Man. The Institute will cover for your deaths. It's done the same on hundreds of other hominid planets, to keep the secret."

"Roland Krebs! *Rollo!* You struck a lady—"

Like a snake striking, the spear leaped to her throat. She strained her head back and said "Ah . . . ah . . . ah . . ." her face suddenly white and her eyes unbelieving.

"Don't hurt her!" Cordice screamed. "We'll *swear* to forget, if you let us go!"

The devil withdrew his spear and laughed. "Swear on what, Cordice? Your honor? Your soul?" He spat. "What man has done, man can undo. You're the living proof!"

"We'll swear by Robadur," Cordice pleaded.

The devil looked off into the sunset. "You know, you might. You just might," he said thoughtfully. "We seal a class of boys to Light Robadur tonight; you could go with them." He turned back. "You're the leader, Andries. What about it?"

"What's it amount to?" Jim asked.

"It's a ritual that turns animals into humans," the devil said. "There are certain ordeals to eliminate the animals. If you're really men you'll be all right."

"What about the women?" Jim's voice was edgy.

"They have no souls. Robadur will hold you to account for them."

"You have great faith in Robadur," Jim said.

"Not faith, Andries, a scientist's knowledge as hard as your own," the devil said. "If you put a Robadurian into a barbering machine he wouldn't need faith to get a haircut. Well, a living ritual is a kind of psychic machine. You'll see."

"All right, we agree," Jim said. "But we'll want our wives unhurt. Understand that, Featherface?"

The devil didn't answer. He shouted and the natives swarmed

around the stakes. Hands untied Cordice and jerked him erect and his heart was pounding so hard he felt dizzy.

"Don't let them hurt you, Wally Toes!"

Fleetingly in Martha's shattered face he saw the ghost of the girl he had married thirty years ago. She had a touch of the living beauty that lighted the face Allie Andries turned on Jim. Cordice said goodbye to the ghost, numb with fear.

Cordice slogged up the dark ravine like a wounded bull. He knew the priests chasing him would spear him like the hunted animal he was unless he reached sanctuary by a sacred pool somewhere ahead. Long since Jim and Leo and the terrified Robadurian youths had gone ahead of him. Stones cut his feet and thorns ripped his skin. Leo and Jim were to blame and they were young and they'd live. He was innocent and he was old and he'd die. Not fair. Let them die, too. His lungs flamed with agony and at the base of a steep cascade his knees gave way.

Die here. Not fair. He heard the priests coming and his back muscles crawled with terror. Die fighting. He scrabbled in the water for a stone. Face to the spears. He cringed lower.

Jim and Leo came back down the cascade and helped him up it. "Find your guts, Cordice!" Jim said. They jerked him along, panting and swearing, until the ravine widened to make a still pool under a towering rock crowned red with the last of sunset. Twenty-odd Robadurian youths huddled whimpering on a stony slope at left. Then priests came roaring and after that Cordice took it in flashes.

He had a guardian devil, a monstrous priest with clay in white bars across his chest. White Bar and others drove him up the slope, threw him spread-eagled on his back, and staked down his wrists and ankles with wisps of grass. They placed a pebble on his chest. He tried to remember that these were symbolic restraints and that White Bar would kill him if he broke the grass or dislodged the pebble. Downslope a native boy screamed and broke his bonds and priests smashed his skull. Cordice shuddered and lay very quiet. But when they pushed the thorn through in front of his left Achilles tendon he gasped and drew up his leg. The pebble tumbled off and White Bar's club crashed down beside his head and he died.

He woke aching and cold under starlight and knew he had only fainted. White Bar sat shadowy beside him on an outcrop, club across hairy knees. Downslope the native boys sang a quavering tone song without formed words. They were mood-sharing, expressing sorrow and fearful wonder. I could almost sing with them, Cordice thought. The pebble was on his chest again and he could feel the grass at his wrists and ankles. A stone dug into his back and he shifted position very carefully so as not to disturb the symbols. Nearby but not in view Jim and Leo began to talk in low voices.

Damn them, Cordice thought. They'll live and I'll die. I'm dying now. Why suffer pain and indignity and die anyway? I'll just sit up and let White Bar end it for me. But first—

"Leo," he said.

"Mr. Cordice! Thank heaven! We thought—how do you feel, sir?"

"Bad. Leo—wanted to say—a fine job here. Your name's in for stat-3. Wanted to say—this all my fault. Sorry."

"No, sir," Leo said. "You were in rapport, how could you—"

"Before that. When I let Martha come and so couldn't make you juniors leave your wives behind." Cordice paused. "I owe—Martha made me, in a way, Leo."

Her pride, he thought. Her finer feelings. Her instant certainty of rightness that bolstered his own moral indecision. So she ruled him.

"I know," Leo said. "Willa's proud and ambitious for me, too."

Martha worked on Willa, Cordice thought. Hinted she could help Leo's career. So she got her spy screen. Well, he *had* been grading Leo much higher than Jim. Martha didn't like Allie's and Jim's attitude.

"I'm going to die, boys," Cordice said. "Will you forgive me?"

"No," Jim said. "You're woman-whipped to a helpless nothing, Cordice. Forgive yourself, if you can."

"Look here, Andries, I'll remember that," Cordice said.

"I'm taking Allie to a frontier planet," Jim said. "We'll never see a hairless slug like you again."

Leo murmured a protest. I'll live to get even with Andries, Cordice thought. Damn his insolence! His heel throbbed and the stone still gouged his short ribs. He shifted carefully and it felt better. He hummed the native boys' song deep in his throat and it helped too. He began to doze. If I live I'll grow my body hair again, he thought.

Jim's voice woke him: *Cordice! Lie quiet, now!* He opened his eyes to hairy legs all around him and toothed beast faces in torchlight roaring a song and White Bar with club poised trembling-ready and no little finger on his right hand. The song roared over Cordice like thunder, and sparks like tongues of fire rained down to sear his body. He whimpered and twitched but did not dislodge the stone on his chest. The party moved on. Downslope a boy screamed and club thuds silenced him. And again, and Cordice felt sorry for the boys.

"Damn it all, that really hurt!" Jim said.

"This was the ordeal that boy Arthur failed, only he got away," Leo said. "Mrs. Cordice kept him on the screen until I could rescue him."

"How'd he act?" Jim asked.

"Trusted me, right off. Willa said he was very affectionate and they taught him all kinds of tricks. But never speech—he got wild when they tried to make him talk, Willa told me."

I'm affectionate. I know all kinds of tricks, Cordice thought. Downslope the torches went out and the priests were singing with the boys. White Bar, seated again beside Cordice on the outcrop, sang softly, too. It was a new song of formed words and it disturbed Cordice. Then he heard footsteps behind his head and Jim spoke harshly.

"Hello, Featherface, we're still around," Jim said. "Mrs. Cordice called you a name. *Krebs,* wasn't it? Just who in hell are you?"

"Roland Krebs. I'm an anthropologist," the devil's voice said. "I almost married Martha once, but she began calling me *Rollo* just in time."

That guy? Cordice opened his mouth, then closed it. Damn him. He'd pretend a faint, try not to hear.

"You can't share the next phase of the ritual and it's your great loss," Krebs said. "Now each boy is learning the name that he will claim for his own in the last phase, if he survives. The men have a crude language and the boys long ago picked up the words like parrots. Now, as they sing with the priests, the words come alive in them."

"How do you mean?" Jim asked.

"Just that. The words assort together and for the first time *mean.* That's the Robadurian creation myth they're singing." Krebs lowered his voice. "They're not here now like you are, Andries. They're present in the immediacy of all their senses at the primal creation of their human world."

"Our loss? Yes . . . our great loss." Jim sounded bemused.

"Yes. For a long time words have been only a sickness in our kind," Krebs said. "But ideas can still assort and mean. Take this thought: We've found hominids on thousands of planets, but none more than barely entered on the symbol-using stage. Paleontology proves native hominids have been stuck on the threshold of evolving human minds for as long as two hundred million years. But on

Earth our own symbol-using minds evolved in about three hundred thousand years."

"Does mind evolve?" Jim asked softly.

"Brain evolves, like fins change to feet," Krebs said. "The hominids can't evolve a central nervous system adequate for symbols. But on Earth, in no time at all, something worked a structural change in one animal's central nervous system greater than the gross, outward change from reptile to mammal."

"I'm an engineer," Jim said. "The zoologists know what worked it."

"Zoologists always felt natural selection couldn't have worked it so fast," Krebs said. "What we've learned on the hominid planets proves it can't. Natural selection might take half a billion years. *Our* fathers took a short cut."

"All right," Jim said. "All right. Our fathers were their own selective factor, in rituals like this one. They were animals and they bred themselves into men. Is that what you want me to say?"

"I want you to feel a little of what the boys feel now," Krebs said. "Yes. Our fathers invented ritual as an artificial extension of instinct. They invented a ritual to detect and conserve all mutations in a human direction and eliminate regressions toward the animal norm. They devised ordeals in which normal animal-instinctive behavior meant death and only those able to sin against instinct could survive to be human and father the next generation." His voice shook slightly. "Think on that, Andries! Human and animal brothers born of the same mother and the animals killed at puberty when they failed certain ordeals only human minds could bear."

"Yes. Our secret. Our *real* secret." Jim's voice shook too. "Cain killing Abel through ten thousand generations. That created *me.*"

Cordice shivered and the rock gouged his short ribs.

"Dark Robadur's sin is Light Robadur's grace and the two are one," Krebs said. "You know, the Institute has made a science of myth. Dark Robadur is the species personality, instinct personified. Light Robadur is the human potential of these people. He binds Dark Robadur with symbols and coerces him with ritual. He does it in love, to make his people human."

"In love and fear and pain and death," Jim said.

"In pain and death. Those who died tonight were animals. Those who die tomorrow will be failed humans who know they die," Krebs said. "But hear their song."

"I hear it. I know how they feel and thank you for that, Krebs," Jim said. "And it's only the boys?"

"Yes, the girls will get half their chromosomes from their fathers. They will get all the effect of the selection except that portion on the peculiarly male Y-chromosome," Krebs said. "They will remain without guilt, sealed to Dark Robadur. It will make a psychic difference."

"Ah. And you Institute people *start* these rituals on the hominid planets, make them self-continuing, like kindling a fire already laid," Jim said slowly. "Culture shock is a lie."

"It's no lie, but it does make a useful smokescreen."

"Ah. Krebs, thank you. Krebs—" Jim lowered his voice and Cordice strained to hear—"would you say Light Robadur might be a *transhuman* potential?"

"I hope he may go on to become so," Krebs said. "Now you know the full measure of our treason. And now I'll leave you."

His footsteps died away. Leo spoke for the first time.

"Jim, I'm scared. I don't like this. Is this ritual going to make *us* transhuman? What does that mean?"

"We can't know. Would you ask an ape what *human* means?" Jim said. "Our fathers bred themselves through a difference in kind. Then they stopped, but they didn't have to. I hope one of these hominid planets will breed on through the human to another difference in kind." He laughed. "That possibility is the secret we have to keep."

"I don't like it. I don't want to be transhuman," Leo said. "Mr. Cordice! Mr. Cordice, what do you think?"

Cordice didn't answer. Why let that damned Andres insult him again? Besides, he didn't know what to think.

"He's fainted or dead, poor fat old bastard," Jim said. "Leo, all this ritual is doing to you is forcing you to prove your human manhood, just like the boys have to. We have our manhood now only by accident of fertilization."

"I don't like it," Leo said. "That transhuman stuff. It's . . . immoral."

"It's a hundred thousand years away yet," Jim said. "But I like it. What I don't like is to think that the history of galactic life is going to head up and halt forever in the likes of old Wally Toes there."

"He's not so bad," Leo said. "I hope he's still alive."

I am, goddamn you both! Cordice thought. They stopped talking.

Downslope the priests' voices faded and the boys sang their worded creation song alone. White Bar went away. The sky paled above the great rock and bright planets climbed to view. Cordice felt feverish. He lapsed into a half-dream.

He saw a fanned network of golden lines. Nodes thickened to

become fish, lizards, and men. A voice whispered: *All life is a continuum in time. Son to father, the germ worldline runs back unbroken to the primordial ocean. For you life bowed to sex and death. For you it gasped sharp air with feeble lungs. For you it bore the pain of gravity in bones too weak to bear it. Ten thousand of your hairy fathers, each in his turn, won through this test of pain and terror to make you a man.*

Why?

I don't know why.

Are you a man?

What is a man? I'm a man by definition. By natural right. By accident of fertilization. What else is a man?

Two billion years beat against you like surf, Walter Cordice. The twenty thousand fists of your hairy fathers thunder on you as a door. Open the way or be shattered.

I don't know the way. I lost the way.

Through dream mists he fled his hairy fathers. But they in him preserved intact the dry wisps that bound him terribly with the tensile strength of meaning. They steadied the pebble that crushed him under the mountain-weight of symbol. All the time he knew it.

By noon of the clouded day thirst was the greater agony. Cordice scarcely heard the popping noises made by the insects that fed on his crusted blood and serum. But he heard every plash and ripple of the priest-guarded water downslope. Heard too, once and again, the death of boys whose animal thirst overpowered their precarious new bondage to the symbol. Only those who can remember that the grass wisps *mean* survive, Cordice thought. Poor damned kids! To be able to suffer and sin against instinct is to live and be human.

Jim's and Leo's voices faded in and out of his fever dreams. His back was numb now, where the rock dug into it.

Rose of sunset crowned the great rock above the pool when White Bar prodded Cordice downslope with his club. Cordice limped and rubbed his back and every joint and muscle of his misused body ached and clamored for water. Jim and Leo looked well. Cordice scowled silence at their greetings. I'll die without their damned pity, he thought. He moved apart from them into the group of native boys standing by the rock-edged pool. Their thin lips twitched and their flat nostrils flared and snuffled at the water smell. Cordice snuffled too. He saw Krebs, still masked in twigs and feathers, come through the rank of priests and talk to Jim.

"You'll all be thrown into the water, Andries. For the boys, Dark

Robadur must swim the body to the bank or they drown. Light Robadur must prevent the body from drinking or they get clubbed. The two must co-act. Understand?"

Jim nodded and Krebs turned back to the priests. These kids can't do it, Cordice thought. I can't myself. He shook the arm of the boy beside him and looked into the frightened brown eyes. *Don't drink,* he tried to say, but his throat was too gummed for speech. He smiled and nodded and pinched his lips together with fingers. The boy smiled and pinched his own lips. Then all the boys were doing it. Cordice felt a strange feeling wash through him. It was like love. It was as if they were all his children.

Then wetness cooled his body and splashed his face. He dog-paddled and bit his tongue to keep from gulping. White Bar jerked him up the bank again and behind him he heard the terrible cries and the club thuds. Tears stung his eyes.

Then he was limping and stumbling down the dark ravine. At steep places the native youths held his arms and helped him. They came through screening willows and he saw a fire near the brush-walled pit. The three women stood there. They looked all right. Cordice went with the boys toward the pit.

"Wally Toes! Don't let them hurt you!" Martha cried.

"Shut up!" Cordice yelled. The yell tore his gummed throat.

The boys faced outward and danced in a circle around the pit. The priests danced the opposite way in a larger circle and faced inward. There was ten feet of annular space between the rings. The priests howled and flung their arms. Cordice was very tired. His heel hurt and his back felt humped. Each time they passed, White Bar howled and pointed at him. He saw Martha every time he passed the firelit area. A priest jumped across and pulled the boy next to Cordice into the space between the rings. Cordice had to dance on away, but he heard screams and club thuds. When he came round again he saw them toss a limp body between the dancers into the pit.

They took more boys and made them kneel and did something to them. If the boys couldn't stand it, they killed them. Even if they did stand it, the priests threw them afterward into the pit. I've got to stand it, Cordice thought. If I don't, they'll kill me. Then White Bar howled and leaped and had him.

Threw him to his knees.

Held his right hand on a flat stone.

Pulled aside the little finger.

Bruising it off with a fist ax! Can't STAND it!

Outrage exploded in screaming pain. Hidden strength leaped roaring to almost-action. Then his hairy fathers came and made him be quiet and he stood it. White Bar chewed through the tendons with his teeth and when the finger was off and the stump seared with an ember the priests threw Cordice into the pit.

He felt other bodies thump beside him and his hairy fathers came very near. All around him they grinned and whispered: *You ARE a man. Your way is open.* He felt good, sure and peaceful and strong in a way he had never felt before. He wanted to hold the feeling and he tried not to hear Jim's voice calling him for fear he would lose it. But he had to, so he opened his eyes and got to his feet. Leo and Jim grinned at him.

"I knew you'd make it, old-timer, and I'm glad," Jim said.

Cordice still had the feeling. He grinned and clasped bloody hands with his friends. All around the pit above their heads the piled brush crackled and leaped redly with flame.

Beyond the fire the priests began singing and Cordice could see them dancing in fantastic leaps. The living native boys struggled free of the dead ones and stood up. He counted fourteen. Smoke blew across the pit and the air was thick and suffocating. It was very hot and they all kept coughing and shifting and turning.

Outside the singing stopped and someone shouted a word. One native boy raised his arms and hunted back and forth along the pit edge. He went close and recoiled again.

"They called his name," Jim said. "Now he has to go through the fire to claim it. Now he has to break Dark Robadur's most holy *Thou shalt not.*"

Again the shout. Twice the boy stepped up and twice recoiled. His eyes rolled and he looked at Cordice without seeing him. His face was wild with animal fire-fear.

Leo was crying. "They can't see out there. Let's push him up," he said.

"No," Cordice said.

He felt a Presence over the pit. It was anxious and sorrowful. It was familiar and strange and expected and very right. His hairy fathers were no part of it, but they greeted it and spoke through him.

"Robadur, Robadur, give him strength to pass," Cordice prayed.

A third shout. The boy went up and through the flame in one great leap. Vast, world-lifting joy swirled and thundered through the Presence.

"Jim, do you feel it?" Cordice asked.

"I feel it," Jim said. He was crying, too.

The next boy tried and fell back. He stood rigid in the silence after the third shout. It was a terrible silence. His hair was singed off and his face was blackened and his lips were skinned back over strong white teeth. His eyes stared and they were not human now and they were very sad.

"I've *got* to help him," Leo said.

Jim and Cordice held Leo back. The boy dropped suddenly to all fours. He burrowed under the dead boys who didn't have names either. Vast sorrow infolded and dropped through the Presence. Cordice wept.

Boy after boy went through. Their feet knocked a dark gap in the flaming wall. Then the voice called *Walter Cordice!*

Cordice went up and through the dark gap and the fire was almost gone there and it was easy.

He went directly to Martha. All her bright hardness and pout were gone and she wore the ghost face. It gleamed as softly radiant as the face of little Allie Andries, who still waited for Jim. Cordice drew Martha off into the shadows and they held each other without talking in words. They watched as the others came out and then priests used long poles to push the flaming wall into the pit. They watched the fire die down and they didn't talk and the dancers went away and Cordice felt the Presence go away too, insensibly. But something was left.

"I love you, Martha," he said.

They both knew he had the power to say that word and the right to have a woman.

Then another long time and when he looked up again the flyer was there. Willa and Allie stood beside it in dim firelight and Krebs was coming toward him.

"Come along, Cordice. I'll dress that hand for you," Krebs said.

"I'll wait by the fire, Walter," Martha said.

Cordice followed Krebs into the forest. His nervous strength was leaving him and his legs felt rubbery. He hurt all over and he needed water, but he still felt good. They came to where light gleamed through a hut of interlaced branches. Leo and Jim were already dressed and standing inside by a rough table and chest. Almost at once the plastigel soothed Cordice's cuts and blisters. He dressed and drank sparingly from the cup of water Jim handed him.

"Well, men—" he said. They all laughed.

Krebs was pulling away the twigs and feathers of his mask. Under it he had the same prognathous face as the Robadurian priests. It wasn't ugly at all.

"Cordice, I suppose you know they can regenerate that finger for you back on Earth," he said. He combed three fingers through his beard. "Biofield therapists work wonders, these days."

"I won't bother," Cordice said. "When do we swear our oath? I can swear now."

"No need," Krebs said. "You're sealed to Robadur now. You'll keep the secret."

"I would have anyway," Jim said.

Krebs nodded. "Yes. You were always a man."

They shook hands around and said goodbye. Cordice led the way to the flyer. He walked hard on his left heel to feel the pain and he knew that it is no small thing, to be a man.

Humanity is usually the hero of the tales humanity tells—often in the form of an individual human being but, sometimes, in the form of humanity as a whole. Since science fiction often deals with an advanced humanity moving out into the Universe, the heroism is many times multiplied and the hubris is squared and cubed.

How much higher can it go, then, than to represent humanity as finally taking on, and, in prospect, defeating the Creator, as in Simak's "The Creator," but with more sophistication? A proper way to end the book.

A LETTER FROM GOD
IAN WATSON

So at last I awoke and saw my universe. Already I knew that something had gone wrong. . . .

I shouldn't be able to tell you this. There oughtn't to be a single simple "I" that can communicate with you. We should wear myriad faces. We should be the Many-in-One, of which each conscious species in the universe is only the most fragmentary reflection—one single attribute of our high self, which is beyond self.

Instead, I awoke to a singleness of being which is far below that High Selflessness. I realized that I had been incarnated from out of my sleeping self quite recently at a single point in space-time. It was the tug of that incarnation—that teasing of a portion of myself out of myself, into a particular shape for a while—it was that, coupled with something watery and oceanic, that had woken me a cosmic moment later. Like the footfall of an intruder in a darkened bedroom.

The bedroom wasn't entirely dark, of course. Galaxies and metagalaxies, crowded with suns, hung all over the place—a very big number of night lights, which was good.

Not dark. But it was empty. At first I thought it was entirely empty; and I shivered with dread at the absence of life.

To be sure, I *had* awoken—like an engine on a rather cold morning started, nonetheless, by a tiny trickle of charge from the battery. But the battery should have been fully charged—brimful with life-energy calling to me. And it wasn't; that tiny pulse was all I'd felt. I knew now how close I'd come to being in a cosmos where no life could ever have awakened me; and I knew how small and limited this present "I" must therefore be.

It took a cosmic moment to locate the life that had awakened me. I was guided by a few more incidents of high consciousness from the same direction—high by your standard, pitifully weak by any other reckoning. I shouldn't have heeded the first tug. I should have turned over in my sleep, and slept through this cosmos till it collapsed! But in the vast silence that single note of life had sounded like a gong. Now that I was awake, I was committed to it; and because of this I was reduced to a single personal ego.

Of course, *you* had no idea that you were the one and only life-form to emerge in this cosmos. Oh, you, with your proud arrays of radiotelescopes: tin ear trumpets harkening vainly for an alien message amid the mindless noise!

Like a vagabond who has precisely one match to light one piece of kindling to keep warm by, I directed myself toward you to cup my hands around that single prick of life-light, and nurse it with my breath.

Let me explain something about the creation of universes.

Your scientists have deduced that each successive cosmos springs into being by a random scattering out of "superspace" of all the material of the previous one after it has collapsed. All the natural laws and physical constants of the previous cosmos vanish entirely, and new laws and constants spontaneously occur. But only certain laws and constants permit a habitable universe to occur—a universe where stars can form at all, and burn for a long time. The majority of universes must necessarily be lifeless ones. Either they last for too short a time, or perhaps no elements heavier than helium ever get the chance to form.

You know the game of pool, or snooker? You send the cue ball cannoning into a triangle of target balls and they all scatter in different directions, depending upon the cue ball's speed and spin and vector. If you had a completely frictionless pool table, the balls would carry on indefinitely, colliding and rebounding, till they all clunked into pockets—after a longer or a shorter time. (I bend the rules. I know.) Well, that first scattering of the balls is a bit—just a *bit*—like the first scattering out of superspace.

Contrary to your notion of random scattering, however, there is *a first deliberate shot* which send the balls of the cosmos flying, establishing the particular laws and constants of each universe.

And the Player? Myself. Or rather, the High Precursor of my present limited self. But it isn't quite so simple. The Player does not stand outside the universe. The precursor is the cue ball and the target balls and the cue as well, not to mention the baize of space-time which the motion of the balls unrolls. At the instant of that first shot from which the cosmos springs, the precursor is torn apart, submerged into the spreading fabric of the game it has selected. Too, it must select angle and speed and spin such that during the course of the game, as the universe evolves, life of one kind or another will come into being: a cosmos of multifarious consciousness out of which—*by means of which*—that precursor will eventually awake and look around, with an awareness far beyond any of its billion tributary components.

A player usually has an opponent, too. Just so here, though in this case the Opponent is also part of the precursor. It is its antiself—and that antiself will also emerge, for unless there is a tension between God and anti-God the universe would be over in a flash. This is where the game gets really interesting.

This time, however, the precursor has miscued direly. The constants are off, the physical laws are wrong.

One world. One inhabited speck in it all—and that speck, I see now, a complete fluke! Not our favorite electromagnetic life—that's ruled out by the current constants—but protoplasmic life, preposterously chemically coded! Existing on a world perilously poised in a tiny habitable zone around a star that has been stable miraculously long! A world with a giant moon to draw tides upon the shore, and life upon the land. A world with an oxygen atmosphere which hasn't burned up the life, but which on the contrary the life has learned to breathe. And where did the oxygen come from, anyway? From life itself. Wild paradox. The odds against such life are vast even in an infinity of worlds.

I see the evidence of searing by a nearby supernova long ago. I see the hammer blow of a comet strike in your Late Cretaceous Period. I see the scars of the Ice Ages—but somehow you escaped from the jaws of the ice calamity again and again, just as you avoided by a hair's-breadth the runaway greenhouse effect of overheating.

I see how consciousness awoke, to awaken me—and how close it is to winking out again as you gobble up forests and food, fuel and fish.

The other consciousness, in your seas—which also, I see, conspired to awaken me—is already gone, turned into perfume and boot-oil, manure and pet food by yourselves.

You have multiplied to starvation point and built sun-bombs to turn your world into a cinder. And here am I, awake, doomed to be cast in your image—since it is the one and only one available;

so, if you all die, in this restricted image I shall hear nothing for almost ever after but the ticking of the quasars and the crackling of the barren suns.

You've flown to your moon, though, in tin cans. You've sent tin cans farther out into the first few inches of that aimless deadness that stretches out all around you, everywhere.

And you're going to destroy yourselves. Would it destroy you, equally, to know that there's nothing else alive out there?

The only hope, as I see it from my hamstrung viewpoint, is for you to survive and spread out into the dead universe, to bring your own life to it, and in so doing to *change yourselves* into all the myriads of other life-forms that are so sadly lacking.

I don't have the micromanipulative ability to pluck the ten thousand matches from your childish hands. My time should be eons, my span whole galaxies! This attention to you is straining my Godly eyes!

How could this miscuing ever have taken place? Perhaps the sheer desolation everywhere else is somehow compensated for by the run of luck you represent. Perhaps this is a bravado universe. Perhaps my precursor meant to cue a universe with no Opponent at all—since one and only one ball must run the course from first to last? A universe designed to fool the Opponent is surely also . . . a universe designed to fool myself!

Would a miracle, of the kind I think I can manage, not completely humiliate my one and only world?

I've made my mind up. I've decided, in an almighty break with tradition, to level with you people; to shake you by the scruff of the neck, to kick you in the ass—out into the galaxy, and into those beyond. (The exact details—the tin cans—I'll have to leave up to you.)

I don't, as I said, have the touch for dealing with individual scruffs of necks; I write large.

So I do just that.

I inscribe most of the foregoing as an open letter on a circular column ten miles high. (Which, to me, is rather like scribing a testament on a grain of rice. But never mind.) I plant this pillar down off the shore of your Florida, near where some of your tin cans take off, though not so closely as to be a hazard. Unfortunately, it does rather dwarf your Vehicle Assembly Building. . . . No offense intended.

And I plant a second ten-mile column with a Russian text near Tyuratam Kosmodrome in your USSR.

I sit back, awaiting the cosmic exodus.

———

Perhaps ten miles is too high, even with your ingenuity—telescopes, balloons with cameras dangling from them . . .

It can't be, surely, that the letters are too large to be recognized as letters?

Well, it takes six weeks before the full text is released—by the Americans, the Russians following suit a few hours later.

The Russians promptly declare that I'm an impostor. According to them, my columns are the handiwork of an alien civilization bent on disenchanting you with the idea of galactic exploration by harping on the emptiness and the absence of life out there. With devastating cunning the Russians point out that on the contrary the sudden appearance of the columns proves that civilizations must abound. And these civilizations can't be too far ahead of Earth, either, or else they wouldn't be worried. They wouldn't stage this hoax of a letter from God, plainly an insult to human savvy.

I guess, pigheaded as it is, I should welcome this reaction, if it succeeds in uniting a squabbling world against an imaginary adversary in the sky; if it sets the starships flying.

The Americans, for their part, decide that if "God" (best left undefined) can post a letter, equally they can answer it. They have great faith in the postal service. Up hum radio messages.

"This is the President of the United States of America speaking to the entity which identifies itself as God, in the sincere hope that you're listening. We appeal to you, on behalf of all the peoples of the Earth of whatever faith, to continue the dialogue you've begun. I'm suggesting no secret communications, but now that you've proved the extent of your powers perhaps radio will suffice? Now, we have some questions we all beg you to answer to elucidate your remark that the universe is the result of a 'miscuing'—and your other statement that no other life-forms exist in the universe apart from ourselves. It's been suggested that this latter statement may be a compassionate, Godly way of making us value our own lives more. . . ."

Around about this point in his radio speech, an awful double mishap occurs—so entirely coincidental that it seems utterly deliberate on my part.

The ten-mile-high column off Florida heels over in the ocean. Falling, it slaps a tidal wave across most of the peninsula, destroying towns and cities—and incidentally all of the launch facilities at the cape. And in the USSR the weight of their column triggers a fearful earthquake in a previously quiet seismic area, wrecking their launch site, too. Shaken loose by the earthquake, that column also topples, hitting the ground with the force of an atom bomb. These two incidents, in their way, seem to me like a cruel recapitulation of the original miscuing of the whole darn cosmos —only this time I was trying to balance two cue sticks upright. . . .

The Russians presently fire rather a large number of missiles out into space, to explode at random, but this cannot do me any harm, of course; I'm not of that nature.

The Chinese choose this moment of depleted Russian strength to attack with their own missiles. They get pretty thoroughly trashed in return, but the USSR is badly trashed, too.

I look on, appalled at what I have wrought.

The Russian and Chinese survivors cry that the extraterrestrial plot to ruin you all has worked. The Americans—and this is worse for my ego, now that I have one—accuse me of downright incompetence. By my own admission I set the universe up ineptly in the first place; now I've proved myself incompetent to have any further hand in it. (And I must honestly admit that this restricted "I," which I am, does fall short of what I'd consider full Godly understanding. . . .)

I withdraw from the tattered world, to lick my wounds for a century or two.

At the end of that century or two, the starships rise from Earth. They inch out, faster than light, into the heavens. Their crews burrow into dead worlds and the dead satellites of dead gas giants. They build habitats. They begin to terraform some worlds so that people may walk upon the surface unprotected, even if it takes five thousand years.

Presently starships fly outward from these new worlds. The sphere of human penetration expands farther and farther.

I switch to high-speed scanning. Millennia fly by, and now the starmen are constantly changing themselves into new and diverse kinds of beings: beings who can inhabit dead worlds without air or water, beings who can swim in gas giants, and coast through raw vacuum. Changing. A hundred forms. A thousand forms.

Like fleas they leap from the woolly spiral of the Milky Way across into Andromeda. They. *You.*

And you are all my Adversary. You are all my Opponent, now. You contribute nothing to my own expansion. None of you. I'm as restricted as I ever was. I can't grow to anything like my full capacity. But *you* aren't restricted.

You're hatching a multibillion-year scheme to survive the collapse of this cosmos and make it through intact into the next, differently cued cycle of existence—to bring me to trial! Worse, to cue the next cycle yourselves so that it starts out right. I'm accused of Huge Frivolity, Negligence, and a Cavalier Attitude.

I hide from you all now in the deepest deeps between the metagalaxies—even if I am, in one sense, still everywhere. *I* hide: this "I" hides from man.

But once this universe reaches its phase of maximum expansion and begins to contract again, I know that wherever I hide we'll all be rushed together in the end. Then you'll catch me, sure as eggs is eggs.

Cosmic eggs are no exception. Particularly when they're all in one basket.